Organizational Communication

Theory and Behavior

Peggy Yuhas Byers
Ball State University
Editor

Allyn and Bacon

Boston • London • Toronto • Svdnev • Tokyo • Singapore

Dedication

This book is dedicated to my father, Edward Yuhas, and the loving memory of my mother, Eleanor Yuhas. They are truly two of the most inspiring, courageous, and loving individuals I shall ever know.

◆

Series Editor: Carla F. Daves
Editorial Assistant: Andrea Geanacopoulos
Editorial-Production Administrator: Joe Sweeney
Editorial-Production Service: Walsh Associates
Composition Buyer: Linda Cox
Manufacturing Buyer: Suzanne Lareau
Cover Administrator: Suzanne Harbison

Copyright © 1997 by Allyn and Bacon
A Viacom Company
160 Gould Street
Needham Heights, MA 02194
Internet: www.abacon.com
America Online: keyword: College Online

Library of Congress Cataloging-in-Publication Data

Organizational communication : theory and behavior / edited by Peggy
    Yuhas Byers.
        p. cm.
    Includes bibliographical references and index.
    ISBN 0-205-17443-4
    1. Communication in organizations.   2. Interpersonal
communication.   3. Communication in organizations—Case studies.
I. Byers, Peggy Yuhas.
HD30.3.0723   1996
302.3'5–dc20   96-24912
                                      CIP

Printed in the United States of America

Contents

PART II   Organizational Life   115

Part III   Contemporary Issues   257

Preface

Understanding the role of communication within the modern organization is vital to its growth and prosperity. It is through observing and understanding how people communicate with each other through words, symbols, and behaviors that we are able to improve our daily activities in such organizations. Whether it be work settings, volunteer social service boards, or community organizations, an understanding of how individuals behave, why they behave as they do, and how human interaction can be improved upon is essential for organizational success. The aim of this book is to provide both students and practitioners with both theoretical and practical information on how people communicate with each other in organizations.

Communication is an important part of life in organizations. Therefore, the study of organizational communication should provide a basis for understanding virtually every human process that occurs in organizations. Organizational communication deals with conflict, persuasion, ethics, roles, rules, culture, networks, diversity, leadership, creativity, and technology. Through the chapters in this book, the reader will be introduced to both theory and pragmatics relating to a variety of facets of communication in organizations.

There are several outstanding features of this book. First, the book addresses many current and important topics in organizational communication such as cultural diversity, gender issues, leadership, technology, and conflict. The book is intended to accomplish four specific goals: (1) to develop an awareness of the process and importance of communication in organizations, (2) to develop an awareness of important theories and how they are applied in an organizational setting, (3) to develop an awareness of oral and behavioral communication skills necessary for effective organizational communication, and (4) to develop an awareness of new and important issues and topics in contemporary organizations.

The book is delineated into four parts or sections. The first section, Communication as a Process, is designed to orient the reader to the process and various facets of communication in organizations. It serves as a foundation upon which to better understand the subsequent chapters in the book. It explores verbal and nonverbal communication and ethics in the organizational setting. The second section of the text, Organizational Life, focuses specifically on organizational behavior issues such as leadership and motivation, conflict management and conflict models, creativity, and persuasion in the organizational setting. The third section, Contemporary Issues, addresses current trends in the study of organizational communication. It focuses on the role of gender, the role of the consultant, the role of cultural diversity, and the role of technology in the organizational setting. The final section, Postscript, concludes the text with a general overview of the development of organizational communication as a field of study and provides useful insight as to the future of organizational communication.

PART I: COMMUNICATION AS A PROCESS

In Chapter 1, The Process and Perspectives of Organizational Communication, Dr. Peggy Yuhas Byers provides a background on communication. The chapter discusses what communication is, the different levels and types of communication in organizations, and different models of communication. It also provides different perspectives on communication in organizations such as classical management theory, human relations theory, human resource theory, systems theory, and chaos theory and the learning organization. Moreover, it provides the reader with a way to look at the process of communication and some of the barriers to effective communication in the organizational setting.

Dr. Susan A. Hellweg, in Chapter 2, Formal and Informal Communication Networks, begins by discussing the definition and importance of communication networks in organizations. She discusses formal networks in terms of functions, structures, roles and descriptors, and informal networks in terms of characteristics, functions, rumor, and the grapevine. The chapter concludes with a discussion of the methods for analyzing formal and informal networks in organizations.

In the third chapter, Nonverbal Communication in Organizations, Dr. Valerie Manusov and Dr. Julie M. Billingsley introduce the reader to nonverbal communication. They present behavioral codes such as proxemics, facial expressions, kinesics, haptics, and vocalics and nonbehavioral codes such as dress, chronemics, and context. They discuss the nature of nonverbal communication, focusing on complexity, the issue of intentionality, levels of meaning, and the influence of the context. Finally, they discuss the functions of nonverbal communication in the organizational setting, focusing on perception and impression management, relational messages, and coordination of interaction.

In Chapter 4, Dr. Ann L. Plamondon discusses Ethics in the Workplace: The Role of Organizational Communication. She begins the chapter with a discussion of value dimensions such as personal and organizational values. A review of ethical theories for analysis is presented and focuses on the approaches for the analysis of ethical choice. The chapter concludes with a description of concrete ethical dilemmas likely to occur in an organizational setting such as conflict of interest, invasion of privacy, keeping confidences, image campaigns, and whistle blowing.

PART II: ORGANIZATIONAL LIFE

In Chapter 5, The Role of Communication in the Leadership Process, Dr. Raymond M. O'Connor, Jr., begins the second part of the book with a thorough review of leadership theories. He begins the discussion with trait theories and takes it through participative theories, behavioral theories, contingency theories, and current research trends in leadership focusing on the role of communication.

In the sixth chapter by Dr. Dale L. Shannon, Conflict Management in Organizations, the reader is presented with a discussion of the differences between destructive and constructive conflict management strategies. Conflict management with regard to the different levels of communication is presented, along with a discussion of the different styles of conflict management. The author provides the reader with conflict intervention techniques for the organizational setting and concludes the chapter with a discussion of the future trends in the research of conflict management.

In Chapter 7, Dr. John Parrish-Sprowl discusses Persuasion In and By Organizations. The author presents theoretical traditions related to persuasion in organizations focusing on the rhetoric traditions, the social science–foundationalist, and the social science–interpretive perspectives. He then discusses internal persuasive contexts such as labor negotiations and organizational change and external persuasive contexts such as advertising, public relations, lobbying, and sales. The author concludes this chapter by discussing the impacts of persuasion on contemporary issues in organizations such as diversity and globalization.

Dr. Angela Trethewey, in Chapter 8, Organizational Culture, defines organizational culture and presents its elements such as language, rites and rituals, stories, heroes, and symbols. She presents the functional, interpretive, feminist, and critical approaches to understanding the influence of the organizational culture on our communication. She concludes the chapter with a discussion of recent trends in the study of organizational culture.

Dr. Timothy Neal Thompson, in the final chapter in this section, Organizational Creation and Evolution, couples organizational communication and creativity. He discusses opportunities for change in the organization through creativity such as sense-making, requisite variety, and enacting order as well as the systems evolutional perspective, equivocality, rules, and cycles of communication. The importance of interaction effects and the relationship of creativity to chaos theory are also discussed. The chapter also presents the reader with a discussion of factors that can either enhance or inhibit creativity in organizations.

PART III: CONTEMPORARY ISSUES

The third section begins with Chapter 10 and a discussion of Gender Issues: Management Style, Mobility, and Harassment. Dr. Cynthia Berryman-Fink begins with an examination of the status of women in contemporary organizations. She focuses on workforce participation, the extent of women in management and the sex segregation of occupations, and salary differences. She discusses the glass ceiling, the function of culture in relation to gender differences, stereotypes of males and females in the organizational setting, and attitudes, abilities and behaviors of male and female managers. Additionally, she presents a review of gender and informal communication such as mentors and networks, a perspective on balancing career and family roles, and information on sexual harassment. The chapter concludes with a discussion of organizational romance and the future of gender influences in organizations.

In Chapter 11, Cultural Diversity and Organizations, Dr. Alberto González, Jennifer Willis, and Cory Young explore the interrelated and expanding global interests of organizations, focusing on our assumptions about cultural diversity in organizations and the changing demographics in the workplace. The chapter also addresses the role of communication in diversity training in organizations, the history of diversity training, specific communication issues, the selection and assessment of diversity training programs, and the organization's response to diversity training. The chapter concludes with a discussion and critique of three specific models of diversity training programs.

In Chapter 12, titled The Organizational Consultant, Drs. James and Ethel Wilcox discuss means for analyzing communication problems in organizations as an organizational consultant. They review the different types of difficulties experienced by contemporary organizations, the different types of client–consultant relationships that directly affect consultation opportunities, and characteristics of an ideal organizational consultant. The chapter concludes with a discussion of suggestions on how the consultant can effectively relate to the client and ethical responsibilities of the consultant.

In Chapter 13, Communication Technologies in Contemporary Organizations, Dr. David R. Neumann begins with a discussion of the information superhighway. He discusses its impact on an organization's daily activities and its impact on information accessibility. Perspectives of the "office of the future" are provided with descriptions of current communication technologies such as teleconferencing, advanced telephone systems, distance education, advanced computer systems, the internet, and the world wide web, as well as speculation about what the future may bring. A review of theories, postulates, and hypotheses related to the impact of technology in organizations is provided along with a discussion relating to the human factors involved in technological communication. The chapter concludes with a discussion of the implications of technology for management and training.

PART IV: POSTSCRIPT

The postscript to the text, How to Think and Talk About Organizational Communication, written by Dr. Phillip K. Tompkins, summarizes and synthesizes much of what the various authors have presented in their respective chapters. He also provides us with an in-depth historical perspective on the development of what we now refer to as "organizational communication." Starting in 1929, and finishing with contemporary perspectives, Dr. Tompkins offers the reader a new way to look at the growth of the field and corresponding stages illustrated by the topics addressed in this book.

There are several people I would like to thank for helping to make this book possible. First and foremost I would like to thank my husband, Bryan, whose wisdom and experience were invaluable to me. Thanks also for reading all my drafts. Gratitude also goes to Jim O'Rourke at the University of Notre Dame, whose advice and support were generously provided on early drafts. I would also like to thank the authors of the various chapters presented in this book. Their expertise, timeliness, and cooperation made the process run smoothly. I am also grateful to Doug Tyler in the art department at Saint Mary's College for helping me with the graphics for this book. Thank you, Joyce Perry, my friend and confidant. Her patience, support, clerical assistance, and unending positiveness helped beyond words. Special thanks also goes out to all my organizational communication students who inspired me to put this book together and also to Nancy Martin who provided a student's perspective on things. Appreciation is also extended to the faculty and staff in the Department of Speech Communication at Ball State University, specifically Cindy and the student workers who helped me put it all together at the end; and also to the following reviewers: D. F. Treadwell, Westfield State College; Dr. Marshall Prisbell, University of Nebraska at Omaha; Nina Jo Moore, Appalachian State University; Richard A. Katula, Northeastern University; Carol R. Berteotti, University of Wisconsin; and Jack Barwind, Syracuse University. Finally, thanks goes to my editor at Allyn and Bacon, Carla Daves, whose confidence and support were unending.

Contributors

Cynthia Berryman-Fink

Dr. Cynthia Berryman-Fink is acting vice provost for faculty affairs and former head of the department of communication at the University of Cincinnati. From 1981–1984, she was a partner in Communication Enhancement Training, a human resources consulting firm. At the University of Cincinnati, she has taught graduate and undergraduate courses in Management Communication, Organizational Communication, Organizational Diversity, and a variety of Small Group Communication courses. She has served as a speaker or consultant to a number of organizations such as Procter and Gamble, Cincinnati Bell, the Internal Revenue Service, Service Merchandise Corporation, Merrill-Dow Pharmaceuticals, Marathon Oil Company, the Environmental Protection Agency, and various hospitals, banks, and educational institutions in the greater Cincinnati area. She has published four books and over twenty articles and book chapters and has presented over thirty papers at international, national, and regional conferences in the areas of organizational communication, personnel, education, and psychology.

Peggy Yuhas Byers

Dr. Peggy Yuhas Byers is an assistant professor in the Department of Speech Communication at Ball State University, Indiana, and has been teaching courses in Organizational Communication, Interpersonal Communication, Small Group Communication, Professional Speaking and Writing, Interviewing, and Research Methods in Communication for over eight years. She has served as a speaker/consultant for a variety of organizations such as Women In Communication. The Center for Business Communication at the University of Notre Dame, and WSBT TV. She has published in the areas of focus groups, interpersonal communication, organizational communication, rhetoric, and statistical analysis. She has presented over fifteen papers at national and regional conferences in the areas of communication apprehension, organizational communication, interpersonal communication, research methods, and mass communication.

Julie M. Billingsley

Dr. Julie Billingsley, a former assistant professor in the Department of Communication at Rutgers University, New Jersey, is now the manager of human resources at Z S Associates in Evanston, Illinois. Her areas of interest are decision-making and conflict interaction, social processes, decision support systems, organizational change, power in organizations, technology, nonverbal communication, and theories of structure in the organization. She teaches graduate and undergraduate courses in Organizational Communication Theory, Small Group Communication, Public Speaking, Administrative Communication, and Communication in the Workplace. Dr. Billingsley has presented workshops for conferences and numerous organizations in the areas of effective speaking, effective work teams, and effective meetings. She has authored book chapters and articles in nonverbal communication, small group communication, and computer-supported meetings, and has presented over twelve papers at international, national, and regional conferences. She has served as reviewer and guest reviewer, member of the editorial board, and reader for a variety of scholarly journals in the area of organizational communication.

Alberto González

Dr. Alberto González, associate professor in the Department of Interpersonal Communication at Bowling Green State University, Ohio, has been teaching at both the graduate and undergraduate levels and researching in the area of intercultural communication for over ten years. Dr. González has authored three books in the areas of culture and communication and over fifteen book chapters and articles. He is an active participant in national and regional conferences with approximately thirty scholarly presentations to his credit. Along with holding offices in both national and regional organizations such as the Intercultural Communication Division of the Central States and Southern Communication Associations, he also is active on the editorial boards of numerous journals. He has been an associate editor, reviewer, and manuscript referee for a variety of journals in the area of intercultural communication.

Susan A. Hellweg

Dr. Susan A. Hellweg has been a professor in the School of Communication at San Diego State University since 1979 in organizational and political communication as well as interviewing. She teaches classes at both the graduate and undergraduate levels. Dr. Hellweg has authored or co-authored eighty papers for scholarly conferences and has over forty publications to her credit. Her work has appeared in a variety of communication and management journals, as well as in books. She is also the senior author of a recently published book covering the presidential debates. She has served on the ICA the Board of Directors, the SCA Legislative Council, and the WSCA Executive Council. Dr. Hellweg has been an associate editor and on the review boards of numerous communication and management journals. Finally, Dr. Hellweg was honored as the outstanding member of the Organizational Communication Division of the International Communication Association for her service contributions.

Valerie Manusov

Dr. Valerie Manusov is an assistant professor in the Department of Speech Communication at the University of Washington. She teaches undergraduate and graduate courses in Interpersonal Communication, Intercultural Communication, Research Methods with an emphasis on quantitative analysis, and Nonverbal Communication, to mention a few. She has authored nine articles in academic journals and book chapters. Dr. Manusov has twice been given special recognition for her scholarship at international and regional conferences and has presented over eighteen conference papers and panel discussions. She has conducted workshops on nonverbal communication for the Educational Media Association of New Jersey and the Communication Studies Network in Sheffield, England. She has won numerous awards and grants for her work in the area of nonverbal communication and has served on editorial and review boards for national, regional, and state journals.

David R. Neumann

Dr. David R. Neumann, assistant professor and chair of the Professional and Technical Communication Department at Rochester Institute of Technology, New York, has been teaching courses in Organizational Communication, Teleconferencing Communications Management, Research Methods, and Persuasion, among others for over eight years. Dr. Neumann has conducted numerous adventure-based team building workshops covering topics such as organizational culture, conflict management, leadership, and problem-solving for a variety of organizations such as IDS Investment Group, Xerox, Kodak, and Guiltspur Exhibit Co. He has published over thirteen articles in the areas of imaging, technology, language, and public speaking in both books and journals. He has presented over twenty papers at conventions both nationally and regionally, in addition to receiving many grants and awards.

Raymond M. O'Connor, Jr.

Dr. Raymond M. O'Connor, Jr. is an assistant professor in the Department of Psychology at Valparaiso University, Indiana. His area of specialization is industrial-organizational psychology, with an emphasis in personnel selection, and testing and measurement. Research areas including leadership, decision-making, occupational stereotyping, and escalation of commitment. His courses, taught at both the graduate and undergraduate levels, include Industrial Psychology, Organizational Psychology, Statistics, General Experimental Psychology, Testing and Measurement, and Learning and Behavior. Dr. O'Connor has developed and administered assessor training and assessment dimension and exercise development programs. He has authored a variety of articles on organizational evaluation and assessment instruments, sex-typed occupations, effects of feedback on performance, and decision making. Additionally, he has presented papers on topics such as testing, occupational stereotypes, statistics, and leadership at both national and regional conferences.

John Parrish-Sprowl

Dr. John Parrish-Sprowl is chair of the Department of Communication at Indiana University Purdue University at Fort Wayne, Indiana. He has been teaching graduate and undergraduate classes for over ten years. His courses range from Organizational Communication, Negotiation and Conflict, Decision Making and Problem Solving, to Theory, Research Methods, Gender and Communication, and Interpersonal Communication. He has published approximately twenty-five scholarly articles and book chapters in addition to numerous presentations at national and regional conferences. In addition, he has consulted and/or conducted training workshops for over sixty different organizations including corporations, universities, and labor unions. Dr. Parrish-Sprowl has also held numerous offices. On the national level he has been on the Legislative Council and has also served as chair of the Applied Communication Section for SCA. At the regional level he has served on the Executive Council and been chair of both the Applied Communication and the Theory and Methods sections of ECA. His work as a scholar, teacher, and consultant has extended into the post-Communist transformation in Poland. Currently, he is doing research and consultation in the area of organizational transformation.

Ann L. Plamondon

Dr. Ann Plamondon, J.D., is professor and chair of the Department of Communication, Dance, and Theatre at Saint Mary's College, Indiana. She has been teaching courses in Ethics, Persuasion, Art and Entertainment Law, Critical Issues in Mass Communication, and Mass Communication Law for over twenty years. She has received both legal and academic scholarship and teaching awards at both Saint Mary's College and Loyola Law School in Louisiana. Dr. Plamondon has authored a book, book chapters, and over twenty scholarly articles and legal briefs as well as several invited papers both nationally and internationally. She was selected as one of only three faculty to represent Saint Mary's College at the three Poynter Center Conferences on Ethics and the Educated Person.

Dale L. Shannon

Dr. Dale Shannon is an assistant professor in the Communication Department at Western Michigan University in Grand Rapids, Michigan. He is responsible for teaching both undergraduate and graduate students in Organizational Communication, Group Communication Processes, Conflict Management, and Research Methods. His areas of interest include organizational communication, negotiation support systems, conflict management, new communication technology, group decision support systems, and quantitative methods. Dr. Shannon has been a speaker and consultant for organizations such as Ameritech Engineers, Interchange Organization, Community Reconciliation Center, and Texaco. He has published two book chapters in the areas of conflict and negotiation. He has also authored a variety of papers presented internationally and nationally in the areas of negotiation support systems, technology, and the conflict process.

Timothy Neal Thompson

Dr. Timothy Neal Thompson is an associate professor in Speech and Communication Studies at Edinboro University in Pennsylvania and is responsible for both graduate and undergraduate students. His courses include Public Relations, Advertising, Conflict Management, Language and Thought, and Organizational Communication. He has held offices in a number of regional and national speech communication organizations over the past ten years. Dr. Thompson has conducted a variety of workshops in public relations, effective communication skills, and creativity for organizations such as Schofield Barracks (Hawaii), Grand Forks Air Force Base, Aberdeen Proving Ground, Davey Tree Company, and the Kent Human Resource Group. He is the author of a forthcoming book on communication, creativity, and change and a variety of book chapters and articles relating to creativity and mass communication. Dr. Thompson has also presented numerous papers at national, regional and state conferences in the areas of creativity, organizational communication, mass communication, and organizational culture.

Phillip K. Tompkins

Dr. Phillip K. Tompkins is currently a professor of communication and comparative literature at the University of Colorado at Boulder. He teaches graduate and undergraduate courses in Organizational Communication, Rhetorical Theory and Criticism, and Philosophy of Inquiry. He has also lectured at the University of Helsinki, Finland, in the School of Economics and Business Administration, and the Helsinki University of Technology. Dr. Tompkins has published five books/monographs, over thirty scholarly articles and commentaries, and has presented numerous papers at scholarly conferences. Dr. Tompkins has received many honors and awards such as the Excellence in Teaching Award at Purdue University and the Robert J. Kibler Memorial Award sponsored by the Speech Communication Association. He is a past president and fellow of the International Communication Association. Finally, Dr. Tompkins has served on the editorial boards of *Communication Theory, Southern Journal of Communication,* the *Howard Journal of Communication, Western Journal of Speech Communication, Communication Monographs, Communication Quarterly,* and *Quarterly Journal of Speech.*

Angela Trethewey

Dr. Angela Trethewey is an assistant professor in the Department of Speech Communication at the University of Washington. She directs research and teaches both undergraduate and graduate students in courses such as Interviewing, Organizational Communication, Communication and Gender, and Feminist Research Methods. Her areas of interest are feminist critique and organizational communication. She is an active participant in national and regional conferences with numerous scholarly presentations. Many of her scholarly papers have received special recognition at national conventions. Dr. Trethewey has also won a variety of awards, for example, the Rawling Merit Award and the Purdue Research Foundation Summer Grant Award.

Ethel M. Wilcox

Dr. Ethel M. Wilcox, a professor in the Department of Communication at the University of Toledo, Ohio, specializes in the areas of organizational, interpersonal, and health communication. She has won the Outstanding Teacher of the Year Award, Master Teacher Award, and the Outstanding Female Faculty Member of the Year Award. For over seventeen years Dr. Wilcox has served as a consultant and conducted workshops and training seminars at organizations such as The Toledo Hospital, Medical College of Ohio, Cincinnati Children's Hospital, Northwest Ohio Consortium of Family Physicians, New England Council of Hospital Pharmacists, Blue Cross/Blue Shield, American Red Cross, and Upjohn Sales. She has also served as a marketing consultant for Timex, Owens-Illinois, Liggett and Myers, and AT&T. She has co-authored two books in interpersonal communication in the health care setting and a variety of book chapters and journal articles on health communication, conflict management, interpersonal communication, and organizational communication. She has also authored over thirty-five papers, covering topics such as organizational communication, interviewing, listening, health communication, and communication competency, which have been presented at both national and international conferences for over eighteen years.

James R. Wilcox

Dr. James R. Wilcox, professor and graduate coordinator in the Department of Interpersonal Communication at Bowling Green State University, Ohio, has been teaching graduate and undergraduate courses in Organizational Communication, Interpersonal Communication, Attitude/Behavior Research, Negotiation and Bargaining, and Health Communication, among others, for over twenty-five years. He has chaired over thirty master's theses and over thirty doctoral dissertations. He has over seventeen publications including books, chapters, and articles in areas such as organizational communication, health communication, organizational culture, conflict management, gender issues, and public address. He has presented over sixty-five papers at international, national, and regional conferences. He has conducted workshops and seminars and been a consultant to numerous Toledo area hospitals, various types of health care facilities, health care providers, and medical students, as well as Owens Corning Fiberglass, Ford, Oldsmobile, General Electric, United Telephone, and Northeast Utilities of Connecticut.

Jennifer Willis

Jennifer Willis is a doctoral student in the Department of Interpersonal Communication at Bowling Green State University. Her research interests are in the areas of intercultural communication and rhetorical criticism.

Cory Young

Cory Young is a master's student in the Department of Interpersonal Communication at Bowling Green State University. Her area of interest is intercultural communication.

▶ Part I

Communication as a Process

▶ 1

The Process and Perspectives of Organizational Communication

PEGGY YUHAS BYERS

Understanding organizational communication is important for a variety of reasons. First, organizations are now paying special interest to the function of communication. As communication scholars Bachrach and Aiken (1977) suggest, most of the daily routines inside organizations entail information exchange and coordination. These activities are critically dependent on effective communication. As employees, we spend the majority of our time either talking or listening. When we are not engaged in these types of activities, we are probably reading, writing, or diagramming. Therefore, it is vitally important that we are able to effectively engage in these communication activities.

Additionally, many organizations hire costly consultants to conduct workshops for employees in a variety of communication areas, such as listening, conflict management, and leadership. Leaders of organizations understand the importance of fostering an understanding of the dynamics of organizational communication throughout every level of management. They believe that an understanding and appreciation for the process of communication is critical to an organization's success.

To fully comprehend the material presented in the following chapters, it is essential that we address in this first chapter some important questions about the relationship between communication and organizations. For example: What is communication? What are the different levels of communication? What are the different types of communication in organizations? What is the process of communication? What are the main models of communication? How does the process of abstracting work and how does that relate to the barriers of effective organizational communication? And finally, what are the traditional and contemporary theoretical perspectives on communication in organizations?

WHAT IS COMMUNICATION?

Communication has traditionally been defined as "behavior." It has been suggested that we "cannot not communicate" (Watzlawick, Beavin, & Jackson, 1967, p. 49), just as we cannot not behave. Behavior has no opposite. According to this perspective, every act, both conscious and unconscious, contains information that is then interpreted by a receiver. Even a decision not to respond to a question or statement from another person is *some* type of response or behavior. The message sent when we are ignored or given the "cold shoulder" is usually loud and clear and easy to interpret.

In response to this perspective, or conception of communication, Sarah Trenholm (1991), a communication theory expert, states that communication is often used as an "explanatory construct." She points out that the word "communication" is used to explain almost everything, as is suggested in the idea presented above. It is used to explain how we talk and how we act. Trenholm acknowledges that geneticists, neurophysiologists, biologists, zoologists, engineers, and computer scientists use its models and vocabulary to describe processes within both living and human-made systems.

Charles Conrad, in his book, *Strategic Organizational Communication: Toward the Twenty-First Century,* defines communication in organizations as "a process through which people, acting together, create, sustain, and manage meanings through the use of verbal and nonverbal signs and symbols within a particular context" (1994, p. 3). This definition places special emphasis on the words "people," "acting together," "meaning," and "context." This definition includes exchanges in every type of communication, from intrapersonal to public; it includes exchanges that create meaning in our minds as the receiver of the message; and it is focused on the context of organizations.

Joining the three notions presented, we can conceive, then, of organizational communication as both behaviors and symbols, generated either intentionally or unintentionally, occurring between and among people who assign meaning to them, within an organizational setting. Organizational communication allows us to explain what individuals in organizations do, how they do it, and what effect it may have on the receiver.

THE LEVELS AND TYPES OF COMMUNICATION IN ORGANIZATIONS

Levels of Communication

In their landmark book, *Pragmatics of Human Communication: A Study of Interactional Patterns, Pathologies, and Paradoxes* (1967), Paul Watzlawick, Janet Beavin, and Don Jackson present their axioms of human communication. One axiom indicates that communication "not only conveys information, but that at the same time it imposes behavior" (1967, p. 51). The notion that communication conveys information and suggests behavior has come to be known as the "report" and "command," or the "content" and "relationship," levels of communication, respectively. The report, or content level of communication, imparts information to the receiver. The "command," or "relationship" level refers to "what sort of message it is to be taken as" (p. 52). The relationship level is metacommunication, in that it communicates how the content of the message is to be interpreted. For example, the two phrases, "Have the report on my desk by Monday!" and "Have the report on my desk by Monday?" both convey the same information. The supervisor wants the employee to have the report in on Monday. The relationship level projected in each, however, is very different. In the first the superior is saying unequivocally that the report must be in on Monday—it is a demand. In the second, however, the supervisor is requesting that the report be turned in Monday—if the employee can get to it by then. The former is a demand, the latter is a request. The relationship between the employees expressed in the two scenarios is quite different. In the first, one is clearly in the one-up position, and in the second, the two are more or less on equal footing. Thus, although the content level of each message is the same, the relationship level is clearly not.

With this information in mind, we can look at the different types of communication as defined by the number of individuals involved. We can see how the number of people included in the act of communication changes the process.

Types of Communication

Intrapersonal Communication

Intrapersonal communication is the communication that occurs inside the individual. It is how we talk to ourselves, or the act of "listening to that little voice that lives in your mind" (Adler & Rodman, 1994, p. 9). We are both sender and receiver, our thoughts and feelings constitute the message, and our brain acts as the channel by processing those thoughts and feelings. Feedback is that information we discard or add. The process of evaluating how we did in our marketing presentation, of analyzing how prepared we are for an interview, or of silently rehearsing how to best ask our boss for a raise are all examples of intrapersonal communication.

Interpersonal Communication

Communication with another person is called interpersonal or dyadic communication. Some scholars imply that this is the most common type of communication (Adler & Rodman, 1994). In interpersonal communication, we function as both a sender and a receiver. The message is the information provided, the channel is usually sight and sound, and feedback is the response provided by each member of the dyad. Interviewing is often thought of as a type of interpersonal communication. Although an interview situation is often more structured than a regular conversation with a friend and may often follow a script (an interview guide with specific questions, for example), it possesses the same qualities and characteristics present in any discussion between two people. Other examples of interpersonal communication in organizations are, for instance, talking with our supervisor about an upcoming sales meeting, standing by the coffee machine discussing the recent company personnel changes, or making a sales pitch to a potential customer.

Small Group Communication

Small group communication occurs whenever a small number of people come together for a purpose. It may be, for example, to solve a problem or to generate new ideas about a product. The difference between a small group and a large group is that in a small group each individual has an equal chance of participating, each can be easily heard, and each can easily interact with all other members of the group. This type of interaction generally becomes difficult after there are more than ten or twelve members. When there are too many members, and each cannot readily communicate with the others, you no longer have a small group.

Small groups consist of several sender/receivers. With the addition of more people, the communication becomes more complicated. There are more chances for misunderstandings to occur. Since the group is together for a specific purpose, the messages are generally a bit more structured than in interpersonal communication; the channels and opportunity for feedback, however, are the same. Examples of small groups in organizations are plentiful. Sales and project teams, the board of directors of the company, and oftentimes small departments function as a small group in which each person can readily communicate with all the members and in which a specific goal or purpose usually exists.

Often in organizations, small group efforts are referred to as "teams." The idea of using groups, or teams, began with the idea of "quality circles" back in the 1980s. Quality circles consisted of a few people who would meet for a few hours a week to discuss problems. Although quality circles still exist today, their popularity has declined somewhat. When we look at contemporary organizations, however, it is clear that teams are still quite popular. For example, companies like Federal Express and IDS, through adopting work teams, have recently boosted their productivity up by 40 percent. Nynex used teams to help in the transition from a highly "bureaucratic Baby Bell to a high-speed cruiser on the I-way" (Dumaine, 1994, p. 86). Teams helped to cut in half the number of engineering difficulties on Boeing's new 777 passenger jet.

The popularity of teams in organizations does not imply that they are useful in every situation. On the contrary, teams are sometimes used where it is neither practical nor necessary. Not all of us work well in teams, some of us may function better on our own. Careful analysis of the problem to be addressed and the individuals to be included in the group are necessary before a team can effectively and efficiently be put to work.

Public Communication

In public communication the speaker (sender/receiver) imparts a message to an audience (sender/receiver). Public communication occurs when the group becomes too large for all to actively participate. The channel is the same as in interpersonal and small group communication (sight and sound), yet may be more exaggerated with a louder voice, more expansive gestures, and perhaps props or visual aids such as flip charts and overheads due to a larger audience. The opportunity for feedback, however, is somewhat limited. Generally, other than the facial expressions and body postures of the audience that can be seen by the speaker, feedback is limited. Most public communication settings are formal, and thus the members of the audience usually do not interrupt the speaker to voice disapproval. Audience members do, however, clap and smile in agreement with the speaker. Public communication within organizations usually does not occur on a daily basis. This type of communication may occur, however, at banquets, award ceremonies, and press conferences, for example.

Communication in the Organizational Context

The traditional types of communication occurring in organizations, like the ones previously discussed, can be further grouped into the primary "forms," or categories of communication in organizations. Raymond Lesikar (1976), who has written extensively on this subject, provides three categories of communication specific to the organizational context as being: (1) internal-operational communication, (2) external-operational communication, and (3) personal communication.

Internal-Operational Communication.   Internal-operational communication consists of "structured communication within the organization directly related to achieving the organization's work goals" (Lesikar, 1976, p. 9). Structure implies that the communication is part of the operation of the organization. The work goals of the organization refer to the primary reason the organization exists—for example, a service organization or a manufacturing organization. Lesikar recognizes that internal-operational communication is carried out through a variety of structured activities. Examples of this type of organizational communication are inter-departmental communications such as sales reports and inventory records, which communicate needs to the production planning department. Other examples are production orders, which communicate needs to the manufacturing department. Additionally, department managers need to inform superiors and subordinates of important information which is most often done through memos and telephone calls. Memos, reports, conversations, and phone calls all intended to serve the function of coordinating efforts and achieving the work goals are related to this form of communication.

External–Operational Communication.   External–operational communication is that communication structured and concerned with achieving the organization's work goals, or interorganizational activity. It is conducted with those entities existing outside the organization (Lesikar, 1976). It refers to the communication the organization engages in with regulatory and governmental agencies and with the public—its customers, vendors, service companies, the press, and the public at large. More specifically, external–operational communication refers to sales and public relations efforts, service follow-ups, and advertising, including brochures, flyers, radio and television spots, and newspaper and magazine pieces. Because every organization is dependent on its environment for success, this type of communication is vital for continued operation.

Organizations usually invest large sums of money in their public communication. It is through this form of communication that customers and the public learn about the organization, its products, and its services. Through public relations and advertising campaigns, the organization can sell itself, its image, and its goods.

Personal Communication.   The final form of organizational communication discussed by Lesikar deals with personal communication. He states that not all communication occurring in organizations is based solely on the task at hand. He defines personal communication as "that incidental exchange of information and feeling which human beings engage in whenever they come together" (1976, p. 11). Because individuals are social beings, we have a continuous need to communicate with others, if for no other reason than to establish and maintain healthy social relationships. Although personal communication is not directly a part of the organization's work goals, it is vital nonetheless.

Talk to those who have worked in organizations in which personal communication was discouraged or in which the personal communication that did occur was mostly negative. They will verify that it had a direct and negative impact on how they functioned in that organization and how well they did their jobs. The ability to engage in rewarding communication with others, simply for the sake of establishing and sustaining personal relationships, is important to the members of any organization. The personal communication we have with others affects our attitudes, beliefs, opinions, and willingness to do our jobs. It has a direct impact on how well we perform our organizational roles.

Now that we have established a working definition of organizational communication and have reviewed the different types and levels of communication in organizations, let us turn to the various models used to explain the process of communication.

MODELS OF COMMUNICATION

Human communication within organizations is a dynamic and ongoing process. Within this book we will assume that communication is a transaction. By this we mean that the process is a complicated one consisting of sender/receivers, noise, and verbal and nonverbal messages to mention a few. Before we more fully explore the idea of communication as a transaction, let us first take an historical look at the development of communication models.

Communication as Action

Perhaps the earliest, best known, and most basic model of communication was developed by Claud E. Shannon and Warren Weaver in 1949. The model was developed in response to World War II, the measurement of electronic signals, and advances in telecommunications.

Figure 1-1 represents a version of the Shannon and Weaver (1949) model. Their original information theory and model are, however, much more detailed than the simple illustration presented. Their model, as does the figure below, represents a mechanistic, or "communication as action" perspective. In this model, a source develops a message consisting of signs. The signs are then transferred to signals, or encoded. The signs are sent over a channel to a receiver who then decodes, or interprets them. The model also consists of noise, which affects the process. Noise is anything that interferes with the message being transmitted. It depicts the communication process as being linear and sequential. A message flows in one direction, in a straight line from sender to receiver. The message eventually comes to a complete stop when it has been decoded.

B. Aubrey Fisher, in his book *Perspectives on Human Communication* (1978), provides a thorough overview of this perspective. He recognizes that in viewing communication as a one-way action, or as a mechanistic process, "the physical elements of communication, [and] the transmission and reception of messages flowing in a conveyor-belt fashion among source-receivers" are the most important components (p. 133). Moreover, he purports that the channel of communication, or how the message is delivered, is the locus of the model. It is the "place of *where* to look in order to explain the communication process" (p. 95).

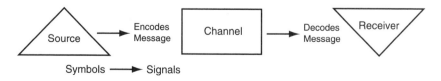

FIGURE 1-1   **Communication as action.**

This way of conceptualizing communication has many implications (Fisher, 1978; Trenholm, 1991). First, as already noted, it assumes that communication is linear or one-way and that each part transfers its functions in a sequential manner. Each component of the system has its own specific function that moves forward to the next component. Each part affects only that part that comes next in line. The second assumption of this perspective is that the elements are "material entities that exist in time and space" (Trenholm, 1991, p. 32). Communication, then, is a process that occurs over time and across space. A final assumption is that the process can be broken down into separate parts and that the sum of the parts is no greater than the whole. In other words, we can study the process by breaking it down and looking at the components one by one and receive a complete picture of communication.

The model presented in Figure 1-1 was originally applied to electronic communication, yet has also been used to describe human, face-to-face communication. Communication is seen as a one-way event. A source sends a message to a receiver. There is no discussion of feedback or response from the receiver in this model. As our knowledge of the dynamics of communication developed, however, our models changed as well.

Communication as Interaction

The Shannon and Weaver model (1949) was criticized for its linearity and lack of feedback. Mass communication experts McQuail and Windahl (1993) note how the components of another model (DeFleur, 1970) adds other ingredients to the mechanistic model thus improving the Shannon and Weaver concept of communication. The notion of feedback in communication brings us to the second type of model—communication as interaction.

Figure 1-2 is a simpler version of the DeFleur (1970) model, a source encodes and sends a message through a channel to a receiver who then decodes it. The receiver, then, becomes a source sending a message or feedback back to the original source over a channel. Noise, or interference, can happen at any point in this process. It is easy to see how this model is more circular than the mechanistic model developed earlier. With the inclusion of feedback, the model becomes two-way, rather than one-way, as is the mechanistic model. The circularity of the process lends itself to interaction rather than to a simple linear action. The two parties interact with each other, rather than act upon each other.

In models presenting communication as an interaction between two individuals, the source is provided with feedback, which allows it then to change and adapt more effectively to the situation at hand. The availability of feedback increases the possibility of isomorphism, or agreement between the meaning intended and the meaning received. In the interaction model, the original source of the message could adapt and rephrase messages so that the intended receiver can achieve a clear understanding of that message.

Even with the addition of feedback to the model, it still isn't complete. The interaction model still portrays communication as a static event. One person is the

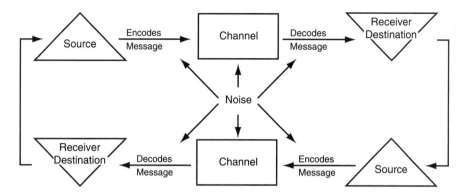

FIGURE 1-2 **Communication as interaction.**

sender and one person is the receiver and they then change roles. It suggests that there are "discrete acts" of sending and receiving, beginning and ending (Adler & Rodman, 1994, p. 17). Communication as interaction models were criticized in that they portray communication as coming back to the original source, full circle, to exactly the same point at which it began. That, as Dance (1967), a communication scholar, notes, is a very inaccurate depiction of the process of communication. The more recent models of communication were developed to reflect more accurately the entire process and dynamic of human communication.

Communication as Transaction

Current models of communication portray with more completeness what we now believe the process of communication to be. More contemporary models show communication as a transaction.

Communication as transaction models, such as the one presented in Figure 1-3 adapted from Dean Barnlund's (1962) model, represent a major change in our conception of human communication. We no longer see the process as being either linear or circular. The crux of the transaction model is that we are, simultaneously and continuously, both sender and receiver. Individuals are both sending and receiving messages simultaneously. We are not first a sender and then a receiver, but continually both.

The model in Figure 1-3 depicts two individuals engaged in a transaction. Each person is both simultaneously a sender and a receiver. Each person emits nonverbal and verbal messages, and each person possesses internal information such as past experiences, attitudes, prejudices, and ideas that influence how messages are encoded and decoded. Each person also perceives external information such as the location, the time, and any cues related to the context that affects how messages are encoded and decoded. Noise is anything that interferes with the transmission or reception of the message. Noise can be physical, such as an airplane flying overhead

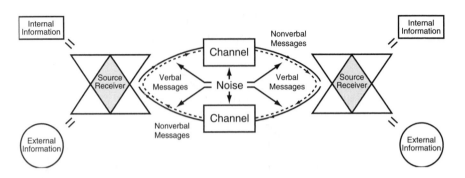

FIGURE 1-3 **Communication as transaction.**

or a loud stereo that inhibits us from hearing the message. It could also be psychological in that we may currently be preoccupied with thoughts about the upcoming sales meeting and therefore not paying attention to what the other person is saying. Finally, the noise could be semantic in that we either do not understand the language used within the message or misinterpret it. These elements, taken together, give us a picture of communication as a transaction.

Now that we understand the elements involved in a communication transaction, let us turn to some principles guiding this process. Hybels and Weaver (1992) suggest three principles of the transactional process: (1) Participants are continuously and simultaneously both sender and receiver. (2) Communication has a past, present, and future. (3) Participants play roles. The first principle implies that even if we are not talking or moving, we are still sending messages. Even when listening to someone complain about a boss, or a new policy, our posture, face, and eyes are still communicating to that individual our approval or disapproval of the complaint. When we receive messages, our response is simultaneously sending a message to the other person; therefore, we are always a sender and a receiver concurrently. The second principle implies that we encode and decode present messages based on what we have experienced in the past. Our past helps us give meaning to information. If our former supervisor, whom we did not get along with, was very young, we may have ill feelings about the next younger supervisor we have. The future also affects how we encode and decode messages. Do we anticipate having future encounters with this person? Will we need to ask this person a favor in the next few weeks? Our anticipated future communication with others influences how we may act and talk around them. Finally, roles, or the parts we play around others, have a direct impact on our communication. Are we taking the role of a peer of equal status or of a supervisor of higher status? How we see our role and the role of the other determines, in part, how we organize and interpret messages. When we take an equal role with our peers, we are different than when we take the higher status role of the supervisor or the professor.

The development of models reflects significant transformations in how we perceive the phenomenon of communication. Starting with the mechanistic, or action, model with its emphasis on linearity, moving to the interaction model with its emphasis on circularity, and ending with the transaction model and its emphasis on simultaneity and internal and external factors, we can see how communication has grown in its complexity. The models presented in this chapter are certainly not the only ones available. They do, however, embody much of the debate over the years concerning the process of communication.

BARRIERS TO ORGANIZATIONAL COMMUNICATION

We have reviewed the fundamentals of communication and the development of communication models. Also, we have looked at how complex communication is when viewed as a transaction between individuals. Given this, we are able to explore the barriers to effective communication with a focus on the context of the organization.

The Process of Abstracting

Alfred Korzybski (1958) proposed his "structural differential" to help explain the process of abstraction, or how we abstract from the "thing" to communicating about it with each other. He was one of the founding fathers of the general semantics movement that studied how we use language and how we relate to reality through the use of symbols, both verbal and nonverbal. He showed us the process of abstraction from the existence of a "thing," to how it is perceived and talked about. Here, first the process of abstracting will be described, then it will be related to the area of organizational communication through a discussion of the resulting barriers to communication and their implications.

As in the simple version of the process of abstracting presented in Figure 1-4, we can see the progression from the existence of a thing, down through the ladder of abstraction.

- *Level 1.* The first level is referred to as the event level. This level assumes a natural existence of something. At this level there is a "mad dance of 'electrons'" (Korzybski, 1958, p. 387) which, when taken together, construct an "event." The event consists of "an infinite number of characteristics" (p. 387) represented in the diagram by the small marks.
- *Level 2.* The second, or object level, is a silent level. The number of characteristics at this point "is large but finite" (p. 387). At this point on the ladder, the object exists apart from anything we say about it. We receive data through our senses, yet have not put anything regarding the event into words.
- *Level 3.* At the third, or descriptive level, we are able to describe the event. We can give it a name and talk about it. We can talk about what it looks, smells, tastes, and feels like. We begin to talk about our perceptions, and to "disregard

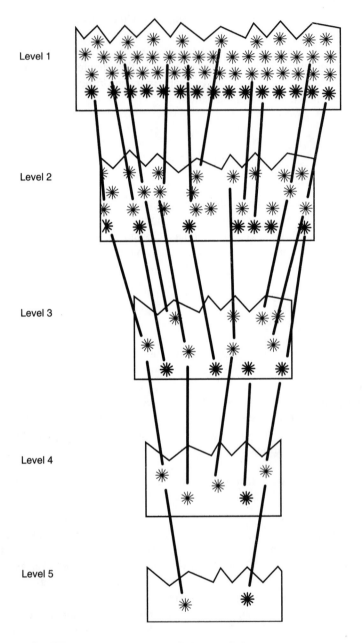

Level 1

Level 2

Level 3

Level 4

Level 5

FIGURE 1-4   **The process of abstracting.**

the accidental characteristics...[and maintain]...characteristics which are of particular immediate interest to us" (p. 387).

- *Level 4.* In the fourth, or inferential level, we are able to make evaluative comments about the object or event. Rather than merely describing it, we are able to judge its worth, goodness, and badness. We begin to infer things about the object. We talk about the abstractions we made at the previous level.
- *Level 5.* From this point on in the process, we continue to make inferences. We make inferences about our inferences and so on. The levels of abstraction continue.

The abstractions continue on indefinitely as we continue to talk about the object or event, with each step becoming more abstract, more removed from the initial thing. It must be noted that at each level, and most profoundly at the first and second levels, we leave out characteristics of the object or event. Since we can never entirely perceive the whole of something, there are literally thousands of characteristics left out that will go unnoticed, neglected, or become forgotten at the next level of abstraction. Those characteristics that we carry with us are referred to as "abstracted characteristics." What began as a conglomeration of millions of stimuli is eventually reduced, through the process of abstraction, to a few features.

Not only does the structural differential show us the process of abstraction and how we talk about reality, it also provides us with ways of overcoming many of the problems, discussed below, associated with this process. As the model of abstraction indicates, we must continually return to the less abstract levels for more accurate information from which to evaluate and describe the situation/behavior at hand. The assumption is that our language and interpretation will be more precise and correct if we continually go back and check them against the "reality" of the situation. We should not rely only on the abstracted characteristics but return also to the less abstract levels for more information. We should become "ideal observers" (Korzybski, 1958), always looking for more information from the less abstracted levels on which to base our perceptions.

Barriers to Communication

We can take the ideas presented in the structural differential, or ladder of abstraction, and relate them to our communication in organizations. Lesikar (1972) points out four traditional ways of looking at barriers to communication in organizations. First, he acknowledges the obvious problems of physical distance brought about by physical growth. More recent, in fact, are those problems created by individuals who no longer even work in the physical confines of the organization itself, as discussed in Chapter 13. It is not difficult to find those who work out of a car or out of a home, rather than an office building. Lesikar notes also that the "separation of communicans clearly contributes to communication difficulty" (p. 41). Second, he refers to those barriers caused by the traditional hierarchy of power and status in organizations. He notes how, more often than not, the lower and upper ranks do not communicate easily with each other. He points out that job specialization is a third source of organizational barriers. Through specializing, individuals identify mostly with those possessing similar specializations. This, he notes, promotes antagonism and problems between and among different groups. Last, he points to the problems created by "information ownership." When gatekeepers keep information to themselves, the organization as a whole suffers.

With knowledge of the difficulties in the process of abstracting, as well as in many of the other problems associated with communication just presented, we can turn to some more specific barriers that result from these two phenomenon.

Implications of Abstracting and Barriers

Reality Is in Process, Unique, and Infinite

There are a number of implications we can apply to organizational communication based on abstracting and the principles of general semantics. First, general semantics suggests that "reality is in process, unique, and infinite" (Lesikar, 1972, p. 44). By "in process" we mean that our conception of what is "real" is always changing. Just as we, as individuals, change from day to day, so do others. Thus, the world is in a constant state of change. The concepts of uniqueness and infinity of reality provide related implications. As we know, no two things are exactly alike or identical. There are an infinite number of variations to things, snowflakes, for example. Lesikar states that "Differences are the rule and similarities the exception" (1972, p. 44). In sum, then, everything and every action and utterance is unique. There are an infinite number of ways things can be said, interpreted, acted on or acted out.

When thinking about reality as constantly changing, with unique components and an infinite number of ways to communicate and interpret messages, we become aware of how difficult it may be to correctly understand others. Related to these notions, Ichheiser (1970) refers to his "mechanisms of rigidity." He discusses two "misinterpretive mechanisms" as being "first, the tendency to stabilize the image of other people in our own mind, and second, the tendency to make this image definite" (p. 77). He believes that we generally assume that people do not fundamentally change, even when the person may have undergone significant transformations. It is through maintaining a stable and consistent image of a person that we are able to predict and understand his or her behavior. Our images of others become static and tend to hold others down, thus not allowing for change and growth.

It is easy to relate this to our communication in the organizational context. For example, perhaps we went to high school with the new employee, Joe. After high school, Joe went to college for a bachelor's degree, then on to graduate school for an advanced degree. During this time, Joe made some far-reaching changes in his attitudes and behaviors. He went from being a lazy, loud, and overbearing bully, to being an educated, mature, responsible, and good-natured adult. Our mechanisms of rigidity make it extremely difficult for us to perceive and accept Joe as the person he is today. We tend to hold on to our old ways of thinking about him. We do not accept the changes he has gone through and the person he has become. As one can conclude, situations such as this can easily lead to rumor, gossip, defamation, and an inability to accurately perceive Joe's worth as a trusted and productive employee.

Communication Is Based on Our Perceptions of Reality

Lesikar (1972, 1976) notes that we can only communicate about that very small part of reality that we perceive. Human perception is limited. As the process of abstracting demonstrates, we perceive only a small part of the reality that surrounds us. Our senses are either incapable of perceiving it or we tend to ignore it. Lesikar writes (1972, p. 45): "Because of our limited perception, rarely can we communicate about the whole of an object or event, for we are not able to perceive all the details of it." We form our opinions about situations, which then become our reality, on only a small portion of the entire situation. Others, who may perceive characteristics, then form different opinions about the same situation.

Ichheiser (1970), a general semanticist, notes that behavior is always determined by two factors: personality characteristics such as attitudes and dispositions and situational characteristics such as time and location. He recognizes that we can never adequately interpret another's behavior when we ignore one or the other. This notion complicates even further the implication described above. Since it is important to consider both the person and the situation, the amount of information we perceive from both, then, is even more limited since there is more to take into account. Ichheiser believes that, more often than not, we tend to attribute a person's behavior to his or her personality and ignore the situation at hand. Moreover, he points out that we often are not in a position to observe and evaluate the situation at hand, thus considerably limiting our perceptual ability. For example, we may see a fellow employee come in late for a meeting and miss a deadline. We may, then, categorize this individual as lazy and ineffectual, when in reality the person may have extenuating circumstances that would make the behavior understandable.

Related to our overemphasis of the personality is the notion that we assume people act the same way in all situations. Ichheiser refers to this as "overestimating personal unity." He believes that we see only a part of the person in any situation and that the person may behave differently in other situations. We perceive a person to be a particular way based, perhaps, on our limited experiences with him or her in that particular situation. We assume the person's personality is unified across situations. Again, we are perceiving only a small part of this person's repertoire of behavior, yet we act upon it as though it pertains to every situation this person encounters. We see a tough and assertive female account representative and assume she behaves the same way with her family, which may or may not be the case.

Along with his discussion of our overemphasis on personality, Ichheiser also discusses a success–failure dichotomy. He states that we often evaluate people by the consequences of their actions, as being either a success or a failure. Because true success and failure depend upon both personality characteristics and situational factors, our over-reliance on personality issues may keep us from correctly evaluating the role of the situation in the person's success or failure. We may say, for example, that a successful boss or employee has all the characteristics that accompany a "successful" person, such as intelligence and motivation, yet fail to see that perhaps this person was simply in the right place at the right time. In this way, again, we are failing to see the whole picture and acting on a few limited perceptions.

Related to this idea of perceiving only a part of the whole, Ichheiser's (1970) concept of "mote-beam mechanism" serves as an example, yet also as an antithesis. Mote-beam, sometimes confused with projection, in which we attribute characteristics we possess to another person who does not possess them, refers to the notion that we perceive certain characteristics in others that we do not perceive in ourselves. For instance, we may perceive and condemn certain attitudes in others such as bigotry and aggressiveness, which we ignore in ourselves. Thus, not only do we perceive and act on a small part of the whole person, but we falsely perceive certain characteristics of the other that we do not admit to possessing in our own self-evaluation. We may assume a successful manager is using sneaky and underhanded methods for increasing production, yet we deny those very same behaviors in ourselves.

Imprecise Relationship of Symbols and Reality

Lesikar (1972) presents a third implication of general semantics and the abstraction process. He notes that to "convey reality accurately would require a language as complex as reality itself. It would have to convey the billions...of variations that exist" (p. 46). Because this is virtually impossible, our language is much more elementary than the reality it describes. Our use of symbols, or language to describe reality, therefore, is imprecise and inexact. We can never truly describe something in total. As noted earlier, we attend to only a few characteristics of the many available to us.

When we talk, for example, about a new product, the sales representative can never *fully* explain the "thing." The salesperson may describe what it looks like, feels like, smells like, what it does, and so on. Yet, due to our inability to perceive many of its characteristics because of the limits of our senses, as well as our lack of vocabulary to describe it, many characteristics will never be discussed. This would be true, for example, of the chemical components in a new brand of ink or the molecular design of a new shampoo.

Uniqueness of Meanings and Perceptions

The fourth implication presented by Lesikar (1972) deals with the notion that not only do we perceive different realities, but we give different meanings to the realities we perceive. He states that our minds are unique in that they "filter" perceptions differently. We each possess our own knowledge, experiences, emotional make-up, pattern of thinking, logic, biases, and such (p. 47). Consequently, then, we each give unique meanings to the information we perceive. Given this, Lesikar believes that "miscommunication is always present" (p. 47).

Ichheiser (1970) believes that it is not the differences of perception, but the lack of awareness of these differences that is most problematic. He states that because we are unique, we will inevitably possess certain limitations that make understanding the behavior of others very complex and often incorrect. He further notes that "we have to realize that other personalities may lie beyond the range of our insight either because they belong to another psychological type, or because they belong to cultural types, or because they belong to another 'situational' type" (pp. 67, 68). By psychological types he means, for example, the difference between extroverted and introverted individuals. Cultural types refers to the different ways members of particular groups perceive social reality, and situational types refers to the influence the situation may have on the individual's behavior.

There will always be some degree of misinterpretation and miscommunication. That is part of the human condition. The general semantics philosophy, and the process of abstraction and its implications presented above, however, equip us with a better understanding of what can go wrong. It provides us with information we can use to combat these communication and perception difficulties and with instruments we can use in the organizational setting to improve our communication with superiors, subordinates, and peers. The information provided above is by no means exhaustive of the barriers to effective communication, but it is, nonetheless, a point from which we can begin to understand the difficulties in the process of effective communication.

Now that we have reviewed what communication is, the problems associated with communication, and what the process of communication may look like, let us focus on the theoretical perspectives, both traditional and contemporary, that examine the role of communication in the organizational setting.

THEORETICAL PERSPECTIVES OF ORGANIZATIONS

Those who study organizations generally believe that the first attempt to analyze communication and organizational activities occurred in the late nineteenth and early twentieth centuries with individuals such as Max Weber, Henri Fayol, and Frederick Taylor. However, if we look deep enough, we can see that the study of organizations and organizing has its root in the field of classical rhetoric (Tompkins, 1987). It is suggested that "what is today called organizational theory (as well as management and administration) is an extension of the classical concerns of rhetorical theory" (Tompkins, 1987, p. 77). For example, Aristotle was probably the first to discuss persuasion through three types of proof: ethos, pathos, and logos. Phillip Tompkins, in his revealing comparison of classical rhetoric and organizational communication theories, suggests that Aristotle's ethos, (a person's character), is like Weber's description of personal or charismatic authority. Aristotle's second proof, pathos (the power to stir emotions), is like Weber's description of traditional authority. The last form of proof, logos (the use of persuasive arguments), is comparable to Weber's rational–legal authority. Although the intent herein is not to provide a detailed comparison of classical rhetoric and organizational theories, it can be seen that there is a striking similarity between many of the concepts presented in this section and those of classical rhetoric.

From the beginning, organizations were looking for better and more efficient ways to "get the job done." Beginning with the traditional perspectives, and continuing on to more recent and contemporary thoughts, we can easily see how the role of communication has changed.

The perspectives presented in this chapter represent a change in thinking by those who study organizations and organizational communication. Beginning with the foundation for analyzing behavior at work with classical theory, to acknowledging the importance of human relations in the workplace, to more contemporary perspectives such as chaos theory, we can see an evolution of thought on our behavior in the organizational setting.

Classical Management Theory

The earliest attempts to understand the complexities of organizations and maximize productivity during the early 1900s were undertaken by Frederick Taylor, an engineer, Henri Fayol, an industrialist, and Max Weber, a social theorist. Taylor, Fayol, and Weber individually developed theories which, when taken together, are referred to as "classical management theory." Daniels and Spiker write (1994, p. 52) that "These three theorists differed from one another in many of the principles that they advocated, but they shared a common idea that effective organizational performance is determined by efficient design of work and organizational structure." To better understand the ideas behind classical management, it is first necessary to review the three theories on which it is based—scientific management theory, administrative theory, and bureaucracy.

Scientific Management Theory

At the turn of the century, through observing workers shoveling iron ore at Bethlehem Steel, Frederick Winslow Taylor, in his classical book, *The Principles of Scientific Management* (1911), noted how some workers used long shovels, some used short ones, some stood straight while others bent their knees. By studying and timing the individual approaches the workers took, Taylor determined he had found the "one best way" to get the job done in order to improve productivity and decrease backaches. His ideas shaped companies and influenced managers for generations. They contributed to massive increases in productivity and the standard of living.

Taylor's focus was not necessarily on the output of work, but on how the work was accomplished. Taylor believed that by analyzing all of the steps in a work process and then by creating standardized procedures for those steps, managers could identify the best method for accomplishing that task, thus guaranteeing maximum efficiency. The individual was a passive part of the "process" for Taylor, almost as if he or she was part of the work apparatus. However, in his book the worker is discussed as an individual. He concerned himself with understanding the motives that influence individuals and realized that effective managers must do more than reorganize work processes, they must also be concerned with the "mental attitude" of the workers. He does believe, however, that individuals' motives can be understood and shaped through scientific control and analysis, much as the work process is understood and controlled.

Principles of Scientific Management Theory

Scientific management, as advanced by Taylor in 1947, has many important principles.

1. There is "one best way" to perform a task or job—Through careful observation and analysis, managers can determine the most efficient way to proceed on a task. Effectiveness should be measured scientifically and objectively.
2. Employees should be scientifically selected and improved—Employees should be hired based on their skill and expertise, and their work productivity should be developed.
3. Workers are monetarily motivated—Workers will increase productivity if they receive more money in return.
4. Management plans the work, and laborers follow through with the plan—Workers take orders from the foreman who is in charge of that particular task. Cooperation rather than individuality should be emphasized.
5. Clearly defined rules, regulations, and roles—Harmony in an organization can be achieved by clearly defined and scientifically based rules and regulations.
6. Loafing should be eliminated—Workers should be serious in giving their best effort.

Scientific management theory, as defined by Taylor, has two essential elements: cooperation and scientific knowledge (Rasberry & Lindsay, 1994). Taylor's ideas significantly transformed work standardization and planning in a variety of areas such as industrial engineering, personnel, and supervision (Kreps, 1990). The role of communication was to help define and plan tasks in the most efficient and effective way possible. It was used as a means for directing and controlling the worker.

Administrative Management Theory

Administrative management theory serves as a guideline for the management of organizations based on strict rules and lines of authority. The focus is on the administrative level of the hierarchy. Henri Fayol pioneered this perspective in the early 1900s. In his book, *General and Industrial Management,* published in 1916, Fayol discusses the organizational hierarchy and the flow of communication within that hierarchy. According to Fayol, people wishing to talk with others on different levels must follow the hierarchy up, over, and down. Horizontal communication with peers in other departments was not permitted—"The chain of command was inflexible and insensitive to the human needs of organization members" (Kreps, 1990, p. 70). The person would need to go up his or her departmental hierarchy and then over to and down the other's departmental hierarchy in order to communicate.

The implications from following a strict chain of communication are clear. Therefore, Fayol developed his "gangplank" theory suggesting that if a person wishes to engage in horizontal communication with a peer in another department, he or she could do so and bypass the departmental hierarchies as long as permission was granted by a supervisor. For Fayol, however, communication in organizations was still a vertical, uni-directional act following formal channels.

Principles of Administrative Management Theory

Fayol (1916) advanced twenty key management ideas related to his administrative theory. In sum, the principles are as follows:

1. Planning is necessary to analyze tasks, design strategies, identify needed materials, and accomplish goals.
2. Through organizing personnel, equipment and resources can be allocated.
3. Managers should command the employees to work toward the organization's goals.
4. Activities of groups should be coordinated to reach the organization's goals.
5. Managers should use control to ensure employees are doing their jobs correctly.
6. Division of labor increases productivity and efficiency.
7. Subordinates should yield to superiors' authority to control.
8. Disciplined employees will submit to rules and regulations, otherwise they will be penalized.
9. Unity of command implies that each employee will have only one superior to report to.
10. Scalar chain implies a clear vertical line of communication between superiors and subordinates following the organizational hierarchy.
11. Unity of direction implies that all organizational members should be working toward the same organizational goals.
12. Organizational members should act in the interest of the organization, not in the interest of individual.
13. Remuneration implies that employees are monetarily motivated and that their work performance is directly related to their earnings.
14. Centralization of power implies that central administration should maintain close control over activities for the most success.
15. All organizational activities should be clearly integrated into the organization's goals. Each activity should have its place in the order of things.
16. All organizational members should be treated equally and fairly.
17. Stability of tenure implies that as long as an employee is doing his or her job correctly and accomplishing assigned tasks, employment should be continued.
18. Managers should stay aware of tasks that need to be done and direct their employees toward those tasks.
19. Esprit de corps implies that when members take pride in their organization, organizational goals can best be achieved.

20. Line and staff functions need to be determined. Staff assist and support line managers who direct and make decisions about how to best accomplish the organization's goals.

Overall, the administrative management perspective of the early 1900s did little to further the role of communication within organizations. Fayol did, however, clearly define the flow and direction of communication in organizations and recognized the necessity of horizontal communication with his gangplank notion. In addition to scientific and administrative management theories, the final component to classical management theory is that of bureaucracy developed by Max Weber.

Bureaucracy

Max Weber is known as the "father of bureaucracy." In *The Theory of Social and Economic Organization* (1947), he describes a bureaucratic organization. As set forth by his eight qualities presented below, we can see that the role of communication in organizations is, again, very orderly and formalized. It follows a clear and rational pattern. Weber's conception of bureaucracy "has almost become synonymous with organizational inefficiency, red tape, and insensitivity" (Kreps, 1990, p. 65). Highly bureaucratic organizations are seen as very formalized, very inflexible, and very insensitive to workers' needs.

Qualities of a Bureaucratic Organization

1. Organizational tasks are accomplished through formalized rules, regulations, and procedures. All tasks and organizational activities are regimented and standardized.
2. Role specialization simplifies workers' activities. Breaking down complex tasks into specialized activities increases worker productivity.
3. The formal hierarchy helps direct employees' interpersonal relationships toward the organization's goals. One's place in the hierarchy is determined by the person's title in the organization and his or her expertise.
4. Technical competence and an ability to perform his or her task is the sole basis on which an individual should be hired and maintained. Job qualifications should be objectively evaluated by management.
5. Organizational tasks are more important than the individuals performing them. Personnel are interchangeable, therefore, the same task could be performed by a variety of qualified individuals.
6. Interpersonal relationships should remain impersonal and professional in order to accomplish organizational goals. Employees should concentrate on organizational goals rather than on their own goals.

7. Clearly defined job descriptions provide all members of the organization a formal outline of their duties and job responsibilities. Management's expectations should be clearly understood by all employees.
8. Organizations should have logical, clear-cut, and predictable rules and regulations to help promote order and to facilitate accomplishing organizational goals. Activities should be rational and predictable.

The government, large organizations, and universities have all been criticized for their red tape and bureaucratic styles. On one hand, organizations that become too bureaucratized and have too many rules, regulations, policies, and procedures can become self-defeating. They may red tape themselves into a static and stifling process. On the other hand, bureaucracy offers organizations a way of standardizing complex industries as long as everything in the process proceeds as it should.

Scientific management, administrative management theory, and bureaucracy form what has been referred to as the classical management perspective. This perspective, in general, promotes ideas such as standardization, organization, strict policies, procedures, job descriptions and regulations, a formal and rational flow of tasks and communication, structure, and social control. It views the worker as a part of the task and as one who is motivated strictly by money. As is seen in the description of each component of classical management theory presented above, communication did not necessarily play a prominent role. It was viewed as part of the worker's task. It was formalized, organized, and restricted only to that communication which helped workers achieve organizational goals.

According to Michael Macoby (1993) and David Freedman (1992), organizational scholars, the work environment has changed so dramatically that what Taylor, Fayol, and Weber purported almost a century ago is no longer applicable to the modern organization. They argue that with the introduction of computers, jobs are not as precise as they once were, and strict formats are a thing of the past. Organizations are becoming more decentralized in efforts to decrease cost and increase productivity. As Freedman (1992) notes, "the more science and technology reshape the very essence of business, the less useful the concept of management itself as a science seems to be" (p. 26). The environment today is often unpredictable, uncontrollable, and uncertain; this was not necessarily the case in the early 1920s. Today, employees can most effectively maximize productivity through the practice of continual learning, and then by making sound judgments and decisions on the available information.

Human Relations Theory

As an attempt to remedy problems encountered as a result of the classical management philosophy and its neglect of the human condition, organizations started to focus more on the employee. The individual and social relationships, which were not seen as being important in earlier perspectives, have now become paramount. The human relations perspective was not intended to change the classical features of organizations. Rather, it was intended to provide tools for managing relationships under the traditional systems of hierarchy and authority (Daniels & Spiker, 1994).

The human relations movement began in the 1930s with experiments that came to be known as the Hawthorne Studies. In 1939 Roethlisberger and Dickson published the findings of their experiments in *Management and the Worker.* The findings gave way to the Harvard-affiliated human relations school of management under the leadership of Elton Mayo. The experiments, conducted at the Western Electric Hawthorne plant in Illinois between 1925 and 1932, were designed to find ways to increase productivity and efficiency. By both increasing and decreasing the illumination of lights in the experimental groups, and maintaining the consistency of illumination in the control group, the researchers found that productivity increased. The results of the study led the researchers to question the scientific and classical ways of thinking. They concluded that it was not the change in illumination at the facility that led to increased productivity, but rather the fact that someone was paying attention to the workers. The extra attention influenced workers to increase their work performance. The workers felt they were important, that someone was studying them. This finding led to other experiments in relay assembly tasks, interviews, and bank wiring observations to further explore this phenomenon.

Human relations is concerned with the interpersonal relationships between employees. The human relations perspective is summed up succinctly with the question: "How can we best achieve and maintain a fair balance between the *things* of production—the machines, the buildings, the materials, the systems—and the *humanity* of production—the workers, the foremen, the managers, the shareholders?" (Sheldon, 1960, p. 7). The aim of management must be to render industry more humane.

Some believe that organizations generally gave only "lip service" to the human relations perspective (Filey, 1960). It has been proposed that the avenue to good human relations applications in organizations should be twofold: (1) "there must be a clear definition of the function of human relations and of its place in the business environment," and (2) "the principles of sound human relations procedure must be understood and applied by all members at *all* levels in the business organization" (p. 35).

The activities of the human relations functions are as follows (Filey, 1960, pp. 39, 40):

1. Management development—Management's attitudes must portray a true commitment to human relations beliefs. They should do more than just role-play human understanding, they should act as role models for their employees.

2. Employee relations—It is important to provide employees with enough information to promote job satisfaction, motivation, and cooperation. Employee relations can be improved through practices such as attitude surveys and employee counseling and policy and practice explanations from superiors.

3. Labor relations—Efforts to promote sound labor–management relations, and a labor contract containing wishes of both labor and management, is key to effective labor relations. Maintaining effective two-way communication between management and labor through collective bargaining and grievance procedures are ways to improve this relationship.

4. Public or community relations—The final function implies that employees come to an organization with attitudes that have already been shaped by their environment. Therefore, to understand an individual's behavior on the job, one must also understand the individual's surroundings. Good public relations, where the individual receives positive information about the organization, are essential to developing sound human relations practices.

The role of communication was still mostly formal in the human relations perspective, but informal systems were recognized as inevitable. Communication was usually downward and used for direction and control. Upward communication was mostly cosmetic in that it was not truly valued by those higher up. Communication was used to guide and provide direction as well as to convey feelings of belongingness (Gibson & Hodgetts, 1991).

Unfortunately, some saw the human relations school of thought as being manipulative. Workers were offered false hopes. They were told they were important, yet managers, who still believed in the classical perspective, continued to treat them as though they were a part of the production machine. The application of human relations principles became superficial and had a tendency to decrease worker performance, rather than increase productivity. These shortcomings led to the emergence of the human resource theory of management.

Human Resource Theory

Near the end of the Second World War, organizational scholars and practitioners began to realize that workers have needs to be met other than those related only to wages or the desire to feel wanted. The human resource perspective, developed in response to these needs, "emphasizes genuine participation in all levels of the organizational hierarchy" (Kreps, 1990, p. 85). Its purpose is to make optimum use of employees, helping them to reach their full potential. This perspective advances the involvement of workers in the day-to-day decisions of the organization. It asserts that workers are motivated by sense of self-worth and not merely by their economic well-being. Workers are interested in meaningful and challenging tasks.

The assumptions behind the human resource perspective are much like those of the human relations perspective. It assumes that people do not inherently dislike work. Moreover, most people are more capable of exercising creativity, responsibility, self-direction, and self-control than their current jobs allow. This perspective suggests that managers need to tap into unused human potential. The worker should be viewed as a resource within the organization. The work environment should promote open participation so that all may contribute. It should also continue to broaden the worker's span of control (Miles, Porter, & Craft, 1966).

The idea of participative management arose from this perspective. It asserts that organizational leaders should, as much as possible, involve the workers in the decision-making process. Likert, in his book, *New Patterns of Management* (1961), proposed four types of management styles: (1) *exploitative-authoritative,* characterized by management's use of tight control and authority; (2) *benevolent-authoritative,* characterized by giving workers the feeling of power, yet not really giving them any control in the organization; (3) *consultative,* characterized by allowing workers to provide information to management, yet without management's really trusting the workers' insight; and (4) *participative,* characterized by the encouragement of workers to contribute in all matters and in decision-making processes.

The styles can be placed on a continuum from highly autocratic to highly democratic. He believed the fourth, or participative style, to be the most successful. The characteristics of this style include the following:

1. The communication between subordinates and supervisors should be open. Each should feel free to solicit ideas and opinions from the other, and each should feel free to discuss problems with the other.

2. Superiors and subordinates should work together to solve problems. Decision-making should be decentralized through all levels of the organization.

3. Communication should flow freely through all channels of communication. Communication should be horizontal, diagonal, and vertical so that it is relatively accurate.

4. Workers' goals should be determined by both superiors and subordinates. The goals should be high, but realistic.

5. Organizational members should exercise self-control. Control in the organization should be decentralized throughout the levels of the hierarchy.

The role of communication in the human resource perspective is important and flexible. It is formal and informal, both of which are deemed important, and vertical, horizontal, and diagonal. It can be used for control, support, organization, and direction. And finally, decision-making is decentralized (Gibson & Hodgetts, 1991).

Much as human relations, human resources has also been criticized for placing too much faith in "the power of its prescriptions for virtually any organizational setting" (Daniels & Spiker, 1994, p. 67). Not every employee in an organization is capable of self-control and responsible behavior. The maturity of the worker plays a large role in whether he or she is capable of handling such responsibilities. As we know, no one style is effective for all workers in all organizations in all settings.

Systems Theory

Knowing that not all organizations are the same, with the same dynamics and environmental influences, organizational scholars and practitioners adopted a systems perspective that acknowledges the interrelationship of the different components both within and outside the organization. By the late 1960s, "theoretical development . . . and organizational analysis seemed to be converging towards a systems-based . . . approach that focused on the adaptability of organizational designs to environmental imperatives" (Reed, 1992, p. 2). While classical theorists perceived of the organization as a machine-like process that operated through control, systems theorists perceived that organizations are more like living organisms with their own life cycles. Systems theory continues to be a pervasive and contemporary perspective on organizations. Communication is seen as the glue holding the systems and subsystems together, allowing for units to function in sync with each other.

Kreps writes (1991, p. 93) that "Systems theory provides a powerful descriptive model of organizational processes." The phrase, general systems theory, was derived to describe the widespread application of the systems perspective to organizations. In his book, *General Systems Theory: Foundations, Development, Applications* (1968), Ludwig von Bertalanffy provides the groundwork for developing a systems perspective for organizations. He suggests that the only meaningful way to study an organization is to view it as a system of mutually dependent parts. He views the organization as a complicated arrangement of related parts interacting and changing to adapt to the environment.

The systems perspective of organizations relies on several important concepts:

1. Input—Input in an organization is what the organization consumes. It can be a variety of things such as raw material, information, or the economy. The function of input is to describe the environment and potential trouble spots and to provide information for decision-making.

2. Output—Output from the organization is what it sends out to the public. This could be in the form of goods or services, public relations campaigns, and other information about the organization and its product.

3. Transformation—The process of taking input and turning it into output is referred to as transformation. It includes the network and subsystems working together.

4. Homeostasis—The reactions of the consumers, or customers to the output, is referred to as feedback. Feedback may be negative or positive and may consist of, for example, product consumption increase or decrease, letters of support or disapproval, and law suits. It allows the organization to maintain balance or homeostasis. Feedback is a homeostatic mechanism that allows all parts to function together.

5. Wholeness—Wholeness refers to the notion that the sum of all the components taken together as a system is greater than the effect of each in isolation or nonsummativity. Wholeness is also referred to as synergy, which implies that the sum of the whole is greater than the sum of the parts. The interdependence of the parts results in something much greater than what could be accomplished if each part worked in isolation.

6. Hierarchy—The relationship among system parts is organized in a hierarchy. This implies that a system is composed of related subsystems working together. The subsystem is composed of sub-subsystems working together and so on down to the most basic elements. The organization itself as a system is a subsystem of the environment or the suprasystem.

7. Openness—A system may be either relatively open or closed. Open systems are characterized as those having active and ongoing exchanges with their outside environment. Closed systems do not have such an exchange. Organizations, with their use of input from the surrounding environment, are classified as open systems. In a stable environment, the organization's process of transforming input into output is relatively routine and steady. It must not, however, ever underestimate or neglect the environment if it wants to continue operating in the future.

8. Equifinality—Equifinality implies that there are a number of ways to arrive at the same end. The output of the subsystem is not totally determined by the contents of the input. The interaction among subsystems allows for a variety of ways of transforming the input for a variety of ends. Organizations can perform numerous activities for a variety of goals.

9. Interdependence—All parts of the system are dependent on all other parts. Each subsystem interacts with other subsystems in cooperation to transform the input into output.

The role of communication in systems theory is dynamic. It is not merely an activity occurring within an organization, nor is it merely a tool for organizational control (Daniels & Spiker, 1994). Rather, communication defines the organization. It is the means through which the subsystems organize themselves and work together. It is the means through which homeostasis is maintained and wholeness is achieved. It flows freely throughout the hierarchy. It is through communication that the values and goals of the organization are understood, that decision making and conflict resolution within the system occur, and that power and leadership are exercised (Tracy, 1989).

Based on this modern view of organizations and the role of communication, organizational practitioners and scholars are turning to a newer, and still somewhat underdeveloped, perspective of organizations. The final perspective discussed in this section relies heavily on systems theory in its view of organizations. It does add, however, some new dimensions.

Chaos Theory and the Learning Organization

Freedman (1992) states: "Put simply, while traditional science focused on analysis, prediction and control, the new science emphasizes chaos and complexity" (p. 26). During the past few decades, managers and scientists have concluded that the work setting and related environments are in a constant state of flux. With the heavy reliance on computers and electronic methods of sending and retrieving information, organizations can hardly keep up with such a fast pace and onslaught of information. Fundamental assumptions about how organizations can best achieve their goals are being questioned as predictability and stability are becoming a thing of the past.

Fred Kofman and Peter Senge (1993), systems scholars, note three fundamental difficulties arising from the traditional ways of understanding organizational behavior. First, they believe that we typically fragment problems down into pieces, yet most of the problems faced by contemporary organizations are increasingly systematic and not truly amenable to such a linear analysis. Fragmentation develops specialists who treat the symptoms rather than the causes. Second, the authors discuss the problems related to competition. They imply that "we have lost the balance between competition and cooperation precisely at a time when we most need to work together" (Kofman & Senge, 1993, p. 9). Management teams and departments compete with each other to determine who is right, who knows more, and who is better, when these are the very people with whom they should be collaborating. Moreover, the authors suggest that our fixation on competition has also reinforced our reliance on quick fix and measurable results. The third problem recognized by Kofman and Senge deals with reactiveness. They assert that many managers believe that management *is* problem-solving. A problem solver is constantly putting out fires, trying to get something to go away.

Rather than trying to systematically analyze and organize organizational behavior, a new perspective, based in part on the system's model, was developed to help better understand the state of our contemporary work environment. Chaos theory, first developed by a meteorologist at MIT named Edward Lorenz and later introduced in the book, *Chaos: Making a New Science,* by James Gleick (1987), provides a new means for understanding organizational behavior.

While developing a computer program simulating weather patterns, Lorenz noted that even minute changes, which one would expect to then cause minor alterations, affected dramatic changes in the weather pattern. The weather was not nearly as systematic as was once thought. The first significant insight provided by chaos theory is that "For all practical purposes, the behavior of even relatively simple physical systems is fundamentally unpredictable" (Freedman, 1992, p. 30). A second significant insight offered by chaos theory suggests that patterns do exist within the seemingly random series of events in these systems. As Freedman (1992) suggests, certain paths are followed more often than others, certain paths, or "strange attractors" occur more frequently than others. These strange attractors allow us to determine, within broad parameters, what a system is likely to do, just not when it is likely to do it.

The emphasis in chaos theory is on how order emerges from the interaction of the parts as a whole, much like systems theory. Complex adaptive systems are those systems occurring in nature that are highly successful, such as a colony of ants, and are central to chaos theory. Freedman (1992) suggests the following ideas as being critical to the principles of chaos theory:

Principles of Chaos Theory

1. Successful organizations function as "complex adaptive systems."
2. These adaptive systems are self-managed. They function as a network of agents acting independently and without any central control.
3. The agents form "communities" that cooperate with each other to perform tasks none could accomplish on their own.

4. The systems become self-organizing in that they learn from feedback and the environment and embed the learning in their actual structure. They continuously rearrange themselves to adapt to changes.
5. Complex adaptive systems permit self-management and learning through flexibility by "flexible specialization." Agents change and adapt based on learning, abandoning old and obsolete behaviors, and acquiring new ones to accommodate the changing situation.

The principles developed in chaos theory represent the majority of contemporary organizational environments. Managers struggle to create order out of a rapidly changing environment and try to cope with perpetual uncertainty. The economy is no longer based on a steady industrial core, but instead on the transference of information. Chaos theorists may not be studying business organizations in particular, however; according to Freedman (1992), their perspective has already had an impact on current thinking and writing in the study of organizations.

Peter Senge, in his book *The Fifth Discipline: The Art and Practice of the Learning Organization* (1990), argues that most people feel lost in their organizations. There is too much information, change is too rapid, and there are too many conflicting demands on employees. They feel they are in a "system over which they have little or no influence" (p. 18). He recognizes that traditionally, as was espoused by scientific management theory, we were taught to break things down and analyze problems in their fragments and components. Therefore, we lose sight of the larger whole, we are unable to see the consequences of our actions. Senge describes what he refers to as the learning dilemma. He states that "we learn best from experience but we never directly experience the consequences of many of our most important decisions," thus creating a "learning horizon" (p. 23). He says it becomes impossible for organizational members to learn from direct experience when the consequences of our actions are beyond our learning horizon.

In contemporary organizations, notes Senge, problems are too complex and time is too short to engage in such behavior. He argues that managers should begin to look at organizations not as machines, but as living things. A more holistic approach focusing on the overall system should be taken. According to Senge, when managers become successful at systems thinking, seeing things as a whole, rather than as separate parts, a "learning organization" develops. Learning organizations are akin to the complex adaptive systems discussed earlier and espoused by chaos theorists. They possess several key principles, listed below.

1. *There is no such thing as a learning organization:* A learning organization is not a thing, it is not an object, building, company, or manual. A learning organization is a "category." It stands as a "medium in which we can articulate new models for living together" (Kofman & Senge, 1993, p. 16). A learning organization represents a view, a vision of how things operate together. It is a "climate that promotes learning" (McGill & Slocum, 1993, p. 74).

2. *The learning organization embodies new capabilities beyond traditional organizations:* Learning organizations are more adaptive and generative than traditional organizations. They seek deeper understandings rather than quick-fix solutions. They possess a commitment to openness and an ability to deal with complexity.

3. *Learning organizations are built by communities of servant leaders:* Leadership in learning organizations is collective. It is those individuals with capabilities regardless of their position in the hierarchy. Servant leaders refers to those individuals who chose to serve, both one another and a higher purpose.

4. *Learning arises through performance and practice:* Creating managerial practice fields, or virtual learning spaces, in which individuals can play and practice is an important part of creating a learning organization. Often this is done through software simulations.

5. *Process and content are inseparable:* In learning organizations the content or issues cannot be separated from the process we might use to learn about them.

6. *Learning is dangerous:* There is anxiety associated with facing the unknown and unfamiliar. The learning necessary for becoming a learning organization is called "transformational learning" (Kofman & Senge, 1993, p. 19). It is not concerned with tools or techniques, but it is concerned with who we are (Kofman & Senge, 1993; Senge, 1990).

Some organizations are taking steps to help managers develop the necessary skills needed to make this type of thinking possible, to create learning organizations. At the Center For Organizational Learning at Massachusetts Institute of Technology, researchers and practitioners are focusing on developing learning organizations. Through the use of software, individuals are able to plan and experiment with seemingly chaotic systems in an effort to understand the consequences of their actions within an organizational setting.

Peter Drucker (1992), an organizational scholar, asserts that modern organizations "must be organized for the systematic abandonment of whatever is established, customary, familiar, and comfortable, whether that is a product, service, or process; a set of skills; human and social relationship; or the organization itself" (p. 96). They will need to "plan abandonment" rather than to hold on to the present way of doing business. He stresses that every organization "has to build the management of change into its very structure" (p. 97). Drucker's conception of the modern organization sounds very much like a learning organization as described above. The process of learning and change is incorporated into the organization's schemata. The CEOs of some of America's fastest-growing companies "are cutting-edge practitioners of the management techniques...[by] learning how to gain strength from failure, and the importance of forging relationships and alliances, while also discovering new ways to unleash creativity" (Serwer, 1994, p. 42). These companies are fast becoming examples of learning organizations. They are not tied to any particular product or idea, but they keep experimenting. Failure is not only expected, but it is almost a requirement until the system comes together with an ever-changing environment (Serwer, 1994).

In sum, we have traced the evolution of perspectives on organizations beginning with the classical perspective, which emphasized accomplishing the task over all else, the human relations perspective, which seemed to emphasize interpersonal relations over all else, and the human resources perspective, which sought a balance between the two. Finally, we conclude with the two contemporary perspectives of systems and chaos theory, which both focus on the relationship among the different facets of an organization. The notion of a learning organization is still in its incubation stage. Only time will tell if modern organizations are willing and able to try and incorporate the learning organization principles into their modes of operation.

Looking ahead to the future, new trends can be predicted. For example, existing theories "may not be able to reflect adequately the realities of the new economic order" (Doktor, Tung, & Von Glidnow, 1991, p. 362). Theories and perspectives developed in the North American culture are becoming obsolete and narrow-minded. Organizational forms and structures that reflect a global awareness and sensitivity will need to be developed. Future management philosophies applicable in a variety of cultural settings also need to be developed.

CONCLUSION

This first chapter is designed to introduce us to some important fundamentals of communication. First, organizational communication is defined. The different levels and types of communication such as intrapersonal, interpersonal, small group, and public communication, are also discussed. Special attention is given to forms of communication occurring specifically within the organizational setting. The process of communication is then presented, focusing on models of communication as action, interaction, and transaction. The process of abstracting and barriers to effective organizational communication are described. Finally, the last section of the chapter presents both traditional and contemporary theoretical perspectives on organizations, focusing on classical management theory, human relations theory, human resource theory, systems theory, and chaos theory and the learning organization. We have seen the role of communication in organizations grow from being only a means to control the worker to becoming the defining central focus and activity within an organization.

GLOSSARY

Administrative management theory—a perspective on management developed by Fayol focusing on the hierarchy in an organization and the importance of communication following the chain of command. The focus is on concepts such as clearly defined worker responsibilities, centralization of power, and coordination of organizational activities.

Bureaucracy theory—a perspective on management developed by Weber focusing on formalized and inflexible roles. Rules and regulations, specialization, rationality, and impersonal relationships characterize this theory.

Chaos theory—a perspective based on systems theory emphasizing how order emerges from the interaction of parts as a whole. It promotes self-organizing through continual rearranging to adapt to new situations.

Classical management theory—a perspective on organizational design and management philosophy based on the scientific, bureaucracy, and administrative management theories. It stresses organization and hierarchy and the use of scientific means for selecting, evaluating, and remunerating workers.

Communication as action—communication flows in a linear, sequential, unidirectional path from sender to receiver.

Communication as interaction—communication flows in a circular path between sender and receiver who adapt their messages through feedback.

Communication as transaction—communication is a process in which participants are simultaneously sender and receiver, each influenced by internal and external factors and noise.

Content level—the report, information contained in the message.

External–operational communication—communication with entities existing outside the organizational setting that is directly related to accomplishing work goals.

Human relations theory—a perspective on management that focuses on satisfying the worker's desire to be a part of the organization. Management's task is to make the worker feel needed and wanted.

Human resource theory—a perspective on management that emphasizes worker participation in organizational decision-making at all levels of the hierarchy.

Interpersonal communication—communication we have with another individual.

Internal–operational communication—structured communication within the organization related to achieving work goals.

Learning organization—an organizational philosophy derived from chaos theory that promotes learning through play and practice.

Intrapersonal communication—communication we have with ourselves.

Organizational communication—both behaviors and symbols, generated whether intentionally or unintentionally, occurring between and among people who assign meaning to them, within an organizational setting.

Personal communication—communication that occurs within the organizational setting that is not related to achieving work goals.

Public communication—communication we have with a large number of people who constitute an audience.

Relationship level—implies how the content of the message is to be interpreted, defines the relationship.

Scientific management theory—a perspective on management developed by Taylor focusing on scientific and objective means for performing tasks and on selecting, developing, and remunerating workers. Utilizes clearly defined rules, roles, and regulations.

Small group communication—communication we have with a small number of individuals where everyone can readily interact with all members of the group.

Structural differential—depicts the process of abstracting from a "thing" to how we talk about it.

Systems theory—a perspective on management that emphasizes viewing the organization as a system rather than as individual components. The focus is on the mutual dependent parts of the organization interacting and adapting to the environment.

CASE STUDY

Adam arrives for work at the National Bank at 7:45 A.M. every day. He is the mortgage department supervisor responsible for eight individuals. Adam has been described as running a tight ship and as being very dogmatic, yet a very personable supervisor. He has developed several employee manuals for the bank, each describing policies, procedures, rules, regulations, and job duties. He is sure to cover everything in detail with new bank employees. Under his supervision, mortgages have increased steadily over the past five years. However, employee turnover in his department has also increased.

On this typical day he first visits the breakroom for some coffee and a quick donut. He stops to have a friendly chat with Leah, his star employee. Adam notices that Leah seems to be preoccupied with something, as her posture and face indicate that she isn't really paying attention to him. Upon returning to his desk he quickly reviews yesterday's activities to see that everything is in order, making notes and writing comments, while mentally preparing himself for the new day ahead. The bank opens at 9:00 and Adam and his staff are ready for the customers. From 9:00 to 12:30 Adam receives potential customers, answers questions from his staff, answers the phone, assists a teller, and generally takes care of business.

At 12:30 Adam has a lunch meeting with the local Rotary Club of approximately fifty members. At this meeting Adam, as the secretary of the organization, delivers the minutes of the last meeting to the members. At 2:00 he returns to work and continues on his daily routine. At 5:30, when the bank closes, Adam gathers his staff and they review the day's accounts to make sure all is in order. He notes that everyone's, especially Leah's, activities for the day were down significantly and mentions to them that he is very dissatisfied and expects that this will not happen again, since they have a positive record to maintain. He also notes that one employee was particularly rude to a potential customer and strongly requests that a letter of apology be mailed to this person at once. At 6:00 he leaves for home.

Discussion

Based on the hypothetical case presented above, which organizational theory is most applicable to Adam's style of management and why? How might it turn itself into a learning organization? Identify how the topics covered in this chapter relate to Adam's day at work.

Topics

The definition of organizational communication, the levels of content and relationship, and the occurrences of intrapersonal, interpersonal, small group, and public communication. Also, internal-organizational, external-organizational and public communication, as well as the models of communication.

REFERENCES

Adler, R. B., & Rodman, G. (1994). *Understanding Human Communication* (5th ed.). New York: Harcourt Brace.

Bachrach, S. B., & Aiken, M. (1977). Communication in administrative bureaucracies. *Academy of Management Journal, 20*(3), 365–377.

Barnlund, D. (1962). Toward a meaning-centered philosophy of communication. *Journal of Communication, 12,* 197–211.

Conrad, C. (1994). *Strategic Organizational Communication: Toward the Twenty-First Century* (3rd ed.). New York: Harcourt Brace.

Dance, F. E. X. (ed.). (1967). *A Helical Model of Communication.* New York: Holt, Rinehart and Winston.

Daniels, T. D., & Spiker, B. K. (1994). *Perspectives on Organizational Communication* (3rd ed.). Dubuque, Iowa: Wm C. Brown Communications.

DeFleur, M. L. (1970). *Theories of Mass Communication.* New York: David McKay.

Doktor, R., Tung, R. L., & Von Glidnow, M. A. (1991). Future directions for management theory development. *Academy of Management Review, 16*(2), 362–365.

Drucker, P. F. (1992). The new society of organizations. *Harvard Business Review, 69* (Sept.-Oct.), 95–104.

Dumaine, B. (1994). The trouble with teams. *Fortune, 130*(5, Sept.), pp. 86–92.

Fayol, H. (1916). *General and Industrial Management.* London: Pitman.

Filey, A. C. (1960). What is human relations? In I. L. Heckmann, Jr., & S. G. Huneryager (eds.), *Human Relations in Management* (pp. 35–45). Cincinnati: South-Western Publishing.

Fisher, B. A. (1978). *Perspectives on Human Communication.* New York: Macmillan.

Freedman, D. H. (1992). Is management still a science? *Harvard Business Review, 70* (Nov.-Dec.), 26–28.

Gibson, J. W., & Hodgetts, R. M. (1991). *Organizational Communication: A Managerial Perspective* (2nd ed.). New York: Harper Collins.

Gleick, J. (1987). *Chaos: Making a New Science.* New York: Viking.

Hybels, S., & Weaver, R. L. II (1992). *Communicating Effectively* (3rd ed.). New York: McGraw-Hill.

Ichheiser, G. (1970). *Appearances and Realities.* San Francisco: Jossey-Bass.

Kofman, F., & Senge, P. (1993). Communities of commitment: The heart of learning organizations. *Organizational Dynamics, 22* (Autumn), 5–23.

Korzybski, A. (1958). *Science and Sanity* (4th ed.). MA: Colonial Press.

Kreps, G. L. (1990). *Organizational Communication: Theory and Practice* (2nd ed.). New York: Longman.

Lesikar, R. V. (1972). A general semantics approach to communication barriers in organizations. In J. O. Harris (ed.), *Current Concepts in Management* (pp. 41–48). Baton Rouge: Louisiana State University, Baton Rouge, LA, Division of Research, College of Business Administration.

Lesikar, R. V. (1976). *Business Communication: Theory and Practice* (3rd ed.). Homewood, Ill: Richard D. Irwin.

Likert, R. (1961). *New Patterns of Management.* New York: McGraw Hill.

Macoby, M. (1993). Managers must unlearn the psychology of control. *Research Technology Management, 36*(1), 49–51.

McGill, M. E., & Slocum Jr., J. W. (1993). Unlearning the organization. *Organizational Dynamics, 22* (Autumn), 67–79.

McGregor, D. (1960). *The Human Side of Enterprise.* New York: McGraw Hill.

McQuail, D., & Windahl, S. (1993). *Communication Models for the Study of Mass Communication* (2nd ed.). New York: Longman.

Miles, R. E., Porter, L. W., & Craft, J. A. (1966). Leadership attitudes among public health officers. *American Journal of Public Health, 56,* 1990–2005.

Rasberry, R. W., & Lindsay, L. L. (1994). *Effective Managerial Communication* (2nd ed.). Belmont Calif: Wadsworth.

Reed, M. (1992). Introduction. In M. Reed & M. Hughes (eds.), *Rethinking Organization: New Directions in Organization Theory and Analysis* (pp. 1–16). Newbury Park: Sage Publications.

Roethlisberger, F. J., & Dickson, W. J. (1939). *Management and the Worker.* Cambridge: Harvard University Press.

Senge, P. M. (1990). *The Fifth Discipline: The Art and Practice of the Learning Organization.* New York: Doubleday.

Serwer, A. E. (1994). Lessons from America's fastest-growing companies. *Fortune, 130* (3), pp. 42–56.

Shannon, C., & Weaver, W. (1949). *The Mathematical Theory of Communication.* Urbana: University of Illinois Press.

Sheldon, O. (1960). The philosophy of management. In I. L. Heckmann, Jr. & S. G. Huneryager (eds.), *Human Relations in Management* (pp. 7–9). Cincinnati: South-Western Publishing.

Taylor, F. W. (1911). *The Principles of Scientific Management.* New York: Harper Row.

Tompkins, P. K. (1987). Translating organizational theory: Symbolism over substance. In F. M. Jablon, L. L. Putnam, K. H. Roberts, & L. W. Porter (eds.), *Handbook of Organizational Communication: An Interdisciplinary Approach* (pp. 70–96). Newbury Park: Sage Publishers.

Tracy, L. (1989). *The Living Organization: Systems of Behavior.* New York: Praeger.

Trenholm, S. (1991). *Human Communication Theory* (2nd ed.). Englewood Cliffs, N.J.: Prentice-Hall.

von Bertalanffy, L. (1968). *General Systems Theory: Foundations, Development, Applications.* New York: George Braziller.

Watzlawick, P., Beavin, J. H., & Jackson, D. D. (1967). *Pragmatics of Human Communication: A Study of Interactional Patterns, Pathologies, and Paradoxes.* New York: W. W. Norton.

Weber, M. (1947). *The Theory of Social and Economic Organization.* (A. M. Henderson & T. Parsons, trans.). New York: Oxford University Press.

RECOMMENDED READINGS

Blackler, F. (1993). Knowledge and the theory of organizations: Organizations as activity systems and the reframing of management. *Journal of Management Studies, 30*(6), 863–884.

Geser, H. (1992). Towards an interaction theory of organizational actors. *Organization Studies, 13*(3), 429–451.

Hales, C. (1993). *Managing Through Organisation: The Management Process, Form of Organisation, and the Work of Managers.* London: Routledge.

Hassard, J., & Pym, D. (eds.). (1990). *The Theory and Philosophy of Organization: Critical Issues and New Perspectives.* NY: Routledge.

Huse, E. F., & Bowditch, J. L. (1973). *Behaviors in Organizations: A Systems Approach to Managing.* Reading, Mass: Addison-Wesley.

Ouchi, W. G., & Price, R. P. (1993). Hierarchies, clans, and theory z: A new perspective on organizational development. *Organizational Dynamics, 21* (Spring), 62–70.

Pfeffer, J. (1991). Organization theory and structural perspective on management. *Journal of Management, 17*(4), 789–803.

Staw, B. M. (1991). Dressing up like an organization: When psychological theories can explain organizational action. *Journal of Management, 17*(4), 805–819.

Tushman, M. L., O'Rielly, C., & Nadler, D. A. (eds.). (1989). *The Management of Organizations: Strategies, Tactics and Analyses.* New York: Harper Row.

▶ 2

Formal and Informal Communication Networks

SUSAN A. HELLWEG

Communication networks in organizations are analogous to the nervous system within the human body or the interstate system that connects cities and towns across the country. Networks provide the means for messages to flow in all directions in the organization so that information can be disseminated or retrieved, tasks can be coordinated and completed, decisions can be made, conflicts can be resolved, and the workforce can be maintained through hiring and performance appraisal processes. Networks allow for the transmission of messages through defined channels, so that information can reach intended receivers in a timely and efficient manner and chaos can be minimized; through such transmissions, an organization achieves some predictability and stability, since employees know where to go to access information and to whom information should be imparted. An organizational communication network represents a pattern of interactions; once such a pattern is established among employees it can be designated as a network.

In any organization there are a multitude of networks through which communication travels. Supervisors and subordinates communicate on a frequent basis as a function of their relationship, as do employee work groups. Networks can operate at the dyadic, group, and organizationwide level. An employee is typically part of a number of networks simultaneously, for example, as a member of a supervisor–subordinate dyad, as a member of a work unit, and with associates across departments to accomplish tasks. In addition to networks within the organization, there are ones that span to entities outside the organization's boundaries; these networks are important to an organization's survival, in the procurement of raw materials, in determining the needs and preferences of consumers, in the marketing of products and services, in staying abreast of government regulations, and in learning about the competition's activities.

Message flow through organizations occurs both horizontally and vertically. Horizontal communication involves employees of relatively the same status in the organization. In contrast, vertical communication by definition involves employees of different hierarchical status, for example, a chief executive officer and a department head. Upward communication is initiated by the individual of lower status; downward communication is initiated by the individual of higher status. Horizontal message flows in organizational networks are typically more frequent than vertical ones; downward communication tends to be more frequent than upward communication.

Formal networks carry officially sanctioned messages that the organization creates. They reflect relationships described in the organizational personnel chart. For example, supervisors and subordinates communicate formally through a reporting relationship. Officially sanctioned organizational messages may take the form of memoranda, bulletins, newsletters, as well as various types of oral communication such as might occur in meetings. The formal communication structure of an organization is systematically established for the transmission of messages through defined relationships. It is therefore relatively predictable and stable.

In contrast, informal networks are situationally derived. They emerge out of immediate needs of organizational members, whether they be functional or social needs. The informal system does not have a permanent structure, rather employees become members of this system as a function of particular issues or situations and then may disband. As a spontaneously emergent structure, the informal network is not consistently initiated by the same employees, nor is it considered an "on the record" vehicle of communication. While the system of formal networks within an organization may serve as a "blueprint" of how employees are supposed to communicate, the system of informal networks suggests how they actually do communicate (Jaccoby, 1968). Formal and informal networks operate in conjunction with one another. The informal system, for example, may function to translate messages that are carried over the formal system. The informal system, because it lacks permanent structural pathways, can move communication messages more quickly than its counterpart, which can get bogged down with the time it takes to develop officially sanctioned messages and with the number of transmitters through which communication must travel. The informal system, carrying "off the record" messages cannot be substituted for the formal system as an official organizational mechanism for disseminating information, making its counterpart a necessity in organizational functioning.

A formal communication system is created by the organizational hierarchy of reporting relationships, while an informal communication system is a determinant of an organizational structure. Because a personnel chart dictates who communicates to whom formally, communication follows an already established organizational structure. In contrast, because the informal system is situationally derived and spontaneous, it creates an organizational structure all of its own. If transparent paper describing the lines of authority that dictate the formal communication system were placed on top of a description of the pathways by which communication takes place informally in the organization, immediate differences might be obvious, particularly in the way that the informal communication system bypasses transmission patterns reflected in the officially sanctioned formal communication system. Figure 2-1 displays how such an overlay might look.

This chapter will focus on formal and informal communication networks in organizations, and will explore their functions and characteristics, their structure and transmission patterns, and their participants. In addition, how these networks can be determined and analyzed will be discussed.

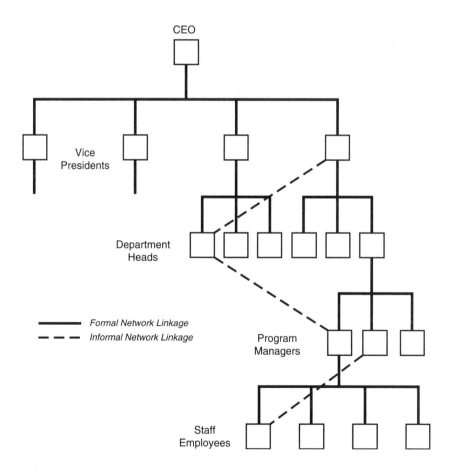

FIGURE 2-1   **Contrasting formal and informal network systems.**

FORMAL COMMUNICATION NETWORKS

Without formal communication networks, an organization would be chaotic. Employees would not get instructions vital to the completion of tasks, nor would they know what tasks needed to be accomplished. The organization would have no systematic means of disseminating or retrieving information essential to its effective functioning. Actions in the organization would be random. Employees would inevitably execute tasks with a great deal of variability, since they would not be consistently aware of company policies and procedures. The feedback system in the organization would become dysfunctional; the organization would have no reliable means to find out how it was doing in the delivery of its products or services, and employees would not receive evaluations of their job performance in any systematic way to reinforce or alter behaviors.

A network can be described functionally in terms of the types of messages it carries. Task or production messages are transmitted through networks that concern task output, including job instructions and performance feedback. Maintenance messages are carried on networks that focus on policies and procedures (e.g., how tasks are to be carried out). Human messages travel on networks that focus on the individual employee (e.g., vacation schedules, company benefit plans, employee attitudes toward the assigned tasks and company policies, recognition of employee accomplishments). Formal networks definitely are concerned with all three types of messages.

Network Structures

The structure of organizational networks reflects the pathways that messages take on them, that is, who communicates with whom and through whom. Obviously, a network can involve any number of persons. It may involve the vertical hierarchy of the organization or the chain of supervisors and subordinates connected to one another; it may consist of subordinates in a work unit discussing company tasks. A formal network has rules about how communication is to take place in terms of prescribed pathways, to whom all communications must go through, whether members initiate communication equally, and so on. Four simplified network structures will be discussed here, though many more are possible.

As shown in Figure 2-2, the chain involves serial transmission from one employee to another until the message reaches its destination. It is centralized in nature, since a network member is central to the message flow. The Y network is also centralized, with three employees in sequence and two others branching off from that structure. The wheel involves a central message unit and separate transmission/reception units in all directions; this structure might fit a small department, with a supervisor and four subordinates. In the case of the circle network, no one employee is central to the message flow, thus it is considered decentralized. The circle is somewhat like the chain, despite the fact that it is decentralized, in the fact that it involves serial transmission of messages. Group member morale tends to be

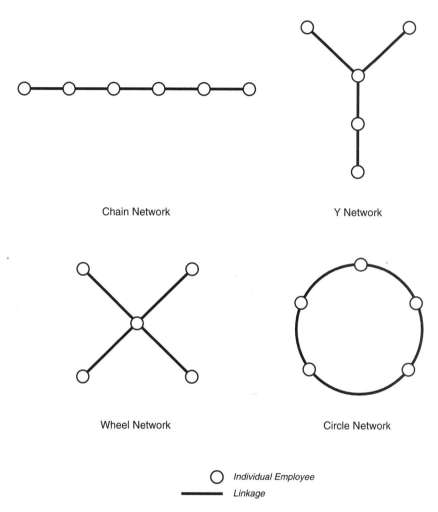

FIGURE 2-2 **Network structures.**

greater in networks that allow for decentralized message control, since members can get better access to one another and do not always have to go through intermediaries.

Network Roles

As members of organizational networks, we play roles as a function of our positioning and the structure of the network involved. A liaison acts as a link between two or more organizational network groups, without belonging to them. As a linking pin, this employee coordinates the activities of the groups passing information from group to group. Typically, a liaison has considerable tenure in the organization. In their position as messengers, liaisons often are the initial sources of information and are considered by others to be highly influential in the organization because they have some control over its information flow. An example of a liaison would be a department head carrying messages between work units organized under that individual's supervision.

A bridge is a member of one network who connects it to another by forming a dyadic relationship with one of the other group's members. Distortion is more likely when a bridge is used to communicate messages rather than a liaison because of the potential intermediaries the information needs to go through to get to its intended destination. An example of a bridge would be a member of the accounting department who meets regularly for lunch with a member of the payroll department, transferring messages from one work unit to another.

A gatekeeper acts as a filter to allow information to pass to a receiver or to screen it out. An example would be a secretary who screens telephone calls to a supervisor; in this way the boss is precluded from experiencing information overload, since there are some telephone calls that the secretary might be able to handle or give to someone else. A gatekeeper obviously is influential in the organization, deciding what will and will not get transmitted further.

An isolate is an individual in the organization who has relatively few communication contacts compared with others. This might happen to an employee who has a highly specialized job function or considerable job autonomy, not reliant on others to complete assigned tasks. An example in an organization would be a researcher not assigned to a research team, but rather basically left alone to accomplish product development. It is also possible for an organization to have an isolated dyad or two people associated with one another, but not dependent to a great degree on others.

A boundary spanner or cosmopolite reaches beyond the boundaries of a network to the outside. For example, customer service representatives span the boundaries of the organization to the public in that they isolate problems with products or services the company provides. In the case of a boundary spanner, the network involved can be within the organization or be the organization itself. The roles ascribed to network members defined above are illustrated in Figure 2-3.

Network Descriptors

A number of descriptors are available to indicate the properties of networks as found in Figure 2.4. Not only do networks differ in their structure and in the positions that employees occupy within them, they also vary in many other ways because of the relationships network members have with one another.

Dominance refers to the degree to which there is an equal relationship among network members. A highly dominant network necessitates that communication be directed to one or a few members, while a lowly dominant network would be one in which communication is relatively evenly distributed. A highly dominant network might occur within a work unit in which a supervisor would be a focal point for

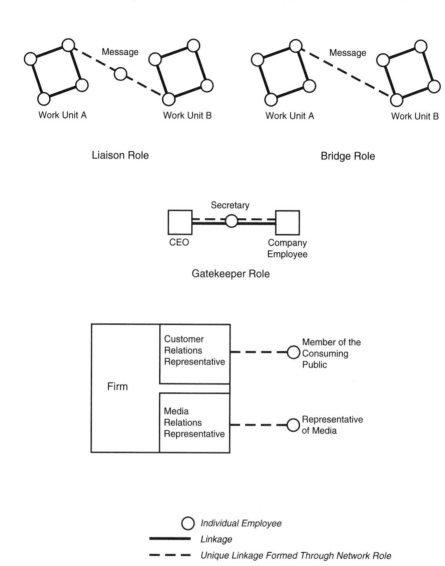

FIGURE 2-3 **Network roles in an organization.**

communication from subordinates. A lowly dominant network might occur in the context of peer employees working on a task together, with no one in the group needing to coordinate work completion.

In contrast, centrality indicates the degree to which a network member is located at the crossroads of the message flow. As discussed earlier, centralized networks would include ones reflecting the chain, the Y, or the wheel structure, since in each case messages consistently flow through a certain individual as they move from one end of the network to the other.

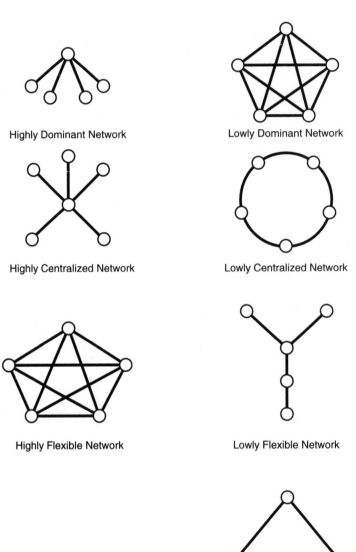

Highly Dominant Network

Lowly Dominant Network

Highly Centralized Network

Lowly Centralized Network

Highly Flexible Network

Lowly Flexible Network

High Reachability Network

Low Reachability Network

FIGURE 2-4   **Properties of organizational networks.**

Flexibility suggests the degree to which a network follows a set of rules about the pathways on which communication must travel. A highly flexible network would allow for variation in these pathways, while a lowly flexible one would consistently use the same transmission patterns. A network that involved a strict chain of com-

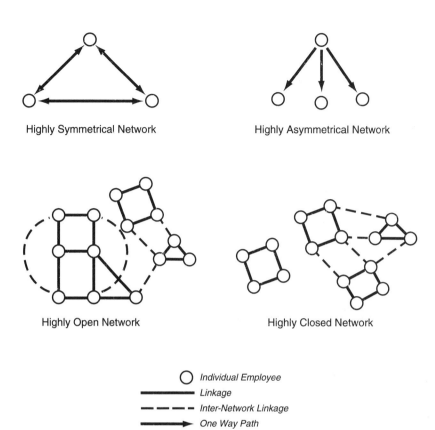

Highly Symmetrical Network   Highly Asymmetrical Network

Highly Open Network   Highly Closed Network

○ *Individual Employee*
—— *Linkage*
– – – – *Inter-Network Linkage*
——▶ *One Way Path*
◀——▶ *Two Way Path*

FIGURE 2-4   *Continued.*

mand would be associated with low flexibility, while a network of department heads might be highly flexible, since the members would all share the same hierarchical status. That is not to say, however, that the degree of flexibility a network possesses is simply associated with the presence of vertical or horizontal relationships.

Reachability involves the number of intermediaries to whom a message needs to travel to get to its final destination. In a chain network, relatively high reachability would be involved (depending upon how many members the network entailed) as opposed to the wheel network, which is likely to be characterized by fewer intermediaries. As the number of individuals through whom a message must pass increases, distortion of that message is likely to increase; therefore, in the case of high reachability (in which there are relatively more intermediaries involved), message distortion is potentially greater than for low reachability (in which the message can get more directly from source to receiver). An organization that is highly structured with many hierarchical levels is more likely to be characterized by networks with high reachability.

Network strength is measured by the frequency and duration of communication between participants. A supervisor holding relatively lengthy weekly staff meetings and individual meetings with workers would have a relatively strong network, whereas a supervisor who rarely was in contact with workers because of travel demands and subordinate job autonomy might have a less strong network.

Reciprocity suggests that network members agree about the nature of their linkages. For example, a subordinate may be more likely to remember one-on-one contacts with a supervisor than the supervisor who has to manage a staff of forty individuals and there is little, if any, individual contact. If, in recalling the nature of their network relationship, the supervisor and subordinate were providing different answers to the relative frequency with which they communicate, who initiates these communication episodes, etc., then low reciprocity would be ascribed to the dyad. Noting unreciprocated networks is important in understanding how employees perceive their relationships.

Symmetry is the degree to which communication in a network is equally shared between members, so that a two-way link exists. In contrast, asymmetry involves an unequal relationship between network members, such that one communicates significantly more than another, suggesting more of a one-way path. The latter might prevail in a supervisor–subordinate relationship in which the supervisor tended to request information from the subordinate and the subordinate complied.

Openness refers to the degree to which a network is characterized by linkages to its outside environment. An open network would have a multitude of connections to other networks in the system; a closed network would keep more to itself, perhaps because of functional autonomy, not needing messages from the outside to achieve its objectives and not needing to send messages outside to acquire information, services, or goods. In Figure 2-4, the network descriptors discussed are illustrated in terms of relative property levels.

INFORMAL COMMUNICATION NETWORKS

Informal communication networks are "people" networks. Rather than following the pathways that reporting relationships (as reflected in personnel charts or policy manuals) dictate, informal networks operate in a unpredictable manner. Employees may choose to communicate with other organizational members through informal means because of proximity (e.g., co-workers); because one perceives that the other is a reliable and knowledgeable source, because there is friendship and thus they trust one another with information; because they know each other outside of the workplace; or because they see each other at the time that such communication is needed (e.g., waiting for a committee meeting to start). For the purposes of this chapter, the term "informal communication networks" will be used synonymously with the term "grapevine." While perhaps it could be argued that informal communication networks (e.g., communication involving dyadic members discussing personal matters or widespread discussion about whether the company softball team can win the championship in competition with the various district offices) represents a broader term than grapevine (e.g., rumor transmission among various employees about potential layoffs in the pattern like a grapevine), both terms embody communication of an unofficial nature that is spontaneous and situationally derived.

Informal communication systems are an important and necessary part of an organization. Without them, employees are left to fill in gaps until the official word is disseminated, they may not feel any sense of ownership of information, and morale may decline. Informal networks allow employees to express themselves in ways that the formal networks would not; they play an important role in humanizing the organization, giving the employees a sense of belonging, allowing them to discuss concerns outside of the on-the-record system. In addition to providing an outlet for employees to express their feelings and to get messages from the formal networks translated into terms they understand, they offer the means for management to tap into employee sentiment and to find out what their concerns are, so that the formal networks can be properly responsive. Informal networks become especially busy when employees perceive the need for information, such as in a crisis, and thus may even feel that management is purposefully withholding information. Informal communication systems are particularly prevalent in organizations that foster secrecy (Yoder, 1970). Informal communication systems are primarily oral in nature.

Grapevine Participants

While there is no consistent pattern in organizations in terms of initiators of informal communication, individuals who serve as "communication centers" are strategically located in the pathway of informal communication transmissions. Secretaries may serve in this function (Davis, 1969; Kaufman, 1977), since they are gatekeepers and are often sought after for information. Likewise, network liaisons, as communication centers, may function as key participants in grapevine activity.

Grapevine transmission can be initiated and stopped anywhere in an organization (Goldhaber et al., 1979). Perhaps surprisingly, while the grapevine is often regarded as a worker system, it has been found to be equally active among management personnel (Davis, 1954); this is an interesting finding in light of the fact that management has control of the formal communication networks. Employee gender likewise does not seem to be a factor in grapevine activity (Kaufman, 1977; Marting, 1969).

Effects of Grapevine Activity on Organizational Functioning

Informal communication networks can serve a number of positive functions. However, when rumors are transmitted that are not substantiated by fact an organization can become dysfunctional. Rumors represent incomplete information; employees may feel inclined to second-guess the missing information. Likewise, informal communication may lead to the leaking of information before the organization is ready to disseminate it (e.g., layoff plans), causing severe morale problems; in this case, the information may be inaccurate and it is not emanating from the appropriate authorities.

Factors Involved in Rumor Dispersion

A number of factors play a role in whether a rumor gets perpetuated or is discontinued. These would include the importance of the message (e.g., a potential corporate merger versus a new company logo) (Boss, 1965), the ambiguity of the message (e.g., whether the details about potential layoffs are sketchy or not) (Mandel, 1972), the need for information (e.g., in a crisis) (Boss, 1965), the withholding of information by management that employees believe they need (e.g., personnel realignments) (Mandel, 1972), the credibility of the transmitters (e.g., whether the employee giving out the information is someone others believe based on past experiences), who the rumor involves (e.g., the chief executive officer versus an assembly line worker not well known to others), and its timeliness (e.g., whether the information is presently of use to its receivers).

Factors Contributing to Grapevine Message Distortion

Several factors are involved in the distortion of messages moving the organizational grapevine, largely because they represent incomplete information. Condensation or leveling occurs when the sender reduces the amount of information being communicated, because, for example, it cannot all be retained. Information salience, or sharpening, entails the highlighting of some parts of the information when it is transmitted to another employee; typically, this highlighting involves the information that the source feels is most important. Closure, or adding, consists of filling in gaps by a source so that the story looks more complete. Finally, selective perception, the only factor listed here involving the receiver of grapevine information in the distortion of message content, pertains to picking out pieces from what is being communicated and forgetting about others.

Grapevine Transmission Patterns

Keith Davis (1953), who has been largely identified with grapevine research in the communication discipline, found that grapevines can follow a single-strand chain pattern, where A communicates the information to B, who transmits it to C, etc., a gossip chain pattern, where A procures the information and communicates to all other workers, a probability chain pattern, where A provides the information randomly to F and D, who further this information in a likewise manner taking into account the laws of probability. Grapevines generally follow a cluster transmission pattern, where A communicates the information to two other employees, with the pattern duplicating all over the organization.

The pattern Davis has described is essentially analogous to an actual grapevine, with pathways moving from branch to offshoots. Rumors tend to move horizontally in an organization (Sutton & Porter, 1968), since in all likelihood employees feel more comfortable transmitting this type of information among their peers.

Types of Organizational Rumors

Several types of rumors have been identified as prevalent in grapevine activity: anxiety rumors, wish-fulfillment rumors, and wedge-driving rumors (Hershey, 1966). Another category that might be added to this list is social rumors. Anxiety rumors reflect sources of uneasiness for employees. An example would be a rumor pertaining to the possibility that cost-of-living raises will not come in the near future. Wish-fulfillment rumors suggest particular employee desires. An example of this type of rumor would be one that focused on the possibility that collective bargaining processes might lead to higher salaries. Wedge-driving rumors are a function of divisive elements in the organization or disunity among employees. An "us versus them" attitude might be reflected in the rumor statement. An example of a wedge-driving rumor would concern employee perception that corporate executives receive better benefits plans than they do. Finally, social rumors would involve information about particular employees in a social context (e.g., whether a female employee is pregnant).

Control of the Organizational Grapevine

Informal communication networks can be functional and dysfunctional depending upon the effects of the messages being communicated and the message content itself, in terms of its timeliness in connection with the formal communication networks, the completeness of the information being transmitted and the speculative activity that results, the appropriateness of the message itself, etc. Research suggests that once a rumor is determined to be credible, organizational events are aligned to fit it and support what it is communicating (Davis, 1961), suggesting that rumors can significantly affect organizational reality and functioning.

It would seem important for members of management to seek out ways to control the organizational grapevine to the degree that it is possible and appropriate. First, management needs to be sensitive to employee sources of anxiety. If rumor transmission becomes very active, management should recognize this as a signal that employees are lacking information they feel they need. Second, management needs to provide important information to employees openly, honestly, and quickly to reduce speculation. Through such communication, management will be seen as responsive to employee needs, and employee morale will not be damaged. Third, if management can locate key communicators among the employee ranks, these individuals can be used to disseminate information, since employees will tend to believe these individuals. Finally, management can combat the organizational dysfunctioning through rumor activity designed to make sure that employees get the information they need. A proactive stance on management communication, rather than a reactive one after rumors have begun, can enable an organization to function more as a unit, rather than as an entity of divisive elements uncertain of an organization's motives, actions, and plans. Some researchers (e.g., Weinberg & Eich, 1978) have investigated the establishment of a rumor control center as an intervention agent, with the intent of squelching inaccurate information traveling in an institutional system and replacing it with verified data. Some organizations have implemented such systems (Goldhaber, 1979).

METHODS OF ANALYZING FORMAL AND INFORMAL COMMUNICATION NETWORKS

Network analysis involves systematic research to determine the pathways that communication takes in an organization. One form of such research is residential analysis, which requires the investigator to conduct observations of communication behavior within the organization. A second form of network analysis would consist of the distribution of questionnaires to organizational members who would, through the process of recall, indicate with whom they communicate, how frequently, and for what purpose; the questionnaire could ask the respondents whether such communication took place through the formal or informal structure and how important the subject felt these communication episodes were. A third type of network analysis would entail the maintenance of a communication diary by employees as communication episodes occurred for a specified period of time (e.g., a week), noting the initiator of the communication, the channel involved, the function of the communication, its length, and an evaluation of its usefulness, timeliness, importance, accuracy, etc. The latter two types of analysis described have been used in a number of studies based upon instrumentation developed by the members of the International Communication Association (Goldhaber & Rogers, 1979).

Finally, ECCO (Episode Communication Channels in Organizations) Analysis, developed by Davis (1952), specifically examines grapevine patterns of transmission in an organization in connection with targeted messages. Questionnaires, for example, are distributed to employees, asking them to indicate if they are cognizant of a particular message, from whom they received it, to whom they transmitted it, the time elements involved, the location of the communication between transmitter and receiver, the channel utilized, and accuracy and distortion considerations. From this, the investigator can determine the patterns of message flow. While this instrument taps network patterns for particular communication episodes, it does not assess overall communication patterns. Therefore, the selection of the targeted communication episode is vitally important in making any suggestions about typical message flows.

CONCLUSION

This chapter has provided a description of how formal and informal communication networks function in organizations. Formal networks were identified as those through which officially sanctioned organizational messages travel along the preestablished routes defined by a corporation's personnel chart. In contrast, informal networks were characterized as being spontaneous, situationally derived, nonpermanent, people networks that carry unofficial messages in an unpredictable manner. In connection with formal networks the chapter offered distinctions among various network structures (chain, Y, wheel, circle), network roles (liaison, bridge, gatekeeper, isolate, boundary spanner), and network descriptors (dominance, centrality, flexibility, reachability, strength, reciprocity, symmetry, and openness).

In a discussion of informal networks or the organizational grapevine, the chapter outlined potential participants on the grapevine, system transmission patterns, types of organizational rumors, effects of grapevine activity on organizational functioning, control of the organizational grapevine, and factors contributing to rumor dispersion and grapevine message distortion. Finally, the chapter described methods of analyzing formal and informal communication networks in organizations through observations, employee questionnaires designed to gather information globally about network behaviors or in connection with specific communication episodes, or employee diaries of communication behavior over a period of time.

GLOSSARY

Anxiety rumors—rumors that deal with subjects that produce anxiety among employees (e.g., potential layoffs).

Asymmetry—a descriptor for a network characterized by unequal relationships among members, such that the communication path tends to be more one-way (e.g., between a supervisor and workers) than two-way.

Boundary spanner—an employee who reaches out beyond the confines of a network (e.g., a workgroup) to the outside, either internally to employees not part of the network or externally to customers, government representatives, media personnel, other organizations, and the like.

Bridge—a member of a network who connects that network to another through a dyadic linkage with one of the other group's members.

Centrality—a network property that reflects the degree to which a member is positioned at the crossroads of the message flow; a highly central network being indicated by network information moving consistently through a certain individual to get to its destination.

Chain network—a type of network structure that is characterized by serial transmission of a message from one employee to another until it reaches the intended receiver.

Circle network—a type of network structure in which no individual member is at the center of the message flow.

Communication diary—an audit instrument used by employees over a specified period of time to record their particular communication episodes with other organizational members.

Dominance—a descriptor for a network that reflects the degree to which communication is directed to one or a few group members; a highly dominant network being one in which communication is not evenly distributed, with much of it going, for example, to a supervisor.

Downward communication—message flow that moves from a higher level authority to those of lesser hierarchical status (e.g., supervisors to subordinates).

ECCO (Episode Communication Channels in Organizations) analysis—a systematic means to examine grapevine patterns in an organization through the use of questionnaires asking employees about a particular communication episode.

Flexibility—a network descriptor that indicates the degree to which set rules are followed for message transmission, with a highly flexible network being more spontaneous than its counterpart.

Formal networks—systematically established structures that carry officially sanctioned messages through defined relationships that an organization creates (e.g., announcement of a corporate merger, change in company policy, or new product line; performance appraisal interview between a supervisor and subordinate; a corporate committee meeting).

Gatekeeper—a network role requiring the employee to act as a filter of information as it passes through to another individual, preventing message overload for the latter (e.g., a secretary assigned to a department head).

Grapevine—a situationally derived message system on which informal communication (e.g., rumors) travels.

Horizontal communication—message transmission between employees of approximately the same hierarchical status in the organization (e.g., two assembly workers).

Informal networks—a spontaneously emergent communication structure that ignores the formal reporting relationships in an organization and involves employees as functional and social needs arise (e.g., a group of workers speculating about impending layoffs).

Isolate—a network role involving an employee who has relatively few communication contacts in the organization because of job autonomy, functional specialization, and the like.

Liaison—a network role that involves an individual who takes messages to and from networks without being a member of them, thus acting as a linking pin between them.

Openness—a network property reflecting connections beyond the boundaries of a network to other networks, a highly open network being one well connected to the outside environment.

Reachability—the number of intermediaries in a network it takes for a message to move from its source to its receiver; high reachability meaning relatively more such individuals than for low reachability.

Reciprocity—a network descriptor indicating the degree to which parties in a network agree over the nature of their linkages; high reciprocity being associated with high agreement.

Residential analysis—a form of network analysis requiring the investigator to enter the organization and observe network patterns.

Social rumors—rumors that focus on social activities and relationships involving employees (e.g., whether an employee is pregnant).

Strength—a network property reflecting the length and duration of interaction in a network relationship (e.g., between a supervisor and subordinate), such that high levels of interaction frequency and duration would indicate a high-strength network relationship.

Symmetry—a network descriptor suggesting equal interaction among network members, such that a two-way path exists between participants.

Upward communication—message transmission that moves from individuals relatively low in the organizational hierarchy to those of higher status (e.g., from a subordinate to a supervisor).

Vertical communication—downward or upward message transmission occurring between individuals of different hierarchical status in the organization.

Wedge-driving rumors—rumors that are divisive in nature, such as ones involving labor versus management, white collar versus blue collar employees, or workers in different departments.

Wheel network—network structure consisting of a central message unit and separate transmission/reception units in all directions (e.g., a supervisor and four subordinates).

Wish-fulfillment rumors—rumors that reflect the desires of employees (e.g., about possible pay raises).

Y network—a network structure that looks like the letter "Y," involving a central message unit and branching units.

CASE STUDY

A female employee of the XYZ Corporation, a manufacturing company in the rural Midwest, was physically accosted as she entered the corporate facility very early in the morning to work on some paperwork quietly before the rest of the staff in her department were to arrive. She greeted the guard at the gate and then proceeded to her office. Word spread quickly through the employees that the attack had taken place. Many questions abounded as the employees talked among themselves: How is she? What happened? How could this happen to someone in this company? Did the security guard not hear any trouble? How did the perpetrator get in the building? What is the company going to do about it? Are we safe to work here? Will this ever happen to anyone else here?

Corporate executives started immediate meetings to establish what had happened and what the company should do about it. This investigation involved talking to a number of individuals, including the police who responded to a 911 call from a janitor in the building at the time. In addition, with the collection of this information, the company needed to make a number of decisions: What do we tell the employees about this incident? What channels do we use to communicate this information? Who should provide the information to the employees? How do we control the rumors going around while we are in the decision-making process? How do we protect the privacy rights of the individual involved? How do we take steps to make sure this never happens again? How do we reassure employees of their safety at the facility? How do we deal with the press when they start making inquiries of us? In order to examine these decisions, the chief executive officer, vice presidents, and other key executives, as well as those close to the situation (e.g., corporate security staff, personnel director, public affairs director), met separately and collectively.

Employees were becoming increasingly anxious and were turning to others in their departments, particularly their supervisors, for answers. Rumors reflecting the anxiety of employees were flying in all directions. Formal channels would need to respond, but only after decisions had been made, since anything management would say could be construed as fact. Consistent statements by members of management was imperative. Relying on informal networks to carry the message would be an unacceptable answer because not only would it make management look unresponsive, messages transmitted informally are uncontrollable, may become distorted as they move through the system, and do not represent officially sanctioned content. At the same time, until management was ready to respond officially to the incident, employees could talk of nothing else, out of their concern for the victim, disbelief that the incident had occurred on the site, and doubts about their own safety on the premises.

Given this scenario, how might the corporation respond? Specifically, what should be communicated, by whom and through what channels, providing the needed information in a timely manner and yet involving those individuals who need to be involved in the decision-making process; controlling employee anxieties about their own safety without making light of the situation; respecting the privacy rights of the victim; and making the company responsive to the internal and external communities.

REFERENCES

Boss, B. M. (1965). *Organizational Psychology.* Boston, Mass.: Allyn & Bacon.

Davis, K. (1952). *Channels of personnel communication within the management group.* Unpublished dissertation, Ohio State University.

Davis, K. (1953). Management communication and the grapevine. *Harvard Business Review, 5,* 43–49.

Davis, K. (1954). Communication within management. *Personnel, 31,* 212–218.

Davis, K. (1961). The organization that's not on the chart. *Supervisory Management, 6,* 2–7.

Davis, K. (1969). Grapevine communication among lower and middle managers. *Personnel Journal, 48,* 269–272.

Goldhaber, G. M. (1979). *Organizational Communication.* Dubuque, Iowa: William C. Brown Communications.

Goldhaber, G. M., Dennis, H. S. III, Richetto, G. M., & Wiio, O. A. (1984). *Information Strategies: New Pathways to Management Productivity* (rev. ed.). Norwood, N.J.: Ablex.

Goldhaber, G. M., & Rogers, D. P. (1979). *Auditing Organizational Communication Systems: The ICA Communication Audit.* Dubuque, Iowa: Kendall/Hunt.

Hershey, R. (1966). Grapevine: Here to stay but not beyond control. *Personnel, 43,* 62–66.

Jaccoby, J. (1968). Examining the other organization. *Personnel Administration, 31,* 36–42.

Kaufman, M. M. (1977). *A study of grapevine communication patterns in sales-oriented organizations.* Unpublished dissertation, Georgia State University.

Mandel, J. E. (1972). Informal organization and communication as they exist with the formal organization and their effect upon communication. *The Administrator, 2,* 10–12.

Marting, B. J. (1969). *A study of grapevine communication patterns in a manufacturing organization.* Unpublished dissertation, Arizona State University.

Sutton, H., & Porter, I. W. (1968). A study of the grapevine in a government organization. *Personnel Psychology, 36,* 78–82.

Weinberg, S. B., & Eich, R. K. (1978). Fighting fire with fire: Establishment of a rumor control center. *Communication Quarterly, 26,* 26–31.

Yoder, D. (1970). *Personnel Management and Industrial Relations.* Englewood Cliffs, N.J.: Prentice-Hall.

RECOMMENDED READINGS

Eisenberg, E. M., Farace, R. V., Monge, P. R., Bettinghaus, E. P., Kurchner-Hawkins, R., Miller, K. I., & Rothman, L. (1985). Communication Linkages in Interorganizational Systems: Review and Synthesis. In B. Dervin & M. J. Voigt (eds.), *Progress in Communication Sciences* (Vol. 6, pp. 231–261). Norwood, N.J.: Ablex.

Hellweg, S. A. (1987). Organizational grapevines. In B. Dervin & M. J. Voigt (eds.), *Progress in Communication Sciences* (Vol. 8, pp. 213–230). Norwood, N.J.: Ablex.

Monge, P. R., & Eisenberg, E. M. (1987). Emergent communication networks. In F. M. Jablin, L. L. Putnam, K. H. Roberts, & L. W. Porter (eds.), *Handbook of Organizational Communication: An Interdisciplinary Perspective* (pp. 304–342). Newbury Park, Calif.: Sage.

Rice, R. E., & Richards, W. D., Jr. (1985). An overview of network analysis methods and programs. In B. Dervin & M. J. Voigt (eds.), *Progress in Communication Sciences* (pp. 105–165). Norwood, N.J.: Ablex.

Richards, W. D., Jr. (1985). Data, models, and assumptions in network analysis. In R. D. McPhee & P. K. Tompkins (eds.), *Organizational Communication: Traditional Themes and New Directions* (pp. 109–128). Beverly Hills, Calif.: Sage.

Rogers, E. M., & Kincaid, D. L. (1981). *Communication Networks: Toward a New Paradigm for Research.* New York: The Free Press.

Wigand, R. T. (1988). Communication network analysis: History and overview. In G. M. Goldhaber & G. A. Barnett (eds.), *Handbook of Organizational Communication* (pp. 319–359). Norwood, N.J.: Ablex.

> ▶ 3

Nonverbal Communication in Organizations

VALERIE MANUSOV AND JULIE M. BILLINGSLEY

While waiting for her bus, one of the authors was gazing absently at the free news-papers available for passengers. She was pulled out of her daze by the headlines of an employment circular advertising an article on "Interview-Fluent Body Language." As the bus pulled up, she grabbed a copy of the paper and read the article during the ride to work. It was much as she feared. The article was touting "the way to achieve hiring success" by using one's eyes, face, and gestures to communicate a positive image.

In many ways, the article was better than some of its predecessors. Although it used the simplified term "body language," it showed that we employ a number of cues that go far beyond body movements as part of our nonverbal presentation. Much like other portrayals of nonverbal communication, however, it assumed that using specified cues will have a particular, and certain, effect. Indeed, the article provided several lists discussing those behaviors to use (e.g., an "eyebrow flash" when greeting the interviewer, mirroring the interviewer's positive behaviors) and those to avoid (e.g., sweaty hands, too much or too little gaze). Using these appropriate behaviors, the author guaranteed, will improve the readers' chances of getting the jobs they desire.

While nonverbal behaviors are an important set of behaviors, and they do have the potential to send messages, enhance impressions, and influence hiring, they, like all aspects of communication, work in a more complex way than was portrayed in the employment newspaper. This chapter is designed to introduce the reader to the nature of nonverbal behavior, particularly within the organizational context, with the hope that it will increase the reader's understanding of the nonverbal system. Discussion focuses on the following: (1) the types of behaviors that can be called "nonverbal communication," (2) the nature of nonverbal behavior, and (3) the functions that nonverbal behaviors fulfill in organizational contexts. Greater sensitivity to the complexity of nonverbal actions, rather than lists of the "best" behaviors, should provide communicators with more success in using, and appreciating, nonverbal cues.

KINDS OF NONVERBAL BEHAVIORS

Within any interaction, we have a range of behaviors available to help us communicate. We usually think of language as the primary message carrier, but other cues are also at work, affecting what we come to believe is communicated. Those actions, other than the spoken word, that are part of how we create meaning in social interactions are aspects of the nonverbal or paralinguistic communication system (Burgoon, Buller, & Woodall, 1989).

Generally, a given nonverbal cue does not occur on its own, but rather works in tandem with language and other nonlanguage behaviors (Patterson, 1987). Instead of constructing the meaning of a message from one behavior (e.g., prolonged gaze), communicative understanding usually is derived from a range of cues functioning in concert. Behaviors are typically understood as "a pattern of action that will accomplish the representation of meaning" (Kendon, 1983, p. 20). It is usually only when a series of actions occur during the same interaction that we come to believe that a particular message was communicated.

For example, when trying to show their customers that they are credible, sales staff are likely to try to speak fluently, gaze with regularity, and make their nonverbal behaviors consistent with their words. Likewise, when trying to determine if a job candidate will "fit in" with the company, an interviewer will look for a combination of cues such as dress, vocal style, and facial characteristics that reflect whether the candidate's style appears similar to other employees. Rather than focus on a single cue, in most cases we both act (encode) and interpret (decode) others' actions using multiple channels or codes. Further, social meanings (i.e., messages carried by nonverbal behaviors on which most people would agree) are also typically derived from a cluster of communication cues.

In order to understand what elements are part of the nonverbal system, however, it is useful to discuss particular cues as if they were separate from one another. Furthermore, although they are more likely to occur in concert with other behaviors, single cues can occasionally influence meanings on their own. One way to categorize these individual nonverbal behaviors to better understand the range in the nonverbal network is to put them in one of two groups: behavioral and nonbehavioral codes.

Behavioral Codes

When we talk to others, we engage in one form of communicative action. There are many other behaviors that are "performed" in our conversations, however. Those cues that can be seen as dynamic and changing within a given interaction are the behavioral cues associated with nonverbal communication. These include body movements (kinesics), use of space (proxemics), facial expressions and eye behavior, touch (haptics), and vocal cues (vocalics).

Kinesics

The behaviors that most closely correlate with the popular term "body language" are kinesic cues (Birdwhistell, 1970). These include actions that we engage in with our bodies, such as gesturing, leaning, and walking. Gestures often accompany speech and can help illustrate or augment a point (e.g., holding our hand up to a certain point to indicate another's height) or regulate the flow of conversation (e.g., a listener may motion with his or her hand to indicate that the speaker should hurry, or people might raise their hands during meetings to show their desire to speak). Other gestures, known as adaptors, are movements that typically reflect an internal state. For example, playing with our hair may denote nervousness or boredom, and rubbing our face can show confusion or fatigue.

Some gestures may substitute for language. For example, emblematic gestures (such as "thumbs up" or "thumbs down") are likely to be used in the absence of spoken words. These emblems are unlike other types of nonverbal behaviors in that they typically have a clear, language-like meaning. Interestingly, although the use of particular emblems varies between cultures, most cultures have some way of gesturing interpersonal control (an important aspect of organizational behavior), current state or condition, and evaluation of another (Kendon, 1988). Our posture and the ways in which we walk, known as gait, may also reflect internal states such as moods, feelings about the person we are interacting with, and our personal attributes. Head, trunk, and foot movements, body position, and orientation towards or away from another are all behaviors encompassed by the kinesic system.

Body movements may have many implications in organizations. For example, one group of researchers conducted a study to measure the effect on customers of kinesic behaviors used by sales staff (Sommers, Greeno, & Boag, 1989). They found that the "customers" (this study was conducted in a laboratory with the participants acting as sales staff or customers) were more likely to be influenced by "salespeople" who used more body movements than by those whose kinesic behaviors were limited. The researchers concluded that people respond better to "happy, joyful" behaviors and that these are linked with increases in kinesic cues as well as other nonverbal and verbal behaviors.

Proxemics

The study of our use of personal space is known as proxemics (Hall, 1966). Proxemic behavior refers both to how we use a given territory as well as how far or close we are likely to stand to others. Research on the former has found that we actively "mark" our territories by placing certain objects, or artifacts, to show that a given space is ours (Becker, 1973). For example, employees are likely to put markers in their offices to show ownership of the area, and others are likely to respect those signifiers of ownership. In addition, artifacts and other environmental cues serve to reflect particular aspects of an organizational culture (Gagliardi, 1990).

In addition to territory as an aspect of our use of space, there are also particular rules for how close we should or should not stand in relation to another. These edicts depend on the nature of the interaction. In business contexts, for example, the most likely "distance zones" to be used are the casual–personal and the social–consultative zones (Hall, 1966). The former is used typically when interacting with known, but nonintimate, others, and the latter is most likely to be employed in impersonal business transactions. Although Hall provides ranges commonly used for these zones, the specific distance used will depend on the culture within which the behavior occurs, the idiosyncrasies of the interactants, and the nature of the topic discussed.

A number of studies have looked at the connection between use of space and perceptions of people in organizations. In his review of the research in this area, Leary (1990) concluded that how close we stand to another during an interaction can influence another's perception of our leadership potential. Increased closeness (along with more touch, formal attire, and posture) was linked with others' views that a person had greater status. Further, Gagliardi (1990), a researcher studying organizational culture, discussed the famous Hawthorne experiments and the "influence ... made possible by the change in setting ..., and of the symbolic value that this change had taken on for [the workers] in terms of 'spatial language'" (p. 6).

Facial Expressions and Eye Behavior
Two of the behaviors seen as particularly important nonverbal cues are facial expressions and gaze behavior. Indeed, researchers coined the term "facial primacy" to highlight the importance that expressions have on initial interactions (Knapp & Hall, 1992). Although they play a role in many communicative functions, facial behaviors are most strongly associated with emotional expressions, which are also known as affect displays. Some scholars argue that certain facial expressions are universal: ways of showing happiness, sadness, and anger can be recognized across a range of unrelated cultures (e.g., Ekman & Friesen, 1986).

The study of eye behaviors, called oculesics, shows that the eyes are also linked with emotions. In addition, however, patterns of gaze or lack of gaze are seen as important in coordinating interactions, assessing feedback, and learning about another's character. For the latter, the ties between gaze patterns and status and leadership are particularly noteworthy in the organizational context. More than any other behavior, however, unusual gaze patterns (e.g., not looking at another) are likely to be interpreted as sending a particular message (e.g., dishonesty or shame) even if there are no other communication cues available. These may be due to stereotypes that we hold about the nonverbal behaviors linked with deception (Leathers, 1992).

Studies on facial and eye behavior found a number of connections between these cues and organizational effects. For example, researchers Ketrow and Perkins (1986) noted that greater levels of employee eye contact led to increased customer satisfaction, more positive perceptions of the transaction, and more positive views of the business institution. Further, research revealed that actual job candidates who used more eye contact and smiling (along with more head movements) were accepted more often for advertised positions than those who used less of the behaviors (Forbes & Jackson, 1980).

Haptics

The use of touch to communicate is known as haptics. Touch is seen to be an important cue for both biologic (Montagu, 1978) and communicative reasons (Jones & Yarbrough, 1985). There are also very powerful rules dictating when touching is appropriate, and violations of these norms can lead to negative evaluations of the person enacting the behavior. What a touch comes to mean, however, depends on a variety of factors including who does the touching, where on the body the touch occurred, and the nature of the touch. These meanings or functions include such things as emotional displays, playfulness, influence, and responsiveness.

Touch is particularly important to study in the organizational context because of its ties to status (Henley, 1977) and sexual harassment (Hickson, Grierson, & Linder, 1991). A given touch can be seen as showing friendship, intimacy, or an assertion of one's power. Deciphering between these meanings is often difficult, and the ambiguity allows interactants to arrive at very different conclusions regarding what a particular touch "meant."

Increased touch has been found to interact with a number of organizational outcomes. For example, occasional touches have been found to increase sales (Heslin, Whittler, & Abella, 1989). However, Hickson and his colleagues (1991), who studied nonverbal behaviors in a different context, noted that repeated use of touch over time by one person is likely to lead to perceptions of sexual harassment (see Chapter 10). Thus, touching, more than other behaviors, may have extreme positive and negative effects.

Vocalics

Although the spoken word is seen as an aspect of language, the other things that we do with our voices are part of our vocalic behavior, or paralanguage. Sighs, tone, speed or tempo, volume, silence, pitch, and vocal quality are all considered part of the paralinguistic system (Giles et al., 1987; Trager, 1961). Although they can occur independently of language (e.g., sighing, silence), these vocal cues typically work alongside speech to alter the meanings of the spoken words.

For example, a supervisor might tell his or her employee to "Get someone to do the job now." If the speaker puts vocal emphasis on the word "someone" he or she is implying that the employee just needs to get another to do the job; who does the job is not important as long as it gets done. Putting the stress on the term "now," on the other hand, indicates that the job should be done quickly; the urgency of the task is most important.

Vocal cues are also used in assessments of another's character. Although few vocal behaviors are reliable indicators of actual personality characteristics, they are often part of stereotyping others as confident, outgoing, dishonest, personable, and the like (Knapp & Hall, 1992). Further, vocal cues are important in discerning emotions and moods. Other aspects of paralanguage, such as an accent, act as markers of group and regional affiliation (Thakerer & Giles, 1981). These cues can also denote or signify our membership within an organization or a part of the organization.

Much of the work in this area has focused on the ways in which vocalics influence character perception in various professional contexts. For example, Barge, Schlueter, and Pritchard (1989) studied the vocal cues used by attorneys. They concluded that several aspects of vocalics are likely to interfere with perceptions of credibility. These behaviors included disfluencies, inappropriate speed, pitch, range, and intonation, "faulty articulation," and lack of warmth and dynamism.

Summary

There are a range of cues that can be seen as active behaviors that we can perform within any given interaction. Because actions like eye behavior, personal space, and vocal pitch can change from moment to moment, they provide a powerful source of meaning that may vary throughout an interaction. As can be seen from the studies in this area, behavioral cues are most likely to have an effect on organizational perceptions when they occur in clusters. These groups of behaviors include nonbehavioral cues as well.

Nonbehavioral Cues

Although most of the cues that we associate with nonverbal communication are behavioral, there are others that may be important contributors to the meaning of an interchange but cannot adequately be described as "active." Three nonbehavior cues are dress and appearance, the use of time (chronemics), and the environment.

Dress and Appearance

Within the organizational context, few areas have been as researched as dress and appearance. Indeed, organizational researchers Noesjirwan and Crawford (1982) argue that dress is the most important component of image. There are numerous guides to "Dressing for Success," some of which derive from scholarship in this area (e.g., Molloy, 1977). Other investigations have focused on clothing, body size, colors, height, and facial hair and the influence that they are likely to have on such things as hiring and salary level.

One area within this larger category focuses on overall attractiveness. A person's attractiveness becomes important because we tend to assume that those who are more attractive than others are more likely to be sociable, intelligent, friendly, and successful (Herman, Zanna, & Higgins, 1986). Indeed, because they are often treated as having those characteristics and are invited to engage in more interactions, attractive people often come to have more social skills than those who are less attractive.

A large amount of research has been conducted investigating the influence of physical appearance within the organizational context. Researchers Bardack and McAndrew (1986), for example, found that attractiveness and clothing are both important to hiring in simulated studies; of the two sources of information, attractiveness was seen as more important than dress. When physical attractiveness is the only judgment criterion, those with higher levels of attractiveness are more likely to be hired than those with lower levels (Carlson, 1967). Other researchers suggest, however, that dress and attractiveness by themselves do not generally increase the likelihood of such things as being hired, but when two candidates are equal in ability (the most important hiring criterion), the one with greater perceived attractiveness is more likely to get the position (Chung & Leung, 1988).

Chronemics

An often overlooked cue in the nonverbal system is the use of time to communicate. Arriving early or late, doing one or more things simultaneously, and how quickly a task is performed are all part of chronemics, or time, as a source of communicative information. In addition, the use of time is linked with status, perceived personality characteristics, and beliefs about what is or is not important to another (McGrath & Kelly, 1986).

For instance, it is more likely that an interviewer will keep an interviewee waiting than vice versa. The assumption is that the person with greater power or control has the right to influence when interactions begin and end. Further, if an interviewee shows up early, an interviewer might use this information to make judgments about the other (e.g., he or she is anxious or really wants the job). In addition, if the interviewer does several things at the same time as he or she speaks with the interviewee, the latter is likely to think that the interview is not that important to the interviewer.

One particularly noteworthy study in this area was done by Word, Zanna, and Cooper (1974). They looked at the effects of race similarity on time granted to interviewees. Their results suggested that white interviewers were more likely to conduct longer interviews with whites than they were with blacks. The interviewers also tended to use a range of more "positive" cues with the white than with the black candidates. The authors concluded that nonverbal cues, such as use of time, are tied to the stereotypes we hold about others.

The Environment

The structure of our environments is likely to both affect communication patterns (i.e., who talks to whom, what they talk about) and work as a communication tool (i.e., to express status, show a desire to change the nature of a relationship with another, and reflect organizational norms). The environmental cues that may work in these ways include such things as furniture arrangement, color, temperature, textures, and architectural design (Altman & Chemers, 1988).

Within a work environment, certain areas are "marked" for use in given ways. For example, one corridor may be for offices and another region for conferences. Some office spaces are "open" (no walls, doors), and others are more traditionally "closed." These features are likely to affect the kind of communication that occurs within a particular environment. We may also choose certain cues to communicate particular messages about ourselves. Putting a large desk between ourself and others who come into an office, for example, may be done purposefully to show a degree of distance from others and to reflect our place in an organizational hierarchy.

The ways in which an environment is structured often reflects and encourages a particular organizational culture or climate (see Chapter 8). Discussing the role of the environment in creating and recreating a certain corporate culture, organizational observer Gagliardi (1990) contends that "every detail of the setting reminds us, physically and symbolically, with all the motionless and unmovable persistence of objects, what we are, what we do, what we cannot do" (p. 15). Thus, the environment has the potential to go beyond its basic function and both influence and present a view of an organization to those inside and outside the corporate boundaries.

Summary
Nonbehavioral cues such as physical appearance and environmental structures and forms are unlikely to change over the course of an interaction. These cues are, however, important in how they affect the nature of the conversation. The use of time also works differently than other behavioral cues in that it provides a structure for the interaction rather than being something that occurs within an interchange. Most importantly, nonaction codes are likely to affect what kind of communication patterns emerge within an interaction and the topics of that communication.

THE NATURE OF NONVERBAL BEHAVIOR

As has been seen, there are a wide range of behaviors that count as part of our nonverbal communication repertoire. As also noted, nonverbal cues typically do not occur in isolation, but rather work in combination to enable certain communicative meanings and functions to occur. Discussing them separately helps show the range of cues available in the nonverbal system, but determining what any given cue comes to mean is usually based on its relationship to other behaviors and contextual cues. This idea reflects an important point about how nonverbal communication works, but it is not how we often think about the communication potential of nonverbal cues.

The upcoming section shows that nonverbal behaviors do not typically work in the manner that they are often portrayed and in the way that many of us (inaccurately) use them. To show more about the nature of nonverbal behavior, this section focuses on the complexities of the nonverbal communication system by highlighting

(1) the ambiguity of nonverbal behaviors, (2) the role of intentionality and control behind nonverbal messages, (3) the levels of meaning involved in any interpretation of nonverbal codes, and (4) the influence that context and culture have on the meaning of nonverbal messages.

The Ambiguity of Nonverbal Behaviors

Early writing on nonverbal cues emphasized a communication system that was both straightforward and transparent. For example, in his book, *Body Language,* Julius Fast (1970) put forward the thesis that we could learn to read others' nonverbal behaviors in order to discover their intentions and their degree of (primarily sexual) interest in the observer. Further, Freud (1959) asserted that our hidden thoughts and beliefs inevitably "ooze" from us nonverbally despite our best efforts to control this leakage.

The argument that nonverbal behaviors are somehow "windows to the soul" suggests that there is a direct connection between a given nonverbal cue and a particular internal state or emotion. Further, it implies that we cannot and do not control our nonverbal display. These assumptions are often well accepted, and they are behind the argument that in cases in which nonverbal channels contradict a spoken message, it is more accurate to interpret the nonlinguistic cues (Mehrabian & Wiener, 1967). We believe, after all, that words reflect what people want us to hear, whereas nonspoken cues relay a person's actual character and state of mind.

But do nonverbal behaviors work this way? To say that a given behavior reflects a particular internal state or trait means that nonverbal cues act as signs or signals of that specific disposition. Whenever there is a direct and innate link between something (e.g., feeling happy) and a given indicator (e.g., a smile), the latter is said to be a "signifier" for the former (known as the "referent"). This view of nonverbal behavior suggests that nonlanguage cues are clear and unambiguous: a given sign always and only represents a particular, singular meaning.

Although there are other ways that we could think about nonverbal cues, when we view another's behavior we may be inclined to judge that it is a direct reflection of some aspect of the other's character, mood, feeling, or belief. We may feel that we have access to what is really going on inside the other's mind or heart. But we are also likely to be wrong. While sometimes a given cue may signify a certain state, there are at least two other options for the behavior's origin.

First, the cue may potentially be a signifier of other dispositions (e.g., the smile may be linked inherently with sarcasm, relief, and/or embarrassment). In this situation, the ambiguity (and the meaning potential) of nonverbal cues is reflected in the number of possible referents with which a given cue is linked "naturally." That is, it is difficult to know the "true" meaning of a given behavior because any one cue can be connected with a range of possible innate meanings.

Second, the smile may be assigned its meaning by the culture or group in which it occurs (Ekman & Friesen, 1986). For example, Americans often smile to show their displeasure; it is an agreed upon way to indicate disagreement without actually stating that we are unhappy with another. Further, smiles are often used by cultural groups as masks for other felt emotions. In the American culture, for instance, we may smile to cover embarrassment. In Japan, people are likely to smile as a way to shield sadness.

In situations in which the meaning for a behavior comes, not from some inherent link between a behavior and its referent but from a link imposed on it by the rules of a culture or social group, the behavior is a symbol for a given meaning rather than a sign (Cronkhite, 1986). The message value for a given cue or cues is created by an arbitrary ("non-natural") agreement among users. The range of possible meanings that can be assigned to a given behavior is limited only by the people who use it.

Thus, any nonverbal behavior has a large range of possible message values (Manusov, 1990). In addition to the numerous meanings that can be associated with a particular behavior inherently, there are a number of things that a behavior may "come to mean" because a given culture has agreed on what the cue will symbolize. Because any behavior can be both a sign and a symbol of many ideas, traits, intentions, beliefs, feelings, states, and other messages, a particular nonverbal action cannot be assigned one meaning automatically. This range of meanings makes nonverbal cues potentially, and commonly, ambiguous.

An example may help to clarify this. We see a person across the room who has his or her arms crossed. Crossed arms could indicate that the person is angry, cold (either physically or dispositionally), ill, or wishes to show his or her authority. It may be that crossed arms are a comfortable place to keep one's arms, they help the speaker to keep from gesturing too much, or the speaker feels a need to protect him or herself. It may also be a symbol, decided upon by the person and another in the room, that it is time to leave.

To decide among these meanings (and other possible interpretations), we may look to other interaction cues. A behavior only becomes less ambiguous when there are other sources of information (e.g., temperature, conversation topic, information about the speaker's background, and other nonverbal cues such as a tapping foot and a scowl) that help to place it in a particular context (Burgoon, Buller, & Woodall, 1989). Even with the other cues, however, we always have to "read the mind" of the other. As will be seen, this kind of mind reading is likely to be affected by our own beliefs, intentions, and character.

Any given cue is in itself ambiguous; more information is needed to decide the ultimate meaning of that nonverbal behavior. Knowing that any given behavior may be a sign or a symbol for a range of meanings, however, broadens our view of the message potential behind the nonverbal communication system. It is also likely to decrease our belief that a certain behavior clearly "shows" what another is like or what he or she feels.

Degrees of Intentionality and Controllability

One characteristic of nonverbal behavior that may alter the degree to which a particular cue or set of cues is ambiguous is based on how purposefully the behaviors are encoded. As mentioned, although we often overlook it, nonverbal cues can be sent intentionally as part of a communicative message. Inherent in the idea that behaviors can be agreed upon symbols for a particular message is the argument that we must be able to use our actions purposefully.

Behaviors that are used intentionally (i.e., we mean to show someone that we are angry and use certain cues with that purpose in mind) are more likely to be read accurately than cues that are less intended (i.e., leaks of actual feelings or cues that are encoded without direct intent [Motley, 1986; Motley & Camden 1988]). This may be because intentional behaviors are likely to be more exaggerated and redundant than unintended behaviors. Because of their defined character, "strategic" or intentional cues are more likely to be read the way that the encoder wishes than are spontaneous or unintended behaviors.

To help show how this works in interactions, we can explore a typical job interview. Most interviewees are likely to think carefully about what clothes to wear to an interview, and they expend energy to present a certain physical image. Interviewees are likely to give themselves enough time to arrive early, and while waiting they may purposefully show that they are excited about the interview. Both before and during the interview, they will tend to sit formally and straight, try to look "attentive" (use more eye contact, smile more, nod often), and attempt to sound competent (speak fluently, at a solid pace, and look facially sincere). The interviewer will probably see these behaviors and interpret them with a similar meaning to what the encoder intended.

Although some of the behaviors mentioned above may be unintended (i.e., competence may "show through" certain behaviors), at the minimum we try to exaggerate or augment our natural attributes. More likely, however, we attempt to establish messages with a specific intent, and we use nonverbal means of doing so. Furthermore, depending on our skill at sending messages, others are likely to read that we are, for example, interested and excited about the job.

Certain behaviors are more controllable and are therefore easier to use with a greater degree of intentionality. According to psychologists DePaulo and Rosenthal (1979), nonverbal codes fall into a hierarchy of controllability. The face and eyes are seen as most likely to be controlled. This is followed by kinesics and then vocalic cues. Microexpressions, brief facial cues that are often not noticeable to an observer, are the hardest to monitor and control. Although all behaviors can be controlled and used with intent, most of us are more likely to learn those skills associated with the face and are less likely to monitor our vocal cues.

Some cues are sent without conscious intent, of course; indeed, many times we use cues that show something that we are not aware of or that we would rather hide. Rosenthal's (1985) work on expectancy effects helps to highlight this. In his early work, the researcher found that when we have a particular belief about another (e.g., that the other is intelligent or unintelligent), these beliefs or expectancies are likely to show through certain behaviors. That is, when interacting with another person who we think has particular characteristics, we respond to that other with behaviors that express our knowledge and opinion about his or her action or character. So, if we believe that another is kind, our facial expressions, body movements, and vocal tone are likely to be more pleasant. This may occur even when we are trained to monitor our actions.

What makes this all the more striking is that others respond to our expectancy-based behaviors. When a person is repeatedly treated as being a certain kind of person, he or she may begin to act in a way that is consistent with the treatment he or she receives. Rosenthal (1988) calls this the Pygmalion Effect, or the tendency to be molded by the expectations of others. Although other researchers (e.g., Swann, 1987) have found that we only respond to expectancy behaviors if we do not already have a strong sense of who we are, research on expectancies shows an important potential for nonverbal cues.

Thus, nonverbal behaviors can be encoded with degrees of intent and control (Motley, 1986). These range from unintended behaviors that we do not know we are using to highly controlled behaviors sent with a particular purpose. To say that we can, and do, sometimes control our nonverbal cues does not imply that we are doing so to create artificial images of ourselves (although, of course, this is sometimes the case). Rather, more of the time we use nonverbal "displays" to highlight our overall communicative intent.

For example, if a supervisor wishes to show a subordinate that he or she has done a good job, the former may purposefully walk to the latter's desk, smile at him or her, and use "happy" or excited vocal cues. These are all part of the supervisor's intention to show the employee that he or she has done well and that the supervisor is pleased with the performance. This combination of somewhat exaggerated cues is likely to be an unambiguous message for the employee. Although the supervisor may not think with complete consciousness about the behaviors he or she is using, the behaviors are still part of a purposeful message "package."

As was argued, nonverbal behaviors have a rich message potential and may be encoded with different degrees of intent. A given nonverbal behavior is likely to be more "readable" if it occurs alongside other cues that can be seen to imply the same meaning or function; it also becomes less ambiguous if it is communicated with intent. Many times, however, nonverbal cues occur without (and sometimes despite our attempts at) control. The degree of intent both alters the form of the behaviors (e.g., their readability) and the meanings underlying them.

Levels of Meaning

In addition to differences in the degree of intentionality behind a nonverbal message, we are also likely to make choices about whether another person encoded his or her behaviors purposefully. Indeed, communication researchers Manusov and Rodriguez (1989) argued that people in formal interactions (e.g., a bank teller and customer) are more likely to assume that the other was acting with a high degree of intent rather than that the other's behaviors indicated only an unintended meaning. Thus, in addition to there being different degrees of encoded intent, there are also differences in perceived intent.

This is important in at least two ways. First, knowing that we make judgments of another's intentionality implies that the decisions are a part of how we determine the meaning for behavior (Manusov, 1990). For example, if a customer assumed that an employee's positive greeting behaviors were done purposefully, the meaning given to the cues could be that the employee valued the customer's business, the employee was trained to act positively, and that the employee liked the customer and wanted to show this to him or her. If the customer assumed that the behaviors were not intentional, he or she would choose from a different pool of meanings. This would include such things as the employee is a nice person, is in a good mood, or is attracted to the customer. While there is some overlap between these meanings, the degree of intentionality assumed by the perceiver varies somewhat and leads to a different interpretation for the action.

In addition to allowing or excluding certain meanings, the fact that we make choices about others' degree of control and purpose underlying their use of nonverbal cues shows that the "meaning" of nonverbal cues occurs at many levels. That is, we have talked about the encoding or sending of particular behaviors to create a given message (e.g., wanting to show interest in a job). But judgments about what another means also lie in the receiver or decoder of a message. Thus, at minimum, two levels of meaning occur concurrently in any interaction. While one person wishes to create a particular impression, the other is making interpretations about the other's character. Further, it cannot be assumed that what a person meant to imply by certain nonverbal behaviors is what the other person read in those cues.

The receiver or interpreter's view of a message relies on the attributions given to the set of behaviors by the perceiver. "Attributions" refer to how we make sense of or determine the cause for a given action. They are part of our overall cognitive system that helps us make sense of the world around us. According to various attribution theorists (e.g., Heider, 1958; Jones & Davis, 1965), in our everyday lives we act as "lay scientists" who search for the reasons why they, and others, acted the way they did. This attribution-making has been found to occur most often when a behavior becomes particularly noticeable, either because it is negative or because it is different from what another might expect (Pszyszynski & Greenberg, 1981).

Besides the fact that only certain types of behaviors are likely to instigate attribution-making, attributions also tend to be biased because they reflect the attributors' own goals, beliefs, and motives. Thus, for example, we are likely to view the causes of our own negative behaviors in a way that makes us less responsible, but we tend to place the blame on others for the same actions. This is based, in part, on the perspective of the attribution-maker (e.g., looking out at another or in towards oneself), and it is motivated by needs to defend our sense of self. Further, we make attributions in ways that are consistent with our feelings for the other person (e.g., we are kinder in our views of others if we like them and less benign in the meaning or cause we ascribe if we do not like them).

In addition, the type of attribution made for another's behavior is likely to influence how the attributor responds to the other person. For instance, if a person wears a bright-colored suit to an interview, the interviewee may make an attribution as to why the interviewee wore what he or she did. The interviewer may attribute the behavior to the person's character (i.e., that the bright color represents a happy disposition) or to the fact that the interviewee doesn't know the rules (i.e., at the company only blue or grey suits are worn). If the first attribution occurred, the interviewer may respond well to the interviewee. In the second case, the interviewer might act less positively.

Clearly, attributions are an important part of how we make sense of the things that happen around us, including but not limited to nonverbal cues. Research suggests that such attributions are likely to occur regarding the intentionality of nonverbal behaviors, however. For example, sometimes we mirror one anothers' behaviors, either purposefully or inadvertently. This has been associated with feelings of closeness and rapport (Tickle-Degnan & Rosenthal, 1992). If we believe that another mirrored our behaviors with intent (a common suggestion for people to increase sales; DePaulo, 1992), we are likely to judge that person more negatively than if we perceived the other used the same behaviors unintentionally.

In the second case (judging the cues as unintentional), we typically think that the behaviors represented actual rapport and good feelings. In the first case (seeing the mirroring as intended), however, we may feel manipulated and view the other negatively (Manusov, 1992). Similarly, researchers have found that if people sit too close to us on purpose, we are likely to judge them and interpret their behavior more harshly than if they sat too near because they had no other choice (O'Connor & Gifford, 1988). Although we tend to believe that a person who uses intentional nonverbal cues has more social ability than one who does not, we are also likely to be concerned about the former's sincerity.

What makes this even more complex is the fact that different types of receivers are likely to make different sorts of judgments about what a behavior means. Specifically, if the receiver is part of the interaction (i.e., that person is talking to the other about whom he or she is making an attribution), the attributor is likely to make more positive judgments about what a behavior means. This is known as the positivity bias (see Manusov, 1993). If the receiver is looking from the outside of an interaction, however, the attributions are more typically negative (Kellermann, 1989). These biases act as systematic distortions in the ways we interpret nonverbal cues.

There are a number of explanations that have been offered for positivity and negativity biases. First, if we have a chance to interact with another, the latter's behaviors become more personalized. Seeing another as an individual often makes us judge him or her more kindly. Second, when we are interacting with another, our views of that person are influenced by the fact that he or she is communicating with us. Thus, our interpretations for the other's behaviors benefit from viewing that person kindly; after all, he or she was behaving in reaction to us. Observers do not have this same self-driven motivation.

Third, when we evaluate others from within an interaction, we are attempting to do more than judge the meaning of their actions. We are also, for instance, trying to create an impression and to help the conversation run smoothly. Observers, on the other hand, have only one focus: they are trying to make sense of the other and his or her behaviors. The cognitive "busyness" of interactants versus observers results in a different, and usually kinder, focus (Gilbert & Osborne, 1989). Finally, interactants are given the opportunity to ask questions of one another, talk about their reactions, and be responded to by the other. This gives them an opportunity to negotiate the meaning of their behavior and alter the other's view of their character, and such negotiation is likely to lead to more favorable outcomes (Swann, 1987). Observers cannot engage in this more dynamic meaning-making.

As can be seen, attributions, or receivers' interpretations for others' behaviors, are important sources of meaning within any communicative exchange. They coexist with the encoders' view of what they believe has been communicated and are strongly influenced by the perceptions or biases of the decoder. Besides the encoder's and decoder's perspectives on a message's content, however, there are at least two other levels of meaning. These are negotiated and social meanings.

Occasionally a certain behavior stands out to us. Indeed, we may ask one another about the meaning behind a particular cue (Stamp & Knapp, 1990). Negotiated meanings occur when the definition of the behavior stems from this conversation. Often part of metacommunication (i.e., talking about one's communication), negotiated meaning allows us to work together to build the meaning for a given behavior, and it ensures a greater level of coorientation (i.e., similarity of perspectives) in our meaning for the cue. Such negotiated meaning may differ from both the source's and the receiver's initial belief about what was denoted by the particular behaviors.

For example, a superior may notice that a subordinate does not seem to be working on a task very quickly (an aspect of chronemics). The supervisor may judge inwardly, or make the attribution, that the employee does not care about his or her job. At the same time, the employee may believe that he or she was doing what he or she should (i.e., trying to do the task carefully). Later, in a performance evaluation session, the superior may comment on the employee's use of time. This comment may lead them into a discussion of why the subordinate was "wasting time." Through a give-and-take between the two communicators, the message for the way the employee used time may be reinterpreted to mean that the employee was being diligent, but perhaps was overly concerned with detail. They may decide that a good employee ought to do the job carefully, but should not take too much time with any one task. In this case, the negotiated meaning is a middle ground between the encoder's and the decoder's original interpretations. Further, both interactants are likely to take away similar meanings from the interaction.

We are only likely to talk about the meaning for nonverbal behaviors when the cues appear to be highly unusual or the meaning given to them by one or the other interactant is uncertain. Although we do not very often talk specifically about what a behavior means, the fact that we can metacommunicate, and potentially alter what the behaviors come to mean, shows another message level that is possible for a set of nonverbal cues.

There is one final level of meaning that can be given to any nonverbal behavior— the social or cultural level. According to nonverbal researcher Burgoon and her colleagues (1989), many sets of nonverbal cues may have a "typical" meaning that is ascribed to the behaviors by people in a culture or social group. When most people would agree on a meaning for certain behaviors, the cues are seen to have a more clear, socially defined message. Looking at the meanings that most cultural members would be likely to give to a set of behaviors is known as the "message orientation."

Despite the idiosyncrasies that we usually bring to our interpretations of nonverbal messages, certain cues or sets of cues are likely to be seen in similar ways by most people. A lack of eye contact, for example, is most commonly viewed negatively and is seen as a violation of expected behavior (Burgoon et al., 1985). Likewise, certain facial expressions or gestures are likely to be interpreted similarly by most members of a particular group or culture.

According to researcher Burgoon and her colleagues (1989), "The message orientation centers on the behaviors and sets of behaviors that form the 'vocabulary' of nonverbal communication in a particular 'language' community" (p. 17). It also suggests that certain interpretations for nonverbal cues are preferred within any given communication group and that many meanings are given habitually to certain behaviors because they are so commonly associated with one another for a particular group.

Although this last level of meaning that can be assigned to nonverbal behaviors implies that perhaps there is some degree of a "body language," it should be interpreted within the framework of all of the places in which meaning can be created. Any given nonverbal cue or set of cues can have a meaning that exists within the mind of the person who enacted the behaviors. Simultaneously, meanings are formed within the thoughts of perceivers who make attributions as to why another acted in a given way. Further, we can discuss together what a particular behavior meant and derive a new interpretation from this exchange. Overarching all of this is a network of common interpretations shared by a group of communicators who learn the more standard ways of taking meaning from certain nonverbal cues.

Thus, the particular "message" content of nonverbal cues exists in a number of places. Depending on which of the meanings each interactant holds for a behavior, however, he or she is likely to react to the behaviors in diverse ways.

Culture and Context

The message orientation to nonverbal cues underscores a vital issue in understanding the nature of nonverbal behaviors: the meanings and use of nonverbal behaviors are culture and context bound. Although there may be some limited universal meanings given to certain emotional expressions (i.e., that most people in different cultures see smiles as part of expressing happiness), the majority of meanings for nonverbal cues are framed by the social or cultural group in which it occurs.

This framing occurs in at least two ways. First, cultural and contextual demands largely dictate which nonverbal behaviors are seen as appropriate within a given situation. They state the preferred rules that guide the use of nonverbal cues. For example, we have talked about low levels of eye contact and have stated that people typically judge limited eye contact as negative. In particular, it may be seen as indicating dishonesty or disrespect. This judgment is typically American, however. In other cultures (e.g., Mexico), limited eye gaze is the appropriate way to show respect to a person of higher status. Using the type of extended gaze that listeners are expected to use in the United States would be considered inappropriate within other cultures.

The guidelines for using nonverbal cues within a given culture are known as the "display rules" for that behavior (Ekman & Friesen, 1986). Display rules are the edicts for when, where, and with whom people are expected to use particular kinds of nonverbal cues. These rules change across cultures, as indicated above, as well as during different contexts within a culture.

For instance, there is an expectation that we sit close to others when the setting is described as "romantic." Choosing a seat far away from our partner in that type of context usually indicates that we do not want to be close to the other or are trying to compensate for the intimacy of the situation by acting in less intimate ways. In a business meeting, however, a larger distance is required between people. Only when two people need to talk secretly in this context, or if they wish to express a high degree of solidarity, would they be likely sit as close as two people would within a more intimate setting. These expectations, and the meanings given to violations of them, are based on cultural rules.

The edicts that develop within any particular culture are dictated in large part by the nature of the culture. All cultures are said to have "world views," which are frameworks for making sense of the things that occur around us. Burgoon and colleagues write: "To the extent that cultures hold different world views (e.g., different social, religious, moral, and political values), their communication patterns may manifest these differences" (1989, p. 26). Thus, a culture that believes that privacy is a particularly important value is likely to create proxemic rules that emphasize greater distance from others. Similarly, in societies that value personal expressiveness, it would be predicted that we would engage in a greater range of facial expressions and gestures.

Although cultures are typically thought of as occurring across political borders, organizations are also seen as developing their own cultures (see Chapter 8). Rules for acceptable nonverbal behaviors can therefore emerge within different organizational contexts. Indeed, Munter (1993), a writer discussing organizational effectiveness, argued that using appropriate nonverbal behaviors is a key component of constructive managerial communication. He combined the political and organizational definitions of culture by asserting that effective managers "resist applying their own culture's nonverbal meanings to other cultures" (p. 76).

As in the case of political cultures, the corporate culture's world view is also likely to affect the emergence of rules and the meanings that are attached to them (Gagliardi, 1990). An organization with greater concern for secrecy, for instance, may create physical environments that discourage interaction. One that values innovation may create rules that encourage greater discourse.

Besides creating the rules for using nonverbal cues, cultures shape the interpretations for particular behaviors. As mentioned in the discussion on kinesics, all cultures have certain behaviors that they use as emblems. But the types of behaviors used, and the meanings given to those behaviors, originates and makes sense only to people from that culture or those who have learned the cultural interpretations. Knowing that the thumb and forefinger circled symbolizes that everything is "okay" is part of learning the American code system. That particular gesture has no meaning in most cultures, although in a few cultures it has a very different, and highly negative, meaning.

In addition to the culture within which nonverbal behaviors occur, its physical and communicative context also has an important effect on the meaning and appropriateness of the behaviors. A behavior that occurs within one context may take on diverse meaning from an action that happens in a different situation, and it may be more or less ambiguous depending on the context.

Touch, for example, has a range of meanings within the U.S. culture that emerge in different contexts. If we have been dating someone for a while and he or she takes our hand during dinner, the touch is likely to be seen as a sign of affection and intimacy. If our boss takes our hand during a performance evaluation, the behavior may be interpreted in a number of ways. It may show actual affection, although other cues would have to exist for this to be seen as appropriate; it may indicate remorse over an upcoming firing decision. The behavior may be meant to comfort the employee, or it may be a show of greater status. As can be seen, the behavior, in this case touch, takes on a different range of meanings based on the context within which it occurs. The context itself may also decrease or increase the ambiguity of the behavior. In the first scenario, touch is an expected part of an intimate dinner. In the second setting, touch is less expected, and the possibility of what the behavior means is increased.

Culture (whether defined by political, psychological, or organizational boundaries) and context (identified by physical features, type of interaction, and other communicative information that is available) are both vital influences on what behaviors are expected and what the behaviors may ultimately mean. This aspect of the nature of nonverbal behavior emphasizes the largely symbolic, or arbitrary, aspect of nonverbal cues.

Summary

Nonverbal behaviors are often seen as easy-to-read links to natural, inner dispositions. As has been seen, the nature of nonverbal communication is far less clearly defined. The meanings of nonverbal cues are largely ambiguous and are only able to take on more "reliable" meaning when studied as clusters of behaviors. In addition, behaviors may emanate from internal, uncontrolled factors; but nonverbal cues are encoded with different levels of intent and control. They are also interpreted at a number of levels, including the encoder's view, the receiver's perspective, negotiations within the interaction, or definitions of social commonalities. Finally, nonverbal cues are rule-governed, and these rules (and the interpretation for the behaviors) are affected by the culture and the context within which they occur.

FUNCTIONS OF NONVERBAL BEHAVIORS

Despite the complex picture we have painted of the nature of nonverbal cues, they can be and are used with accuracy during communicative exchanges. Indeed, nonverbal cues perform a number of important functions for us in our everyday interactions—"Functions are the purposes, motives, or outcomes of communication" (Burgoon, Buller, & Woodall, 1989, p. 22). Many of these functions have already been mentioned in the examples we have provided above, and they include such things as expressing intimacy, controlling the type and amount of communication, and making judgments of others.

Within organizational contexts, there are a number of functions served, in part at least, by nonverbal cues. Of particular note are the goals of person perception and impression management (i.e., how we judge others as well as how we work on showing particular aspects of ourselves), relational messages (i.e., the ways in which nonverbal cues express the nature of the relationship between individuals), and the coordination of interaction (i.e., how nonverbal cues allow us to engage in interactions with one another). These will be discussed in turn.

PERSON PERCEPTION AND
IMPRESSION MANAGEMENT

Perhaps more than any other aspect of nonverbal communication, the role that non-language cues have in creating an impression of another or for oneself is an important function in organizational contexts. This section will focus on the role of impression formation (person perception) and impression management (image creation) in organizations.

Impression formation is the process perceivers perform when they make judgments of others (Schneider, Hastorf, & Ellsworth, 1979). As people get to know one another, part of what they do is to try to assess what the other is like. We do this to decide how best to act with this other person, to discern if he or she is the type of person that we want to get to know better, and to figure out how to interpret his or her behaviors.

Simultaneously, we are also trying to allow others to see what we are like and to portray a desirable image of ourselves, a process known as impression management. According to Goffman (1959), a sociologist who studied human behavior, we work actively to "play out" our chosen self-presentations during interaction with others. Like actors in a drama, we seek to perform our given roles and identities in ways that are likely to enhance our image and our outcomes.

In most interactions, people are concerned with both impression formation and impression management, and the functions are served simultaneously. Within the research on organizational communication, the study of these two interrelated goals focuses largely on job interviews.

Interviews

Job interviews and their connection to nonverbal communication channels make up the area most widely researched by scholars interested in nonverbal behaviors and organizations. Interestingly, interviews have not been found to be a very reliable way to find people who will be effective employees, yet they are used as an important source of information in hiring decisions (Gifford, Ng, & Wilkinson, 1985). Even though the interview itself is not as valid a method as we would hope, nonverbal cues are a relatively important factor within them.

As with most other communicative functions, nonverbal cues typically work in tandem to perform a particular goal. Thus, a range of behaviors are typically seen as important in creating a "favorable outcome" during interviews. Increased eye contact, smiling, gestures, head nods, high energy level, speech fluency, and modulated voice have all been found to be important cues in interviews (Edinger & Patterson, 1983; McGovern, 1976). Indeed, these cues are consistently linked with the likelihood of hiring (Forbes & Jackson, 1980).

Other studies investigated the relative importance of these nonverbal cues. That is, certain researchers asked whether the above mentioned nonverbal cues are more important than what a person says within an interview; but the results on this question are mixed. Some scholars (e.g., Clowers & Fraser, 1977; Tepper & Haase, 1978) found that nonverbal cues are more important than language on effectiveness ratings for both interviewees and interviewers, leading them to claim that nonverbal behaviors are the primary modality for judgments of another. Others argue that nonverbal cues, while important, are not the most critical components of interview decisions.

This latter research suggests that there are other important mediators in the interview process that will affect the overall role of nonverbal cues. First, nonverbal cues may only become important when applicants cannot be judged on ability alone. For example, when candidates have similar aptitudes for a position, nonverbal cues are used to make hiring decisions; but when one person has greater ability for the job, he or she is likely to be hired despite any differential use of nonverbal cues (Chung & Leung, 1988).

Second, nonverbal cues are often limited in impact because most of us use similar cues to one another (DePaulo, 1992). Perhaps because of popularized books on the importance of our nonverbal image in interviews, most of us learn to dress and act in ways that encourage perceptions of competence and likability. Thus, in cases in which aptitude is equal, nonverbal skill is also likely to be similar. It is only in situations in which one person uses "effective" nonverbal cues, and the other does not, that the cues are likely to have an important influence.

A third reason why the use of nonverbal behaviors in interviews is not straightforward deals with levels of meaning. Researchers discovered that interviewers may use different cues in judging interviewees than interviewees intentionally manipulate in order to create an impression for this interviewer (Gifford, Ng, & Wilkinson, 1985). Although both applicants and employers relied on similar nonverbal cues to determine or express social skill, they used different cues in presentations of motivation. Specifically, interviewees employed dress and upper body movement as part of showing motivation, but interviewers looked towards smiles, gestures, and time talked as indicators of the applicant's motivation for the job.

Overall, most of us believe that nonverbal cues are an important part of the impression-making that occurs in interviews. Their role is not overwhelming, however. Because ability is the first factor employed in hiring decisions, because most of us are similar in our use of nonverbal cues in job interviews, and because perceivers (interviewers) and impression managers (interviewees) may use different cues in their roles, the impact of nonverbal cues in the employment interview becomes somewhat modified.

Other Contexts

As mentioned, much of the research investigating how nonverbal cues work in impression formation and management focuses on interview settings. These communicative functions are important in other areas of organizational life, however. Sales, for example, rely in part on the images created by the sales staff on the product or service, the company, and the salesperson. As noted previously, some research suggests that certain nonverbal cues by sales staff may be more influential on sales than others. In particular, appearing to be happy or joyful is likely to increase the likelihood of a sale (Sommers, Greeno, & Boag, 1989).

In general, the research in this area, and in other contexts involving interaction between employees and customers, implies that creating certain images may increase the effectiveness of employees. For example, one study investigated cues associated with "nonverbal conviviality" and found that use of certain nonverbal behaviors increased people's satisfaction with customer-contact personnel (Martin, 1986). In addition, researchers reported that increases in eye contact leads to greater client satisfaction (Ketrow & Perkins, 1986).

Underlying these studies is the (very controversial) belief that increases in satisfaction are likely to mean that customers are likely to buy more and return to the company with their future needs. Scholars argue that what is occurring in impression formation and management in customer/employee contexts is the search for "surrogate" cues for quality that encourage people's satisfaction (Parasuraman, Zeithaml, & Berry, 1985). Thus, certain behaviors used by the employees signal that the organizational member is a certain type of person. For the potential customer, this type of person is likely to represent a company with good products and services.

As has been seen, less research investigates the role of nonverbal behavior in customer contact. What has been done primarily rests on the belief that nonverbal cues are linked (either actually or in others' minds) with certain personality characteristics. These also include such things as leadership (Leary, 1990), competence (Barge, Schlueter, & Pritchard, 1989), and managerial style (Baird & Bradley, 1979).

Relational Messages

Not only do we try to create images of ourselves or determine attributes of others, we also use nonverbal cues to create and determine the nature of the relationship between people in an interaction. Relational messages are determined at the dyadic (two person) level of the interaction; they reflect the type of relationship people have, or desire to have, with one another. These relationships can be differentiated in a number of ways, also known as relational topoi (Burgoon & Hale, 1987). Indeed, there may be up to twelve dimensions on which relationships can be defined. Of particular importance to the organizational context, however, are messages of power, intimacy, and immediacy.

Power.   As always, a number of cues typically work to reflect the type of relationship people have. Greater power is typically linked with control over the use of cues in a given interaction. Therefore, we may show our degree of status over another by holding the meeting in our office, dictating the time the meeting will occur, keeping the other waiting, and using either greater or lesser eye contact than the other (Burgoon, Buller, & Woodall, 1989). The person with less power shows this status by accepting the rules that have been set down.

To show equal levels of power, people in relationships will use different behaviors. There will probably be a similar amount of "setting the agenda," and each is likely to use the same degree of eye contact, gestures, and vocal variation. Indeed, several theories from interpersonal communication research suggest that matching, or using the same communicative behaviors as another, is likely to show more solidarity and equality between individuals (Giles et al., 1987).

Power relationships that are well established (e.g., a boss and an employee) are likely to play out easily in nonverbal displays, with each of us accepting and enacting cues that are appropriate for our position. Sometimes, however, power may be "negotiated" as we try to use behavioral "moves" that show greater or lesser power. That is, if two people both want to show greater status than is given to the other, each person is likely to follow the other's power display with a similar, or increased, nonverbal expression of his or her own status or power.

Supervisors may also attempt to "negotiate" a more balanced or comfortable relationship with their subordinates by increasing the rapport in their interactions. Five nonverbal behaviors are linked with a person's attempt to build rapport with another: smiling, appropriate touch, affirmative head nods, immediacy (involvement) behaviors, and gaze (Heintzman et al., 1993). Managers who are successful in building rapport through these nonverbal means are also likely to be perceived as trustworthy and attractive and to increase their workers' satisfaction. According to the researchers, these characteristics also tend to increase compliance and productivity.

Intimacy.   The discussion of rapport suggests that in addition to power another important relational message is the degree of intimacy or closeness within a relationship. Intimacy is likely to be communicated nonverbally through closer proximity, quieter and more pleasant vocal tones, greater eye contact, and increased touching. Although intimacy is not usually seen as a part of relationships within organizations, it does occur.

In addition to professionalism, many times work relationships also have a personal side; that is, we often date or are friends with people who work in the same company (Dillard & Miller, 1988). This is usually an accepted, and easily incorporated, part of organizational life, but it may become complicated in at least two ways.

First, what is an expected part of the behavior between friends or intimates (e.g., more touching, different vocal tones) may not be accepted behavior in the organizational context. Thus, relationships can be threatened because we need to know how to switch between appropriate roles. In daily interactions at work, these rule structures may become mixed up, or we expect behaviors that occur in the more informal contexts also to occur within the organizational setting.

Second, we may find it difficult to know how to create a new type of relationship outside of the corporate context with our established organizational relationships. Thus, working out a transition into having another type of relationship may be difficult. This becomes even more complicated when only one person wishes to move to a more intimate nonwork relationship or when the two people involved have different organizational status. Sometimes important close relationships emerge from this negotiation. Other times, the same behaviors are seen as sexual harassment (Bingham, 1991).

Immediacy.   Throughout the literature on interviewing and sales, a range of cues is commonly mentioned that work together to send a similar relational message. When people act in ways that show that they are interested or involved in a conversation, they are reflecting a high degree of immediacy (Andersen, 1985). Although too much immediacy may not be effective, in general, increased levels of immediacy cue use typically link with better organizational outcomes.

Researchers Sommers, Greeno, and Boag (1989), for example, found that customers responded well to "happy, joyful" behaviors used by salespeople. These cues included more body movement and positive facial displays. Similarly, immediacy cues (shown through greater levels of eye contact, positive facial displays, and touch) may be associated with higher customer satisfaction levels (Ketrow & Perkins, 1986), increased likelihood of hiring (Forbes & Jackson, 1980), and better sales (Heslin, Whittler, & Abella, 1989).

What is more, changes in immediacy cues are likely to affect other interactants' behaviors. The most common tendency is for increases or decreases in the immediacy level of one person's cues to be matched or reciprocated by the other interactant (Manusov, 1995). Thus, if an interviewer acts with low immediacy cues, an interviewee is likely to use fewer immediate behaviors. This may affect both interactants' satisfaction with the interview.

Although matching is the most common reaction to changes in immediacy, the actual nature of the response will depend on a number of factors. Researchers studying these reactions or accommodation processes assert that the ways in which one person responds to another's behaviors depends on interaction functions (i.e., whether the focus is on a task or relationship discussion [Patterson, 1982]), the ways in which the behaviors are labeled (Andersen, 1985), the size of the behavioral violations (Cappella & Greene, 1982), and the degree to which the person is seen as "rewarding" to the other interactant (Burgoon & Hale, 1987). In some cases, for example, we may react to another's immediacy behavior by compensating for very high levels with few immediacy cues if we feel that this will help balance the conversation (Argyle & Dean, 1965).

Other Relational Messages

In addition to power, intimacy, and immediacy, relational messages may also include the degree of formality established between people, the level of comfort, the extent to which a relationship is focused on social or task goals, and the like. Any of these may also play out in our behaviors at work.

Coordination of Interaction

As mentioned, power relationships are often defined by who calls a meeting and where that meeting is held. When nonverbal elements work to influence the nature of an interaction, this is seen as the function of coordinating interaction, or conversational management. Two of the most important ways in which nonverbal cues work to coordinate interaction include (1) the effect of nonverbal structure on patterns of interaction and (2) the ways in which nonverbal cues allow conversational flow.

A great deal of work in small group communication (a common format of organizational behavior) has looked at how things, such as the seating arrangement, influence communication patterns, and this area of study is known as small-group ecology (Knapp & Hall, 1992). Researchers have found, for example, that there is a link between leadership and seating position. Specifically, elected leaders are likely to place themselves at the head position at a rectangular table. When there is no appointed leader, the person who is in this seating position is likely to become an emergent leader (Strodtbeck & Hook, 1961). This is based largely on the fact that facial orientation and communication are likely to be directed toward this position.

Indeed, seating positions are important in other ways as well. Meetings that occur at round tables where visibility and orientation are equal for all interactants may encourage a balanced level of communication (Knapp & Hall, 1992). In conferences that occur at long tables, information has to flow through those seated near the middle of the table. As well, office location increases or decreases the amount of communication that the office holder receives. Those with centrally located offices are situated to engage in greater interaction. Offices in the corners, although sometimes associated with greater status if they are large and have multiple windows, are less likely to be a frequent part of the communication flow.

The structure of offices may also affect the type and amount of communication that occurs within them. For example, desks that are placed between people are likely to reduce the amount of communication that occurs; they may also affect how at ease people are in that environment (White, 1953). It has been argued that desks located between people act as barricades to communication (Zweigenhaft, 1976). Nonverbal researchers Knapp and Hall (1992) assert, however, that at times these barricades are seen as appropriate reflections of a person's status and of the relationship between interactants.

In addition to the way they interact with our position and set of particular communication patterns, nonverbal cues are used within interactions to allow the conversation to occur. Knapp and Hall write that "Conversations begin, and they are eventually terminated. Between these two points, however, it is necessary to exchange speaking and listening roles, that is, to take turns" (1992, p. 383).

Much of our turn-taking tasks rely on nonverbal indicators. To show that the speaker can keep his or her turn and that they are still engaged in the interaction, listeners tend to nod their heads and use vocal fillers (e.g., saying "uh huh" or "mmm"), also known as back channels. When they are ready to turn the floor to another, speakers are likely to reduce their rate and pause. Listeners who wish to take the floor will often use an "audible inhalation," a breath that signifies an attempt to speak. In meetings in which many people may wish to talk, we often need to raise our hands to "get the floor" (our turn at speaking).

These behaviors, and others, occur typically below our level of consciousness, but they allow the "stuff" (the meaning and content) of interactions to occur. Because of their importance in monitoring and allowing conversations, nonverbal cues provide an invaluable function in organizational contexts.

Summary

Although many functions occur within organizations and are influenced, at least in part, through nonverbal channels, we have mentioned what we see to be three of the most important. These include how nonverbal cues work within the person perception and impression management contexts, how they influence the establishment and interpretation of relational definitions, and the ways in which they work to affect the flow of interaction.

CONCLUSION

Our intent in this chapter was to introduce readers to the potential of nonverbal communication as a message system, with a particular emphasis on how those behaviors work within the organizational context. As was seen, nonverbal behaviors include a plethora of behavioral and nonbehavioral cues. These behaviors can be natural extensions of internal dispositions, but more often they are symbolic of a particular meaning and are encoded with some degree of purpose and intent.

What the behaviors ultimately come to mean is influenced by the encoder's intent, the decoder's attributions, overt negotiations of meaning, and socially-defined or typical interpretations attached to certain cues. These cues usually occur next to one another, and together they enable communicators to perform particular interactive functions (i.e., impression formation and management, the reflection or creation of relational definitions, and the coordination of interaction).

In unveiling nonverbal communication in this way, we tried to highlight the ambiguity and complexity of the nonverbal system. At the same time, we use nonverbal cues everyday as we engage in observation and communication. Keeping in mind that nonverbal communication is not as straightforward as we sometimes think it is, there are some ways of using nonverbal cues more effectively than they are typically employed.

Suggestions for Improving Nonverbal Communication

1. As we have repeated, using multiple cues in attempting to encode or decode a meaning increases the chance that the behaviors will be communicated consistently.
2. Behaviors that are encoded with specific intent and directed toward another are likely to be less ambiguous than cues used with no intent and control.
3. Thinking about the ways our own biases or experiences may influence our interpretations of others' behaviors may keep us from making the wrong conclusions about the meaning of those cues.
4. Talking about, or negotiating the meaning of, ambiguous cues is likely to lead to more shared understanding than trying to mind read or assume that another has interpreted one's behaviors accurately.
5. Watching communication over time, rather than making quick judgments, is likely to lead to greater accuracy.
6. Looking for other cues beyond nonverbal behavior (such as what the person is saying) usually helps to ground those cues in a particular context and makes them less ambiguous.

7. Understanding that people from other cultures may have very different rules and interpretations for nonverbal cues can keep us from making erroneous judgments about them or their behaviors.
8. Realizing that nonverbal cues may be a part of different functions should encourage people to think about the range of meanings possible for the behaviors.
9. Understanding what cues are seen as appropriate (e.g., what to wear or how to act in a job interview), is based on sensitivity to an organization's culture.

GLOSSARY

Chronemics—the use of time to communicate and the ways in which time affects communication.

Display rules—cultural edicts for when, where, and with whom one uses nonverbal communication behaviors. This is usually applied to emotional displays.

Emblems—gestures that have a direct verbal translation (e.g., fingers in a V to signify peace).

Haptics—the use of touch as communication.

Kinesics–the use of body behaviors such as gesture, lean, and walk as communication.

Proxemics—the use of space and territory as part of nonverbal communication.

Relational messages—behaviors that occur in communication encounters and define the way that people see their relationship with one another.

Signifiers—actions or behaviors that stand for something else but have a natural relationship with the thing they represent.

Symbols—actions or behaviors that stand for something else but have an arbitrary relationship with the thing they represent.

Vocalics—also known as paralanguage, these are cues associated with the voice that are part of nonverbal communication.

CASE STUDY—THE NEW HIRE

Victoria's Story

Victoria Chelton was very pleased to be starting a new job. She had just finished secretarial training, and she knew jobs were scarce. On her first day, Victoria arrived ten minutes early, eager to make a good impression with her boss, Mr. Landrell, a manager in the marketing department. She had to stop at personnel first to complete some forms. This took about half an hour. As she got off the elevator on the fifth floor, she smiled and nodded to several women who were standing by the elevator. She asked one of them for directions to Mr. Landrell's office, and after a brief pause, the woman gave her the information. When she arrived at the office, Victoria knocked on the open door. Mr. Landrell immediately stood up from his large desk and came to the door to shake Victoria's hand. He directed Victoria to one of the "visitors' chairs" and then leaned against the desk next to her, making Victoria feel right at home. They spent the next fifteen minutes going over her duties. Victoria made a list of these duties, and on a few occasions, Mr. Landrell leaned over her to check this list. This really helped Victoria understand her duties, and she responded by smiling and speaking pleasantly. Mr. Landrell then showed Victoria to her desk, and she began work.

Marge's Story

Marge Fenton had been with the company for four years, and in that time, she had seen seven secretaries come and go. She figured that something was going on with Tom Landrell and his secretaries, but nobody ever said anything about it. When the new secretary came in, Marge was surprised that she was so late, but not surprised at how she looked. Marge commented to a friend: "Here comes another young looker for Tom to feed on. Have you noticed, all his secretaries are young and naive?" Her friends laughed, and they went on with their work. Later, Marge looked into Tom's office. She noticed that Tom was acting pretty chummy with Victoria.

Tom's Story

Tom Landrell had the worst luck with secretaries. They seemed to come and go faster than the seasons, and he really needed to find a good one to keep up with the workload. He hoped this new one would work out and be okay to work with; he spent so much time at work that he needed to be compatible with his staff. When Victoria showed up at his door, he was pleased that she was so pretty, thinking that she could liven up things around here. Sitting on the edge of his desk, as he tends to do, Tom went over Victoria's duties. He watched her closely to get a sense of her intelligence and personality. She seemed nervous, so he tried to be reassuring to her. As he did so, she responded with what seemed like flirting behavior. Tom wasn't quite sure what to do about that, but he said nothing. Later, he escorted Victoria to her desk, and he went on with the rest of his duties.

    Discussion: What nonverbal cues were at play in this scenario? What meanings and functions were attached to the behaviors? What factors may have led to so many different meanings for the same behaviors? Was one of these interpretations best? Why?

REFERENCES

Altman, I., & Chemers, M. M. (1988). *Culture and Environment.* New York: Cambridge University Press.

Andersen, P. A. (1985). Nonverbal immediacy in interpersonal communication. In A. W. Siegman & S. Feldstein (eds.), *Multichannel Integrations of Nonverbal Behavior* (pp. 1–36). Hillsdale, N.J.: Lawrence Erlbaum.

Argyle, M., & Dean, J. (1965). Eye-contact, distance, and affiliation. *Sociometry, 28,* 289–304.

Baird, J. E., & Bradley, P. H. (1979). Styles of management and communication: A comparative study of men and women. *Communication Monographs, 46,* 101–111.

Bardack, N. R., & McAndrew, F. T. (1986). The influence of physical attractiveness and manner of dress on success in a simulated job interview. *The Journal of Social Psychology, 125,* 777–778.

Barge, J. K., Schlueter, D. W., & Pritchard, A. (1989). The effects of nonverbal communication and gender on impression formation in opening statements. *The Southern Communication Journal, 54,* 330–349.

Becker, F. D. (1973). Study of spatial markers. *Journal of Personality and Social Psychology, 26,* 439–445.

Bingham, S. (1991). Communication strategies for managing sexual harassment in organizations: Understanding message options and their effects. *Journal of Applied Communication Research, 19,* 88–115.

Birdwhistell, R. (1970). *Kinesics and Context: Essays on Body Motion Communication.* Philadelphia: University of Pennsylvania Press.

Buck, R. (1984). *The Communication of Emotion.* NY: Guilford.

Burgoon, J. K., Buller, D. B., & Woodall, W. G. (1989). *Nonverbal communication: The unspoken dialogue.* NY: Harper & Row.

Burgoon, J. K., & Hale, J. L. (1987). Validation and measurement of the fundamental themes of relational communication. *Communication Monographs, 54,* 19–41.

Burgoon, J. K., & Hale, J. L. (1987). Nonverbal expectancy violations: Model elaboration and application to immediacy behaviors. *Communication Monographs, 55,* 58–79.

Burgoon, J. K., Manusov, V., Mineo, P., & Hale, J. L. (1985). Effects of eye gaze on hiring credibility, attraction, and relational message interpretation. *Journal of Nonverbal Communication, 9,* 133–146.

Cappella, J. N., & Green, J. O. (1982). A discrepancy-arousal explanation of mutual influence in expressive behavior for adult–adult and infant–adult dyadic interaction. *Communication Monographs, 49,* 89–114.

Carlson, R. E. (1967). The relative influence of appearance and factual written information on an interviewer's final rating. *Journal of Applied Psychology, 51,* 461–468.

Chung, P., & Leung, K. (1988). Effects of performance information and physical attractiveness on managerial decisions about promotion. *The Journal of Social Psychology, 128,* 791–801.

Clowers, M. R., & Fraser, R. T. (1977). Employment interview literature: A perspective for the counselor. *Vocational Guidance Quarterly, 26,* 13–26.

Cronkhite, G. (1986). On the focus, scope, and coherence of the study of human symbolic activity. *Quarterly Journal of Speech, 72,* 231–246.

DePaulo, B. M., & Rosenthal, R. (1979). Ambivalence, discrepancy, and deception in nonverbal communication. In R. Rosenthal (ed.), *Skill in Nonverbal Communication: Individual Differences* (pp. 204–248). Cambridge, Mass.: Oelgeschlager, Gunn & Hain.

DePaulo, P. J. (1992). Applications of nonverbal behavior research in marketing and management. In R. S. Feldman (ed.), *Applications of Nonverbal Behavioral Theories and Research* (pp. 63–88). Hillsdale, N.J.: Lawrence Erlbaum.

Dillard, J. P., & Miller, K. (1988). Intimate relationships in task environments. In S. Duck (ed.), *Handbook of Personal Relationships* (pp. 449–465). New York: John Wiley.

Edinger, J. A., & Patterson, M. L. (1983). Nonverbal involvement and social control. *Psychological Bulletin, 93,* 30–56.

Ekman, P., & Friesen, W. V. (1986). A new pan-cultural facial expression of emotion. *Motivation and Emotion, 10,* 159–168.

Fast, J. (1970). *Body Language.* New York: M. Evans.

Forbes, R., & Jackson, P. (1980). Nonverbal behavior and the outcome of selection interviews. *Journal of Occupational Psychology, 53,* 65–72.

Freud, S. (1959). Fragment of an analysis of a case of hysteria. *Collected Papers,* Vol. 3. New York: Basic Books.

Gagliardi, P. (ed.). (1990). *Symbols and Artifacts: Views of the Corporate Landscape.* Berlin: Walter de Gruyter.

Gifford, R., Ng, C. F., & Wilkinson, M. (1985). Nonverbal cues in the employment interview: Links between applicant qualities and interviewer judgments. *Journal of Applied Psychology, 70,* 729–736.

Gilbert, D. T., & Osborne, R. E. (1989). Thinking backward: Some curable and incurable consequences of cognitive busyness. *Journal of Personality and Social Psychology, 57,* 940–949.

Giles, H., Mulac, A., Bradac, J. J., & Johnson, P. (1987). Speech accommodation theory: The first decade and beyond. In M. L. McLaughlin (ed.), *Communication Yearbook 10* (pp. 13–48). Newbury Park, Calif.: Sage.

Goffman, E. (1959). *The Presentation of Self in Everyday Life.* Garden City, N.Y.: Doubleday/Anchor Books.

Hall, E. T. (1966). *The Hidden Dimension.* Garden City, N.Y.: Doubleday/Anchor Books.

Heider, F. (1958). *The Psychology of Interpersonal Relations.* New York: John Wiley.

Heintzman, M., Leathers, D. G., Parrott, R. L., & Cairns, A. D. (1993). Nonverbal rapport-building behaviors' effects on perceptions of a supervisor. *Management Communication Quarterly, 7,* 181–208.

Henley, N. M. (1977). *Body Politics: Power, Sex, and Nonverbal Communication.* Englewood Cliffs, N.J.: Prentice-Hall.

Herman, C. P., Zanna, M. P., & Higgins, E. T. (eds.). (1986). *Physical Appearance, Stigma, and Social Behavior: The Ontario Symposium,* Vol 3. Hillsdale, N.J.: Lawrence Erlbaum.

Heslin, R., Whittler, T., & Abella, R. (1989). When salespeople touch customers: Reactions and perceptions. *Proceedings of the Society for Consumer Psychology.*

Hickson, M., Grierson, R. D., & Linder, B. (1991). A communication perspective on sexual harassment: Affiliative nonverbal behaviors in asynchronous relationships. *Communication Quarterly, 39,* 111–118.

Jones, E. E., & Davis, K. (1965). From acts to dispositions: The attribution process in person perception. In L. Berkowitz (ed.), *Advances in Experimental Social Psychology,* Vol. 2 (pp. 219–267). New York: Academic Press.

Jones, S. E., & Yarbrough, A. E. (1985). A naturalistic study of the meanings of touch. *Communication Monographs, 52,* 19–56.

Kellermann, K. (1989). The negativity effect in interaction: It's all in your point of view. *Human Communication Research, 16,* 147–183.

Kendon, A. (1983). Gesture and speech: How they interact. In J. M. Wiemann & R. P. Harrison (eds.), *Nonverbal Interaction* (pp. 13–45). The Hague: Mouton.

Kendon, A. (1988). How gestures can become like words. In F. Poyatos (ed.), *Cross-Cultural Perspectives in Nonverbal Communication* (pp. 131–141). Toronto: Hogrefe.

Ketrow, S. M., & Perkins, K. *Operator Eye Contact and Client Satisfaction in Computer-assisted transactions.* Paper presented to the Speech Communication Association, Chicago, Ill., November 1986.

Knapp, M. L., & Hall, J. A. (1992). *Nonverbal Communication in Human Interaction* (3rd ed.). Orlando, Fla.: Holt, Rinehart, & Winston.

Leary, M. R. (1990). Self-presentational processes in leadership emergence and effectiveness. In R. A. Giacalone & P. Rosenfeld (eds.), *Impression Management in the Organization* (pp. 363–374). Hillsdale, N.J.: Lawrence Erlbaum.

Leathers, D. G. (1992). *Successful Nonverbal Communication: Principles and Applications* (2nd ed.). New York: Macmillan.

Manusov, V. (1990). An application of attribution principles to nonverbal messages in romantic dyads. *Communication Monographs, 57,* 104–118.

Manusov, V. (1992). Mimicry or synchrony: The effects of intentionality attributions for nonverbal mirroring behavior. *Communication Quarterly, 40,* 69–83.

Manusov, V. (1993). "It depends on your perspective": Effects of stance and beliefs about intent on person perception. *Western Journal of Communication, 57,* 27–41.

Manusov, V. (1995). Reacting to changes in nonverbal behavior: Relational satisfaction and adaptation patterns in romantic dyads. *Human Communication Research, 21,* 456–477.

Manusov, V., & Rodriguez, J. S. (1989). Intentionality behind nonverbal messages: A perceiver's perspective. *Journal of Nonverbal Behavior, 13,* 15–24.

Martin, W. B. (1986). Defining what quality service is for you. *Cornell Hotel and Restaurant Administration, 26,* 32–38.

McGovern, T. V. (1976). The making of a job interviewee: The effect of nonverbal behavior on an interviewer's evaluations during a selection interview. *Dissertation Abstracts International,* 4740B.

McGrath, J. E., & Kelly, J. R. (1986). *Time and Human Interaction.* New York: Guilford Press.

Mehrabian, A., & Wiener, M. (1967). Decoding of inconsistent communications. *Journal of Personality and Social Psychology, 6,* 108–114.

Molloy, J. T. (1977). *The Woman's Dress for Success Book.* Chicago: Follet.

Montagu, A. (1978). *Touching: The Human Significance of the Skin* (2nd ed.). New York: Harper & Row.

Motley, M. T. (1986). Consciousness and intentionality in communication: A preliminary model and methodological approaches. *Western Journal of Speech Communication, 50,* 3–23.

Motley, M. T., & Camden, C. T. (1988). Facial expression of emotion: A comparison of posed expressions versus spontaneous expressions in an interpersonal communication setting. *Western Journal of Speech Communication, 52,* 1–22.

Munter, M. (1993, May-June). Cross-cultural communication for managers. *Business Horizons,* 69–78.

Noesjirwan, J. A., & Crawford, J. M. (1982). Variations in perceptions of clothing as a function of dress form and viewer's social community. *Perceptual and Motor Skills, 54,* 751–757.

O'Connor, B. P., & Gifford, R. (1988). A test among models of nonverbal immediacy reactions: Arousal-labeling, discrepancy-arousal, and social cognition. *Journal of Nonverbal Behavior, 12,* 6–33.

Parasuraman, A., Zeithaml, V. A., & Berry, L. L. (1985). A conceptual model of service quality and its implications for future research. *Journal of Marketing, 49,* 41–50.

Patterson, M. L. (1982). A sequential functional model of nonverbal exchange. *Psychological Review, 89,* 231–249.

Patterson, M. (1983). *Nonverbal Behavior: A Functional Perspective.* New York: Springer-Verlag.

Patterson, M. L. (1987). Presentation and affect-management functions of nonverbal communication. *Journal of Nonverbal Behavior, 11,* 110–122.

Pszyszynski, T. A., & Greenberg, J. (1981). Role of disconfirmed expectancies in the instigation of attributional processing. *Journal of Personality and Social Psychology, 40,* 31–38.

Rosenthal, R. (1985). Nonverbal cues in the mediation of interpersonal expectancy effects. In R. L. Street & J. N. Cappella (eds.), *Sequence and Pattern in Communicative Behaviour* (pp. 85–102). London: Edward Arnold.

Rosenthal, R. (1988). Interpersonal expectancies, nonverbal communication, and research on negotiation. *Negotiation Journal,* 267–281.

Schneider, D. J., Hasorf, A. H., & Ellsworth, P. C. (1979). *Person Perception.* Boston: Addison-Wesley.

Sommers, M. S., Greeno, D. W., & Boag, D. (1989). The role of nonverbal communication in service provision and representation. *Service Industries Journal, 9,* 162–173.

Stamp, G. H., & Knapp, M. L. (1990). The construct of intent in interpersonal communication. *Quarterly Journal of Speech, 76,* 282–299.

Strodtbeck, F. L., & Hook, L. H. (1961). The social dimensions of a twelve-man jury table. *Sociometry, 24,* 397–415.

Swann, W. B. (1987). Identity negotiation: Where two roads meet. *Journal of Personality and Social Psychology, 53,* 1038–1051.

Tepper, D. T., & Haase, R. F. (1978). Verbal and nonverbal communication of faciliative conditions. *Journal of Counseling Psychology, 25,* 35–44.

Thakerar, J. N., & Giles, H. (1981). They are—so they spoke: Noncontent speech stereotypes. *Language and Communication, 1,* 255–261.

Tickle-Degnan, L., & Rosenthal, R. (1992). Nonverbal aspects of therapeutic rapport. In R. S. Feldman (ed.), *Applications of Nonverbal Behavioral Theories and Research* (pp. 143–166). Hillsdale, N.J.: Lawrence Erlbaum.

Trager, G. L. (1961). The typology of paralanguage. *Anthropological Linguistics, 3,* 17–21.

White, A. G. (1953). The patient sits down: A clinical note. *Psychosomatic Medicine, 15,* 256–257.

Word, C. O., Zanna, M. P., & Cooper, J. (1974). The nonverbal mediation of self-fulfilling prophecies in interracial interaction. *Journal of Experimental Social Psychology, 10,* 109–120.

Zweigenhaft, R. (1976). Personal space in the faculty office: Desk placement and student-faculty interaction. *Journal of Applied Psychology, 61,* 529–532.

RECOMMENDED READINGS

Burgoon, J. K., Buller, D. B., & Woodall, W. G. (1989). *Nonverbal Communication: The Unspoken Dialogue.* New York: Harper & Row.

DePaulo, P. J. (1992). Applications of nonverbal behavior research in marketing and management. In R. S. Feldman (ed.), *Applications of Nonverbal Behavioral Theories and Research* (pp. 63–88). Hillsdale, N.J.: Lawrence Erlbaum.

Gagliardi, P. (1990) (ed.). *Symbols and Artifacts: Views of the Corporate Landscape.* Berlin: Walter de Gruyter.

Knapp, M. L., & Hall, J. A. (1992). *Nonverbal Communication in Human Interaction* (3rd ed.). Orlando, Fla.: Holt, Rinehart, & Winston.

Leathers, D. G. (1992). *Successful Nonverbal Communication: Principles and Applications* (2nd ed.). New York: Macmillan.

Ethics in the Workplace: The Role of Organizational Communication

ANN L. PLAMONDON

In his oscar winning performance as Gordon Gekko in *Wall Street,* Michael Douglas characterized the ethical philosophy of the 1980s in his speech at the stockholders' meeting of Teldar Paper (Stone, 1987):

> *Greed... is good. Greed is right. Greed works. Greed clarifies, cuts through and captures the essence of the evolutionary spirit. Greed, in all of its forms, greed for life, for money, for love, knowledge, has marked the upward surge of mankind, and greed, you mark my words, will not only save Teldar Paper but that other malfunctioning corporation called the U.S.A.*

The scandals that resulted from adherence to this philosophy have been headline news: Wall Street insider trading; savings and loan failures; Iran-Contra; Congressional banking and post office improprieties; falsification of medical research data. The public response has been to demand accountability from individuals and organizations in every sector of society, business, government, and nonprofit institutions.

Organizations have put matters of ethics on the agenda for re-evaluation. In 1989–1990, the Center for Business Ethics at Bentley College sent a questionnaire to the chief executive officers of the *Fortune 1000* list of industrial and service corporations. Of the 24 percent of corporations responding, 93 percent reported taking steps to instill ethical values in routine operations, and 50 percent reported plans to expand the incorporation of ethical values (Center for Business Ethics, 1992). The objectives of these efforts were threefold: to become a socially responsible organization; to provide guidelines for the conduct of organizational members; and to ensure compliance with the law. The most often reported means of accomplishing these objectives was the development of a code of ethics for the organization.

Reliance on organizational codes of ethics is by no means adequate to ensure ethical conduct. Indeed critics of such codes have maintained that they frequently have little to do with ethical behavior. An analysis of eighty-four codes drawn from a survey sent to organizations appearing in the *Business Week 1000* revealed three clusters of admonitions: "Be a dependable organizational citizen"; "Don't do anything unlawful or improper that will harm the organization"; and "Be good to our customers" (Robin et al., 1990). These provide little guidance for such pressing ethical issues as conflicts of interest, employee rights, confidentiality, sexual harassment, discrimination, whistle-blowing, and protection of the environment. What is needed is a method of evaluating situations from a broad philosophical perspective. This can only be accomplished by the application of ethical theories. This chapter will first describe four traditional ethical theories and then apply them to some of the most serious ethical dilemmas arising in organizational communication.

PHILOSOPHICAL ETHICAL THEORIES

Kant's Categorical Imperative

Immanuel Kant was appointed Professor of Logic and Metaphysics at the University of Königsberg in 1770. From 1781 to 1798 he wrote philosophical treatises that were to change the history of Western thought. His ethical philosophy was in complete disagreement with Gordon Gekko's ethical philosophy of self-interest. The opening words of his earliest work on moral philosophy are: "Nothing can possibly be conceived in the world, or even out of it, which can be called good without qualification, except a *good will* (Kant, 1949, p. 11). Kant's meaning is that things commonly thought to be good, money, love, knowledge, power, for example, can be misused and, therefore, are not good without qualification. He maintained that a good will is one that chooses to perform an action solely because it is intrinsically right and not because of some advantage that the action might bring to oneself or to others. This led him to distinguish hypothetical from categorical imperatives. Hypothetical imperatives are actions one must take in order to bring about a certain result; one must engage in training exercises if one is to become a great athlete. Categorical imperatives, on the other hand, are actions that one must take because they are good in themselves and not good as a means to a further end. According to Kant only categorical imperatives are moral imperatives.

Our conduct is guided by maxims, subjective principles that set rules for actions. The foundation of Kant's (1949) ethical philosophy is respect for law. The main characteristic of law is its universality. Hence, our maxims for action must be ones that can be universalized (p. 38): "There is therefore but one categorical imperative, namely, this: '*Act only on that maxim whereby thou canst at the same time will that it should become a universal law*'" (p. 38).

Thus, the categorical imperative provides a test to which one can put all subjective maxims. One has merely to ask whether he could will that his subjective maxim should become a universal law. Kant gives an example involving the telling of lies. Suppose that a person borrows money, knowing that he will not be able to repay it. Yet he promises to repay the money (a lie), because if he fails to do so, he will not receive the loan. Kant maintained that this subjective maxim of making a false promise could not pass the test of the categorical imperative (1949, pp. 39–40):

> *Now this principle of self-love or of one's own advantage may perhaps be consistent with my whole future welfare; but the question now is, Is it right? I change then the suggestion of self-love into a universal law, and state the question thus: How would it be if my maxim were a universal law? Then I see at once that it could never hold as a universal law of nature, but would necessarily contradict itself. For supposing it to be a universal law that everyone when he thinks himself in a difficulty should be able to promise whatever he pleases, with the purpose of not keeping his promise, the promise itself would become impossible, as well as the end that one might have in view in it, since no one would consider that anything was promised to him, but would ridicule all such statements as vain pretenses.*

Since the maxim cannot be universalized, it must be rejected. What is ethical is capable of being universalized. One cannot make exceptions for oneself in the name of self-interest or greed.

The criterion of universalizability provides the form that correct ethical judgments must take. Kant also gave another formulation of the categorical imperative that provides content, namely, how we are to treat ourselves and other persons. He argued that one makes laws for oneself by using the categorical imperative, but other persons are also centers of self-legislation. This self-legislation is the source of human dignity and of one's obligation to others. Persons are the only entities having absolute value, and they should be treated as such: "Accordingly the practical imperative will be as follows: *So act as to treat humanity, whether in thine own person or in that of any other, in every case as an end withal, never as a means only*" (p. 46). One must never use another person merely as a means to one's own selfish ends.

Kant applies this formulation of the categorical imperative to the same example of making false promises. If a person makes a promise in exchange for some benefit, and either has no intention of keeping the promise or has reason to believe he will not be in a position to keep the promise, he uses the promisee (the absolutely valuable end) as a mere means to a relative end (the benefit).

The relevance of Kant's categorical imperative to contemporary moral problems is obvious. All of the scandals with which we began this chapter fail the test of the categorical imperative. One cannot universalize the maxims of insider trading, outrageously risky loans, writing checks that are not covered by deposit, falsifying data, and so on. In addition, all of these actions use other persons merely as a means to self-advantage (power, fame, money), disregarding other persons as valuable ends in themselves.

Kant's admonition to place ultimate value in persons has been compared to the view of the Jewish theologian Martin Buber (Purtill, 1976). Buber distinguished two fundamental kinds of relationships between persons. The ideal kind of relationship between persons is an "I-Thou" relationship. But sometimes persons engage in "I-It" relationships with another person, the kind of relationship appropriate to an object. This is tantamount to Kant's conception of treating another person merely as a means. "I-Thou" relationships are characterized by respect, mutuality, honesty, lack of pretense, lack of manipulation, and accepting responsibility for others. "I-It" relationships are characterized by self-centeredness, deception, exploitation, manipulation, pretense, and appearance; all involve the use of persons merely as a means to personal gain. These concepts will have special relevance to a discussion later in this chapter of ethical communication in organizations.

Utilitarianism

Utilitarian theories derive their name from their acceptance of the "principle of utility" or "greatest happiness principle" (Bentham, 1970). Historically this type of ethical theory can be traced to Epicurus in Ancient Greece. Modern developments of the theory occurred in the nineteenth and twentieth centuries. What is agreed upon by utilitarians is that the rightness or wrongness of actions depends upon the good or bad consequences produced by the actions. This notion places them in sharp contrast with the ethical philosophy of Kant. John Stuart Mill (1957) explicitly addresses what he sees to be a flaw in Kant's approach:

> *This remarkable man [Kant], whose system of thought will long remain one of the landmarks in the history of philosophical speculation, does... lay down a universal first principle as the origin and ground of moral obligation; it is this: "So act that the rule on which thou actest would admit of being adopted as a law by all rational beings." But when he begins to deduce from this precept any of the actual duties of morality, he fails, almost grotesquely, to show that there would be any contradiction, any logical (not to say physical) impossibility, in the adoption by all rational beings of the most outrageously immoral rules of conduct. All he shows is*

that the consequences of their universal adoption would be such as no one would choose to incur. (p. 6)

Mill (1957) insists that actions are not good because they flow from a good, amiable, brave, or benevolent person, because "these considerations are relevant, not to the estimation of actions, but of persons" (p. 26). What matters is the set of circumstances produced by the action of the person.

Utilitarians are not in agreement as to what constitutes good and bad consequences. Some theorists, like Epicurus and Bentham, argued that good and bad consequences are to be calculated by the quantity of pleasure or pain produced by the actions. Such theories are called hedonistic utilitarianism. Some twentieth century philosophers, for example, G. E. Moore, insisted that "good" was a term incapable of definition (Moore, 1962). They are known as ideal utilitarians. Mill represents a middle ground, sometimes referred to as quasi-ideal utilitarianism. Although he agrees with Bentham that "actions are right in proportion as they tend to promote happiness" (p. 10) and that happiness refers to the presence of pleasure and the absence of pain, he makes a distinction between the quantity and quality of pleasure. In addition to the bodily pleasures persons share with animals, persons are capable of higher pleasures associated with their higher faculties: the pleasures of feelings, imagination, and intellect (p. 11). Hence, for Mill (1957), the right action is one that produces "whether we are considering our own good or that of other people...an existence exempt as far as possible from pain, and as rich as possible in enjoyments, both in point of quantity and quality" (p. 16).

The utilitarian position is to be sharply distinguished from the philosophy of greed and self-interest. Indeed Mill (1957) maintains "that the happiness which forms the utilitarian standard of what is right in conduct is not the agent's own happiness but that of all concerned. As between his own happiness and that of others, utilitarianism requires him [the agent] to be as strictly impartial as a disinterested and benevolent spectator" (p. 22). The view is not to be confused with altruism; the moral agent is, rather, benevolent, regarding himself the same (neither more nor less than) as any other person.

Contemporary moral theorists draw a further distinction between "act" and "rule" utilitarianism. In general, act utilitarianism is the view that "the rightness or wrongness of an action depends only on the total goodness or badness of its consequences, i.e. on the effect of the action on the welfare of all human beings," (Smart, 1973, p. 4) whereas rule utilitarianism is the view that "the rightness or wrongness of an action is to be judged by the goodness or badness of the consequences of a rule that everyone should perform the action in like circumstances" (p. 9). In brief, the distinction raises the question whether each ethical situation should be regarded as unique or whether there are rules of action that tend to promote the well-being of humanity. Although Mill did not explicitly note this difference, he did anticipate it by considering an objection to his theory in that there is rarely time to calculate the consequences of an action for the general welfare before performing it. Mill responded that the history and experience of the human race are instructive about the general tendencies of actions to produce good or bad consequences.

Smart (1973) argued that the fundamental kind of utilitarianism is the act variety. This is because it seems inappropriate to a utilitarian theory to obey a rule just because it has maximized the general welfare in the past if it no longer does, or if it does not maximize happiness in the particular circumstances at hand: "[W]ho would say that we ought to keep to a rule that is the most generally optimistic, even though we knew that obeying it in this particular instance would have bad consequences" (p. 44).

That is not to say, however, that rules do not have an important role to play even in an act utilitarian theory. Rules that tend to maximize the general happiness should be thought of as "rough guides" to action, especially when the moral agent is in a position to act in an habitual manner or does not see a pressing need to consider the situation in which one finds him- or herself any different from a prior situation in which the rule worked.

Returning to our earlier examples, this analysis seems to work well. As a rule, insider trading does not produce the best consequences for persons operating in a free market economy. That is why it is illegal as well as immoral. Lying to Congress and diverting funds to causes that are not approved by elected representatives of the people does not optimize the general welfare. In fact, it undermines the democratic process. Falsifying research data on alternative treatments for breast cancer does not maximize happiness. Rather it robs persons of fundamental medical choices about life-threatening situations.

There is a problem, however, in regarding act utilitarianism as more fundamental than rule utilitarianism. It arises in considerations of justice. As a rule, it is clear that the well-being of humanity is maximized when justice is served. But could there be a situation in which the sacrifice of an innocent person could instead bring about the greatest well-being of the greatest number? Hypothetical situations have been suggested. Suppose the sheriff of a town could prevent serious riots by framing and executing an innocent person. Suppose, in addition, that the scapegoating conspiracy were never found out. The general welfare would be enhanced because the population would believe that justice was done. Riots would not occur endangering the life and property of many citizens. Only the innocent man would suffer (Smart, 1973). Should an act analysis be considered more fundamental than a rule analysis in this case? Utilitarians tend to answer that the example is sheerly a logical possibility and not likely to be a factual one (Smart, 1973). Indeed one is hard pressed to find real situations in which all of the factors come together in ways that the hypothetical example suggests. However, justice and the possibility of the sacrifice of individuals for the good of the many do remain problems for the theory.

Ross's Prima Facie Duties

Oxford University professor, Sir W. D. Ross, developed his ethical philosophy in conscious opposition to both utilitarian theories and the Kantian theory. He introduces his objection to utilitarianism in the form of an example. Suppose that a person has promised to meet a friend for a social engagement, but on the way to the agreed upon meeting point, he sees a serious accident and is in the position of being able to bring relief to the victims. Utilitarians hold that the person's duty is to bring relief to the suffering of the accident victims because it brings more happiness into existence. Ross (1930) thinks there is a better analysis of why the promise should be broken in order to relieve suffering:

> *It may be said that besides the duty of fulfilling promises I have and recognize a duty of relieving distress, and when I think it is right to do the latter at the cost of not doing the former, it is not because I think I will produce more good thereby but because I think it the duty which is in the circumstances more of a duty. . . . If . . . I could bring equal amounts of good into being by fulfilling my promise and by helping some one to whom I had made no promise, I should not hesitate to regard the former as my duty. Yet on the view that what is right is right because it is productive of the most good I should not so regard it. (p. 18)*

Ross maintains the the essential problem of utilitarianism is that this theory does not "do justice to" what he calls "the highly personal character of duty" (p. 22). By this Ross means that persons have moral duties *because* they stand in morally significant relationships to one another. Some of these morally significant relationships are: promisee—promisor; creditor—debtor; spouse—spouse; parent—child; friend—friend; countryman—fellow countryman (p. 19). Utilitarian theories, on the other hand, assume that there is only one morally significant relationship—being a possible beneficiary of another's actions.

According to Ross, there are circumstances and relationships that have moral significance. These circumstances lead one to recognize certain duties that Ross calls prima facie duties, duties "at first glance" or "upon first examination." He lists six such duties (p. 21).

1. Duties of fidelity
2. Duties of gratitude
3. Duties of justice
4. Duties of beneficience
5. Duties of self-improvement
6. Duties of non-maleficence

Duties of fidelity arise from the agent's own past actions. Ross thinks they fall into two categories. The first is explicit and implicit promises. One has a duty to keep explicit promises that one has made, and one also has the duty to keep implicit promises that arise from undertaking certain actions. For example, in entering into communication, interpersonal, public or mass, there is an implicit promise to tell the truth. A second kind of duty of fidelity is reparation for one's past wrong actions.

Other duties, duties of gratitude, rest upon the past actions of other persons. When a person does a service for another, a morally significant relationship is created, and the recipient of the service owes a duty of gratitude. The duties of beneficence and non-maleficence seem to account for what utilitarians argue is our duty. Ross agrees that we have a duty to others to bring about happiness and minimize pain. However, it is not the production of goodness that makes the act good; acts of benevolence and not injuring others are intrinsically good. Duties of self-improvement refer to improvement in virtue and intellect, not material comfort. Duties of justice are confined to the distribution of happiness according to merit.

Ross does not claim that this list is exhaustive. He does insist that the prima facie duties in his list are self-evident, known the same way we know a geometrical or arithmetical truth. This means that we know it is our duty to keep promises, not to harm, etc. without any further need of proof or evidence.

Our duty to act in a specific way may be traceable to more than one prima facie duty. For example, our duty to obey the law can be seen to arise from gratitude, implicit promises, and beneficence. Gratitude is involved because of the benefit one receives from living in a particular society. When one assumes residence in a society, one makes an implicit promise to obey its laws. Finally, many societal laws are based on utilitarian principles; they are ways of acting that tend to maximize the happiness and minimize the misery of most members of that society.

Nor does Ross attempt to rank or give a definitive priority of certain prima facie duties over others. This brings him to his disagreement with Kant. Ross maintains that Kant's philosophy leaves no room for exceptions to duty. For example, when confronted with the earlier ethical dilemma of breaking a promise or relieving the suffering of victims of an accident, Ross assumes that Kant cannot justify breaking the promise. This is because, of course, promise breaking cannot be universalized. Indeed, this is one of the very examples used by Kant to illustrate his theory. Ross believes that it is counter to our intuition to think that promise keeping is right in all circumstances. This means that although it is self-evident that the prima facie duties are always duties incumbent upon moral agents, prima facie duties may come into conflict. In this case the duty of fidelity is in conflict with the duty of beneficence.

The possible, indeed inevitable, conflict of prima facie duties leads Ross to distinguish them from our "actual or absolute" duty. When there is no conflict, one should act according to the *prima facie* duty or duties underlying the circumstances, and one can be certain that one is doing the right thing. But when there is a conflict, this certainty disappears (Ross, 1930, pp. 30–31):

> *Where a possible act is seen to have two characteristics, in virtue of one of which it is prima facie right, and in virtue of the other prima facie wrong, we are (I think) well aware that we are not certain whether we ought or ought not to do it; that whether we do it or not, we are taking a moral risk. We come, in the long run, after consideration, we think one duty more pressing than the other....*

Although prima facie duties are always incumbent upon persons, sometimes a choice has to be made between two or more conflicting prima facie duties. Ross believes that by intuition and moral reflection, the moral agent will come to see that one of the prima facie duties is more pressing under the circumstances. In the earlier example, beneficience is more pressing than fidelity. However, in another set of circumstances, it is possible that fidelity may be more pressing than beneficience. Although Ross never attempts a ranking among prima facie duties, he seems to regard the duty not to harm as the one most likely to be most pressing or "most stringent" in most circumstances (p. 22).

Rawls: Justice, Fairness, and Rightness

Professor John Rawls of Harvard University developed a contract theory of ethics in the tradition of Locke, Rousseau, and Kant. In a contract type of theory, the social and moral order is founded on convention or agreement, the contract. Unlike earlier philosophers, Rawls does not regard the contract as one to set up a particular kind of society or particular form of government. Rather, the original agreement involves the choice of the principles of justice for the society (1971, p. 11):

> *They are the principles that free and rational persons concerned to further their own interests would accept in an initial position of equality as defining the fundamental terms of their association. These principles are to regulate all further agreements; they specify the kind of social cooperation that can be entered into and the forms of government that can be established. This way of regarding the principles of justice, I shall call justice as fairness.*

In other words, the content of the agreement is the acceptance of "certain moral principles" (p. 16).

The contractual situation is not a real one, but a hypothetical one. Rawls is asking moral agents to imagine stepping out of reality into what he calls an "original position." In this original position, the person is functioning behind a "veil of ignorance." Although the parties to the agreement have an understanding of politics, of economics, of sociology and of human psychology, each person is ignorant of the age, gender, race, class, physical condition, intellectual or artistic capabilities that he or she will have when leaving the original position. In this situation, Rawls assumes that "[s]ince all are similarly situated and no one is able to design principles to favor his particular condition, the principles of justice are the result of a fair agreement or bargain" (p. 12). Each person will treat each other person equally as a moral agent. Information that would allow persons to act in a biased manner would be lacking. There will be no advantage and no envy. Indeed the agents would be motivated naturally to strive to protect the disadvantaged. The decisions that persons reach in this situation will represent ultimate fairness and rightness.

What principles of justice would be chosen behind this "veil of ignorance"? Rawls thinks it would not be a principle of utility. The motivation is not a desire to maximize total interests but to reach the best situation possible "by free exchange consistent with the right and freedom of others to further their interests in the same way" (p. 119). If utility results, it is a matter of coincidence, not one of reasoned choice.

In Rawls' view, two principles of justice would be chosen. The first principle asserts the necessity of equal liberty: "Each person is to have an equal right to the most extensive total system of equal basic liberties compatible with a similar system of liberty for all" (p. 250). He mentions specific liberties from the Bill of Rights (p. 60):

1. Freedom to vote
2. Freedom of speech and thought
3. Freedom of assembly
4. Freedom to own personal property
5. Freedom from arbitrary arrest
6. Freedom from unreasonable search and seizure

The second principle of justice states the justification of any social and economic inequality: "Social and economic inequalities are to be arranged so that they are both (a) to the greatest benefit of the least advantaged and (b) attached to offices and positions open to all under conditions of fair equality of opportunity" (Rawls, 1971, p. 83). The second part of this principle assures equal access to the hierarchy of authority and responsibility in society.

Rawls maintains that the primary goods are liberty, opportunity, wealth, and self-respect. The two principles of justice form the basis for self-respect. Self-respect is bound with Rawl's conception of the good for any person, which he defines as "the successful execution of a rational plan of life" (p. 433). Success is not to be measured in any absolute sense. Rather it is relative to an individual's talents and resources. An analysis of the concept of self-respect reveals four factors:

1. A belief in one's own worth
2. A belief that one's plan of life is a worthy one
3. A belief in one's ability to carry out the chosen plan of life
4. Appreciation and confirmation by associates

In brief, the principles of justice, chosen behind the "veil of ignorance," provide the foundation for the self-worth, the good, of each person in society.

Rawls' (1971) concept of the veil of ignorance has interesting applications for ethical decision-making in organizations. The next section of this chapter will be devoted to the application of the ethical philosophies of Kant, utilitarians, Ross, and Rawls to specific ethical dilemmas in the workplace.

ETHICS APPLIED TO THE WORKPLACE

The results of several polls suggest that public perception of ethics in organizations is not a positive one. Since the mid-1970s Gallup Polls measuring attitudes toward professional organizational behavior "reveal a consistent pattern of public skepticism" (Jaksa & Pritchard, 1994, p. 45). This skepticism would appear to be well founded in view of the fact that "[b]etween 1970 and 1980, 11 percent of the largest American firms were convicted of lawlessness, including bribery, criminal fraud, illegal campaign contributions, tax evasion, or price-fixing" (Velasquez, 1990, p. 229).

Two key suggestions have been made as to why unethical organizational behavior is so widespread. First, some unethical behavior occurs because individuals are greedy, power hungry, or evil (Velasquez, 1990, p. 229). Second, and perhaps more important, many individuals whose personal ethics would be judged unimpeachable subscribe to a different set of ethics in the workplace. In a sociological study based on interviews with managers, Jackall (1990) uncovered "moral rules-in-use" and "rules for survival and success" which are "highly contextual and moral guidelines that managers divorce from their own set of personal beliefs" (p. 206). Employees also follow these rules in order to succeed in the organization. "As a result, bureaucratic work causes people to bracket, while at work, the moralities that they might hold outside the workplace or that they might adhere to privately and to follow instead the prevailing morality of their particular organizational situation" (p. 210). In brief, much organizational misbehavior results from organizational cultures.

A recent study concludes that individuals *knowingly* violate their personal codes in responding to organizational pressures (Sims, 1992, p. 507). One reason that this happens is that organizations develop counternorms—"accepted organizational practices that are contrary to prevailing ethical standards" (Sims, 1992, p. 507). Five important counternorms were identified (p. 508):

1. "Be secretive and deceitful" versus "Be open and honest"
2. "Do whatever it takes to get the job done" versus "Follow the rules"
3. "Use it or lose it" versus "Be cost-effective"
4. "Pass the buck" versus "Take responsibility"
5. "Grandstand" versus "Be a team player"

This does not purport to be an exhaustive list of situations in which the organizational cultural climate is not supportive of ethical behavior on the part of its members. Five cultural climates will be described that pose serious ethical dilemmas for organizations.

A Climate of Broken Organizational Promises

In 1992 Gilchrist and Van Hoeven published a study based on interviews with subjects employed at over forty organizations. Interviewees were asked to identify "ordinary" breaches of ethics in their organizations. Ordinary was meant to refer to situations that occur in everyday organizational life, as opposed to the extraordinary organizational events that make headline news. The conduct most often reported as unethical involved failure to keep a promise. The subjects described promises that were later openly rejected (Gilchrist & Van Hoeven, 1992). An example was a promise to pay designers on commission. After calculating the actual costs of fulfilling this promise the first month, the promise was withdrawn. "Eventually all designers quit the company. One designer sued. The work of the designers was then placed on other employees, with no adjustment in their other work duties or in their compensation" (p. 119).

Other instances of failure to keep a promise involved inconsistencies between promises and organizational action. A company promised to reward education with promotion. Two years after receiving an advanced degree, the employee remained at the same level. No explanation was ever given. In another company the chief executive officer stressed the quality of its product in corporate communication, yet the managers insisted that "the bottom line is profit, profit, profit, reduce costs and increase sales. Work them harder" (Gilchrist & Van Hoeven, 1992, p. 121).

This type of promise breaking would be considered wrong by all of the ethical philosophies considered above. Kant's account of promise breaking has already been discussed. Promise breaking is not a maxim that can be universalized. In addition, promise breaking uses individuals, the truly important ends, for further ends. In the examples given, the promises were made with the intention of increasing profits. Sissela Bok (1978) details the way in which the deceived person is used: misinformation reduces the choice of the promisee, and there is a transfer of power from the promisee (choosing among alternatives) to the promisor. This situation is coercive in a fundamental way.

Ross would recognize a special relationship between the employer and the employee and a second special relationship based on the promise itself. There does not seem to be a conflict of prima facie duties. The employers may have intended to fulfill a duty of beneficience, but the withdrawal of the promise violates the duty not to harm as well as the duty of fidelity.

A utilitarian analysis would also find the promise breaking unethical, not because of any intrinsic wrongness with respect to the action, but because of the consequences produced. Considering a rule perspective, promise keeping tends to bring maximum happiness to society. An act utilitarian analysis gives the same results. In the situations described, the breaking of the promise led to harm in the organizational community. In the case of the designers: all quit, one sued, and the remaining workers were forced to take on additional work without compensation. This clearly did not maximize happiness in the situation. In the cases of broken promises about advancement with education and about attention to quality, employees clearly suffered in terms of morale. This, in turn, leads to harm, not benefit, in the community under consideration.

In Rawls' (1971) original condition, would the participants to the contract choose situations supporting the breaking of promises? It seems to be inconceivable.

Bok (1978) has argued that some measure of truthfulness in communication is necessary for the very existence of society (pp. 18–19):

> *Imagine a society, no matter how ideal in other respects, where word and gesture could never be counted upon. Questions asked, answers given, information exchanged—all would be worthless. Were all statements randomly truthful or deceptive, action and choice would be undermined from the outset. There must be a minimal degree of trust in communication for language and action to be more than stabs in the dark. This is why some level of truthfulness has always been seen as essential to human society, no matter how deficient the observance of other moral principles. Even the devils themselves, as Samuel Johnson said, do not lie to one another, since the society of Hell could not subsist without truth any more than others.*

A principle supporting the rightness of keeping promises would be chosen for the possibility of any society. Other principles would also be chosen to ensure fairness in that society.

Given the presumption of the rightness of keeping promises, one lesson for organizational behavior would seem to be that promises should not be lightly made. Too often promises are made with an intention of bringing about a short term result (usually profit) and without adequate research into the ramifications of keeping the promise.

A Climate in Which No One Takes Responsibility

Sometimes the structure and functioning of an organization contributes to a situation in which the acceptance of responsibility can be avoided by its members at all levels as well as by the organizational entity itself. Using causality and volition as criteria for determining responsibility, Seeger (1992) describes the possibilities for denying responsibility at three levels.

At the individual level, there are several ways a person might disassociate himself from an outcome deemed to be unethical. First, a person could deny that he had access to information that the questionable activity was occurring. Second, because most organizations are complex and highly departmentalized, disassociation may be made because no one department is singly responsible for the event. The event is the outcome of many decisions coming from departments acting independently of each other. A third possibility is that the individual is carrying out the directives of persons who have the organizational authority to give them.

The Iran-Contra controversy illustrates the first and third kinds of attempts to avoid responsibility at the individual level (Seeger, 1992, pp. 176–177):

> *Information was tightly controlled so that individuals possessed only that information necessary for them to execute their specialized duties.... The planned absence of any specific documentation indicating that superiors*

had been officially informed about the operation allowed those at the top of the hierarchy to avoid accountability.... This "fall guy" plan sought to shield responsible agents from responsibility. By portraying themselves as out of the informational loop, organizational participants may plausibly deny responsibility.

In addition, Oliver North claimed that he was following the orders of his superiors and that he had not "violated an order in 23 years" (Seeger, 1992, p. 178). Clearly there were willful ethical violations occurring by persons in at least two organizations, the National Security Council and the Central Intelligence Agency, yet it was difficult to pinpoint the responsibility. A variation of the excuse of carrying out orders of superiors in the hierarchy can take place at the organizational level. This occurs when a person disassociates himself from the unethical action by claiming to follow organizational policy. This is especially ironic when the policy referred to is the organization's stated code of ethics.

A third level is an environmental one: "Organizations exist in a larger environment and are dependent upon that environment for resources" (Seeger, 1992, p. 179). Individual and organizational blame can be deflected by holding the environment responsible. This frequently takes the form of shifting responsibility to the state of the economy, to allegedly burdensome government regulations, to advancing technology, or to sharp competition. In this way, an organization can attempt to change its status from villain to victim; the organization itself is a victim of larger environmental factors.

It is clearly unethical when a situation is created in which it is not possible to identify responsible individuals. Applying Kant's categorical imperative, one could not universalize a maxim to avoid responsibility for one's actions. In addition, persons avoiding responsibility most often also are using other persons as a means to some further end. In the Iran-Contra scandal, some individuals in both the National Security Council and the Central Intelligence Agency were using members of Congress and the American citizens to bring about their goal of supplying aid to the Contras in Central America. Their tactics involved deception, exploitation, manipulation, pretense, and lack of respect.

A utilitarian analysis also rejects the avoidance of responsibility. The fact that there is an issue of responsibility at all indicates that some bad consequences have come about: Iran-Contra, the Challenger explosion, exploding Pinto cars, Exxon oil spills, and so on. These consequences bring pain and unhappiness to many individuals; in the case of the Iran-Contra affair, there was the possibility of undermining a democratic society with a secret government. If no one can be held responsible for these unwanted consequences, there is no incentive to act responsibly in the future. Accepting responsibility is a deterrent to acting in ways that cause misery to society.

Failure to accept responsibility also violates many of the prima facie duties. Although the specific prima facie duties involved may vary depending on the situation, duties of fidelity, reparation, justice, self-improvement, beneficience and non-maleficence are likely to be involved. Consider the Exxon Valdez oil spill. The organization tried to avoid responsibility by focusing on the drinking problem of Captain Hazelwood. Within the organization, there must be many persons responsible for making false promises about the adequacy of the plan for cleaning oil spills. Justice and reparation are combined. Exxon's attempts to diffuse blame amount to a failure to make the required reparation to the fishing and other industries, thereby resulting in an injustice. This in turn, causes harm and fails to benefit. Finally Ross is clear that self-improvement is largely moral improvement; avoiding responsibility is tantamount to denying one's status as a moral agent.

In Rawls' view, justice, fairness, and rightness are inextricably intertwined. Justice and fairness are incompatible with the avoidance of responsibility. In the original position, it would not be possible to contract for a principle that assigned responsibility to no one. Such a choice would not be in the self-interest of any participant to the contract and could not be chosen.

A Climate of Denying Participation and Dissent

Traditional patterns of hierarchical structure and superior–subordinate authority relationships still exist in many organizations. In the Gilchrist and Van Hoeven (1992) study referred to earlier, a second cluster of employee complaints focused on managerial attitudes that "those at the top are somehow superior to others in the organization" (p. 121). At the center of the characterization of these actions as unethical was the lack of employee input into decision-making. This occurred at all levels. Examples were given that ranged from regulations about parking, to the timing of resignations, to participation in determining the organizational image (Gilchrist & Van Hoeven, 1992).

On the other hand there has been a significant trend towards participative management in other organizations (Apple, 1992). While there is no single definition of "participative management," most definitions emphasize responsibility for decision making. This, in turn, is likely to involve trust, the sharing of information, respect, and joint problem-solving (Likert, 1967). The aim of adopting a system of participative management is "to make organizations more productive (hence profitable) and to increase employee satisfaction" (Apple, 1992, p. 184). Some case studies have reported such successes.

A corollary to adopting a system of participative management is to adopt an attitude of tolerance for dissent (Apple, 1992, p. 189):

> *The two concepts [participation and dissent] are opposite sides of the same coin. If employees are permitted or encouraged to offer input into decision-making, goal setting, innovation, etc. then their input must be free to disagree with that of others in the organization. Participation must be genuine, not pseudo-participation. Employees must feel free to speak their own mind apart from the opinions of management.*

The difficulty of adopting a tolerance for dissent is that it seems to undercut loyalty and managerial discretion, which are deeply ingrained organizational concepts in the traditional view of hierarchical structure.

However, it can be argued that there is no necessary incompatibility. Dissent is not equivalent to activities like boat-rocking and whistle-blowing. These are simply two of the more extreme forms of dissent. Apple writes that "Other options include gentle persuasion, oblique hints, recruiting allies for political maneuvering, and neutral presentation of 'objective' information" (1992, p. 190).

Indeed participation and dissent can be seen as important traditions in the ethics of communication. Nilsen (1966) claimed that "without significant choice there is no morality" (p. 35). According to Nilsen, significant choices are: (1) voluntary choices, (2) choices based on all available and relevant information, (3) choices made with knowledge of alternatives and the short and long-term consequences of the alternatives, and (4) choices made with awareness of motivation. They are bound up with the democratic concept of the marketplace of ideas (Nilsen, 1966, p. 45):

> *If there is free and unhampered expression of opinions, the many competing interests, by presenting their respective views and arguments and criticizing others, will provide the kind of information and critical appraisal that will make possible for the listeners the most constructive choices.*

Like Kant, Nilsen believes that rational choice is the foundation of human dignity: "If we feel that such decision making is most consistent with our own human dignity, with our nature as autonomous personalities, then it is the kind of decision making we must seek for others, else we violate the fundamental ethical principle of impartiality" (p. 38). This was the argument used by Kant to give content to the categorical imperative. Rawls explicitly connects his original condition to Kant's view of autonomous action. The veil of ignorance guarantees that "[t]he parties arrive at their choice together as free and equal rational persons" (Rawls, 1971, p. 252). Because one does not know what his or her position will be after the choices are made, the possibility of dissent will be chosen for the protection of each person.

Ross would also accept the notion of significant choice as part of the meaning of the duty of self-improvement. Significant choices are bound up with the maximization of individual potential and thereby with moral and intellectual improvement.

A rule utilitarian justification also can be given for the imperative of employee dissent. The rule of promoting significant choice in organizations as well as in society at large is one which tends to maximize the well being of members.

A Climate Requiring Whistle-Blowing

When organizations engage in illegal behavior or behavior that is considered to be highly unethical, an individual may "blow the whistle" and reveal the conduct to a regulatory agency or to the news media. More precisely, "[w]histleblowing can be defined as a communicative act which is (1) intentional, (2) responsive, (3) accusatory, (4) public, (5) support seeking, (6) via various media, (7) refutational, and (8) straining a contractual agreement" (Jensen, 1987, p. 321). In the literature the act is considered "pure" if it occurs while the whistle-blower is still a member of the organization. If the person reveals the unethical or illegal activity only after resigning or being fired, he is considered an alumnus whistle-blower (Stewart, 1980). Typical situations involve defective designs in automobiles, industrial dumping of toxic waste into the public water supply, fraud in the use of tax money in government contracts, and the sale of chemically camouflaged spoiled meat (Nadar, Petkas, & Blackwell, 1990).

A 1992 study analyzed 276 questionnaires distributed to subjects in the Syracuse, New York, area to ascertain employee attitudes about whistle-blowing (Callahan & Collins, 1992). The researchers found strong support for the whistle-blower, especially if the activity was illegal and internal channels of the organization had been tried before the whistleblower made the information public.

This view is not shared by everyone. A former chief executive officer at General Motors has been quoted as saying (Stewart, 1980, p. 93):

Some of the enemies of business now encourage an employee to be disloyal to the enterprise. They want to create suspicion and disharmony, and pry into the proprietary interests of the business. However this is labeled— industrial espionage, whistle blowing, or professional responsibility—it is another tactic for spreading disunity and creating conflict.

In addition to the problem with loyalty, there is also a breach of confidentiality. Hence, it is not surprising that whistle-blowers are often fired from their organizations.

In an analysis of twenty-five cases of "pure" whistle-blowing, Stewart (1980) found a typical pattern. The organizational member expresses concerns first within the hierarchy of supervisors, then, only when no action is taken, makes them public. The person is then isolated by superiors from other organizational members and is finally fired or forced to resign.

Some whistle-blowers act out of bad faith or inaccurate information, but many times whistle-blowers act in the public interest by revealing organizational behavior that is harmful (Nader, Petkas, & Blackwell, 1990, p. 156):

In the past ... whistle-blowing has illuminated dark corners of our society, saved lives, prevented injuries and disease, and stopped corruption, economic waste, and material exploitation. Conversely, the absence of such professional and individual responsibility has perpetuated these conditions. In this context, whistle-blowing, if carefully defined and protected by law, can become another of those adaptive, self-implementing mechanisms which mark the relative difference between a free society that relies on free institutions and a closed society that depends on authoritarian institutions.

Are there criteria for distinguishing ethical from unethical whistle-blowing? There is a great deal of agreement that five conditions must be present (Nadar, Petkas, & Blackwell, 1990; James 1990; Jensen, 1987).

1. The harm to the public is serious and considerable.
2. The internal channels of the organization have been tried and exhausted.
3. Accurate evidence of wrongdoing has been collected and documented.
4. Public knowledge of the wrongdoing will force organizational changes and rectify the situation.
5. The harm caused to the organization, its members, and stockholders is outweighed by the public harm.

The presence of these factors seems to warrant the concurrent breaches of loyalty, confidence, and contracts.

It seems difficult to apply Kant's categorical imperative in this situation. This is because, as Ross argues, Kant's theory seems to leave no room for exceptions to duty. Clearly one could not universalize a maxim of action to breach loyalty, or confidence, or contracts. On the other hand, one could not universalize tolerating the continuation of the injustice and harm caused by the organizational behavior. Thus, it is questionable that there is one, clear, right answer; all the alternatives appear to be wrong.

A consideration of the remaining philosophical ethical theories reveals clearer answers. The five criteria fit a utilitarian analysis well. They are targeted to alleviate serious societal harm. At the same time they balance the harm brought about to the organization, and they attempt to save the organization harm by giving it an opportunity to correct the situation on its own terms without public embarrassment. Hence, they aim at producing the maximum good. A possible detrimental side effect has been noted. Would acceptance, especially in the form of legal protection for whistle-blowers, lead to an "informer ethos?" James (1990, p. 187) writes:

> *A society that encourages snooping, suspicion and mistrust does not conform to most people's idea of the good society. Laws that encourage whistle-blowing for self-interested reasons, such as the federal tax law which pays informers part of any money that is collected, could help bring about such a society.*

This does suggest that the protective laws need to be narrowly tailored, focusing on protecting the whistle-blower from unjust retaliation, not providing reward. "It is unlikely that state or federal laws of this type would promote an informer society" (James, 1990, p. 187). Ross would view the situation as a classic one involving conflicts of prima facie duties. The principal conflict is between the duty of fidelity (based on loyalty, keeping confidences, honoring contracts made) and the duty of non-maleficence. Confining ethical whistle-blowing to those circumstances meeting the five criteria make the choice of the "actual or absolute" duty simpler. The more pressing duty would seem to be non-maleficence, not to harm.

In Rawls' view the essential question is one of justice and rights. The organization's conduct must be balanced against the right of the public to know about the dangerous and unjust practices of the organization. Rawls' philosophy does not protect unjust behavior. It would seem that in the original position, the parties to the contract would want protection for whistle-blowing (at least whistle-blowing meeting the five criteria). Behind the veil of ignorance, they do not know their position in society. Any one person could be the person harmed by the organization's conduct. Hence they must choose principles that would protect the least protected member of society.

A Climate of Cultural Relativism: Multinational Organizations

In the 1990s many organizations operate in a global environment. As a result they face cultural standards in other countries that seem to be at odds with ethical standards in the United States. For example, a manager for an organization newly opening in Japan might receive valuable gifts from a Japanese supplier. Whereas this is a standard business practice in Japan, such practices in the United States would raise questions about bribery. Or suppose a multinational organization distributes pesticides. Should this organization take a large inventory of pesticides that have recently been banned by the Environmental Protection Agency and sell them to countries which do not have laws against their use? Or consider the treatment of the labor force in foreign countries. Should foreign employees have the same rights as their American counterparts: a safe working environment, the right to organize, the right to be free from gender discrimination, and so on? The host country does not require these rights for workers and guaranteeing them is expensive. Would their provision negate the benefit of operating in a foreign country? Would failure to provide them constitute exploitation?

These examples raise questions about the possibility of ethical standards that transcend cultures. Multinational organizations often defend their questionable actions by arguing that there are no transcendent values. What is right in Japan is right in Japan. What is right in Mexico is right in Mexico. It is inappropriate to look for organizational values that would be correct for Japan *and* Mexico *and* the United States. This is known as the theory of ethical relativism. This theory insists that there are no absolute moral standards such as those given in the philosophies of Kant, Ross, Rawls, and utilitarians. The theory takes as its evidence the alleged fact of cultural relativism, the differing cultural standards among countries. Accounts of differing cultural standards have been collected by anthropologists over a long period of time; the differing organizational cultures in foreign countries are manifestations of wider cultural values.

Critics of ethical relativism have strong arguments (Purtill, 1976). First, basing ethical relativism on cultural relativism presupposes that truth is intrinsically connected to agreement. This is a patently false supposition. It is not true even in science. Witness the universal agreement of the scientific community prior to Copernicus that the sun and all the planets revolved around the earth. Truth and agreement have no necessary connection. A second kind of argument insists that the theory is contrary to our actual moral judgments. In particular, ethical relativism does not allow for comparisons among different societal values or for recognition of moral improvement in a single society. The values in Nazi Germany cannot be said to be worse than those in contemporary America because there is no overriding standard by which that comparison can be made. The abolition of slavery in the United States cannot be considered moral progress because there is no absolute standard for this judgment. Surely these ideas are counterintuitive.

Other critics have attacked ethical relativism by denying that cultural relativism is itself a fact (Bowie, 1990). They have characterized cultural differences as superficial only, not reflective of genuine ethical disagreements (Bowie, 1990, p. 376):

> *[T]here are certain basic rules that must be followed in each society; e.g. don't lie, don't commit murder. There is a moral minimum in the sense that if these specific moral rules aren't generally followed, then there won't be a society at all.*

This can be extended to multinational organizations. They must follow the moral rules necessary for the very existence of a society. In addition, there is an implicit minimal morality in the marketplace (Bowie, 1990, p. 377):

> *[I]f contract breaking were universalized, then business practice would be impossible. If a participant in business were to universally advocate violating contracts, such advocacy would be self-defeating, just as the universal advocacy of lying and cheating are self-defeating in a given society.*

Also bribery, theft, fraud, and kickbacks would be prohibited under the minimum standards for organizational practice (Bowie, 1990, p. 377). Others have isolated a single minimal ethical principle for professionals derived from the Hippocratic Oath (Drucker, 1973, p. 368): "Above all, not knowingly to do harm".

Another argument against ethical relativism is that certain minimal standards that transcend nations have been found. There are moral principles that have been agreed to and formalized in international treaties (Bowie, 1990). These range widely in subject matter, for example, from general, fundamental human rights to the specific "moral" and "economic" rights of copyright protection.

These minimal moral standards are reflected in the philosophical approaches to ethics. Kant, like Bowie, bases morality on actions that can be universalized. Kant, of course, requires much more in extending his philosophy to the treatment of persons as valuable ends in themselves. Ross's prima facie duties very likely represent duties that can be found in any society. However, what one society may interpret as a duty of fidelity or a duty of beneficience may differ from that of another. In addition two of the prima facie duties, beneficience and non-maleficence, incorporate the utilitarian standard. Finally, what Rawls seeks to accomplish in the original contractual position is the establishment of minimal standards required for a just society.

CONCLUSION

This chapter has focused on four philosophical ethical theories and the application of these theories to moral dilemmas in organizational communication. For Kant, moral imperatives are categorical imperatives, actions that one must take because they are good in themselves. Moral imperatives involve maxims for action that can be universalized. Both act and rule utilitarians maintain that the rightness or wrongness of actions depends upon the good or bad consequences produced by the actions. Act utilitarians consider each moral situation as unique, whereas rule utilitarians emphasize rules of action that tend to promote the well-being of humanity. According to Ross, moral duties arise from morally significant relationships. Ross calls these duties prima facie duties. Prima facie duties can come into conflict. Thus, there can be exceptions to duty, and the moral agent should choose the more pressing duty under the circumstances. Rawls considers justice to be the prime moral obligation. Just ways of acting can be determined by imagining moral agents to be behind a veil of ignorance. No one is aware of his or her individual situation after leaving this original position. Each person will, therefore, treat each other person equally.

If an organization is serious about instilling ethical values it should focus on its ethical climate. The climate should be one that fosters honesty, integrity, fidelity, fairness, caring, respect, and accountability. The mere presence of a code of ethics for the organization will not suffice for ethical conduct. Any code must be examined for substantive ethical values. The values reflected should encompass some philosophical concepts: universalizibility or utility or self-evident duties or fairness. The presence of any one of these principles would prevent the kind of behavior that has brought many organizations a bad reputation. Above all, organizations should abandon the ethical view of self-interest and greed.

GLOSSARY

Actual duty—according to Ross, the most pressing or stringent duty incumbent upon a moral agent in a given situation.

Categorical imperative—according to Kant, a statement that an action is intrinsically necessary: act A is good in itself.

Cultural relativism—the report that what is moral and normal differs from one society or culture to the next.

Ethical relativism—the philosophical theory that there are no absolute moral standards.

Hypothetical imperative—according to Kant, a statement that one action is necessary to bring about a desired result: act A is good to bring about result B.

Original position—in the philosophy of Rawls, the hypothetical situation in which members of society contract for the moral, political, and economic principles that will govern their lives.

Prima facie duties—actions that are obligatory and binding "upon first examination." According to Ross, there are six kinds of prima facie duties.

Principle of utility—the greatest happiness principle of utilitarian theories; acts are right in so far as they tend to promote happiness.

Veil of ignorance—according to Rawls, persons in the original position are operating in ignorance of their social, economic, physical, and mental condition after leaving the original position.

CASE STUDY

During Congressional hearings in the spring of 1994, two researchers, Victor DeNoble and Paul Mele, testified that they had been hired in the early 1980s by Philip Morris to conduct experiments that would lead to the development of a substitute for nicotine. Because nicotine puts stress on the heart, the substitute substance would need to be protective of the heart, while at the same time productive of a nicotine-like "high." Their experimental design involved allowing rats to administer nicotine to themselves by pressing a lever. They found that the rats pressed a lever to receive nicotine up to 90 times in a 12-hour period as compared with pressing a lever to receive saline solution only 12 times in the same time period. When the nicotine was combined with a substance produced in the burning of cigarettes, acetaldehyde, the rats pressed the lever up to 500 times in the 12-hour period. The researchers took this to be evidence of the addictive quality of nicotine. Shortly after they reported their results to Philip Morris in April 1984, their experiment was halted. Upon coming to work one day, they found the equipment, the animals, and the data missing. They also alleged in the testimony that attempts to publish their findings were obstructed (Gregory, 1994, p. 58).

Discussion: What kind of organizational ethical climate is suggested by halting the experiments? How would Ross view the morality of the organization? Should the researchers have blown the whistle in 1984?

REFERENCES

Apple, C. (1992). Ethical dimensions of employee involvement: Issues in social contract, equality and dissent. In J. Jaksa (ed.), *Proceedings of the 1992 National Communication Ethics Conference* (pp. 184–196). Annandale, Va.: Speech Communication Association.

Bentham, Y. (1970). *An Introduction to the Principles of Morals and Legislation.* Edited by Y. H. Burns & H. L. A. Hart. London: Althone Press.

Bok, S. (1978). *Lying: Moral Choice in Public and Private Life.* New York: Pantheon Books.

Bowie, N. (1990). Business ethics and cultural relativism. In P. Madsen, & J. Shafritz (eds.), *Essentials of Business Ethics* (pp. 366–382). New York: Meridian.

Callahan, E., & Collins, J. (1992). Employee attitudes toward whistleblowing: Management and public policy implications. *Journal of Business Ethics, 11,* 939–948.

Center for Business Ethics. (1992). Instilling ethical values in large corporations. *Journal of Business Ethics, 11,* 863–867.

Drucker, P. (1973). *Management: Tasks, Responsibilities, Practices.* New York: Harper & Row.

Gilchrist, J., & Van Hoeven, S. (1992). Employees's accounts of broken organizational promises. In J. Jaksa (ed.), *Proceedings of the 1992 National Communication Ethics Conference* (pp. 111–128). Annandale, Va.: Speech Communication Association.

Gregory, S. (1994, May 9). Is that smoke, or do I smell a rat? *Time,* p. 58.

Jackall, R. (1990). Business as a social and moral terrain. In P. Madsen, & J. Shafritz (eds.), *Essentials of Business Ethics* (pp. 206–212). NY: Meridian.

Jaksa, J., & Pritchard, M. (1994). *Communication Ethics: Methods of Analysis* (2nd ed). Belmont, Calif.: Wadsworth Publishing Company.

James, G. (1990). Whistle-blowing: Its moral justification. In P. Madsen, & J. Shafritz (eds.), *Essentials of Business Ethics* (pp. 160–190). New York: Meridian.

Jensen, J. (1987). Ethical tension points in whistleblowing. *Journal of Business Ethics, 6,* 321–328.

Kant, I. (1949). *The Fundamental Principles of the Metaphysic of Morals.* (T. Abbott, trans.) New York: The Liberal Arts Press (Original work published 1785).

Likert, R. (1967). *The Human Organization.* New York: McGraw-Hill.

Mill, J. (1957). *Utilitarianism.* (O. Piest, ed.) New York: The Bobbs-Merrill Company (Original work published 1861).

Moore, G. (1962). *Principia Ethica.* London: Cambridge University Press.

Nader, R., Petkas, P., & Blackwell, K. (1990). The anatomy of whistle-blowing. In P. Madsen, & J. Shafritz (eds.), *Essentials of Business Ethics* (pp. 153–159). New York: Meridian.

Nilsen, T. (1966). *Ethics in Speech Communication.* Indianapolis: Bobbs-Merrill.

Purtill, R. (1976). *Thinking About Ethics.* Englewood Cliffs, N.J.: Prentice-Hall.

Rawls, J. (1971). *A Theory of Justice.* Cambridge: Harvard University Press.

Robin, D., Giallourakis, M., David, F., & Moritz, T. (1990). A different look at codes of ethics. In P. Madsen, & J. Shafritz (eds.), *Essentials of Business Ethics* (pp. 212–227). New York: Meridian.

Ross, W. (1930). *The Right and the Good.* Oxford: The Clarendon Press.

Seeger, M. (1992). Responsibility in organizational communication: Individual, organizational, and environmental accounts. In J. Jaksa (ed.), *Proceedings of the 1992 National Communication Ethics Conference* (pp. 172–183). Annandale, Va.: Speech Communication Association.

Sims, R. (1992). The challenge of ethical behavior in organizations. *Journal of Business Ethics, 11,* 505–513.

Smart, J. (1973). An outline of a system of utilitarian ethics. In J. Smart & Williams, B. *Utilitarianism: For and Against* (pp. 1–74). Cambridge: Cambridge University Press.

Stewart, L. (1980). "Whistle Blowing": Implications for organizational communication. *Journal of Communication, 30,* 90–101.

Stone, O. (director). (1987) *Wall Street* [Film]. Hollywood, Calif.

Velasquez, M. (1990). Corporate ethics: Losing it, having it, getting it. In P. Madsen, & J. Shafritz (eds.), *Essentials of Business Ethics* (pp. 228–244). New York: Meridian.

RECOMMENDED READINGS

Arnett, R. (1988). A choice-making ethic for organizational communication: The work of Ian I. Mitroff. *Journal of Business Ethics, 7,* 151–161.

Bok, S. (1982). *Secrets.* New York: Pantheon Books.

Johannesen, R. (1990). *Ethics in Human Communication* (3rd ed.). Prospect Heights, Ill.: Waveland Press.

Matthews, J., Goodpaster, K., & Nash, L. (eds.). (1985). *Policies and Persons: A Casebook in Business Ethics.* New York: McGraw-Hill.

Seeger, M. (1992). Ethical issues in corporate speechwriting. *Journal of Business Ethics, 11,* 501–504.

Thompson, D. (1987). *Political Ethics and Public Office.* Cambridge: Harvard University Press.

Toulmin, S. (1988). *The Abuse of Casuistry: A History of Moral Reasoning.* Berkeley: University of California Press.

Valesquez, M. (1982). *Business Ethics: Concepts and Cases.* Englewood Cliffs, N.J.: Prentice-Hall.

Werhane, P. (1985). *Persons, Rights, and Corporations.* Englewood Cliffs, N.J.: Prentice-Hall.

▶ Part II

Organizational Life

▶ 5

The Role of Communication in the Leadership Process

RAYMOND M. O'CONNOR, JR.

It is your first day on the job. You are at your desk for only ten minutes when one of your colleagues hurries by and says, "We have a team meeting in fifteen minutes." When you enter this work group meeting, which includes seven other individuals and yourself, how will you recognize the group's leader? The easy way, of course, is to rely on the formal titles and assigned roles that each person in the group holds. In other words, whoever has the title of manager, supervisor, project leader, department head, and so forth would be the one you identify as the leader.

Imagine, however, that after several team meetings you realize that the flow and content of the group's interactions seem to be dominated by another individual, the manager's top assistant. The way that this person takes charge of the situation makes you realize that the manager is clearly not the team leader. As a result, you decide that even though the manager has the formal stature, the real leader of this team is the manager's assistant—the one who usually "runs the show."

LEADERSHIP: A DEFINITION

In many organizations, we would not find the type of disparity that is described in this scenario. Often, the individual who possesses the formal authority is also the most influential. However, as our example above points out, this is not always the case. In some situations, we are more likely to identify the individual who exercises the most influence over the group as its leader. This points to the importance of developing a definition of leadership that focuses on the process itself, rather than emphasizing traditional indicators of leadership such as position in the hierarchy or formal bureaucratic titles. Therefore, our definition of leadership will be one that is accepted by many experts in the field of leadership research: *Leadership* is the process whereby one individual influences other group members toward the attainment of defined group or organizational goals (Yukl, 1989). It should be noted that although there is still controversy in the literature surrounding the issue of whether leadership and management are the same thing (see Kotter, 1990; Mintzberg, 1979), the focus of the present chapter is on the role of communication in the leadership process. Since communication is an integral process for both managerial and leadership-related activities, this argument becomes a moot point for our purposes. Therefore, these two terms will be used interchangeably throughout this chapter.

One significant element of this definition is worth elaborating on. Specifically, we are referring to the fact that leadership is a process that involves influence. Although a leader can draw on a variety of techniques for exerting this influence, it is safe to say that most of them will involve communication. Therefore, communication is fundamental to the influence process that takes place through leadership. A recent study on managerial effectiveness showed that effective communication is seen as an important part of a managers' activities, and those managers who are most sensitive to communication issues are generally perceived as effective leaders (Daft, Lengel, & Trevino, 1987). In fact, an analysis of performance data showed that managers who were sensitive to communication issues consistently received their company's highest performance appraisal ratings. Clearly, communication plays an important role in determining a leader's effectiveness, and this fact can be readily seen in many of the prominent leadership theories. In fact, even though these theories may differ with respect to which aspects of a leader's behavior are most important, they all recognize the importance that communication plays in determining a leader's effectiveness.

IS LEADERSHIP REALLY THAT IMPORTANT?

In today's society, the notion that effective leadership is a key ingredient in determining organizational success has come to be accepted as a truism. Most people would agree that successful leaders anticipate change, actively identify and exploit opportunities, motivate their followers to higher levels of productivity, provide feedback for improving poor performance, and generally lead the organization toward the attainment of its goals and objectives. In fact, this view is by no means restricted to the world of business. It applies equally well to politics, sports, government, and the countless other organizations that shape our daily lives.

But is this view justified? Do leaders really make a critical difference in shaping the success of an organization? All we need to do is look at the salary schedules of leaders versus nonleaders to see that organizations certainly think they do. Leaders are routinely paid significantly higher salaries than those in nonleadership positions. For example, the head of General Motors is paid more than $1 million annually. In contrast, the highest skilled auto worker may only earn around $50,000 a year (Robbins, 1991). In addition, the more responsibility a leader has, the more that individual earns. Clearly, organizations place a high value on effective leadership.

The research literature also supports the hypothesis that leadership is important to organizational success. A recent review of over fifty years of research in this area determined that effective leadership is a key factor in organizational performance (Motowidlo, 1992). In fact, another review (Day & Lord, 1988) conducted four years earlier concluded that the research shows "a consistent effect for leadership explaining twenty to forty-five percent of the variance on relevant organizational outcomes." Clearly, both academicians and business professionals recognize the importance of leadership for enhancing organizational performance and effectiveness.

Given the significance placed on leadership in both the research literature and the popular press, it becomes important to address the question of what makes for an effective leader. This chapter will attempt to shed some light on this important issue. We will begin by presenting a historical review of many prestigious theories of leadership effectiveness. Throughout this review, we identify specific areas within these theories where the importance of communication is paramount. Finally, it will be argued that regardless of which theory you believe is most plausible, communication will always play a central role in the leadership process. Suggestions for enhancing leader effectiveness through communication will be offered.

LEADERSHIP THEORIES: A HISTORICAL REVIEW

The Trait Approach

Are some people born to lead? A quick review of many historical leaders would suggest that the answer to this question is yes. Great leaders of the past and present— Mahatma Gandhi, Joan of Arc, John F. Kennedy, Martin Luther King, Jr., Mother Theresa, Margaret Thatcher, Nelson Mandela—do seem to be different from ordinary human beings. For example, they all seem to possess high levels of motivation and ambition along with a clear sense of direction and vision. It was this reasoning that led to the logic of the trait approach.

Stated simply, the trait approach assumes that the way to understand what makes some people more effective as leaders is to measure these people on a wide variety of psychological, social, and physical variables and note how they differ from nonleaders. In fact, early research on traits adopted a "great man theory" (Stogdill, 1974).

According to this approach, great leaders possess key traits that set them apart from most other human beings. All we need to do is determine what these traits are and then we will be able to select those people who will be the most effective leaders.

As the research on trait theory progressed (primarily during the 1930s and 1940s), more and more traits were identified as potentially important determinants of leadership. A large number of studies were published, and the results became increasingly mixed and murky. In 1948, Ralph Stogdill, one of the earliest leadership scholars, published a review of the trait literature that was so damaging that it significantly reduced the amount of trait studies published subsequently (Stogdill, 1974). To summarize, in 1948 Stogdill concluded that the research did not show any simple pattern of traits that was both strongly and consistently related to leadership.

The search for leader traits was not entirely fruitless. A number of specific traits have been shown to be modestly, but inconsistently, associated with leadership. One primary example of such a trait is intelligence (Fiedler & Leister, 1977), which does appear to have a moderate positive correlation with leadership effectiveness. It appears that less intelligent leaders will not be as effective as more intelligent leaders. However, other researchers (e.g., Ghiselli, 1971) have argued that there is good reason to believe that this is an inverted-U relationship. According to this logic, a moderate amount of intelligence appears to be optimal for efficacious leadership. If leaders are not intelligent enough, they will not be effective. On the other hand, leaders who are too intelligent will have difficulty communicating and relating to their followers, and this will also reduce leader effectiveness. Therefore, the most effective leaders are those with a moderate amount of intelligence, seemingly because they will be able to communicate most effectively with their subordinates.

Research has also linked a variety of other traits to successful leadership. For example, recent reviews of the leadership literature have suggested that leaders can be characterized along dimensions such as task persistence, self-confidence, dominance, and the ability to influence another's behavior, to name a few (Stogdill, 1974; Yukl, 1981). In addition, one relatively surprising finding that has been reported suggests a small positive correlation between leader effectiveness and height, suggesting that taller people make better leaders. Although no theoretical explanation for this correlation has been discovered, it may reflect the notion that many people prefer to "look up" to their leaders.

In summary, the trait approach to understanding leadership never came close to fulfilling its initial proclamations. Although some traits did appear to be correlated with leadership, these correlations were usually so small and inconsistent as to be inconsequential. For a variety of reasons, including inadequate theorizing, inadequate measurement techniques, and the failure to account for situational factors, this research was not successful enough to provide a general trait theory. Although there has been some renewed interest in traits during the past decade (e.g, Kenny & Zaccaro, 1983), a major movement away from traits came about as a result of Stogdill's 1948 review. Leadership research from the late 1940s through the 1960s took a new perspective that emphasized leader behaviors rather than traits.

The Behavioral Approach

As interest in the trait approach to leadership dwindled, researchers turned their attention to behavioral perspectives. They wondered if there was something unique in terms of the specific behaviors that leaders demonstrated. It was hoped that this approach would provide more definitive answers about the nature of leadership. For the most part, this approach was reasonably successful and added much to our understanding of how leaders behave and how their behavior affects their followers.

In addition, researchers interested in leader behaviors recognized that the implications of such an approach were potentially much more rewarding than the implications of trait theory. As mentioned earlier, if trait theories were successful, they would have provided a basis for *selecting* the "right" person for a role involving leadership. Trait theories assume that leadership is inborn: You either have it or you don't. Therefore, trait theories would allow us to pick the best potential leader for a given position. However, the implication of trait theory is that those individuals who do not possess the appropriate traits will *never* be effective leaders.

Behavioral theories, in contrast, assume that the observed differences in leader effectiveness result from specific behaviors that the leader performs, rather than innate characteristics of the leader. If these studies could identify specific distinguishing behaviors that help separate leaders from nonleaders; then, by implication, we would be able to *train* people to be leaders. We could design specific programs that could implant these effective behaviors in those individuals who wanted to be leaders.

Autocratic versus Participative Styles

Think about the different bosses you have encountered in your life or career. Can you remember one that really seemed to be a "control freak?" The boss who wanted to make all of the decisions, tell people exactly what to do and how to do it, and be in control of all things at all times. In contrast, have you ever encountered a boss who allowed employees a great deal of freedom and responsibility?—A boss who was open to suggestions, actively solicited subordinates' input, and gave subordinates great latitude in determining the best way to do the job. If you have ever had bosses like these, then you have firsthand experience with two sharply distinct styles of leadership: autocratic and participative.

One of the earliest studies of leader behavior examined the relative effectiveness of these two leadership styles (Lewin, Lippett, & White, 1939). They also investigated a third leadership style, laissez-faire; in which the leader takes a "hands-off" approach to influencing subordinates. Ten-year-old boys were randomly assigned to one of three groups involved in hobby activities after school hours. These activities included things like making toy boats and papier-maché masks. Each group was under the supervision of an adult (employed by the experimenters) who behaved in either a democratic, autocratic, or laissez-faire style.

In the democratic condition, the leader allowed the group to decide who was to perform which task, permitted the boys to pick their own work partners, gave specific feedback on how to improve craftsmanship, and tried to be an involved member of the group. In contrast, the autocratic leader decided what was to be done without consulting the boys. He assigned specific tasks to each individual, assigned work partners, was subjective in his praise, and remained detached from the group's activities. The laissez-faire leader was very isolated from the activities of the group. He gave the boys complete freedom to do what they wished and provided information only when he was specifically asked.

The results of this study suggested that the boys' reactions to the task were greatly influenced by the style of leadership to which they were subjected. Boys in the democratically led group were more satisfied and displayed less aggression toward one another than did boys in the autocratically led group. Additionally, independent judges rated the quality of the output to be highest in the democratically led group, although the boys under the autocratic leader tended to produce more items. Additionally, boys in the autocratically led group developed a tendency to stop working and engage in horseplay whenever the leader left the room. This tendency was not observed in either of the other two groups. To summarize, leadership style had a significant impact on the boys in terms of performance, attitudes, and behavior.

University of Michigan Studies

In a series of leadership studies conducted at the University of Michigan (see Kahn & Katz, 1960), researchers investigated more specific behaviors that generally fell into one of two categories: (1) production-oriented and (2) employee-oriented. Production-oriented leadership, also called concern for production, task-focused leadership, or initiating structure, involves behaviors that are focused on getting the task done. A production-oriented leader is one who provides advice, for example, on task performance, answers questions, specifies roles. In contrast, employee-oriented leadership, also called concern for people or consideration, focuses on supporting individual workers in their activities and involving workers in the decision-making process. A boss who demonstrates great concern for his or her workers' satisfaction and commitment to the job is an employee-oriented leader. In general, the results of these studies strongly favored leaders who were employee-oriented in their behavior. Employee-oriented leaders were associated with higher group productivity and higher job satisfaction. Conversely, production-oriented leaders tended to be associated with low group productivity and lower work satisfaction.

The Ohio State Studies

At approximately the same time as the University of Michigan research, a series of studies in leadership at Ohio State University classified individuals on two dimensions: (1) initiating structure, which is similar to production-oriented leadership, and (2) consideration, which is similar to employee-oriented leadership (Stogdill & Coons, 1957). Initiating structure refers to the degree to which a leader structures his or her own role and subordinates' roles toward accomplishing the group's goal. This structuring can occur through a variety of practices, including scheduling the work, assigning employees to specific tasks, and maintaining certain standards of performance, Consideration, on the other hand, refers to the degree to which a leader emphasizes subordinates' needs through two-way communication, respect for subordinates' ideas, the creation of mutual trust, and consideration of the subordinates' feelings.

It is important to point out that these two dimensions of leader behavior are considered to be independent of one another. In other words, a leader may possess either a high or low predisposition toward each dimension. The combination of these two dimensions for an individual suggests that several different types of leaders can be identified (see Figure 5-1). For example, Manager A in Figure 5-1 would be described as being moderately concerned with production but lacking in concern for the feelings of his or her employees. Manager B, on the other hand, would be described as highly considerate of his or her subordinates, but lacking a concern for employee production. Finally, Manager C is devoted to maximizing both production and employee well-being. In fact, it was the style of Manager C (high on both consideration and initiating structure) that was predicted to be the most effective combination of leadership behaviors. This has come to be known as the high-high hypothesis.

Research on the Ohio State dimensions of consideration and initiating structure have provided support for this hypothesis. Questionnaires completed by both leaders and subordinates have shown that high consideration was related to lower rates of grievance filings and lower turnover (Fleishman & Harris, 1962). However, beyond

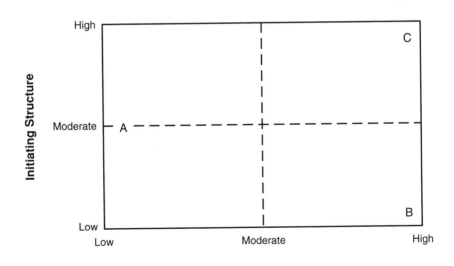

FIGURE 5-1   **Ohio State Leadership Dimensions.**

a certain point, increases in supervisory consideration did not appear to decrease turnover and grievances any further. In addition, the study found that highly considerate leaders could structure work more without risking an increase in grievances. In other words, supervisors could compensate, to some extent, for using a high degree of initiating structure if they also increased their considerateness.

In contrast, leaders who are low on consideration cannot eliminate their negative impact by showing less concern for production. It appears that low consideration has a strong and persistent negative effect on leader-subordinate relationships (Fleishman & Harris, 1962). In addition, other research has rather consistently shown that low consideration is associated with employee dissatisfaction with supervisors.

Even though early results suggested that the combination of high initiating structure and high consideration constitute the most successful leadership style, more recent studies have not always corroborated this finding (Larsen, Hunt, & Osburn, 1976). A review of more recent research suggests that scholars have shifted their focus to specifying those conditions under which consideration and initiating structure *are* related to employee performance and job satisfaction (Kerr, Schriesheim, Murphy, & Stogdill, 1974). Their efforts have resulted in the identification of three broad classes of variables that appear to moderate the relationship between leadership behaviors and various outcome measures (i.e., performance, job satisfaction, organizational commitment). These include (1) subordinate characteristics, such as competence, experience, and job knowledge; (2) supervisor characteristics, such as the relationship that a leader has with his or her superiors in terms of influence, attitude similarity, and behavior similarity; and (3) task characteristics, which include things such as task importance, task meaningfulness, and autonomy in performing the task.

Regardless of which behavioral approach you adhere to, one significant point always seems to emerge. In order to apply the ideas inherent in behavioral theories, effective communication skills are essential. Specifically, these theories argue that a manager must show a high level of both concern for production (initiating structure) and concern for people (consideration). In other words, the leader must not only possess these attributes, but be able to effectively communicate their concerns to their employees. In fact, this is often a critical step in training programs that incorporate behavioral theory concepts.

The Managerial Grid

One specific example of a training program based on the behavioral perspective is known as Grid Organization Development (Blake & Mouton, 1978, 1982). The application of Grid Organization Development is relatively straightforward. The first step consists of a grid seminar—a five-day training session during which an organization's line managers (who have already been trained in the appropriate theory and skills) help other organizational members analyze their own leadership styles. This is done by using a specially designed questionnaire that measures people with respect to concern for production and concern for people. A participant's standing on each dimension is scored with a number from 1 (low) to 9 (high). The combination of scores on these dimensions is then used to identify the leader's style.

Managers who score low on both concern for people and concern for production are scored 1,1 and are referred to as impoverished managers. A manager who is highly concerned with people but has little concern for production is scored 1,9 and is described as having a country club style of leadership. In contrast, leaders who show the opposite pattern—high concern for production but little interest in people—are scored 9,1 and are said to have a task management style. Managers scoring moderately on both dimensions, the 5,5 pattern, are said to have a middle-of-the-road management style. Finally, there are individuals who are high on both concern for people *and* concern for production, those scoring 9,9. This combination of behavioral styles is referred to as team management, which is very similar to the high-high hypothesis developed by the Ohio State researchers.

In team management, the leader shares participation in goal setting, problem-solving, and decision-making. He or she encourages open feedback and critique and advocates the importance of confronting and resolving differences, rather than ignoring them. The 9,9 leader demonstrates initiative, inquires fully into the background and status of projects and problems, engages in constructive problem-solving behavior, and develops relationships with subordinates that are characterized by mutual trust and respect. It is this style that is predicted to lead to the most successful outcomes, such as increased performance and job satisfaction.

After a leader's position on the grid is determined, a training program is begun to increase both concern for production and concern for people in an effort to move the leader closer to the desired 9,9 approach. This training initially consists of organizationwide team training to help work group members interact more effectively with one another. It is then expanded to help reduce conflict between groups that are often working closely together. Subsequent training includes efforts to identify the extent to which the organization is meeting its strategic goals and then comparing this performance to some ideal reference point. Next, the organization develops and implements plans to meet these strategic goals. Finally, the organization continuously assesses progress towards these goals, and problem areas are quickly identified and corrected. The significant role that communication plays in this training should be evident.

Clearly, the effective use of Grid Organization Development involves a significant investment on the part of the organization. But how valid is this method for actually improving leader effectiveness? Although there are some who question the utility of Grid Training as a method for increasing leader effectiveness (Larson, Hunt, & Osburn, 1976; Nystrom, 1978 , the balance of the evidence seems to suggest that when implemented properly, Grid Training can be an effective tool of organizational change. For example, one study evaluated the effects of the 9,9 style on the performance of college students on a task involving arithmetic and work problems (Tjosvold, 1984). Results showed that the subjects would work hardest when the leader was both warm and showed a high concern for productivity, but would exert the least amount of effort when the leader was warm and showed a low concern for productivity (in fact, they would tend to goof off more in this latter condition). In addition, the subjects liked the leader more and expressed greater willingness to work with this person when the leader was high on concern for people. A recent review (Porras & Berg, 1978) identified a number of field studies that also suggested that this technique can be a useful method of developing leader effectiveness.

Summary of Behavioral Theories

Overall, the behavioral approach to leadership has contributed substantially to our understanding of this important concept. As we will see, many of the current theories of leadership still incorporate the dimensions of concern for people and concern for production somewhere in their framework. Unfortunately, in trying to specify a set of leader behaviors that would be effective in *all* situations, these studies overlooked the enormous complexities of individual behavior in organizational settings. In the long run, they all failed at their initial task, that is, to identify universal leader-behavior/ follower-response relationships. It soon became obvious that certain leader behaviors were more effective in some situations than in others. In fact, in some situations only a very specific type of leader behavior is appropriate (consider as an example the situation in which a work environment is so disorganized and chaotic that only a production-oriented leader could straighten it out!!). It quickly became clear to those studying leadership that the prediction of leader effectiveness was more complex than isolating a few traits or preferable behaviors. The failure to obtain consistent results led to another shift in focus, towards identifying the situational factors that are important in understanding leader success. This emphasis on situational concerns spawned the development of our third main leadership perspective—the contingency approach.

Contingency Theories of Leadership

Leadership does not take place in an environmental or social vacuum. Actually, leaders attempt to exert influence on their subordinates in a variety of specific situations. These situations can vary across a great number of dimensions, so it is reasonable to expect that no single leadership style or approach is going to be effective in every situation. Therefore, we could hypothesize that the most useful leadership strategy will probably change from one situation to the next.

This logic represents the underlying rationale behind contingency theories. Contingency theories start with one central assumption: a leader's contribution to successful performance by the work group will depend on both the leader's style and the characteristics of the situation. In order to fully understand leadership effectiveness, we cannot simply look at the leader's style, although this certainly is an important factor. We must also evaluate the situational factors that might moderate the leader's effectiveness. Acceptance of this perspective is at the core of a classic model of leadership proposed by Fred Fiedler (1967), a very prolific and heavily cited author in the area of leadership.

Fiedler's Contingency Model

Fiedler was one of the first proponents of a leadership model that made specific provisions for the role of situational factors in the leadership situation. He maintained that leadership effectiveness depends on the match between the leader's style and the situation. He devised a special way of measuring a leader's style that focused on the leader's personality. Specifically, he described the leader's style in terms of a dichotomous personality trait: task versus relationship motivation. He then went on to describe the situation in terms of its favorableness for the leader, from highly favorable to highly unfavorable.

Task Versus Relationship Motivation. It should be clear that task and relationship motivation closely parallel those concepts discussed under the behavioral approaches to leadership. Task motivation is comparable to the production-centered and initiating structure behavior identified by previous research. Similarly, relationship motivation is analogous to the employee-centered and consideration behaviors from previous approaches. The main difference is that while previous approaches viewed these orientations as behavioral and therefore subject to change, Fiedler argued that task versus relationship motivation is a personality trait that is essentially constant for any given individual.

A leader's degree of task or relationship motivation is measured by a questionnaire known as the least preferred co-worker scale (LPC). In filling out the LPC scale, a leader is asked to think of all the people with whom he or she has ever worked and select the least preferred co-worker. Respondents are then asked to describe their least preferred co-worker by marking a series of sixteen scales anchored at each end by a positive or negative quality. For example, the following item is similar to those found on the LPC scale:

Difficult	___	___	___	___	___	___	___	___	Facile
	8	7	6	5	4	3	2	1	

Notice that the more positive evaluative term is given an 8, while the negative term would receive a 1. Therefore, the higher numbers on the scale are associated with a more positive evaluation of the least preferred coworker. Respondents who describe their least preferred co-worker in consistently negative terms receive a low LPC score, whereas those who use consistently positive terms receive a high LPC score.

Fiedler hypothesized that a person's description of a LPC said more about that person than anything else. He believed, for example, that everyone's least preferred co-worker is equally "unpleasant" and that differences in the descriptions of the co-worker actually represent differences in personality traits among the respondents. He argued that low-LPC leaders are more concerned with task-relevant problems, whereas high-LPC leaders are more concerned with interpersonal relations. Although this assumption has certainly been challenged in the literature (Schriesheim, Bannister,

& Money, 1979), the LPC scale and Fiedler's Contingency Model continue to be a widely used approach to understanding leadership effectiveness.

Situational Favorableness.   Any given leadership situation will be multifaceted. According to Fiedler (1967), the single most important situational dimension for a leader is situational favorableness. Situational favorableness refers to the general notion of how easy or difficult a setting might seem to be for a manager. Fiedler proposed that favorableness is determined by three specific features of the situation:

1. Leader-member relations—The extent to which the group trusts and respects the leader and is willing to follow his or her directions.
2. Task structure—The degree to which the task is clearly specified and defined (structured) as opposed to ambiguous and unclear (unstructured).
3. Position power—The extent to which the leader has official organizational power, that is, how much control over rewards and punishments that the leader has as a result of their position.

According to Fiedler, the better the leader-member relations, the more highly structured the job, and the stronger the position power, the more control or favorableness the situation has.

Once we have identified the leader's LPC score and evaluated the favorableness of the situation, Fiedler proposes matching the leader's style to the situation to achieve maximum leadership effectiveness. A recent review of over 170 studies tends to support Fiedler's predictions (Strube & Garcia, 1981). Specifically, low-LPC (task-oriented) leaders tend to perform better in situations that are either very favorable or very unfavorable. High-LPC (relationship-oriented) leaders tend to perform better in situations of moderate favorability. Although these findings have enjoyed overwhelming replication, there is still no satisfactory explanation as to why these relationships exist (Fiedler, 1984).

Fortunately, this has not stopped Fiedler from proposing an effective training program to help organizations apply his model—*Leader-Match Training* (Fiedler, Chemers, & Mahar, 1977). This program is a self-taught process that uses a programmed learning text. First, the manager completes the LPC scale and situational favorableness measures. Next, the leader is taught how to match his or her LPC level to the leadership situation that exists. But remember that Fiedler views an individual's leadership style as being fixed. Therefore, there are really only two ways to improve leader effectiveness: either change the situation to fit the leader or replace the leader with someone whose leadership style is more appropriate to the situation. Overall, research evidence supports the effectiveness of the leader-match approach to improving leadership effectiveness (Fiedler & Mahar, 1979; Strube & Garcia, 1981).

Although undoubtedly the most popular, Fiedler's LPC theory is only one of many contingency theories of leadership. In general, these theories differ according to the specific situational factor that is deemed most important for leadership effectiveness. In Fiedler's theory, it was the amount of control a leader had over the situation. In path-goal theory (House & Mitchell, 1974), the key situational factors are the personal characteristics of the subordinate and the characteristics of the environment. In situational-leadership theory (Hersey & Blanchard, 1982), the primary situational determinant of a leader's effectiveness is the followers'(or subordinates') maturity. In the Vroom-Yetton normative model of leadership (Vroom & Jago, 1988), the significant situational determinant involves the nature of the decision that a leader needs to make.

Regardless of their focus, the contingency theories all start with the assumption that a particular leadership style will only be effective in certain situations. As with previous leadership theories, the role of communication can be seen throughout these perspectives. We have to identify and measure the leader's style, identify and measure the key situational variables, and then train the leader to match the situation to his or her specific leadership style. All of these processes require effective communication skills, and this will become even more apparent as we review more recent approaches to leadership. These newer theories differ from their ancestors in that they focus on specific aspects of the leadership situation rather than trying to paint a "broad brush" picture of this concept we call leadership.

Recent Approaches to Leadership

Most of the leadership theories we have considered thus far share the underlying presumption that we can identify one appropriate "leadership style" that will always be effective. Regardless of whether that style is determined by a leader's personality traits, by his or her specific behaviors, or by a matching of the leader's style to situational factors, it is hypothesized that we will be able to determine what effective leadership is and apply that understanding to help leaders motivate their subordinates more effectively. Implicit in this perspective is the assumption that leaders will treat all of their subordinates in the same way. In other words, once a leader has found his or her best leadership style, then that style can be applied to all followers in a consistent fashion. More recent approaches to leadership, however, have begun to question this assumption. In fact, these theories all tend to focus on the nature and importance of the leader–follower interaction. We will review two specific examples of this new approach to understanding leadership effectiveness.

Vertical Dyad Linkage Theory
Do leaders treat each and every one of their followers in exactly the same way? Informal observation would suggest that this is not the case. Consider any previous jobs that you have held. Did the leader act differently towards some members of the work group than others? Did some employees seem to be more favored by the leader than other employees? If you answered yes to these questions, then you are familiar with the foundations of vertical dyad linkage (VDL) theory (Dansereau, Cashman,

& Graen, 1973; Graen & Cashman, 1975). This theory posits that the individual relationships between a leader and his or her subordinates will be a primary determinant of effective leadership.

According to Graen and his associates, leaders form a distinct exchange relationship with each one of their subordinates. As part of these exchange relationships, leaders offer valued outcomes such as seeking input into decisions, giving advice, providing support, and allowing for open two-way communication. In response, subordinates will reciprocate with increased commitment and loyalty to the leader as well as with extra effort on the leader's behalf. The model contends that each relationship, or linkage, that exists between the leader and a subordinate is likely to differ in quality. Stated differently, the same supervisor may have fairly warm, open, and trusting relationships with some subordinates and poor interpersonal relationships with other subordinates. Specifically, Graen and his associates postulate that early in the history of the interaction between the leader and a specific subordinate, the leader implicitly categorizes that subordinate into either an "in group" or an "out group." Although it is not entirely clear how a leader determines who is in and who is out, a recent study (Duchon, Green, & Taber, 1986) suggests that leaders tend to choose in-group members because they have a higher level of competence than out-group members and also because they share certain personal characteristics with the leader (such as sex, age, and personality characteristics). It is interesting to note, however, that most out-group members would probably argue that factors such as favoritism, ingratiation, and dirty politics are more important in determining in-group status than issues such as competency (Vecchio, 1988).

Members of the in-group are generally allowed a great deal of autonomy on how they perform their job. They are frequently given special duties and tend to enjoy added amounts of responsibility. They are often invited to participate in managerial decision-making. In essence, they have been elevated to the level of trusted assistant. Out-group members, on the other hand, generally receive less of the supervisor's time and attention. They are supervised within the narrow terms of their formal employment contract. They enjoy none of the special duties, privileges, or perks generally reserved for in-group members. VDL theory makes very specific and straightforward predictions about these relationships: subordinates who are in-group members will have higher performance, higher satisfaction, and less turnover than employees who are out-group members.

Overall, the research designed to test VDL theory has generally been supportive. Specifically, there is substantial evidence to suggest that leaders do differentiate among subordinates in terms of status and that these distinctions are far from random (Duchon, Green, & Taber, 1986). Also, there is extensive support for two of the model's central predictions. Specifically, research has consistently shown that members of the in-group will enjoy higher levels of satisfaction and performance than out-group members (Graen, Novak, & Sommerkamp, 1982; Scandura & Graen, 1984; Vecchio & Gobdel, 1984). In terms of in-group status being related to lower turnover, however, the research evidence is mixed (Ferris, 1985; Vecchio, 1985).

Although the leader–subordinate relationship may be important in determining one's intentions to quit, there appear to be more practical concerns, such as the availability of another job, that will exert much more influence on an employee's actual decision to quit.

Thus, it appears that there is a growing body of evidence to support the notion that leader–member relations can have a powerful effect on employee performance and job satisfaction. Given this fact, the next logical question appears to be obvious—Can we do anything to enhance the nature of these relationships? A recent study on this topic suggests that the answer is yes (Graen & Scandura, 1987). Subordinates in a large government department were asked to fill out a questionnaire on which they rated the quality of their relationship with their supervisor, how satisfied they were with his or her leadership, and how satisfied they were with their jobs. After this measure was taken, managers were given special training designed to help them develop the skills needed to establish positive (in-group) relations with their subordinates. Subordinates then filled out the same questionnaire at a later date. Results indicated that the training appeared to help: subordinates reported better relations with their leaders and higher satisfaction after the leaders had been through this special training. In addition, the positive gains were greater for those who initially reported poor relations with their supervisor than for those initially reporting good relations.

In summary, the research on VDL suggests that a leader's relationship with individual subordinates can play an important role in determining the satisfaction and performance of these individuals. In addition, training supervisors with the skills necessary to enhance these dyadic relationships appears to strongly influence the leaders' effectiveness. In fact, the role of leader–member relations has begun to receive attention in other contemporary approaches to understanding leadership. One specific example of this is the attributional model (Mitchell & Wood, 1980), which focuses on the leaders' attributions regarding the causes behind subordinates' behavior. In particular, this theory focuses on the leaders' attributions concerning their subordinates' current performance.

Attribution Theory

Before reviewing the literature on leaders' attributions for subordinate performance, we must first step back and discuss the general concept of attributions. A large body of evidence (see Harvey & Weary, 1981) suggests that whenever we observe another's behavior, we attempt to determine the causes behind that behavior. Why did your teacher decide to give a pop quiz on Friday afternoon? Why did your best friend tell you that she couldn't go out on Saturday night because she had to wash her hair? Why did mom and dad turn your bedroom into a den less than one month after you left for college? In other words, one thing we frequently want to know about others is why they have acted in a particular way. Attribution theory provides a framework for understanding how we come to conclusions about the causes of another person's behavior.

Attribution theory (Heider, 1944, 1958) suggests that whenever we observe someone else's behavior, we try to determine if that behavior was caused by internal or external factors. Internally caused behaviors are ones that are believed to be under the personal control of the individual. Externally caused behaviors, on the other hand, are seen as resulting mainly from situational factors. For example, when a student is late for class, we might attribute this behavior to the fact that she was caught in a traffic jam or held up by a train. These would represent external attributions because we are assuming that the behavior was caused by situational factors that were beyond the student's control. On the other hand, if we attributed this student's lateness to the fact that she overslept because she was partying until the wee hours of the morning, we would be making an internal attribution.

Obviously, the type of attribution (internal or external) we make for another's behavior has important implications for our subsequent interactions with that individual. If you decide that someone has acted in a specific way because of internal causes (i.e., their personality traits or their general attitudes), you will probably expect that person to behave in the same way on future occasions, and you may adjust your relationship with him or her accordingly. In contrast, if you decide that the person has acted in a specific way because of external causes (i.e., some event or situation in his or her life), you will probably realize that the person's behavior might be very different under other circumstances and therefore not expect him or her to behave in the same way at other times. Given the potential implication of attributions for understanding leader–subordinate relationships, it is important to identify those factors that lead to either internal or external attributions.

What are the factors that influence our decision to attribute a behavior to internal or external causes? A large body of research evidence (see Kelly & Michela, 1980) suggests that we tend to evaluate the behavior in terms of its degrees of consistency, consensus, and distinctiveness. Consistency is the degree to which the same person behaves in the same way at different times. High consistency implies that the person does behave the same way at other times. Consensus is the extent to which other people in the same situation behave in the same way. High consensus means that other people behave in the same way in this situation. Distinctiveness is the extent to which the same person behaves in the same way in other situations. If the person does not behave this way in other situations, distinctiveness is said to be high. According to attribution theory, information about these three factors is combined to form the basis for our decision on whether a behavior was caused by internal or external determinants. More precisely, if consistency, consensus, and distinctiveness are all high, we conclude that the person's behavior most likely stemmed from external causes. In contrast, if consistency is high but consensus and distinctiveness are low, we conclude that the behavior probably resulted from internal causes. Let's consider a concrete example of how this attributional process actually works.

Suppose you join a group of fellow students for lunch at a local restaurant. During the course of eating lunch, one of your fellow students is continuously complaining about the quality of the food, the service, and the restaurant in general. In trying to understand the cause of her complaining, you notice that other members of the group are also complaining about these issues (consensus is high), your friend has complained about this restaurant whenever you have been here in the past (consistency is high), and your friend generally does not complain like this at other restaurants (distinctiveness is high). Therefore, you would be most likely to attribute your friend's behavior to external causes (this must really be a poor restaurant). On the other hand, if no one else is complaining about the restaurant (consensus is low), your friend has also complained about this restaurant at other times (consistency is high), and your friend seems to complain about any restaurant you go to (distinctiveness is low), then you would be more likely to attribute your friend's behavior to internal causes (she is just a "picky" person when it comes to eating out). As mentioned earlier, the research evidence overwhelmingly supports the validity of these predictions (see Kelly & Michela, 1980).

Implications for Leadership Theory

Clearly, attributional processes could potentially play a central role in understanding leader effectiveness. After all, leaders observe the performance of their followers and attempt to understand the causes behind that performance. More specifically, the leader usually wants to know why this behavior met, exceeded, or failed to meet his or her expectations (Lord & Maher, 1989). In fact, research suggests that leaders are most likely to do this when faced with unexpected actions by their followers: actions which the leader cannot readily explain (Hansen, 1980). With respect to the work environment, this means that leaders are most likely to engage in attributional thinking when confronted with poor performance (Mitchell & Wood, 1980). More importantly, it also means that a manager's decision on how to deal with poorly performing subordinates will be largely determined by whether that performance is attributed to internal or external causes.

If a supervisor perceives poor performance as stemming from external causes, such as a lack of required materials or equipment, then efforts to improve performance will focus on rectifying the external situation. Materials can be ordered and equipment can be fixed or replaced. If, on the other hand, the supervisor believes that poor performance is related to internal factors, such as a lack of motivation or effort, then attempts to improve performance will focus on the employee and may include training, reprimand, transfer, or termination. As an example, consider one of the earliest studies conducted in this area (Mitchell & Wood, 1980). In this study, nursing supervisors were given brief accounts of errors committed by subordinates. These incidents described errors that arose from either internal causes (lack of ability or effort) or from external causes (work environment is too demanding). After reviewing the incidents, supervisors indicated what type of action they would be likely to take in each situation. Consistent with attribution theory's predictions, supervisors were more likely to direct corrective action toward the environment if they perceived the errors as resulting from external causes, but more likely to direct corrective action toward the nurses if they believed the errors as arising from internal causes. Clearly, a leader's attribution about a follower's behavior has significant implications for how the leader will treat that follower in future situations.

THE ROLE OF COMMUNICATION IN CONTEMPORARY LEADERSHIP APPROACHES

In both of the leadership theories we have just discussed, the primary focus is on the relationship between the leader and the subordinate. VDL theory cites this relationship as the fundamental determinant of leader effectiveness, whereas attributional theory examines one key element of this relationship—the leader's attributions of a subordinate's performance. Given the emphasis on leader–follower relations, the importance of communication should be self-evident. In order for leaders to develop effective relationships with their followers, they must have good communication skills. As a matter of fact, it doesn't really matter which theory of leadership effectiveness you adopt. The one common thread running throughout all of these theories is that the interaction between a leader and his or her subordinates is paramount in determining how effective that leader will be. Therefore, the importance of developing adequate communication skills should be *the* primary concern for any leader who is trying to enhance his or her ability to effectively lead and motivate employees. We will close this chapter by offering some suggestions that leaders can use for enhancing their communication skills.

COMMUNICATION STRATEGIES FOR BECOMING A BETTER LEADER

Have you ever listened to a professor or speaker who spoke so clearly and eloquently that there was no question in your mind about what that person was communicating? On the other side of the coin, have you ever finished listening to someone speak only to realize that you have absolutely no idea what he or she was talking about? If you have experienced situations like these, then you can certainly appreciate the importance of clear and effective communication. Unfortunately, good communication skills are not inborn; nor are they easily acquired. Effective leaders often work long and hard at perfecting their communication skills. Therefore, we offer the following recommendations to help you get a head start on developing effective interpersonal communication skills.

Keep the Language Simple

Did you know that the author of this chapter is an "I/O psychologist" who has a significant interest in the areas of "T & M" and "OB?" Have you ever had a "roomie" who was interested in "rushing" a fraternity or sorority because he or she thought it would be fun to go "Greek?" Have you ever gone bowling and picked up a "7-10 spare" or perhaps bowled a "turkey?" If so, then you recognize that our everyday speech is often peppered with very formal jargon that is specific to a particular area of interest. In fact, just about every organization, social group, profession, and field tends to have its own jargon—its own specialized language.

Obviously, the use of jargon is inevitable whenever individuals from the same field or social group communicate with each other. In fact, this kind of specialized communication is very important. It provides an easy way for people within the same field to share complex ideas in a relatively straightforward manner (from the perspective of those who understand the jargon, of course). It also allows members of that field to quickly recognize one another by virtue of the fact that they all "speak the same language." For example, anyone with training in industrial/organizational psychology would quickly recognize that the acronyms T & M and OB refer to the fields of testing and measurement and organizational behavior, respectively. Clearly, jargon can be very useful for enhancing communication within a particular field. The problem occurs when that jargon is used with individuals outside of that specific area; those individuals for which the jargon either has a very different meaning or no meaning at all (How many of you read the term OB at the beginning of this section and wondered why I was interested in obstetrics?).

A potent example of how jargon can lead to confusion is illustrated by a study of one large organization (Kantner, 1977). Kantner noted that within this organization, a COMVOC (which is a jargon term for common vocabulary) developed among the members of this organization. For example, in certain departments of the organization, it wasn't unusual to find "fast-trackers" who "shoot from the hip" in order to go for "the big win." Unfortunately, employees in other departments of the organization who didn't understand this jargon often felt out of place. This lack of understanding not only occurred between departments, but also extended to relationships between organizational members and their families. In fact, the wives of male executives were able to identify over one-hundred work-related terms and phrases that they did not understand. As a result, these women indicated that they often had great difficulty understanding what their spouses did on the job. Thus, even though jargon may be helpful for communicating with others in your field, it certainly doesn't help when trying to get your point across to those outside of your profession.

The implication of all of this is that to be an effective communicator one must be careful to avoid jargon. In fact, we can extend this reasoning by arguing that verbal communication between people should always attempt to use language that is short, simple, and to the point. In other words, a good communicator should adopt the K.I.S.S. principle when communicating with others—**K**eep **i**t **s**hort and **s**imple (Borman, 1982). People are better able to understand messages that do not overwhelm them with too much information at once. A good communicator is sensitive to this fact and actively monitors his or her audience for signs that they are being overloaded with too much information.

The importance of clear and concise communication was emphasized in our earlier discussion of leader traits. You may recall the contention that there is an optimal level of intelligence that is needed for effective leadership (Ghiselli, 1971). It was argued that higher levels of intelligence will actually reduce leader effectiveness. The reason for this is that highly intelligent leaders tend to use an inordinate amount of technical language and jargon, thereby making it very difficult for their followers to understand what the leader is saying. After all, leaders will only be able to get their ideas across if they package them in doses small and simple enough to be understood. Therefore, a leader's effectiveness will be directly related to his or her communication skills.

Be an Active, Attentive Listener

Although it is important for a leader to be able to communicate in a way that is understandable to others, it is just as important for the leader to work at being a good listener. Even though listening to others takes up a large percentage of the time spent communicating, research suggests that people tend to actually pay attention to and comprehend a small percentage of the information that they receive in the course of doing their jobs (Rowe & Baker, 1984).

Most people tend to think of listening as a passive process that involves taking in information that is sent by others. However, if listening is going to be done correctly, it must be a much more active process. For example, the listener should ask questions when he or she doesn't understand something, and should nod or signal the communicator when he or she is understanding. These simple and subtle types of cues provide communicators with critical feedback about the extent to which they are getting the message across to you. As a listener, you can do your share to help the communication process by providing such cues so that the communicator knows if you are understanding the information being presented. Asking questions, nodding, smiling, and putting the speaker's ideas into your own words are helpful ways of paying attention and making sure that you are correctly taking in the information being presented.

The importance of good listening skills for effective leadership has been well-documented in the research literature. For example, effective listening skills appear to be related to how quickly a person rises in the organizational hierarchy (Sypher, Bostrom, & Seibert, 1989). In addition, a recent study (Penley et al., 1991) suggests that good listening skills are strongly related to managerial performance. Apparently, well-developed listening skills play an important role in one's ability to succeed as a manager and become an effective leader. A recent article by well-known management consultant, Nancy K. Austin (1991), provides some insight into why listening skills are so important.

According to Austin, when you invite people to talk to you about their problems on the job, you are making an implicit promise to listen to them. Of course, if you do listen and don't like what you hear, you may feel defensive toward the speaker and be more interested in speaking up and "setting the record straight." According to Austin (1991), this is the challenge of listening. Good listeners will resist these temptations and pay careful attention to the speaker. If they cannot do so, they will admit the problem and reschedule another opportunity to get together at a time when they can listen more effectively. In addition, Austin argues that a good leader should be an "equal-opportunity listener." In other words, you should not only pay attention to those individuals whose position and status command your attention, but also to anyone at any level in the organization. A good listener will make sure that he or she makes the time to listen to all individuals in a patient and democratic fashion. The basic assumption behind these suggestions is that people at any job level may have something important to say and that they will feel good about you as a leader if you show appropriate consideration to them. Austin goes on to note that by listening to your employees, you are saying, "You are smart and have important things to say; you are worth my time." Sending such a message to subordinates is essential to establishing the kind of open, two-way communication that is so critical to effective leadership.

Although research has clearly established the importance of good listening skills, many people tend to be insensitive to how others perceive their listening abilities. A recent survey of employees in the hospitality industry (Brownell, 1990) found that almost all the managers indicated that they felt their listening skills were either "good" or "very good." Unfortunately, the data also indicated that most of the manager's subordinates disagreed. In addition, it was also shown that those managers who were rated as better listeners were almost always the managers who had been trained in listening skills. Thus, it appears that the most effective leaders are going to be those who display appropriate listening skills, and training in these skills can significantly enhance a leader's proficiency in this area.

Create a Supportive Climate for Communication

The final recommendation applies to the overall environment in which leader–follower communication takes place. All too often, communication between a manager and employee is likely to take place in a defensive climate (Whetton & Cameron, 1984). In fact, research suggests that the vast majority of employees believe that communication between themselves and their organizations is nowhere near as good as it should be (McCathrin, 1990). For whatever reasons, people are either unwilling or unable to communicate their ideas and feelings to upper-level managers. It appears that part of the problem involves the lack of available channels for upward communication as well as people's general reluctance to use those channels that do exist. What can organizations and their leaders do to develop a supportive climate so that employees feel comfortable communicating with their leaders?

To begin with, organizations can make use of employee surveys. Surveys can be used to gather information about employees' attitudes and opinions on key areas of organizational operations. Administering these questionnaires at regular intervals can be quite useful for identifying changes in attitudes as they occur. In fact, such surveys tend to be quite effective when their results are shared with employees. This is especially true when employees' ideas are then used as the basis for modifying the way things are done in the organization.

A second set of techniques that can help foster communication between leaders and their followers are "brown bag" and "skip level" meetings. These are methods designed to facilitate communication between managers and employees who don't usually get together simply because they are at different organizational levels (McCathrin, 1990). Brown bag meetings are nothing more than informal get-togethers held over breakfast or lunch. The participants bring their meal from home (hence the term brown bag) and sit down to discuss what is going on in the corporation. The informal nature of these meetings is designed to foster the open sharing of ideas. Eating your lunch out of a bag tends to serve as an equalizer and to create a climate in which all parties feel that they are on the same level.

Skip level meetings are designed to accomplish the same objectives. These are generally gatherings of employees and their superiors who are at least two levels higher in the organizational hierarchy. The basic premise behind skip level meetings is that new lines of communication can be opened by bringing together individuals who are two or more levels apart—individuals who usually don't come into contact with one another. From the leader's perspective, skip level meetings also provide an opportunity to develop effective leader–subordinate relationships with individuals who are lower in the organizational hierarchy.

A third approach to fostering effective leader–subordinate communication involves the use of suggestion systems. Oftentimes, employees will not offer their ideas for improving the organizational situation because they either don't know how to reach the appropriate people or, even worse, they don't feel that they will be listened to. As noted earlier, anything that a leader can do to show his or her employees that their ideas count and that they are being listened to will help enhance that leader's effectiveness. To overcome these problems and provide a conduit for employees' ideas, many organizations use suggestion boxes. In addition, employees are often rewarded for their successful suggestions, generally with a flat monetary reward or some percentage of the money saved by implementing the suggestion. A prime example of how suggestion systems can enhance the communication environment is provided by the Eastman Kodak Company (Bergerson, 1977). Kodak's approach represents the oldest continuously running suggestion system, having gone into effect in 1898. At that time, a worker received a $2 reward for pointing out the advantages of washing the windows in the company's production department. Since then, Kodak has received over two million suggestions from its employees, including one that resulted in an award of $47,800 to the man who suggested mounting film boxes on cards for display racks in retail stores.

One final approach to developing a supportive climate for communication is through corporate hotlines—telephone lines that are staffed by organizational personnel ready to listen to employees' comments, answer their questions, take their suggestions, etc. A nice example of this can be seen in the "Let's Talk" hotline that AT&T developed to help deal with employee anxieties at the time of the company's antitrust divestiture (Taft, 1985). By providing employees with this kind of easy access to information and personnel, an organization and its leaders can benefit in many ways. It not only shows employees that the company and its leaders care about them, it also encourages employees to voice their concerns before an issue becomes too serious. In addition, by keeping track of the kinds of questions and concerns that employees raise, the organization has a barometer of what types of issues are on employees' minds. This type of information is invaluable for improving organizational conditions and promoting effective leader–follower relationships.

CONCLUSION

Leadership is the process whereby one individual influences other group members toward the attainment of defined group or organizational goals. Although leaders may use a wide variety of strategies for exerting such influence, it is safe to say that all of these influence attempts involve communication. Therefore, a leader's communication skills will play a pivotal role in determining his or her effectiveness. In fact, the importance of communication skills is highlighted in many of the prominent leadership theories.

Early research on leadership tried to identify key traits that set leaders apart from other people. Although some traits were shown to be related to leadership effectiveness (i.e., intelligence), the overall research paradigm was quickly abandoned in favor of studying leader behaviors. The results of this research led to the identification of two key categories of leader behavior: initiating structure and consideration. These behavioral clusters were so consistently related to important organizational outcomes that many leadership training programs were based upon them (e.g., Grid Organization Development). Despite the excitement surrounding the initial success of behavioral theories, it soon became evident to leadership researchers that the situation in which leadership takes place will have a significant moderating effect on the relationship between leadership style and performance outcomes.

This new focus on situational factors led to the development of contingency theories, which attempted to specify the situational factors that will determine leader effectiveness. For example, Fiedler's LPC theory argues that a task-oriented leader will be most effective under conditions of low or high situational favorability. In contrast, people-oriented leaders will be most effective when there is moderate situational favorability. Contemporary leadership theories are even more specific in their focus, highlighting particular aspects of the leader–follower relationship. Although the prominent leadership theories may differ according to what aspects of leadership are most significant, they all recognize the importance that communication plays in determining a leader's effectiveness.

Our review of the leadership literature suggests some straightforward recommendations for enhancing a leader's communication skills. To begin with, a leader must avoid using jargon. It makes it very difficult to communicate with those who "don't speak the language." In addition, leaders need to take an active role in developing their listening skills. Research clearly indicates that more effective leaders are usually more effective listeners. Finally, a leader can endeavor to create a supportive climate for leader–follower communication. Activities as diverse as suggestion boxes, brown bag lunches, and employee surveys can all function as methods for making the communication process less intimidating.

In summary, the suggestions given above represent ways in which organizations and their leaders can help to break down the barriers that frequently inhibit the flow of information from lower-level personnel to upper-level managers. Given the significant role of communication in the leadership process, these recommendations should not only serve to enhance the communication process, but should also strongly influence the effectiveness of organizational leaders. As noted earlier, those managers who are most sensitive to communication issues are generally rated the most effective leaders (Daft, Lengel, & Trevino, 1987).

Therefore, regardless of what leadership theory one believes is correct, good communication skills will always play a key role in determining leadership effectiveness.

GLOSSARY

Autocratic (leadership style)—a style of leadership in which the leader strictly controls subordinates and makes all the decisions unilaterally.

Consideration—actions by a leader that demonstrate concern with the welfare of subordinates and attempt to establish relationships with them. Also called concern for people and employee-oriented behaviors.

Contingency theories—theories that suggest that a leader's contribution to successful performance by the work group depends on both the leader's style and the characteristics of the situation.

External attribution—identifying an individual's behavior as being due to situational factors that were beyond the individual's control.

Great man theory—the view that leaders possess special traits that separate them from others and that these traits are related to their effectiveness as leaders.

High-high hypothesis—the belief that high levels of both consideration and initiating structure would combine to produce the highest level of leader effectiveness.

Initiating structure—leader behaviors that are designed to enhance productivity or task performance. Also called concern for production and production-oriented behaviors.

Internal attribution—identifying an individual's behavior as being due to personal factors that are unique to that individual's personality.

Jargon—the specialized or technical language of a trade, field, profession, or social group.

K.I.S.S. Principle—an acronym for keep it short and simple, a basic principle of communication advising that messages should be as short and simple as possible.

Leadership—the process whereby one individual influences other group members toward the attainment of defined group or organizational goals.

Least preferred co-worker scale (LPC)—a questionnaire that measures how leaders characterize their feelings about a person with whom they have worked least effectively.

Participative (leadership style)—a style of leadership in which the leader permits subordinates a considerable degree of autonomy in completing routine work activities and also permits them to take part in decision-making.

Situational favorableness—the notion of how easy or difficult a situation may be for a leader. Three factors, leader–member relations, task structure, and position power, combine to represent a wide range of possible situations.

Vertical dyad linkage (VDL) theory—a theory suggesting that leaders form different relations with various subordinates and that the nature of such dyadic exchanges can exert strong effects on subordinates' performance and satisfaction.

CASE STUDY

Susan Bilsner was the type of individual who was always on top of things. She was always the best in her class at school, held many leadership positions, and was a very active and popular student. Upon graduation, she went to work for her uncle's sporting goods store, Sports R Us. Within one year, the company was so impressed with her that she received awards for best attendance and "most productive new employee." In fact, her supervisor even convinced the organization to send her back to school to get an M.B.A. so they could groom her for a top management position. She graduated with honors at the top of her class and returned to Sports R Us to assume the role of production vice-president.

Bilsner had read all about the potential problems of assuming a new leadership position while in graduate school. She was determined to avoid them. She knew that the previous vice-president, Murray Almans, was essentially an absentee autocrat. He had run the division from his office at the top of the building, far above the factory floor. Once or twice a day, he would summon a secretary from the offices on the second floor and send a memo to one group of workers or another. But for the most part, he chose to remain detached from his production unit and make all the decisions himself.

Bilsner's first order of business was to change all of that. She set up her office on the second floor, where she could look out her always-open office doorway and see down onto the factory floor. Instead of eating lunch by herself, she spent the time down on the factory floor, walking around, talking to subordinates, and organizing groups. Although the workers (many of whom had fifteen to twenty years seniority) were surprised by her new policy and reluctant to volunteer for groups, Bilsner persevered. Within a short period of time, she had created a worker award group, a Suggestion of the Month group, and a management relations group. Each group met twice a month, once with Bilsner and once without. She encouraged each group to identify goals and develop plans for reaching those goals. She provided as much support for their activities as she possibly could.

Unfortunately for Bilsner, this was the last thing her employees wanted. In fact, within two months of her arrival, the entire management relations committee resigned. Bilsner talked with her employees and discovered that although they liked her, they were not interested in her new management style. They preferred things the way Almans had run the department in the past. Although they hardly ever saw him, they knew he would never "get in their hair." One employee's comments present an eloquent summary of the employees' reactions to the new "participative management" style: "If you are giving us a choice, Ms. Bilsner, then we would rather go back to the old way of doing things. After you have been in one place doing the same thing for twenty years, the last thing you want is to do is learn a new way of doing it."

Discussion: 1. What type of leadership style does Susan Bilsner have? 2. Was her experience at Sports R Us what you would expect given the research literature on leadership? Why or why not? 3. Could Bilsner have instituted these changes without eliciting such a negative reaction from the workers? If so, how? 4. What would Fiedler's contingency theory predict about Susan's chances of success in applying her new management approach? 5. How could effective communication have helped Bilsner in her effort to create a new climate at Sports R Us?

REFERENCES

Austin, N. K. (1991). Why listening's not as easy as it sounds. *Working Woman,* 46–48.

Bergerson, A. W. (1977). Employee suggestion plan still going strong at Kodak. *Supervisory Management, 22,* 32–36.

Blake, R. R., & Mouton, J. S. (1978). *The New Managerial Grid.* Houston, Tex.: Gulf Publishing Co.

Blake, R. R., & Mouton, J. S. (1982). A comparative analysis of situationalism and 9,9 management by principle. *Organizational Dynamics, 24,* 20–43.

Borman, E. (1982). *Interpersonal Communication in the Modern Organization* (2nd ed.). Englewood Cliffs, N.J.: Prentice-Hall.

Brownell, J. (1990). Perceptions of effective listeners: A management study. *Journal of Business Communication, 27,* 401–415.

Daft, R. L., Lengel, R. H., & Trevino, L. K. (1987). Message equivocality, media selection, and manager performance: Implications for information systems. *MIS Quarterly, 11,* 355–366.

Dansereau, F., Cashman, J., & Graen, G. (1973). Instrumentality theory and equity as complementary approaches in predicting the relationship of leadership and turnover among managers. *Organizational Behavior and Human Performance, 12,* 184–200.

Day, D. V., & Lord, R. G. (1988). Executive leadership and organizational performance: Suggestions for a new theory and methodology. *Journal of Management, 14*(3), 453–464.

Duchon, D., Green, S. G., & Taber, T. D. (1986). Vertical Dyad Linkage: A longitudinal assessment of antecedents, measures, and consequences. *Journal of Applied Psychology, 71*(1), 56–60.

Ferris, G. (1985). Role of Leadership in the Employee Withdrawal Process: A Constructive Replication. *Journal of Applied Psychology, 70*, 777–781.

Fiedler, F. E. (1967). *A Theory of Leadership Effectiveness.* New York: McGraw-Hill.

Fiedler, F. E. (1984). *The Contribution of Cognitive Resources and Behavior to Leadership Performance.* Paper presented at the annual meeting of the Academy of Management, Boston, Mass.

Fiedler, F. E., Chemers, M. M., & Mahar, L. (1977). *Improving Leadership Effectiveness: The Leader-Match Concept.* New York: John Wiley.

Fiedler, F. E., & Leister, A. F. (1977). Leader Intelligence and task performance: A test of a multiple screen model. *Organizational Behavior and Human Performance, 20*, 1–14.

Fiedler, F. E., & Mahar, L. (1979). The effectiveness of contingency model training: A review of the validation of leader match. *Personnel Psychology, 29(1)*, 45–62.

Fleishman, E. A., & Harris, E. F. (1962). Patterns of leadership behavior related to employee grievance and turnover. *Personnel Psychology, 15*, 43–56.

Ghiselli, E. (1971). *Exploration in Managerial Talent.* Santa Monica, Calif.: Goodyear.

Graen, G., & Cashman, J. (1975). A role-making model of leadership in formal organizations: A developmental approach. In J. G. Hunt & L. L. Larson (eds.), *Leadership Frontiers.* Kent, Ohio: Kent State University Press.

Graen, G., Novak, M., & Sommerkamp, P. (1982). The effects of leader-member exchange and job design on productivity and satisfaction: Testing a dual attachment model. *Organizational Behavior and Human Performance, 29*, 109–131.

Graen, G., & Scandura, T. A. (1987). Vertical dyads linkages theory of leadership. In A. Kiesier, G. Reber, & R. Wunderer, (eds.), *Encyclopedia of Leadership.* Kernerstrasse, FRG: C. E. Paeschel Verlag.

Hansen, R. D. (1980). Common sense attribution. *Journal of Personality and Social Psychology, 39*, 996–1009.

Harvey, J. H., & Weary, G. H. (1981). *Perspectives on Attributional Processes.* Dubuque, Iowa: Brown Publishing.

Heider, F. (1944). Social perception and phenomenal causality. *Psychological Review, 51*, 358–374.

Heider, F. (1958). *The psychology of Interpersonal Relations.* New York: John Wiley.

Hersey, P., & Blanchard, K. H. (1982). *Management of Organizational Behavior: Utilizing Human Resources* (4th ed.). Englewood Cliffs, N.J.: Prentice-Hall.

House, R. J., & Mitchell, T. R. (1974). Path-goal theory of leadership. *Journal of Contemporary Business, 3*, 81–98.

Kahn, R., & Katz, D. (1960). Leadership practices in relation to productivity and morale. In D. Cartwright & A. Zander, (eds.), *Group Dynamics: Research and Theory.* Elmsford, N.Y.: Row, Peterson.

Kantner, R. M. (1977). *Men and Women of the Corporation.* New York: Basic Books.

Kelly, H. H., & Michela, J. L. (1980). Attribution theory and research. *Annual Review of Psychology, 31*, 457–501.

Kenny, D. A., & Zaccaro, S. J. (1983). An estimate of variance due to traits in leadership. *Journal of Applied Psychology, 68*, 678–685.

Kerr, S., Schriesheim, C. A., Murphy, C. J., & Stogdill, R. M. (1974). Toward a contingency theory of leadership based upon the consideration and initiating structure literature. *Organizational Behavior and Human Performance, 12,* 62–82.

Kotter, J. P. (1990). *A Force for Change: How Leadership Differs from Management.* New York: The Free Press.

Larson, L. L., Hunt, J. G., & Osburn, R. (1976). The great hi-hi leader behavior myth: A lesson from Occam's razor. *Academy of Management Journal, 19,* 628–641.

Lewin, K., Lippitt, R., & White, R. K. (1939). Patterns of aggressive behavior in experimentally created social climates. *Journal of Social Psychology, 10,* 271–301.

Lord, R. G., & Maher, K. (1989). Perceptions in leadership and their implications in organizations. In J. Carroll (ed.), *Applied Social Psychology and Organizational Settings.* Hillsdale, N.J.: Lawrence Erlbaum.

McCathrin, Z. (1990). The key to employee communication: Small group meetings. *The Professional Communicator, 10(1),* 6–7, 10.

Mintzberg, H. (1979). *The Nature of Managerial Work* (2nd ed.). Englewood Cliffs, N.J.: Prentice-Hall.

Mitchell, T. R., & Wood, R. E. (1980). Supervisors' responses to subordinate poor performance: A test of an attributional model. *Organizational Behavior and Human Performance, 25,* 123–138.

Motowidlo, S. (1992). Leadership and leadership processes. In M. D. Dunnette (ed.), *Handbook of Industrial/Organizational Psychology* (2nd ed.). Palo Alto, Calif.: Consulting Psychologist Press.

Nystrom, P. C. (1978). Managers and the hi-hi leader myth. *Academy of Management Journal, 21,* 325–331.

Penley, L. E., Alexander, E. R., Jernigan, I. E., & Henwood, C. I. (1991). Communication abilities of managers: The relationship to performance. *Journal of Management, 17,* 57–76.

Porras, J. I., & Berg, P. O. (1978). The impact of organization development. *Academy of Management Review, 3,* 249–266.

Robbins, S. P. (1991). *Organizational Behavior: Concepts, Controversies, and Applications.* Englewood Cliffs, N.J.: Prentice-Hall.

Rowe, M. P., & Baker, M. (1984). Are you hearing enough employee concerns? *Harvard Business Review, 62,* 127–135

Scandura, T., & Graen, G. (1984). Moderating effects of initial leader-member exchange status on the effects of a leadership intervention. *Journal of Applied Psychology, 70(3),* 428–436.

Schriesheim, C. A., Bannister, B. D., & Money, W. H. (1979). Psychometric properties of the LPC scale: An extension of Rice's review. *Academy of Management Review, 4,* 287–294.

Stogdill, R. M. (1948). Personal factors associated with leadership: A survey of the literature. *Journal of Psychology, 25,* 35–71.

Stogdill, R. M. (1974). *Handbook of Leadership: A Survey of Theory and Research.* New York: The Free Press.

Stogdill, R. M., & Coons, A. E. (eds.), (1957). *Leader Behavior: Its Description and Measurement.* Columbus, Ohio: Ohio State University Bureau of Business Research.

Strube, M. J., & Garcia, J. E. (1981). A meta-analytic investigation of Fiedler's contingency model of leadership effectiveness. *Psychological Bulletin, 90,* 307–321.

Sypher, B. D., Bostrom, R. N., & Seibert, J. H. (1989). Listening, communication abilities, and success at work. *Journal of Business Communication, 26,* 293–303.

Taft, W. F. (1985). Bulletin boards, exhibits, hotlines. In C. Reuss & D. Dilvis (eds.), *Inside Organizational Communication* (2nd ed.). New York: Longman.

Tjosvold, D. (1984). Effects of leader warmth and directiveness on subordinate performance on a subsequent task. *Journal of Applied Psychology, 69,* 222–232.

Vecchio, R. P. (1985). Predicting employee turnover from leader-member exchange. *Academy of Management Journal, 28,* 478–485.

Vecchio, R. P. (1988). *Organizational Behavior.* New York: The Dryden Press.

Vecchio, R. P., & Gobdel, B. C. (1984). The vertical dyad linkage model of leadership: Problems and prospects. *Organizational Behavior and Human Performance* Vol 34. 5–20.

Vroom, V. H., & Jago, A. G. (1988). *The New Leadership: Managing Participation in Organizations.* Englewood Cliffs, N.J.: Prentice-Hall.

Whetton, D. A., & Cameron, K. S. (1984). *Developing Management Skills.* Glenview, Ill.: Scott, Foresman.

Yukl, G. A. (1981). *Leadership in Organizations.* Englewood Cliffs, N.J.: Prentice-Hall.

Yukl, G. A. (1989). *Leadership in Organizations* (2nd ed.). New York: Academic Press.

RECOMMENDED READINGS

Bass, B. M. (1985). *Leadership and Performance Beyond Expectations.* New York: The Free Press.

Bryman, A. (1986). *Leadership and Organizations.* London: Routledge and Kegan Paul.

Conger, J. A. (1989). *The Charismatic Leader.* San Francisco: Jossey-Bass.

Kotter, J. P. (1988). *The Leadership Factor.* New York: The Free Press.

Mintzberg, H. (1979). *The Nature of Managerial Work (2nd ed.).* Englewood Cliffs, N.J.: Prentice-Hall.

Tichy, N. M., & Devanna, M. A. (1986). *The Transformational Leader.* New York: John Wiley.

Vroom, V. H., & Jago, A. G. (1988). *The New Leadership: Managing Participation in Organizations.* Englewood Cliffs, N.J.: Prentice-Hall.

Yukl, G. A. (1989). *Leadership in Organizations (2nd ed.).* Englewood Cliffs, N.J.: Prentice-Hall.

▶ 6

Conflict Management in Organizations

DALE L. SHANNON

How important is conflict management in organizations? Managers report spending approximately 20 percent of their daily time dealing with some form of conflict (Baron, 1989; Thomas & Schmidt, 1976). In addition, successful managers exhibit more behaviors related to conflict management than unsuccessful managers (Luthans, Rosenkrantz, & Hennessey, 1985). Conflict management, therefore, is an important topic to consider in organizational communication and organizational effectiveness. Not only do we have the word of researchers and writers, however, on the importance of conflict management in organizations, stop and think for yourself, how prevalent is conflict in the workplace? How important is it for organizations to have people knowledgeable in conflict management? Our system of business would be drastically different without proper conflict management.

Conflict management in organizations is a rich and productive area of research. Relevant research can be found in many areas, such as business, communication, psychology, and sociology, to name a few. While researching the same phenomenon of conflict management in organizations, this body of literature is difficult to integrate because of its disparate definitions of conflict and the variety of topics and variables that are the foci. Putnam (1986), a noted scholarly researcher, argues that conflict research also differs as to whether it is deterministic or interactive. Deterministic approaches treat communication as a static variable, conflict is a product of structural variables. Interactive approaches treat communication as a product of the interaction between the parties. Conflict, therefore, arises within this interaction.

With this in mind, this chapter is not intended in any way to be a comprehensive literature review. It is intended as a heuristic device for the readers, providing an awareness of the subject matter and enough information for us to begin asking purposeful questions. In other words, it is hoped that after reading this chapter you will have enough knowledge about conflict management to begin asking questions about what else you do not know.

This chapter consists of six major sections. The first section introduces us to the myriad definitions for conflict that exist in the literature. The second section examines the characteristics of constructive and destructive conflict management. Sections three and four define and present research on different levels of conflict and styles of conflict management. The fifth section provides information on some of the many conflict intervention forms that exist. The sixth section looks at some future directions for conflict management research on communication technologies. Following this sixth section is a brief summary.

CONFLICT DEFINITIONS

Intuitively, we seem to know conflict when we see it. Everyone can probably think of several personal examples of conflict in the workplace. Who has not been reprimanded by a supervisor for doing or not doing something? Aside from this type of knowledge, however, how does the scholarly research literature define conflict? Does the scholarly research literature agree or disagree on what conflict is? This section explores a variety of conflict definitions.

Conflict as an area is so broad that many different workable definitions exist. Scholars even disagree about what constitutes conflict (Fink, 1968). Rather than arguing the strengths or weaknesses of the various definitions, this chapter begins with a presentation of some of the various perspectives whereby conflict management is studied. It is hoped that a discussion of the various perspectives will lead us to a deeper understanding of the concept. This deeper understanding should begin to lead us to ask those questions about what we do not know.

Pondy (1967), a noted organizational scholar, identifies four broad categories of definitions for the term conflict in the research literature. The term is used describe (1) antecedent conditions (e.g., scarce resources), (2) affective states (e.g., stress, tension, hostility, anxiety, etc.), (3) cognitive states (e.g., cognitive conflict or the awareness of conflict), and (4) conflictful behavior (e.g., passive resistance to overt aggression). This section provides examples of research using each of these four perspectives of conflict definitions. For each study cited, notice what variables are considered important and how that might translate to other situations.

Antecedent Conditions

Conflict conceptualizations that include antecedent conditions as all or a part of the definition view conflict as the logical result of these preexisting conditions.

Coser, in the book *Continuities in the Study of Social Conflict* (1967), defines conflict as "a struggle over values and claims to scarce status, power, and resources in which the aims of the opponents are to neutralize, injure, or eliminate the rivals" (p. 8). This definition of conflict contains elements of the antecedent condition category.

Negotiation research often uses scarce resources as a source of conflict. Shannon's work (1992, 1993) provides examples of such a use. Shannon suggests that conflict arises between labor and management negotiators over contract issues. For most of the issues whatever labor "wins" management "loses." For example, determining what percentage of a hospital and benefit plan will be covered by workers and what percentage will be covered by management establishes money as the scarce resource that neither party wants to lose.

Research focusing on antecedent conditions is concerned with the effect of pre-existing conditions on conflict. As such, the primary focus is not on the individuals or the communication in the conflict. An example of a situation that defines conflict by antecedent conditions would be a conflict over scarce resources. Suppose office workers are in conflict over who gets which vacation time because there is not enough "good" vacation time to go around. Changing the antecedent condition, in this case, the amount of vacation time, would change the conflict.

Affective States

The majority of conflict research using the affective states conceptualization of conflict concerns intrapersonal conflict, or conflict within an individual. Because the focus of this chapter is organizational conflict, it does not include intrapersonal conflict as a topic.

An example of conflict research including an affective states perspective that does not involve intrapersonal conflict is provided by Bell (1979). Bell (1979) investigates the effect of arguments containing either substantive or emotional content on the quality of decision-making. She concludes that the affective content of messages does not affect the flexibility of persons in a group decision-making context.

Research focusing on affective states is concerned with the emotional states of the individuals involved in the conflict. As such, the focus of this research is on information internal to one or both of the parties involved in the conflict. An example of a situation that would be defined as a conflict using the affective states definition would be an employee trying to leave the office early one afternoon to go on vacation. Just as the employee is about to leave his desk, his manager walks up and assigns him two major projects to complete before the day is over. Because the employee is under time pressure to leave, the additional work would create hostility and have an impact on how he dealt with his manager. The researcher interested in this situation would focus on how the employee's hostility affected the conflict.

Cognitive States

Thomas (1990), a noted conflict researcher, provides a definition of conflict fitting in the cognitive states perspective and writes, "The process that begins when one party perceives that the other has negatively affected, or is about to negatively affect, something that he or she cares about" (p. 653). The cognitive states perspective concerns the cognitive process of one or both of the individuals in the conflict. Pinkley and Northcraft (1994), and Wall and Nolan (1987), serve as two examples of research using the cognitive states perspective.

Pinkley and Northcraft (1994) investigate the influence of cognitive frames of disputants on the conflict process and outcomes. Conflict frames, much like eyeglass frames, are the lenses through which disputants approach a conflict (Pinkley, 1990). Pinkley and Northcraft find that cognitive frames influence the type and amount of settlement between disputants.

Wall and Nolan (1987) focus on the amount of perceived inequity and perceived conflict and their influence on group satisfaction and conflict management style. They suggest that perceived inequity and perceived conflict are positively related and that perceived inequity is associated more with conflict avoidance than with integrative conflict management.

Research focusing on cognitive states is concerned with how the individuals involved in a conflict process information and how that processing of information influences the conflict process and outcomes. As such, the focus of this research is on information internal to one or both of the parties involved in the conflict. The work of Wall and Nolan (1987) can be used as an example. If a manager thinks, or perceives, that there is inequity between how she is treated and how her peers are treated, this will increase her perception of the amount of conflict. In other words, the more inequity the manager feels, the more conflict she also feels. Wall and Nolan also indicate that this manager would be more likely to try to avoid the conflict, rather than attempt to work out a joint settlement.

Conflictful Behavior

Pondy's (1967) fourth definition of conflict involves the behaviors of the individuals. Deutsch (1973), a noted conflict researcher, broadly defines conflict as the occurrence of incompatible activities. Schwenk (1990), exploring the differing effects of conflict in for-profit and not-for-profit organizations, identifies Pondy's (1967) behavior category as the basis of the conflict definition used in that research. Results indicate that high conflict is associated with high quality for the executives of non-profit organizations, but with low quality for executives of for profit organizations.

Research focusing on conflictful behavior is concerned with the external actions of the individuals involved in the conflict. As such, the focus of this research is on external, observable behaviors of one or both of the parties involved in the conflict. For example, we could use amount of yelling as the conflictful behavior to focus on.

We may be interested in how the amount of yelling affects whether the parties continue the conflict management process or abandon it. With this perspective, we could then watch a variety of conflicts, measure the amount of yelling, and note whether the parties continue or abandon the conflict.

Research, however, does not have to limit the definition of conflict to one of Pondy's (1967) four categories. More general definitions of conflict that encompass several of Pondy's categories are being used (Thomas, 1990). One of the more widely cited definitions is provided by Hocker and Wilmot in their text *Interpersonal Conflict* (1995). They state that "conflict is an expressed struggle between at least two interdependent parties who perceive incompatible goals, scarce resources, and interference from the other party in achieving their goals" (p. 21). Similarly, Hellriegel, Slocum, and Woodman in *Organizational Behavior* (1989), refer to conflict as "any situation in which there are incompatible goals, cognitions, or emotions within or between individuals or groups that lead to opposition" (p. 448). Putnam and Poole (1987), noted researchers, identify three general characteristics of conflict present in many definitions: interaction, interdependence, and incompatible goals.

Pondy (1967) advocates viewing conflict as a dynamic process that involves all four of the definitions presented earlier. Conflict begins with a latent stage (conditions), moves into perceived conflict (cognition), then into felt conflict (affect), then manifest conflict (behavior), and finally into conflict aftermath (conditions). As we can see, conflict can be defined in many different manners. In reading conflict research we should be aware of the conflict definition that the researcher is using. Without a solid understanding of the variety of approaches to conflict, we would never be able to make sense of the vast literature that exists. The ability to change view points, to look at or approach conflict from a different definition, is a useful skill to develop.

Conflict Resolution Versus Conflict Management

Before continuing to the next section, an important distinction must be clarified. The conflict literature makes use of two terms, management and resolution, sometimes, unfortunately, interchangeably. A distinction exists and must be made clear between conflict resolution and conflict management. While some may consider this nothing more than an exercise in semantics, conflict resolution and conflict management are two distinctly different processes from differing points of view. Conflict resolution stems from the perspective that conflict is bad, negative, to be avoided. If conflict can not be avoided, however, it must then be resolved. This perspective treats conflict as if it were an undesirable, abnormal occurrence. Hawes and Smith (1973), in a critique of assumptions underlying conflict communication research, discuss this perspective as viewing conflict as a time disruption in an otherwise peaceful system. Conflict resolution carries with it the notion that the conflict will be terminated, that it will cease to exist. You will usually hear people use phrases such as "We can't accomplish anything until we get this conflict resolved." Conflict resolution also assumes that conflicts should be reduced or avoided. Sometimes, however, conflict needs to be escalated, to be brought to everyone's attention so it may then be properly managed. Conflict resolution views conflict as inherently negative. Goldhaber, in the text book *Organizational Communication* (1993), states that the negative connotations associated with organizational conflict are a result of the early interpretations of the Hawthorne Studies and the human relations form of management discussed in Chapter 1.

Conflict management, on the other hand, views conflict as an inevitable factor of interaction. Because conflict is inevitable, it is viewed as neither inherently positive nor negative. Under the conflict management perspective what becomes important is how the conflict is managed. Conflicts may be managed in such a way as to create a positive situation, or they may be managed in such a way as to create a negative situation. Persons versed in conflict management understand that there can be benefits as well as costs in conflict. If a conflict is productively managed, new ideas or information may be learned, new insights may be gained, and lessons for handling future conflicts may be learned. If a conflict is not productively managed, ideas and information may be lost, possible gains may be lost or actual losses may occur, and a habit for unproductive conflict management could be formed.

The distinction between conflict management and conflict resolution is not universally recognized. We, therefore, must be aware of the distinction and attempt to decipher from the text of each study whether the study approaches conflict from the resolution or management perspective. It should be apparent that this chapter, given its title, approaches conflict from the conflict management perspective. Additionally, we need to assist others we come in contact with in the differences between conflict resolution and conflict management. It will take a concerted effort to bring this to everyone's attention.

DESTRUCTIVE VERSUS CONSTRUCTIVE CONFLICT

Defining conflict as inherently neither positive nor negative, the distinction between constructive and destructive conflict lies entirely in the manner in which the conflict is managed. This section will explore some of the distinctions between destructive and constructive methods of conflict management.

Deutsch (1973) compares destructive and constructive conflict with competitive and cooperative conflict. While this comparison is simplistic, it is useful for illustrative purposes. In a destructive conflict the parties are competing with each other, trying to defeat the other(s), and ultimately, to "win" the conflict. In a constructive conflict the parties are cooperating or working with each other, they are interested in reaching an agreeable outcome, and they need the other(s) to remain a viable entity after the conflict has subsided. This is not to indicate, however, that any particular conflict is entirely destructive or constructive.

Destructive Conflict Management

Destructive conflict management is recognized, among others things, by its expansion and/or escalation of the conflict, issues, and emotions. Destructive conflict can oftentimes become independent of the situations that precipitated the conflict and may likely continue after the initial causes have been resolved, forgotten, or become irrelevant (Deutsch, 1973). Also, parties in a destructive conflict are likely to be less flexible in their approach (Folger, Poole, & Stutman, 1993).

Escalatory conflict spirals are the most recognizable form of destructive conflicts (Hocker & Wilmot, 1991). Such spirals are characterized by overt expressions of the conflict that build upon one another. The interaction in escalatory conflict spirals becomes self-perpetuating (Folger et al., 1993). If the parties involved do not break the cycle of the spiral, the ultimate end is destruction of the relationship (Wilmot, 1987).

Parties involved in a destructive conflict often see the conflict as a win or lose situation. The only way to win is to make the other party lose. Hocker and Wilmot suggest that the best index of a destructive conflict is when one or more of the parties has a strong desire to get even, a tit-for-tat mentality. An example of this would be an employee stealing from his or her employer because of the employer's refusal to grant him or her a raise—"Because I did not get the raise, I am going to steal from the company." This could begin an escalatory conflict spiral if the employer responds—"Since we suspect you are stealing, we will not grant you any additional raises or privileges." Which the employee could respond to by stealing more, and inevitably being fired—the ultimate destruction of the relationship.

Constructive Conflict Management

Deutsch (1973) presents three reasons why a cooperative process assists in constructive conflict management. First, a cooperative process allows for open and honest communication that enables the parties to gain a more meaningful and accurate description of the conflict they are facing. This allows the parties to combine their information and to reduce the possibility of misunderstandings, confusion, and mistrust. Second, a cooperative process encourages the parties to look for mutually beneficial solutions. Because the parties have a better understanding of each other's needs, they can jointly work out a solution. Finally, a cooperative process leads to a more friendly, open atmosphere, which focuses more on similarities rather than differences. The cooperative process begins to stimulate the convergence of the parties' beliefs and values.

Constructive conflicts, sometimes referred to as productive conflicts, "are characterized by a transformation of the elements of conflict" (Hocker & Wilmot, 1991, pp. 37–38). One or more of the following elements would change as a result of constructive conflict: the manner in which the conflict is expressed (from "you have a problem" to "we have a problem"), the perceptions of incompatible goals and/or scarce resources (from "either you get what you want or I get what I want" to "is there a way we can both get what we want?"), the degree of interdependence between the parties (from "I do not need you" to "we need each other"), and the type of cooperation and/or opposition between the parties (Hocker & Wilmot, 1991).

Parties involved in a constructive conflict often see the conflict as a situation in which all parties involved can win. This win/win outlook serves as a guide for the parties, oftentimes becoming a self-fulfilling prophecy.

Hocker and Wilmot (1991) characterize the communication in a constructive conflict as demonstrating cooperation between the parties, involving more satisfying exchanges between the parties, and seeing positive attributions associated with the other parties.

Overall, destructive conflicts usually leave the parties dissatisfied with the results, feeling as if they lost. Constructive conflicts usually leave the parties with a positive feeling, a satisfaction that something positive was the result of the conflict. Parties involved in constructive conflict usually feel better about themselves, the other parties involved, and the conflict management process, while parties involved in a destructive conflict have negative feelings about themselves, the other parties involved, and the conflict management process.

LEVELS OF CONFLICT

Organizational conflict may be encountered on many different levels. The levels that are considered in this chapter include interpersonal, intragroup, intergroup, and interorganizational. A brief clarification on the use of the term "level" is in order. Level is not used to indicate any qualitative difference among the levels—interorganizational is not inherently better or worse because it is a higher level. Putnam and Poole (1987) use the term "arenas of organizational conflict" to indicate the same concept as is indicated by the present use of the term "level".

The separation of organizational conflict into these four levels does not imply that they are distinct and uniquely different from each other. As Thomas (1976) argues, many properties of conflict can be generalized across these four levels. This chapter, however, presents research that indicates there are also differences between the various levels. The following sections provide a definition for each level of organizational conflict and present research on the various levels.

Interpersonal Conflict

Interpersonal conflict in organizations refers to conflict between two organizational members. While any two members of an organization may find themselves in an interpersonal conflict, much of the research on interpersonal conflict in organizations centers on the superior–subordinate relationship. This may in part be because of the previously cited research, which reports that managers spend approximately

20 percent of their daily time dealing with conflict (Baron, 1989; Thomas & Schmidt, 1976). It also should be noted that at this level the research is focusing on individuals, not aggregates, collectives, or representatives.

Most people employed in an organization should have little trouble thinking of an instance of interpersonal conflict within their organization. A quick example from the world of retail could be two employees in conflict over who gets to handle which customers. Joe is upset because he feels that Sue is taking all of the customers who appear most likely to buy expensive items and leaving him the browsers. Because each works on commission, Joe feels he is losing money to Sue. This would present us with a situation ripe for an interpersonal conflict.

Using the various definitions for conflict outlined by Pondy (1967), most interpersonal conflict in organizations has been studied as either the affective or cognitive states of the individuals involved. This, in essence, replaces actual conflict behavior and communication with perceived conflict behavior and communication, as can be seen in the Joe and Sue conflict from the previous paragraph.

Baron (1988) serves as an example of research in interpersonal conflict in an organization. Baron, while defining conflict by the behavior, looks at how the other party interprets that behavior (a cognitive states perspective), to see if apparent sincerity of the message influences attributions. Results indicate that when we believe the opposition is being sincere we will have less negative reactions to that party than if we believe the other party is not being sincere (Baron, 1988).

James, Chen, and Goldberg (1992) use perception of conflict in an interpersonal setting as an independent variable to measure the relationship between organizational conflict and individual creativity. Results indicate that when we are working on a task within our area of primary interest, perceived conflict promotes creativity. On tasks outside of a our area of interest, however, perceived conflict reduces creativity.

Intragroup Conflict

Intragroup conflict is oftentimes thought of as interpersonal conflict in a group setting. To some degree this is accurate. Intragroup conflict, however, differs from interpersonal conflict because a group is more than a collection of individuals. A group possesses an identity and qualities of its own apart from the identities and qualities of its individual members (Fisher & Ellis, 1990). Intragroup conflict is conflict between individuals, pairs, or small collectives within an existing group. Intragroup conflict can hurt group cohesion, decrease productivity, and produce a negative group attitude (Rosenfeld, 1973).

At the intragroup level, factors such as roles, history, climate, and culture begin to function in the conflict management process. The group's task, social, and emotional processes determine the causes of conflict and how the group resolves that conflict (Hellriegel, Slocum, & Woodman, 1989).

Intragroup conflict research is less widely researched than other levels. Fisher and Ellis, in their text, *Small Group Decision Making: Communication and the*

Group Process (1990), discuss opinion deviation and role deviation as two forms of intragroup conflict. Opinion deviation is a group member disagreeing with other group members about the content of ideas. A role deviate, on the other hand, "is a type of person who is not desired by other group members" (Fisher & Ellis, 1990, p. 258).

Putnam (1986) discusses the different impacts of opinion and role deviation on the group. Other group members will increase their participation with an opinion deviate, trying to exert pressure on her or him to conform to the majority opinion. A role deviate, however, is all but ignored by the group.

Bonar and Vaughn (1994) focus on middle managers as a group and discuss conflict within that particular group. They discuss several causes of intragroup conflict: differing perceptions regarding jobs, differing images of the group, differing models of control, differing professional aspirations, and differing measures of success.

An example of intragroup conflict from the world of academe would be a college department (the faculty of which would be defined as a group) in conflict over curriculum changes. One segment of the faculty wants to increase standards. They argue that the current curriculum does not provide enough challenge to be considered anything other than "advanced high school." A second segment of the faculty argues that their college should be geared more towards the academically challenged student and that raising standards would be contrary to that mission. A final segment of the faculty does not want to discuss standards because those discussions always become heated and that particular segment of the faculty does not like friction among colleagues. This would definitely be a situation ripe for intragroup conflict.

Intergroup Conflict

Unlike the previous levels, intergroup conflict focuses on aggregates rather than individuals. While intragroup conflict can involve an aggregate of the larger group, most of the research focuses on individuals within a group. Intergroup conflict assumes the group acts as a unified whole and overlooks the notion of individual group members (Putnam & Poole, 1987).

Putnam and Poole state that the context in which the groups exist and the relationships that link the groups together are the major components of intergroup conflict. Neilsen (1972), in discussing how to manage intergroup conflict, lists several reasons intergroup conflict may occur. Included are differing personal characteristics, differing interpretations of reward and status distribution within the organization, differing perceptions and experiences, and competition for scarce organizational resources.

Intergroup conflict research can take one of two foci. One focus is the interaction between the opposing groups, the other is to look at the effects of intergroup conflict within the groups. Tjosvold, Dann, and Wong (1992) study interactions between groups. In a service organization, they found that cooperative goals and open discussion of opposing views contribute to the servicing of customers, completing tasks, and strengthening expectations of future collaboration between the groups. They argue that conflict between groups can be important to establishing coordination between them, but that conflict between groups with competitive goals is not beneficial.

Intergroup conflict also impacts the groups internally. External conflict is a possible source to increase group cohesion (Hersey & Blanchard, 1993; Napier & Gershenfeld, 1985; Rosenfeld, 1973). Hersey and Blanchard, organizational behavior scholars, state that intergroup conflict creates a more task-oriented atmosphere, productivity can increase, and the leadership becomes more autocratic.

Interorganizational Conflict

Many of the same dynamics that operate in intergroup conflict are also present in interorganizational conflict. Conflict at this level, however, is affected more by the institutional environment in which the conflict takes place (Van de Ven, Emmett, & Koenig, 1980). Organizational environments, however, are too broad of a topic to warrant inclusion in this chapter.

STYLES OF CONFLICT MANAGEMENT

Conflict management styles, or modes, are the approaches we usually take in managing a conflict. Whether these styles are learned behaviors we can choose to use or not, or traits that we have, is in question (see Folger et al., 1993; Putnam, 1988) but of no relevance to this discussion. Thomas (1988) presents the use of the terms "individual's profile" or "individual's mix of modes" as the solution to the state/trait quandary. Profiles or mixes, argues Thomas (1988), reflect both an individual's predispositions and differences in the kind of situations faced. Folger and colleagues (1993) argue for the notion that styles refer to categories of behavior rather than types of people.

Conflict management styles originates with the seminal work of Blake and Mouton's (1964) managerial grid. Hall (1969) and Thomas (1976) both modify Blake and Mouton's grid. These models lay out five conflict management styles situated on two dimensions. Blake and Mouton labeled the dimensions as concern for results and concern for people. The five styles are withdrawal, forcing, smoothing, compromising, and confronting. Table 6-1 presents the three conflict management styles typologies.

A person using the withdrawal style is considered to be low on both concern for results and concern for people. This person considers leaving the conflict as more important than maintaining relationships or achieving results. A person using the forcing style is considered to be high on concern for results and low on concern for people. This person considers results to be the important factor, regardless of how others feel about those results. Smoothing is considered as high on concern for people and low on concern for results. This person wants others to feel good, so she or

TABLE 6–1 **Three Conflict Management Style Typologies.**

Author	Dimensions	Styles
Blake & Mouton (1964)	Concern for results Concern for people	Withdrawal Forcing Smoothing Compromising Confronting
Hall (1969)	Personal goals Relationships	Lose-leave Win-lose Yield-lose Compromise Synergistic
Thomas (1976)	Assertiveness Cooperativeness	Avoiding Competing Accommodating Compromise Collaborating

he does not push for his or her desired outcomes in hopes of making the other parties feel good. Compromising is considered as middle on both dimensions. This person gives in a little on the desired results and gives a little on the relationship. Confronting is considered as high on both dimensions. This person wants to achieve the best results possible while still maintaining positive relationships.

Hall's (1969) revision includes changing the dimensions to concern for personal goals rather than concern for results and concern for relationships instead of concern for people. The five styles change to lose-leave (withdrawal), win-lose (forcing), yield-lose (smoothing), compromise, and synergistic (confrontation).

Thomas's (1976) revisions include renaming the dimensions as assertiveness, which is concern for own goals, and cooperativeness, which is concern for other's goals. The five styles change to avoiding (withdrawal), competing (forcing), accommodating (smoothing), compromise, and collaborating (confrontation).

Numerous instruments have been developed to measure conflict management styles on two dimensions. The influence of Blake and Mouton (1964), Hall (1969), and Thomas (1976) is evident in almost all. Following is a discussion of some of the styles and models presented by researchers and writers.

Rahim (1983, 1985) labels the two dimensions as concern for self and concern for others. The five styles are avoiding (withdrawal), dominating (forcing), obliging (smoothing), compromise, and integrating (confrontation). In addition, he presents information concerning the amount of conflict in addition to the conflict management style.

Putnam and Wilson (1982) present the Organizational Communication Conflict Instrument (OCCI). The OCCI was developed as a direct measurement of concrete communication behaviors, something that was believed to be missing from earlier works (Putnam & Wilson, 1982). The OCCI results in three factors, or family of strategies, that a party in a conflict can use. The strategies are labelled as non-confrontation strategies, solution-oriented strategies, and control strategies. Nonconfrontation strategies manage conflict indirectly through avoiding, sidestepping, and/or downplaying the conflict, an equivalent to avoiding and smoothing. Solution-oriented strategies manage conflict by a combination of compromise and confrontation. Control strategies manage a conflict through direct persuasion, equivalent to Blake and Mouton's (1964) forcing. Because the OCCI measures concrete behaviors rather than conceptual or theoretical beliefs, no dimensions are required to underlie the strategies.

Sillars and colleagues (1982) use the two dimensions of directness of communication and competitiveness of communication as the basis for their instrument to measure conflict management styles. The three main categories of conflict management behavior are avoidance, distributive, and integrative. Avoidance tactics attempt to minimize conflict interaction. Distributive tactics are competitive and/or individualistic behaviors. Integrative tactics are cooperative behaviors that seek to resolve the conflict.

Other researchers question the two dimensional approach popularized by Blake and Mouton (Knapp, Putnam, & Davis, 1988; Nicotera, 1993). Womack (1988), writing in a special issue of *Management Communication Quarterly* dedicated to communication conflict research, highlights many of the problems with two dimensional models. These problems range from internal reliability (low consistency between questions supposedly measuring the same concept), high intercorrelations among the styles (difficult to separate the styles because they are related), social desirability (we may answer in a particular manner because we believe that we should answer that way to look good, not because we actually believe that particular answer), and unclear factor structures (the components that make up the models could be interpreted in different fashions, the results are not perfectly clear). The argument against two-dimensional approaches essentially is that they do not do a good job of representing reality. Rather than assuming two dimensions, Nicotera had subjects write descriptions of their conflict-handling strategies. Using this grounded theory approach, one researcher presented a three-dimensional model of conflict handling behavior (Nicotera, 1993). The three dimensions are attention to one's own view, attention to the other's view, and emotional/relational valence. The first two dimensions share many commonalities with the earlier two-dimensional models. The addition of the third dimension, a relational dimension, creates unique new possibilities.

Pinkley (1990) and Pinkley and Northcraft (1994) do not claim to present a model to categorize conflict management behavior, although their results do suggest such an approach. They identify three conflict frames of reference that parties use during a conflict. The three frames are a relationship versus task frame, emotional versus intellectual frame, and cooperate versus win frame (Pinkley & Northcraft, 1994).

From this discussion of the variety of conflict management styles researchers are investigating, the most important information to retain is that a variety of styles of managing conflict do exist. No particular style is best suited for every conflict episode. Instead, we need to be aware of the variety of options that we have when managing any given conflict. We need to be aware of what works and does not work in certain situations and with certain parties. That is the key to long-term effective conflict management.

INTERVENTIONS

Up to this point, this chapter presents background information on the conflict management process in an organization. This section focuses on practical information on various interventions to assist in the management of conflict, first presenting some macro approaches to conflict management and then presenting micro conflict management information according to the four levels of conflict discussed earlier. As previously cited, Thomas (1976) argues that many properties of conflict can be generalized across these levels. Therefore, any of these strategies may be useful at any given level, regardless of under which level it is discussed.

Macro Perspectives on Conflict Management

What this chapter discusses as macro perspectives on conflict management could also be considered as phase models for conflict management. In other words, they are various stages or phases through which conflict progresses.

One such model is presented by Borisoff and Victor in their text *Conflict Management: A Communication Skills Approach* (1989). Borisoff and Victor's model for effective conflict management consists of five stages: assessment, acknowledgment, attitude, action, and analysis. The first stage involves assessing the nature of the relationship between the participants, background to the conflict, and possible courses of action for the conflict. Recognition that the parties may have differing beliefs, values, goals, and personalities is the goal of the second stage, acknowledgement. An individual examining his or her attitudes toward the other party is the intent of the third stage. Action involves the verbal and nonverbal interchange between the parties in working out the conflict. The final stage, analysis, occurs throughout the conflict process, but is also an important final stage. The parties involved should be sure that the outcome of the conflict is one with which they can live and by which they can abide.

Interpersonal Conflict Management

Much of the research and writing on conflict management focuses on the interpersonal level. Management of conflict at the interpersonal level usually focuses on a variety of skills, techniques, and tactics that one or more of the individuals involved in the conflict can use to reduce, manage, and in some cases, resolve, the conflict.

Four solid pieces of advice for interpersonal conflict management are advanced by Fisher and Ury in their seminal work, *Getting To Yes: Negotiate Agreement Without Giving In* (1981). While Fisher and Ury present their information as aids for negotiation, the same advice applies to interpersonal conflict. They suggest separating the person from the problem, focusing on interests rather than positions, inventing options for mutual gains, and using objective criteria in decision-making.

Books and training guides for the successful management of interpersonal conflict are common. In one particular book, for example, Katz and Lawyer (1992) present a good compilation of communication skills. Topics covered include stages of skill learning, communication, information sharing, reflective listening, problem-solving, assertion, and conflict management styles. Katz and Lawyer provide an excellent workbook for those interested in developing an awareness of the conflict management skills.

Wall and Callister (1995) review conflict literature and provide practicing managers with a list of seven practical suggestions for conflict management:

1. Do not promote conflict. Conflict in and of itself is not beneficial.
2. A conflict avoided from the beginning by good management is better than a conflict managed.
3. When conflict is addressed, realize that the original cause may now only be a small part of the entire conflict.
4. Reduce the number of identifiable issues down to a manageable set and attempt to set up trade-offs between the parties.
5. Adopt a pragmatic approach. Keep trying to manage the conflicts, noting what works and what does not.
6. When managing conflicts, remember it is important that all parties feel that they are being treated fairly.
7. Conflict management skills can be taught and delegated.

Jurma and Powell (1994) examine the perceived conflict management behavior and effectiveness of managers. Findings indicate that managers adopting a more androgynous gender-role type are perceived by their subordinates as more effective at conflict management than managers adopting either masculine or feminine gender-role types.

Walton (1987), a noted conflict researcher, presents the dialogue approach to managing interpersonal conflicts in organizations. The dialogue approach may be undertaken by the two parties or with the assistance of a third party facilitator. Walton uses the term "dialogue" to refer to the parties directly speaking to each other, focusing on the conflict between them as well as their relationship. Through dialogue, almost a form of psychotherapy, the parties reach a better understanding of themselves, each other, their relationship, and the conflict. The hope is that this better understanding will improve the relationship, resolve or manage the conflict, and reduce the potential for future disabling conflicts.

One method of understanding what is beneficial is to consider what is detrimental. Bach and Wyden, in *The Intimate Enemy* (1969), review many "crazy makers" or unfair fighting techniques. These techniques include kitchen-sinking, gunnysacking, beltlining, monologuing, and sandbagging. Kitchen-sinking involves including every issue into the conflict but the kitchen sink. The hope is that the sheer volume of issues will overwhelm the other party. Gunnysacking is saving up every complaint and grievance until they are unleashed at one point in time. As with kitchen-sinking, sheer volume is overwhelming. Beltlining is striking below the belt, using arguments or issues that fall below the other person's psychological beltline. An interchange between two employees in conflict could include the following example of beltlining, "Just because you slept with the manager does not mean that she will approve your proposal over mine." Monologuing is nonstop talking, a person so verbose that no feedback or discussion can occur. Sandbagging involves setting up verbal traps for someone, hoping that they will fall into them and be used against them later. This can often be detected by listening for phrases such as "but just a minute ago you said..."

Intergroup Conflict Management

When dealing with intergroup conflict, we must remember how intergroup conflict differs from the previous levels. Intergroup conflict deals with aggregates of individuals in conflict and not necessarily individual people. This added group dimension creates some additional possibilities for conflict management.

Researchers usually approach the intergroup conflict management through the use of structural interventions or process interventions (Putnam & Poole, 1987). Structural interventions change organizational structures and resource allocations. Process interventions are directed at the conflict interaction between the groups to either redirect the conflict behavior or reframe the parties' perspectives (Putnam & Poole, 1987). An intervention is good if it is both efficient and high in quality (Brett & Rognes, 1986).

Below are seven strategies for managing intergroup conflict (Neilsen, 1972):

1. Multilevel interaction—Intense interaction between both groups on a variety of issues.
2. Exchange of members—Groups exchange members to enhance understanding of the issues, reduces perceptual differences.
3. Negotiation without consultants—Groups negotiate directly without third party intervention.
4. Third-party consultants—Use neutral, high-status people to mediate between the groups.
5. Use of integrators—Use people both groups respect.

6. Limited interaction—Allow groups to interact only on issues with super-ordinate goals and where decision-making procedures are clearly established.
7. Physical separation—Reduce the groups' opportunities to interact.

Neilsen's strategies are listed in ascending order. If the first strategy proves to be an unsuccessful method of conflict management, the groups turn to the second strategy, and so on.

There are four supportive courses upper managers can take to manage or reduce intergroup conflict (Cliff, 1987). The first course of action is attitude. Upper managers "can make a strong impact by severely discouraging counterproductive comments" (p. 52). The second course of action is to ensure that rewards are based on interdepartmental feedback. Establishing cross-department interaction is the third course of action. Cliff suggests that both professional and social links be established between departments. The final course of action is to establish a cross-departmental jury of one or two representatives from each department to review any issues that have been raised. This jury system helps to prevent minor disagreements from becoming counter productive conflicts.

Interorganizational Conflict Management

Many of the same interventions discussed under intergroup conflict may operate at the interorganizational level. An intervention that may be best suited for conflict management at this level is third party intervention.

Third party intervention is the introduction of a neutral third party into the conflict process who assists the conflicting parties in determining a solution to the situation. The role of the third party can vary from that of a facilitator, helping the parties with the process but not the solution, to that of an adjudicator, settling the conflict based on previous legal precedents.

Third party intervention, in and of itself, can prove effective in the conflict management process. The introduction of a third party may change the destructive elements already at work in a conflict by changing the interpersonal dynamics, physical arrangements, nature of the discussion, and the overall approach to the conflict (Rubin, 1994). Kruse (1995), an organizational development consultant, suggests that the human resources department should play a vital and active role in third party interventions within an organization.

Mediation is a popular form of third party intervention. The role of the mediator is much the same as a facilitator. The mediator assists the parties in the process of managing their conflict without interjecting any personal opinions about possible settlements. In mediation the parties involved are in complete control of determining the possible solutions. Many organizations have set up informal mediation offices as a first step in an internal grievance procedure.

Hocker and Wilmot (1995) highlight three advantages of mediation as a form of conflict management. First, it provides all parties involved a mutual stake in the resolution. Because the parties work out the solution, there is no loser in the conflict. Mediation focuses on the relationship between the parties. Second, mediated solutions are more integrative. A good mediator helps the parties get past specific positions to focus on general interests. This focus helps form creative solutions. Third, mediation is adaptable to many types of conflict.

Arbitration, however, removes some of the control over determining possible solutions from the parties involved and places that decision-making responsibility with the third party. The arbiter listens to the various sides present information regarding the conflict, enters into discussions of possible solutions, then renders a decision on the conflict. Entering arbitration, like mediation, is voluntary. No one can force the parties into the process. Arbitration, however, tends to focus on the content of the conflict and typically does not consider the relational aspects of the conflict (Hocker & Wilmot, 1995). Oftentimes professional athletes go to arbitration over salary disputes.

Relying on the legal system to manage conflicts is a form of adjudication. The judge listens to testimony from the various parties, considers legal precedence, and then renders a decision. In adjudication the third party has complete control within legal guidelines, over the solution to the conflict. Participation in adjudication is not always voluntary. A party may be forced to have its case adjudicated if the other side files a law suit. Adjudication is usually viewed as a win-lose option, thereby heightening the stakes for all involved (Hocker & Wilmot, 1995).

Regardless of the form of the third party intervention, Deutsch (1994) presents four kinds of skills for the third party. Third parties need to develop skills in establishing an effective working relationship with each of the conflicting parties. Second, third parties need to develop skills in establishing a cooperative problem-solving attitude among the involved parties toward the conflict. Development of skills related to encouraging a creative group process and group decision-making is the third kind of skill. The final kind of skill is to have knowledge about the issues involved in the conflict.

FUTURE DIRECTIONS

Organizational communication is influenced by communication technology. Communication can occur under many different circumstances. Years ago the main concerns were the differences between face-to-face, written messages, or telephone. Now we can add to that a growing list of forms of mediated communication (voice mail, e-mail, fax machines, audio-conferencing, video-conferencing, computer support systems, to name just a few). Researchers are investigating the possible effects of various forms of communication technology on the conflict management process. The differences between face-to-face and telephone negotiations were explored in the classic studies of Morley and Stephenson (1977) and Short, Williams, and Christie (1976). Weeks and Chapanis (1976) added written communication via teletype to the combination of face-to-face and telephone. These studies investigate the belief that different forms of communication have different strengths and weaknesses and a best format could be selected for various conflict management situations, depending on the contingencies.

Poole, Shannon, and DeSanctis (1992), scholarly researchers, review myriad literature on communication media and conflict interaction. They provide the following seven points in their summary. First, all media have advantages and disadvantages for supporting conflict processes. Second, face-to-face interaction is less effective at surfacing conflicts than other media, but is more likely to avoid extreme escalation. Third, media that are nonvisual, that is, those that preserve anonymity, will result in more input from the parties, but will not necessarily balance power. Fourth, computer support clarifies procedures and helps with complex tasks while audio is weak with complex tasks. Fifth, audio, text, and computer support lead to greater depersonalization than face-to-face or video, therefore it is easier to focus on the issues and avoid negative climates. Sixth, computer support, except for asynchronous conferencing, generally improves solution quality. Finally, people prefer face-to-face interactions over any other media.

A growing body of literature examines the application of computers to the conflict management process. Examples of research on the use of computers in conflict management include Fraser and Hipel (1981), Nyhart and Samarasan (1989), Sainfort, Gustafson, and Bosworth (1987), and Sycara (1991). Some researchers are investigating the application of computers to the negotiation process, resulting in an area referred to as negotiation support systems (NSS). Examples of NSS research include Jarke, Jelassi, and Shakun (1987), Jones (1988), Poole and colleagues (1990), and Shannon (1992). Computer systems have been applied in conflict management in a number of arenas, including ocean mining (Sebenius, 1981), community conflicts (Susskind & Cruikshank, 1987), collective bargaining (Mumpower, Schuman, & Zumbolo, 1986), and the United Nations (Rothstein, 1979).

Sebenius (1981) provides a good example of an application of the computer to the conflict management process. Countries were attempting to reach agreement on mining of the sea floor. Delegates were spending enormous amounts of time arguing over what should or should not be mined and how it should or should not be mined. After making little progress, a computer model was developed, with the assistance of all involved parties, that simulated the ocean floor. Then, as each delegate would propose a solution, that solution could be modeled on the computer, and the results debated on common grounds. The computer, in this example, served as a reality tester. Because the parties could not initially agree on possible effects, the agreed upon computer model served as their "reality." The delegates could now test a variety of solutions and select the "best" solution.

One form of computer support is referred to as a group support system (GSS). In a study of the impact of GSS on group conflict and conflict management, Miranda and Bostrom (1994) found that GSS-supported groups perceived lower amounts of conflict on the issues and lower amounts of interpersonal conflict than non-GSS-supported groups. While this study is only a preliminary one, the possibility of computers assisting in the conflict management process is intriguing.

Poole, Shannon, and DeSanctis (1992) note that a majority of the research involving communication technology is outcome oriented, that is, how does technology X effect outcome Y? Rather than assume that a nice linear cause–effect connection exists between communication technology and conflict management, however, Poole and DeSanctis (1990) argue that the way social technologies, such as the communication technologies discussed here, are used determine their effects. In other words, outcome-based effects can not be predicted in advance without knowledge of the specific users of the technology.

CONCLUSION

This chapter has presented information on conflict management in organizations. It avoids providing pat answers to simplistic questions. Instead, this chapter is designed to present us with a variety of information on the topic and to leave us with the ability to ask informed questions.

This chapter presents information on the variety of conflict definitions present in the literature and the implications of those definitions. Following this a comparison and contrast of destructive versus constructive conflict management is presented. This is included to highlight that conflict, in and of itself, is neither positive nor negative. It is the manner in which conflict is managed, rather, that determines whether the conflict is destructive or constructive. Four levels, or arenas, of conflict are presented. These levels are interpersonal, intragroup, intergroup, and interorganizational. A discussion of conflict management styles is included that covers the traditional two-dimensional models and introduces some alternative approaches to the conflict management styles debate. The fifth section of this chapter presents intervention strategies that may be useful at each of the levels of conflict previously discussed. Finally, a brief discussion of communication technology's role in organizational conflict management is presented. Throughout this chapter, the importance of conflict management in organizations is never questioned.

GLOSSARY

Affective states—the feelings internal to a person. Examples include stress, tension, hostility, anxiety, etc.

Antecedent conditions—preexisting conditions, for example, scarcity of resources, policy differences, etc.

Cognitive states—the psychological frame of reference a person is using, for example, perception or awareness of conflictful situations.

Conflict—an expressed struggle between at least two interdependent parties who perceive incompatible goals, scarce resources, and interference from the other party in achieving their goals.

Conflict management—the treatment of conflict as inevitable. The important focus is on handling the conflict in a productive manner.

Conflict management style—the approach an individual usually takes in managing a conflict.

Conflict resolution—the treatment of conflict as undesirable. The important focus is on reducing and/or eliminating the conflict.

Conflictful behavior—the observable actions of a party involved in a conflict. Could range from passive resistance to over aggression.

Constructive conflict—conflict that is managed in a productive manner. Often results in better outcomes.

Destructive conflict—conflict that is managed in a harmful manner. Often results in poorer outcomes.

Escalatory conflict spirals—a relationship between two parties characterized by increased levels of conflict that becomes self-perpetuating. If the cycle is not broken, results in the destruction of the relationship.

Intergroup conflict—conflict between two or more groups.

Interorganizational conflict—conflict between two or more organizations.

Interpersonal conflict—conflict between two or more individuals.

Intragroup conflict—conflict within a group.

CASE STUDY

A professor from a local university was asked to assist Hometown Manufacturing, Incorporated (HMI), with some internal conflict problems. After discussions with employees from every aspect of the operation, from president and vice-president to hourly workers, this is how the professor summarized the situation at HMI.

HMI is a family-owned, light manufacturing operation. Marvin, the father, is HMI's president, while Karen, the oldest daughter, is vice-president of sales, and Mark, the oldest son, is vice-president of manufacturing. HMI also employs an office staff of five persons, three sales representatives, and thirty-one hourly workers.

Marvin closely supervises all aspects of the business. He is quick to point out problems to his employees with little concern for how his remarks may affect others, figuring that a productive employee is better than a friend on the job. Karen sees the point her father is trying to make with his direct approach, but she also believes he should show more concern for his employees. Mark does not like the tension present in the factory and will go out of his way to avoid confrontation.

Problems surfaced from complaints raised by the workers. The sales reps felt they were "constantly under the microscope" and were afraid to try anything new, for fear that Karen, or worse yet, Marvin, would get after them. The production workers were complaining about "uneven management practices." Mark would off-handedly mention something that would need attention, but Marvin would come down hard on them for the slightest problem.

Karen thought all the problems were between Marvin and Mark and had tried to work things out between them, but to no success. That is when HMI called in the professor.

Discussion: 1. What conflicts are present in this case? At what level is each operating? 2. Identify the conflict management styles of Marvin, Karen, and Mark. Why do you identify each person as you do? 3. If you were to be hired as a consultant, what advice would you give to HMI? What additional information would help you in this consultation? Why? How could you access that information?

REFERENCES

Bach, G. R., & Wyden, P. (1969). *The Intimate Enemy.* New York: William Morrow.

Baron, R. A. (1988). Attributions and organizational conflict: The mediating role of apparent sincerity. *Organizational Behavior and Human Decision Processes, 41,* 111–127.

Baron, R. A. (1989). Personality and organizational conflict: Type A behavior pattern and self-monitoring. *Organizational Behavior and Human Decision Processes, 42,* 281–297.

Bell, M. A. (1979). The effects of substantive and affective verbal conflict on the quality of decisions of small problem solving groups. *Central States Journal, 30,* 75–82.

Blake, R. R., & Mouton, J. S. (1964). *The Managerial Grid.* Houston, Tex.: Gulf Publishing Co.

Bonar, J., & Vaughn, G. (1994). Derailing intragroup management conflict. *Performance and Instruction, 33*(1), 15–18.

Borisoff, D., & Victor, D. A. (1989). *Conflict Management: A Communication Skills Approach.* Englewood Cliffs, N.J.: Prentice-Hall.

Brett, J. M., & Rognes, J. K. (1986). Intergroup relations in organizations. In P. S. Goodman (ed.), *Designing Effective Work Groups* (pp. 82–106). San Francisco: Jossey-Bass.

Cliff, G. (1987). Managing organizational conflict. *Management Review, 76,* 51–53.

Coser, L. A. (1967). *Continuities in the Study of Social Conflict.* New York: The Free Press.

Deutsch, M. (1973). *The Resolution of Conflict: Constructive and Destructive Processes.* New Haven: Yale University Press.

Deutsch, M. (1994). Constructive conflict resolution. *Journal of Social Issues, 50,* 13–32.

Fink, C. (1968). Some conceptual difficulties in the theory of social conflict. *Journal of Conflict Resolution, 12,* 412–460.

Fisher, B. A., & Ellis, D. G. (1990). *Small Group Decision Making: Communication and the Group Process* (3rd ed.). New York: McGraw-Hill.

Fisher, R., & Ury, W. (1981). *Getting To Yes: Negotiating Agreement Without Giving In.* Boston: Houghton Mifflin.

Folger, J. P., Poole, M. S., & Stutman, R. K. (1993). *Working Through Conflict: Strategies for Relationships, Groups, and Organizations* (2nd ed.). New York: Harper Collins.

Fraser, N. M., & Hipel, K. W. (1981). Computer assistance in labor-management negotiations. *Interfaces, 11,* 22–29.

Goldhaber, G. M. (1993). *Organizational Communication* (6th ed.). Dubuque, Iowa: Brown & Benchmark.

Hall, J. (1969). *Conflict Management Survey: A Survey of One's Characteristic Reaction To and Handling of Conflicts Between Himself and Others.* Monroe, Tex.: Telemetrics International.

Hawes, L. C., & Smith, D. (1973). A critique of assumptions underlying the study of communication in conflict. *Quarterly Journal of Speech, 59,* 423–435.

Hellriegel, D., Slocum, J. W., Jr., & Woodman, R. W. (1989). *Organizational Behavior* (5th ed.). St. Paul, Minn.: West Publishing.

Hersey, P., & Blanchard, K. H. (1993). *Management of Organizational Behavior: Utilizing Human Resources* (6th ed.). Englewood Cliffs, N.J.: Prentice-Hall.

Hocker, J. L., & Wilmot, W. W. (1991). *Interpersonal Conflict* (3rd ed.). Dubuque, Iowa: William C. Brown Communications.

Hocker, J. L., & Wilmot, W. W. (1995). *Interpersonal conflict* (4th ed.). Dubuque, Iowa: William C. Brown Communications.

James, K., Chen, J., & Goldberg, C. (1992). Organizational conflict and individual creativity. *Journal of Applied Social Psychology, 22,* 545–566.

Jarke, M., Jelassi, M. T., & Shakun, M. F. (1987). MEDIATOR: Towards a negotiation support system. *European Journal of Operational Research, 31,* 314–334.

Jones, E. H. (1988). Analytical mediation: An empirical examination of the effects of computer support for different levels of conflict in two-party negotiations. Unpublished dissertation, Indiana University. *Dissertation Abstracts International, 49,* 2849A.

Jurma, W. E., & Powell, M. L. (1994). Perceived gender roles of managers and effective conflict management. *Psychological Reports, 74,* 104–106.

Katz, N. H., & Lawyer, J. W. (1992). *Communication and Conflict Resolution Skills.* Dubuque, Iowa: Kendall/Hunt.

Knapp, M. L., Putnam, L. L., & Davis, L. J. (1988). Measuring interpersonal conflict in organizations: Where do we go from here? *Management Communication Quarterly, 1,* 414–429.

Kruse, A. (1995). Third-party roles in conflict management. *Training & Development, 49*(5), 74–76.

Luthans, F., Rosenkrantz, S. A., & Hennessey, H. W. (1985). What do successful managers really do? An observation study of managerial activities. *Journal of Applied Behavioral Science, 21,* 255–270.

Miranda, S. M., & Bostrom, R. P. (1994). The impact of group support systems on group conflict and conflict management. *Journal of Management Information Systems, 10*(3), 63–95.

Morley, I. E., & Stephenson, G. (1977). *The Social Psychology of Bargaining.* London: George Allen & Unwin.

Mumpower, J., Schuman, S., & Zumbolo, A. (1986). *Analytical Mediation: An Application in Collective Bargaining.* Unpublished paper, SUNY-Albany, Rockefeller College of Public Affairs and Policy.

Napier, R. W., & Gershenfeld, M. K. (1985). *Groups: Theory and Experience.* Boston: Houghton Mifflin.

Neilsen, E. (1972). Understanding and managing intergroup conflict. In J. Lorsch & P. Lawrence (eds.), *Managing Group and Intergroup Relations* (pp. 46–66). Homewood, Ill.: Richard D. Irwin.

Nicotera, A. M. (1993). Beyond two dimensions: A grounded theory model of conflict-handling behavior. *Management Communication Quarterly, 6,* 282–306.

Nyhart, J. D., & Samarasan, D. K. (1989). The elements of negotiation management: Using computers to help resolve conflict. *Negotiation Journal, 5,* 43–62.

Pinkley, R. L. (1990). Dimensions of conflict frame: Disputant interpretations of conflict. *Journal of Applied Psychology, 75,* 117–126.

Pinkley, R. L., & Northcraft, G. B. (1994). Conflict frames of reference: Implications for dispute processes and outcomes. *Academy of Management Journal, 37,* 193–205.

Pondy, L. R. (1967). Organizational conflict: Concepts and models. *Administrative Science Quarterly, 12,* 296–320.

Poole, M. S., & DeSanctis, G. (1990). Understanding the use of group decision support systems: The theory of adaptive structuration. In J. Fulk & C. Steinfield (eds.), *Organizations and Communication Technology* (pp. 175–195). Newbury Park, Calif.: Sage.

Poole, M. S., Shannon, D. L., & DeSanctis, G. (1992). Communication media and negotiation processes. In L. L. Putnam & M. E. Roloff (eds.), *Communication and Negotiation* (pp. 46–66). Newbury Park, Calif.: Sage.

Poole, M. S., Zappa, J., DeSanctis, G., Shannon, D. L., & Dickson, G. (1990, August). *A Theory and Design for Negotiation Support Systems.* Paper presented at the meeting of the Academy of Management, San Francisco, Calif.

Putnam, L. L. (1986). Conflict in group decision-making. In R. Y. Hirokawa & M. S. Poole (eds.), *Communication and Group Decision-Making* (pp. 175–196). Newbury Park, Calif.: Sage.

Putnam, L. L., & Poole, M. S. (1987). Conflict and negotiation. In F. M. Jablin, L. L. Putnam, K. H. Roberts, & L. W. Porter (eds.), *Handbook of Organizational Communication* (pp. 549–599). Newbury Park, Calif.: Sage.

Putnam, L. L., & Wilson, C. (1982). Communicative strategies in organizational conflict: Reliability and validity of a measurement scale. In M. Burgoon (ed.), *Communication Yearbook 6* (pp. 629–652). Newbury Park, Calif.: Sage Publications.

Rahim, M. A. (1983). A measure of styles of handling interpersonal conflict. *Academy of Management Journal, 26,* 368–376.

Rahim, M. A. (1985). A strategy for managing conflict in complex organizations. *Human Relations, 38,* 81–89.

Rosenfeld, L. B. (1973). *Human Interaction in the Small Group Setting.* Columbus, Ohio: Charles Merrill.

Rothstein, R. L. (1979). *Global Bargaining: UNCTAD and the Quest for a New International Economic Order.* Princeton: Princeton University Press.

Rubin, J. Z. (1994). Models of conflict management. *Journal of Social Issues, 50,* 33–45.

Sainfort, F., Gustafson, D. H., & Bosworth, L. K. (1987). *Experimental Evaluation of a Computer Based Conflict Resolution Program.* Paper presented at TIMS/ORSA Joint Meeting, New Orleans, La.

Schwenk, C. R. (1990). Conflict in organizational decision making: An exploratory study of its effects in for-profit and not-for-profit organizations. *Management Science, 36,* 436–448.

Sebenius, J. K. (1981). The computer as mediator: Law of the sea and beyond. *Journal of Public Analysis and Management, 1,* 77–95.

Shannon, D. L. (1992). *Time pressure and negotiation support: A test of a negotiation support system using a complex labor-management negotiation.* Unpublished dissertation, University of Minnesota.

Shannon, D. L. (1993, Nov.). *Communication Based Negotiation Support Systems: Does Negotiation Support Structure Make a Difference?* Paper presented at the meeting of the Speech Communication Association, Miami Beach, Fla.

Short, J., Williams, E., & Christie, B. (1976). *The Social Psychology of Telecommunication.* New York: John Wiley.

Sillars, A. L., Coletti, S. F., Parry, D., & Rogers, M. A. (1982). Coding verbal conflict tactics: Nonverbal and perceptual correlates of the "avoidance-distributive-integrative" distinction. *Human Communication Research, 9,* 83–95.

Susskind, L., & Cruikshank, J. (1987). *Breaking the Impasse: Consensual Approaches to Resolve Public Disputes.* New York: Basic Books.

Sycara, K. (1991). Problem restructuring in negotiation. *Management Science, 37,* 1248–1268.

Thomas, K. W. (1976). Conflict and conflict management. In M. Dunnette (ed.), *Handbook of Industrial and Organizational Psychology* (pp. 889–936). Chicago: Rand McNally.

Thomas, K. W. (1988). The conflict handling modes: Toward more precise theory. *Management Communication Quarterly, 1,* 430–436.

Thomas, K. W. (1990). Conflict and negotiation processes in organizations. In M. D. Dunnette & L. M. Hough (eds.), *Handbook of Industrial and Organizational Psychology* (2nd ed.) (pp. 651–717). Palo Alto, Calif.: Consulting Psychologists Press.

Thomas, K. W., & Schmidt, W. H. (1976). A survey of managerial interests with respect to conflict. *Academy of Management Journal, 19,* 315–318.

Tjosvold, D., Dann, V., & Wong, C. (1992). Managing conflict between departments to serve customers. *Human Relations, 45,* 1035–1054.

Van de Ven, A. H., Emmett, D., & Koenig, R. (1980). Frameworks for interorganizational analysis. In A. R. Negandhi (ed.), *Interorganizational Theory* (pp. 19–38). Kent, Ohio: Kent State University Press.

Wall, J. A., Jr., & Callister, R. R. (1995). Conflict and its management. *Journal of Management, 21,* 515–558.

Wall, V. D., Jr., & Nolan, L. L. (1987). Small group conflict: A look at equity, satisfaction, and styles of conflict management. *Small Group Behavior, 18,* 188–211.

Walton, R. E. (1987). *Managing Conflict: Interpersonal Dialogue and Third-Party Roles* (2nd ed.). Reading, Mass.: Addison-Wesley.

Weeks, G. D., & Chapanis, A. (1976). Cooperative versus conflictive problem-solving in three telecommunication modes. *Perceptual and Motor Skills, 42,* 879–917.

Wilmot, W. W. (1987). *Dyadic Communication* (3rd. ed). New York: McGraw-Hill.

Womack, D. F. (1988). A review of conflict instruments in organizational settings. *Management Communication Quarterly, 1,* 437–445.

RECOMMENDED READINGS

Fisher, R., & Ury, W. (1981). *Getting to Yes: Negotiating Agreement Without Giving In.* New York: Penguin Books.

Folger, J. P., Poole, M. S., & Stutman, R. K. (1992). *Working Through Conflict: Strategies for Relationships, Groups, and Organizations* (2nd ed.). New York: Harper Collins.

Hocker, J. L., & Wilmot, W. W. (1995). *Interpersonal Conflict* (4th ed.). Dubuque, Iowa: William C. Brown Communications.

Katz, N. H., & Lawyer, J. W. (1992). *Communication and Conflict Resolution Skills.* Dubuque, Iowa: Kendall/Hunt.

Thomas, K. W. (1990). Conflict and negotiation processes in organizations. In M. D. Dunnette & L. M. Hough (eds.), *Handbook of Industrial and Organizational Psychology* (2nd ed.) (pp. 651–717). Palo Alto, Calif.: Consulting Psychologists Press.

▶ 7

Persuasion In and By Organizations

JOHN PARRISH-SPROWL

How do we get the customer to buy our product? What is the best way to pitch the next customer? How do we get the employees to work overtime? How do we negotiate a more favorable contract? How can I get co-workers to do their teamwork? These are all questions in the minds of people involved in organizational persuasion. In a competitive world organizational members are constantly confronted with the need to persuade. Over the years communication researchers, teachers, and practitioners alike have been interested in trying to develop useful and creative answers to such questions. In this chapter we will explore some of the ways that persuasion in and by organizations has been analyzed and the implications for such analysis on practice. First the theoretical approaches will be overviewed; then a discussion of some of the various organizational persuasion situations follows.

Communication as a discipline finds its roots in the study of persuasion, and the organizational area is no exception. W. Charles Redding, considered by most to be the primary founder of the study of organizational communication as an area of study, tells a fascinating story of the need to teach public speaking to factory supervisors during World War II so that they could effectively train the wave of new employees who comprised the war time workforce (Redding, 1985). Rosie the Riveter, a character created to convince women that they should leave their homes and enter the factories, was the beginning of a process designed to persuade women that they were obligated to do these jobs and to do them in a particular way. From this point on, organizational communication would grow as an area of study, and persuasion would continue to be a central concern of these studies.

APPROACHES TO THE STUDY OF PERSUASION

During this century communication scholars have followed two broad approaches to the study of persuasion, rhetoric and social scientific. Both of these areas have generated a substantial body of theory and research on the practice of persuasion. Because of our overarching interest in persuasion, as well as other forms of communication, communication scholars tend to develop an interest in both areas of research, even if they primarily conduct their own investigations in one genre or the other. Thus, a brief overview of each tradition is necessary to understand the scope of organizational communication research focused on persuasion.

Rhetoric

Greeks from the ancient city state of Athens, particularly Aristotle, Plato, Isocrates, and Gorgias, have been extremely influential in the study of rhetoric right up to the present. In the book, *The Rhetoric,* Aristotle defines rhetoric as "the discovery of all of the available means of persuasion" (Aristotle, 1954, p. 3). From this we can see that the study and practice of rhetoric is directly concerned with the process of persuasion. In Greece and later Rome the noblemen had a certain freedom of speech. They understood that along with freedom of speech is the freedom to listen. Thus they were acutely aware of the importance of persuasive speaking. By Roman times, rhetoric was considered one of the seven liberal arts and all educated people studied the ways and means of rhetoric. Cicero and Quintilian were two particularly important Romans who wrote on the subject of rhetoric. Since those times rhetoric has not been treated with the same level of importance in the scholarly world. In modern times, however, rhetoric studies have blossomed and spread, perhaps due to the growth of free or relatively free speech societies along with the electronic media necessary to reach the broad population.

When a person is engaged in rhetorical acts we refer to them as a rhetor. Persuasion, when studied from a rhetorical perspective, may be understood as rhetors employing various rhetorical devices as the means of changing attitudes and opinions or gaining compliance to some request. While rhetorical devices may be defined in several different ways, one of the most common schema is derived from Aristotle. He suggests that rhetors may engage in communicative acts that employ the persuasive appeals of ethos, pathos, or logos (Aristotle, 1954). Ethos may be understood as the means by which one establishes credibility. As communicators we attempt to do this in a variety of ways. In a job interview for example, we try to develop a good resume detailing our experience, dress to suggest capability and competence, do background research so that we might both ask and answer questions thoroughly and thoughtfully, attempt fluency and poise, and use good manners and courtesy all in an effort to establish our credibility. Aristotle stated that ethos might well be the most important of the rhetorical areas and this may well be the case (Aristotle, 1954).

Pathos appeals are those directed to the emotions and emotional state of the audience. Such rhetorical efforts are intended to persuade a person by responding to felt needs and desires. For example, management has often used messages that are predicated on an employee's sense of loyalty and obligation to the company. By playing on a sense of guilt, fear, or honor, managers often try to convince employees that they should work beyond the call of duty to meet the needs of the organization, whatever the sacrifice of the worker. These types of persuasive appeals can exert a powerful influence in an organization that fosters a high degree of identification among the workers.

Logos is the type of appeal that engages some type of logically structured reasoning. It is in this rhetorical device that persuasion is comprised of arguments that are the use of sequenced premises, data, and consistency of thought. When attempting to persuade with logos, the rhetor will attempt to provide clear and effective reasoning supported by solid evidence. Thus, when a company does some marketing research to understand how consumers are responding to their commercials, they are seeking data that might be used as a basis for justifying the continuance of either the current series or possibly the development of a new advertising theme for their products.

We may think of these appeals as more thoughtful and/or intellectual, but not necessarily more effective in persuading others to change. While a person may think that he or she may be described as either logical or emotional, all attempts at persuasion contain to some degree each of the three types of appeal, and it is difficult to know what actually leads to attitude or behavioral change. Every persuasive situation contains some dimension of all three rhetorical devices, and remember, the art of rhetoric is the "discovery of all of the available means of persuasion" (Aristotle, 1954, p. 3). Therefore, every rhetor is responsible for choosing the best possible combination of appeals to persuade their target audience.

Roman rhetoricians extended the Greek model of rhetoric, taking it to a new level in the educational life of the Roman citizen. As one source put it, "The Greeks invented rhetoric but the Romans perfected it" (Golden, Berquist, & Coleman, 1983, p. 76). Because the rhetor is responsible for choosing which of the available means of persuasion to employ, Cicero and Quintilian were particularly interested in the qualities of the individual making the choices. Cicero felt that the rhetor should be highly knowledgeable about all things related to the subject at hand, and Quintilian added a concern for the moral and ethical character of the individual (Golden, Berquist, & Coleman, 1983). Taking the ideas together they present a case for competence as an orator being predicated on the qualities of a knowledgeable person possessing solid moral character. As Quintilian put it "no man (sic) can be an orator unless he is a good man (sic)" (Golden, Berquist, & Coleman, 1983, p. 77).

Contemporary rhetorical scholars are not as convinced that capable rhetoricians are necessarily of high moral character, but the issue is one of considerable importance in organizational persuasion. As will be discussed later in the chapter, the perceived ethos of the organization and its members plays a critical role in determinations of the effectiveness of persuasive efforts, especially in advertising, public relations, and sales. The important point that we learn from the Romans is that it is easier to establish credibility in a given situation if one is a knowledgeable person of good character generally. Put another way, an organization is better able to survive a given crisis if it makes an ongoing effort to be a good corporate citizen. The same may be said for individuals as well.

Rhetoric criticism is the study of different rhetoric situations to assess both the artistic qualities and effectiveness of the rhetoric act. Each organizational member, customer, and potential consumer are in some ways rhetoric critics, although their analysis is qualitatively different than the scholarly rhetoric critic, who may use more formal critical frameworks or theory in their assessments. As critics we analyze the persuasive messages that people present to us. In doing so we assess others and they in turn assess us. The Greeks and Romans provide us with useful frameworks to judge both the messages we are thinking of sending and the persuasive appeals made to us.

Although other approaches to rhetoric and rhetoric criticism exist, the Aristotelian model and its derivatives have probably been the most influential in Western thought. Such a model of persuasive communication is useful both for scholars and those engaged in the everyday analysis of what makes for effective persuasive efforts. The tradition of rhetoric studies of persuasion is the oldest in the discipline of communication and except for some interpretive and cultural theories, is different in its approach and design than that of the more contemporary social scientific theories.

At the end of World War II scholars from several disciplines, including communication, began to employ probability statistics in their research to develop models of persuasion and attitude change. Social science models began to grow in importance until they were the predominate form of persuasion studies. This dominance was challenged in the eighties and rhetoric studies regained some of their broad appeal, leaving both in the mainstream of thought for those interested in the study of persuasion. Thus we turn our attention to the social science approaches to understanding persuasion.

Social Science

Adolph Hitler's apparent success as a persuader, along with the development of electronic media, fueled increased interest among social scientists in persuasion. From the late forties through to the present thousands of studies have been conducted in an effort to better understand how persuasion works. Most social science research has focused specifically on the notion of attitude change. In other words, persuasion is considered to have occurred when the target of persuasive efforts has changed their attitude about a particular issue or subject. Because such investigations engage nominological scientific methods in the course of study, the definition of terms for research purposes has been an important point of scholarly debate (Kiesler, Collins, & Miller, 1969). While no universally accepted definition of attitude exists Fishbein and Ajzen (1975, p. 6) suggest that "most investigators would probably agree that attitude can be described as a learned predisposition to respond in a consistently favorable or unfavorable manner with respect to a given object."

Attitudes are formed, in large part, based on a person's beliefs, which may be defined as judgments about what is considered to be true. Put another way, when people accept a piece of data or information as representing a fact they incorporate it in their system of thought as a belief (Fishbein & Ajzen, 1975; Simons, 1986). Added to these two key concepts is the term values, which may be defined as the weighting or importance we place on particular attitudes or beliefs, similar to what Fishbein and Ajzen (1975) refer to as belief strength. When taken together, attitudes, beliefs, and values are at the core of most attitude change research. Researchers have attempted to develop theories that account for changes in our attitudes, beliefs, and values and thus create a scientific explanation for persuasion.

Of particular importance is a set of theories articulated early in this era with names like balance theory (Heider, 1958), congruity theory (Osgood & Tannenbaum, 1955) and the theory of cognitive dissonance (Festinger, 1957). This collection of theories launched many studies and continues to influence the thinking of many social scientists today. Basically, all three of these approaches are equilibrium models. This means that people naturally seek harmony in their thoughts and ideas. Thus if the choice to buy a product is inconsistent with a person's belief structure, that person will either change their beliefs or not buy the product. In this way individuals achieve balance or congruity, hence the names of the theories. Another way of approaching the same idea is to say that a person whose opinion is at odds with the choice they are asked to make experiences cognitive dissonance, and they will either change their attitude or make a choice which creates cognitive consonance.

Predicated on the assumption that people will make rational (logically consistent) choices when confronted with the right information, these models attempt to predict the direction of attitude and behavioral change in a persuasive situation. The following example is simple and leaves out a lot of possibilities, but it illustrates the basic thinking of these models. Imagine that a person is going into a dealership to look at cars, possibly to purchase one. However, the buyer believes that all sales people are dishonest and therefore they should not be trusted. When discussing the purchase of a car with the salesperson, our buyer wants to believe what is being said, but to believe creates dissonance because it is at odds with the belief that the seller is a liar. Our buyer will either not believe the sales pitch and not buy the car, or modify the belief that all sales people are liars so as to justify acceptance of the seller's message.

For several decades research based on equilibrium models dominated the efforts of social scientists to create explanations of attitude change. This is not to say that other models were not developed. Additional approaches of importance include McGuire's inoculation theory (McGuire, 1964, 1969), social judgment theory (Sherif & Sherif, 1967), social learning theory (Bandura, 1972), Ajzen and Fishbein's theory of reasoned action (Ajzen & Fishbein, 1980; Fishbein & Ajzen, 1975), and elaboration likelihood theory (Petty & Cacioppo, 1986). Ajzen and Fishbein's theory has been particularly influential in consumer behavior and advertising research and practice. In recent years elaboration likelihood theory has prompted much research and discussion. Due to their prominence these two theories merit further discussion.

Marketers of products and services, and politicians have used Ajzen and Fishbein's (1980) theory of reasoned action extensively for years. Many believe that this model of persuasion has been useful in assisting organizations in developing successful advertising and public relations campaigns. Basically the theory suggests that people deliberate on important decisions and make choices based on reasoned judgments. This idea is not unique to this theory. What sets Ajzen and Fishbein's approach apart from some other social science theories is that they not only take into consideration the attitudes but the beliefs and values of audiences as well. Simplified, they posit that behavioral intention (e.g., likelihood of purchase) is predictable if we account for, measure, and properly weight attitudes, beliefs, and values among the target audience. By assigning relative weights (levels of importance) to all three they claim that their model better predicts behavior than previous models. Thus marketing research teams are able to make a superior prognosis on the sales of a product using the formula derived from this theory of persuasion compared to those based on the equilibrium of attitudes alone. Because the model's complexity is difficult to illustrate with a brief example, the reader is encouraged to refer to the original sources. Suffice to say here that it is a theory with practical utility albeit one that requires special knowledge to employ.

Elaboration likelihood theory (Petty & Cacioppo, 1986) has spawned a substantial amount of research since its introduction. This approach to persuasion assumes that people do not carefully consider their choices in every situation. The theory suggests that sometimes people are thoughtful and careful in their responses to persuasive messages and sometimes not. The former is referred to as the central route to attitude formation and the latter is the peripheral route. While some claim that the simultaneous processing of messages using both central and peripheral routes is possible, recent research does not confirm this position (Booth-Butterfield et al., 1994). This research suggests that persuaders should consider the likely route that audience members might take in developing their persuasive strategies.

Strategies focused on the central route should elaborate the reasons for agreeing with the persuader by providing several sound arguments along with good information in the attempt to persuade. Sales agents, for example, often engage in this approach. Persuasion along the peripheral route, however, requires much less argument elaboration because it is a situation in which the persuadee is not thinking much about the issues involved anyway. An attractive package, while adding little to the utility of a product, might be sufficiently persuasive when a consumer is using peripheral processing in their purchase decision. Whether a particular individual will use central or peripheral processing is not always easy to discern. For example, Snyder and DeBono (1985, 1989) conducted research which found that when people evaluated consumer products they sometimes considered carefully what the product might do for their image with others and sometimes they did not. This is why firms will often employ strategies focused on both, even though, as the research discussed above suggests, people may not use duo routes simultaneously.

Another line of research by social scientists that focuses on persuasion is a series of investigations into communicative actions known as compliance-gaining strategies. This research was limited to a few studies primarily designed to discover the possible range of strategies one might use until the eighties, when such investigations began to proliferate (Levine & Boster, 1993). Compliance-gaining strategies are the ways in which a persuader attempts to convince the target person(s) to engage in an action they otherwise might not have on their own. Sales agents attempt to gain the compliance of customers as do supervisors of workers. Strategies include such messages as promises, threats, deceit, and pregiving. To illustrate, a supervisor might convince a worker to do an extra good job by using a strategy that involves promising a raise, or a teacher might get students to study more if they employ a strategy that threatens failure of the course.

Some social scientists believe that a good method for understanding human behavior in everyday interactions is to watch people play games designed to simulate real life behaviors (Norton, 1995). These studies are known as game theoretical research. Several different games have been developed over time in an attempt to create a laboratory experience that may give social scientists insight into the communicative choices of people in various situations. The most often used of these games is known as the prisoner's dilemma. This game places two individuals or groups in opposition to each other so that their respective choices affect not only their own future but that of the other as well. This game has been used to examine conflict patterns, trust, and competitiveness among other variables.

The popularity of game theoretical research ebbs and flows over time. Currently, especially in economics, game theory is enjoying unprecedented popularity (Norton, 1995). Many scholars like the studies because they allow the observation of communicative behavior in a controlled setting. Others reject such investigations because they are artificial and may involve actions which may occur only in laboratory games, not in everyday conversation. In other words, many believe that the behavior people exhibit in research settings is not necessarily the same as you could expect to find in real life situations. For example, how one negotiates when playing a game of no real consequence may be completely different than when that same person sits down to negotiate a labor contract. We have reason to believe that people are able to take the importance of the situation into account when making decisions about how to act.

Social scientists, including communication researchers, have conducted a substantial number of studies that observe or analyze human action removed from the real life situations we are attempting to understand. Drawing conclusions about negotiation behavior from observing college undergraduates playing a game is a classic example of this phenomenon. Many criticize the body of scientific findings resulting from the above studies for creating an overly simplistic and therefore inaccurate picture of human communication. These critics believe that to capture the complexity of daily human action you must study people engaged in their natural routines. Thus, to learn about negotiation, these scholars would like to observe actual labor or sales negotiations to develop our knowledge of this type of communication behavior. This concern has led many researchers to pursue an alternative approach to the study of persuasion, especially in organizations. In these investigations, the scientist is a close observer, sometimes even a participant observer, in the setting under study. Rather than doing research under the classic guise of the objective scientist, the investigator is concerned with capturing interaction in as natural a state as possible. Such research is often labeled interpretive or interpretive/critical studies.

Since the early 1980s interpretive studies have grown increasingly more common, particularly in organizational research. Linda Putnam and Michael Pacanowsky (1983) edited a particularly useful, as well as influential, book in this area. The book discusses theory and provides examples of interpretive organizational studies. Often, persuasion is not the specific focus of study although persuasive situations are an important component of the investigation. This is because interpretive scholars generally aim to capture a more wholistic understanding of the context rather than to focus specifically on persuasion. For example, in Pacanowsky's study titled "A Small Town Cop: Communication In, Out, and About a Crisis" (1983) several persuasive issues and situations are presented in his story about being a police officer in a small town, but the issue of persuasion is not directly the concern of the research. In other words, his research is trying to convey a broad interpretation of the interactions that might comprise a small town cop, including but not limited to those we might consider persuasion.

Unfortunately, while persuasion is often a prominent component of interpretative studies, due the nature of such work it is difficult to isolate specific lines of research that focus upon persuasion. Even Jhally's work on advertising (1987), to be discussed further later in the chapter, has a much broader focus than persuasion, even though it is a prominent feature of the work. This difficulty, however, also provides us with an important understanding about persuasion in organizations—that it is often embedded in interactions that include myriad communication issues. Interpretative studies help us to understand persuasion as an aspect of the complexity of everyday conversation rather than as something we can do every now and then, isolated from other activities. For example, when a manager is trying to explain a new work process to employees, we can understand this as an act of training, an informative speech, education, an example of enactment of the managerial role, or an act of persuasion. All are useful perspectives to take on this important situation, making analysis more complex for researchers and participants alike.

As we can see, communication studies have a rich tradition that captures a long history and a wide array of approaches to the study of persuasion. All of these modes of inquiry have been used to examine persuasion in organizations. While interpretative studies lead us to realize that persuasion is pervasive in organizational life, some communication practices that are historically considered to be persuasive in nature will be the focus of attention in this chapter. We will first turn our attention to those organizational practices that involve persuasion with members outside of the organization. These include advertising, public relations, and sales. Next we will turn our attention to internal processes. Because so many organizations are undergoing significant structural changes we will explore the persuasive processes associated with labor relations and organizational change. Finally, we will turn our attention to two important topics that play an important role in both persuasion and organizations—diversity and globalization.

ADVERTISING

Organizations of all types engage in some form of advertising. Sometimes the audience is large, sometimes quite small. For example, producers of consumer products may advertise around the world as Coca Cola does, or a small supplier firm may advertise to a few companies in a specific industry, as many electronic component makers do. Advertisements in the United States appear almost everywhere one looks, on television, radio, magazines, newspapers, books, roadside billboards, regular mail, e-mail, flyers hung around school and the neighborhood, signs in front of businesses, and even public rest rooms. Most people in the United States are exposed to thousands of ads every year of their life. All of these ads are efforts in organizational persuasion aimed at changing or reinforcing a consumer's actions.

Advertisers use a variety of strategies in an attempt to make their persuasive efforts successful. One important concern is to identify and define the target audience (Kotler, 1986). As in all persuasive situations, organizations want to know as much about the audience as is possible. Thus market researchers do surveys, conduct focus groups, and observe consumers to learn all they can. Furthermore, organizations try to know when to advertise, where, in what style, and how often they should repeat the message to create maximum response in the marketplace.

Along with the process of identifying the audience, is the task of designing the message to be conveyed by the advertisement (Wells, Burnett, & Moriarty, 1992). Some treat this as an art form with no rules, while others rely heavily on social science research to assist them in ad development. Not only are the designers concerned with the words of the message but the colors, pictures, and size of the ad as well. For example, the stock brokerage firm Dean Witter uses an antique film style including black and white in their ad, which is designed to suggest that the actor in the ad is really Dean Witter talking in a film clip from the first part of the twentieth century. The intent is to suggest a tradition of concern for each investor, which dates back to a more congenial, less impersonal era. The ad was so effective in design that many who watched it believed the film clip to be authentic.

From the organization's perspective, selling products is the primary, if not the only purpose, of advertising. This statement deserves some clarification. Aside from product advertisements, organizations may also present corporate image and issues advertising. The former consists of commercials designed to enhance the reputation of the organization. The latter includes advertisements that aim to persuade the audience to take a position on an important issue related to the industry of the firm sponsoring the ad. Many authors, as do I, consider these ads to be a form of public relations and as such they will be dealt with in the next section. By exempting these type of ads from the discussion we can state that ads are intended to convince people to buy products and services.

As persuasion however, these messages play a much greater role in society. In recent years several communication researchers have focused on the broader societal implications of advertising's persuasive impact (Jhally, 1987; Leiss, Kline, & Jhally, 1986; Schudson, 1984). At the heart of these investigations is a focus on the role of advertising in the historical development of a consumer culture in the United States. Schudson (1984) observes that when Alexis de Tocqueville visited the United States in the middle of the nineteenth century, materialism was an emerging trend. By 1900 however, advertising had become an established and growing business institution along with a growing influence of consumerism in American culture. By the end of the twentieth century, the United States has become deeply materialistic and not incoincidentally advertising has become a ubiquitous multibillion dollar industry. In terms of historical development, consumerism and advertising have grown in tandem, making a compelling argument that advertising has been instrumental in creating our current highly materialistic culture.

Organizations often argue that advertising is not the reason for cultural developments but rather a reflection of historical trends resulting from other causes. In other words, organizations only promote products and services that people want, and thus advertising only responds to rather than shapes the culture as it evolves. Schudson (1984), however, offers four reasons why advertising has played a part in persuading citizens to pursue consumerism as a way of life. Briefly, his arguments are as follows:

> *First, marketers do not actually seek to discover what consumers "want" but what consumers want from among commercially viable choices (p. 235).*
>
> *Second, marketers do not listen to all people equally (p. 236).*
>
> *Third, marketers assume that since "good advertising kills a bad product," they can do little harm; people will only buy what they find satisfying. This works . . . only if people have enough information available to know what the range of possibilities is and how to purchase wisely (p. 237).*
>
> *Finally . . . responding to discovered, felt needs among consumers is an innocuous activity . . . Obviously, a conscientious marketer would want to circumscribe such a view to say that some goods are harmful and should not be sold or promoted even if people want them (p. 237).*

He adds to this last argument by pointing out that even when a good is acceptable that advertising reinforces the desirability of purchasing and using the product.

Therefore, according to Schudson, advertising not only promotes products but it promotes a consumerist lifestyle as well.

Leiss and colleagues (1986) take Schudson's position even further. They argue that

> *Regarded individually and superficially, advertisements promote goods and services. Looked at in depth and as a whole, the ways in which messages are presented in advertising reach deeply into our most serious concerns: interpersonal and family relations, the sense of happiness and contentment, sex roles and stereotyping, the uses of affluence, the fading of older cultural traditions, influences on younger generations, the role of business in society, persuasion and personal autonomy, and many others. (p. 3)*

According to these researchers, while organizations on the surface may be simply selling goods and services, the results of advertising are much more far-reaching. In persuading us to purchase the various products and services for sale in the marketplace, organizations do much more than sell, they affect every aspect of our lives right down to our self esteem.

Advertisements for women's cosmetics, clothing, and other beauty products provide a clear example of this phenomenon. From an early age women pursue these ads for ideas that might assist them in improving their appearance. Organizations create a steady stream of both perennial and new products that are supposed to help women develop an attractive look. The content of many of these ads suggests what constitutes a desirable state of appearance. However, the look conveyed is one that virtually no woman can reasonably achieve. This is particularly so for women over the age of 25. Consequently, in the name of creating a socially acceptable appearance, many women develop serious health and esteem problems, including eating disorders, depression, and a sense of worthlessness (Wood, 1994). Often, the failure to achieve the desired results with one product leads to the purchase of yet another product such that the conclusion drawn by the consumer is not one that questions the goal as presented by the advertiser but one that is within the range of commercially viable choices. Thus as Schudson (1984) and Leiss and colleagues (1986) suggest, our cultural standards are as likely to emanate from advertising as advertising is to arise from our culture.

Organizations operating in a market economy generally engage in advertising not only to survive, but prosper. We must recognize, however, that such persuasive efforts have a greater effect than to simply inform us about the products and services that are available for purchase. Ads not only persuade us to purchase a particular brand or style, they lead us to choose important dimensions of our lifestyle as well. Perhaps the most important aspect of lifestyle choice is simply that being a constant consumer is a desirable way of life. While many question the value of a consumer culture, our collective actions suggest that as a nation we are persuaded that materialism is good. Organizations depend on our faith in materialism and they will continue to persuade us to purchase goods and services as often as possible. As employees of these organizations we urge others to support the market for our products and services. As consumers, however, we must be thoughtful about our response to advertising. Not only in making the best choice among available products, but in the choice to purchase the product at all.

PUBLIC RELATIONS

Closely related to advertising is another form of external organizational communication, public relations. In essence, public relations consists of an ongoing communication effort to persuade various constituencies that the organization is a desirable community member. Put another way, "Public relations is the use of information to influence public opinion" (Dilenschneider & Forrestal, 1987, p. 5). These constituencies, or publics, may include the general population, legislators, industry members, professional groups, interest groups, or groups of customers. In each case, the organization is attempting to create a positive reputation and environment to ensure the smoothest possible operation. Public relations often involves an array of strategies and potentially uses all mediums of communication. For example, an organization may develop image ads or issues advertisements as discussed above. Also, sponsorship of amateur sporting events such as the Olympics, professional sporting events, or public broadcasting programming may be used. Aside from the use of media, organizations may use more personal forms of public relations including lobbying of legislators, public speeches by corporate leaders, involvement in community groups by executives, and appearances at events such as fairs or conferences. Companies may use any or all of these strategies plus others that they may invent to suit their particular circumstances. The amount of public relations effort depends on the needs of the particular organization.

Some organizations invest very little in public relations. One reason for this may be that the publics that affect the organization may be small and well-defined, allowing employees to do public relations work daily in an interpersonal manner. For example, a small neighborhood business may be able to develop its reputation among the members of the community quite easily with only small expenditures of money. This may include donating money to local charities or sponsoring a little league team. These efforts are meant to create a positive image of the organization as a community member; however, the effectiveness depends greatly on the personal relations of the organizational members and the community. No matter how positive the public relations effort might be, when people know the organizational members they make judgments based on their overall attitude towards the organization not simply on a few acts. In other words, without ethos, the rhetorical act is not likely to be believed as genuine.

Another example of a situation demanding little investment in public relations is that of a small supplier firm with one or two customers. In the auto and electronic industries thousands of such organizations exist. While these firms need to create goodwill in a general sense, they mostly need to focus on cultivating a positive relationship with their customers. This is not to say that they do not need a good public image, just that the situation demands a more limited effort. Such firms do need a good reputation as an employer so that they may attract quality employees. They need a positive relationship with local government authorities who provide security and other services along with zoning and other regulations that affect business. Just as with the neighborhood business, such organizations may only need focused, local efforts in public relations.

Larger organizations, particularly those who operate in a national or international arena, often engage in a much more extensive public relations effort. Many organizations, either individually or bound together with other members of their industry, lobby policy makers in an ongoing effort to create a positive environment for their interests. This occurs at the national, state, and local levels of government. Lobbying by these so-called special interests is important because competing special interest groups are doing the same thing. Unfortunately, this often leads to public policy that does not serve a majority of the public well, but rather the interests of a few at the expense of the many. Some claim that price supports for tobacco growers is an example of such a policy. Only a few people benefit from this expenditure but all pay at least some of the cost stemming from the effects of tobacco usage. Consequently, many believe this to be a policy that reflects public relations efforts not public welfare needs.

When organizations want to develop positive relations with publics other than legislators they may engage in a variety of additional techniques. These include both house organs, which are internal publications, and house ads, which are ads that an organization develops for its own publication, such as an advertisement for programming in a local cable guide produced by the cable company. Perhaps more common is the public service announcement (PSA), which is similar to an ad but is distinguished by who is doing the announcing. PSAs are usually designed to serve charities or nonprofits such as the United Way or your local family service agency. Corporate advertising, designed not to sell products but rather to enhance the image of the organization, is often used as part of an ongoing public relations effort.

Public relations efforts often include live presentations such as speakers or staged events. Probably the most recognizable is the corporate sponsorship of a sporting event such as the Virginia Slims tennis tournament. Organizations will use these and any other techniques deemed appropriate to develop their standing as a community citizen. Just as is true for individuals, most leaders are aware that a good organizational reputation takes a long time to build and only one disaster to destroy.

Organizations who make a genuine attempt to develop quality public relations discover real value in their efforts when disaster strikes. Since 1950 several corporate crises have occurred that have tested the ethos of the organization involved. Particularly notable events include the Tylenol tampering case involving Johnson and

Johnson, the gas leak in Bhopal, India, involving Union Carbide, and the wreck of the Exxon Valdez. In each case public relations experts attempted to manage the crisis so that damage in terms of both cost and organizational reputation was minimized. Many believe that Johnson and Johnson was highly successful in their crisis management whereas Exxon was considerably less so. A major difference between the two situations was Johnson and Johnson's ability to persuade the public that it was acting responsibly and in the public interest and Exxon' s failure to achieve the same result.

Johnson and Johnson launched a rhetorical strategy clearly designed to be proactive and pro-consumer. Briefly, the situation developed when someone died from ingesting Tylenol that was laced with poison. Initially, nobody knew who was responsible for the tampering but rather than wait to see if it was an internal problem, Johnson and Johnson withdrew all of the product from store shelves nationwide and put their chief executive officer on the air to reassure the public that they would make every effort to prevent further problems. Across the nation response to the public relations effort was positive, and Johnson and Johnson was able to recover and continue to dominate the aspirin-free pain reliever market.

Exxon, in contrast, was slow to react, and when they did it was much more defensive and reflected little concern for the public interest. In their situation an oil tanker named the Exxon Valdez wrecked in Prince William Sound, Alaska, and spilled oil over a substantial area. By attempting to defend the organization and absolve themselves of primary responsibility, they took a rhetorical position that placed them in opposition to the public interest. This resulted in significant organizational image problems for Exxon, creating a negative persona that continues to haunt them years after the incident. Further, Exxon discovered that once credibility or ethos has been damaged it is difficult to recover. Thus, the lesson to be learned from these two cases is that effective public relations is well understood as a rhetorical act. Those who discover all of the available means of persuasion will be more effective than those who do not.

PERSONAL SALES

Perhaps no other job is considered more specifically persuasive than a personal sales representative. While advertising almost exclusively uses one of the mass media, and public relations may be a blend of media and face-to-face contact, personal sales tends to be at the other end of the external communication continuum in that it is primarily an interpersonal activity. Often sales positions are referred to as boundary roles because they reside at the interface between the organization and its external customers (Miller, 1995). For this reason many customers think of the sales representative as the embodiment of the organization with whom they are doing business. Thus personal sales is a unique position in organizational life, one that requires excellent relational, organizational, and persuasive skills.

Because sales personnel are in such a focal position a substantial number of books, articles, and stories have been written about the profession. Perhaps the most famous is the Tennessee Williams play *Death of a Salesman.* In this drama sales people are portrayed in an unflattering way, which is consistent with how many feel about the profession. In popular culture a common saying to characterize a person as a liar is to compare them to a used car salesperson. Yet despite the negativity surrounding sales, many hard working honest people are in sales at some point in their career. Possibly because of the general mistrust, we should be particularly impressed with the persuasive talents of successful sales agents. Although a sales position requires a person to complete many different tasks, first and foremost in importance is the act of persuading customers to purchase goods or services.

The importance of sales has resulted in a constant stream of research intended to uncover the keys to successful performance. Much of this has been reports and observations from people who have been successful in sales themselves (Parrish-Sprowl, Carveth, & Senk, 1994). Taken as a whole this group of writings is inconsistent in its advice to the would-be successful sales representative. It is difficult to draw a conclusion as to how one may become a talented seller when the advice covers the broad spectrum of human action. This is most likely because the books and articles reflect what was successful for particular individuals in their own situation, which may not be reflective of what might work in any other circumstance. These accounts are often interesting as well as inspirational, but they do not always give meaningful guidance to the person seeking to understand the persuasive process in sales.

In contrast, social scientists have conducted several investigations seeking to uncover the personal traits an individual might possess that are associated with successful sales (Parrish-Sprowl, Carveth, & Senk, 1994). Despite a number of studies researchers have been unable to identify a set of traits that consistently associate with successful sales. Many scholars believe that this is a function of the interactional nature of sales talk and that examining the traits of the sales agent is a poor approach to gain insight into the persuasive process (Soldow & Penn Thomas, 1984; Spiro & Perreault, 1979; Sprowl, 1985). Furthermore, sales situations are so different from industry to industry that it is not likely that any one set of traits is functional across all types of business.

More recent research in communication has focused on the talk itself for clues into the persuasive dynamic. Investigations into the use of compliance-gaining strategies by sales people suggest that a positive approach as well as image may be important in successful sales (Parrish-Sprowl, Carveth, & Senk, 1994; Parrish-Sprowl, & Senk, 1986). In other words, sales agents who use those strategies that create a positive atmosphere, relationship, and sense of self among the individuals involved are more likely to create successful sales records. It is important to remember that to achieve maximum effectiveness positive strategies must be perceived as genuine rather than fake. While this may seem obvious, a great number of sales representatives do not engage in such strategies for reasons that only they understand.

From a rhetorical perspective we are able to develop additional insight into the construction of persuasive messages in sales. First is the establishment of ethos. We expect sales agents to know their products and their market. People probably have more faith in a sales agent who is familiar not only with their own products but with competing brands as well. This may be especially so if the customer does not have sufficient information to make an unassisted choice. In addition, it is probably easier to achieve a positive approach if sales representatives feels comfortable in their product knowledge because they have a greater capacity to focus on the development of the sales relationship. In addition to knowledge of the product, awareness of the customer's wants and needs plays a valuable role in establishing credibility. Just as with advertising, the sales representative needs to take the time to learn about the customer. While we often spend a substantial amount of money to understand the market for advertising purposes, sales agents often do not correspondingly spend the time necessary to discover the desires of the customer in front of them.

Pathos is important as well. Customers need to feel the positive tone that the salesperson is working to establish. A good emotional climate is highly contextual, which is to say that it is difficult to establish general rules guiding the construction of such an environment. Probably a genuine smile along with a real liking for people is as close as we might get to a general axiom. Even these might not be enough in some situations or even appropriate in others. The best strategy may simply be to keep trying until the relationship feels comfortable. For example, some sales representatives will work with a potential client for months or even years until they finally succeed in selling the prospect.

Providing customers with good reasons to purchase a product may be critical. This may be through direct persuasion, or through supplying the information they need to convince themselves, as is suggested by elaboration likelihood theory. Many salespeople have given reasons to buy to a customer only to hear their words out of the customer's mouth at a later time. Sometimes people like to feel that they were not persuaded, that they take in all of the information and make up their own minds as independent thinkers. Thus the sales agent must give them the arguments necessary for them to decide to buy. Again, as with establishing ethos, listening to the customer describe their wants and needs provides much of the information necessary for the salesperson to construct the reasoning that ultimately persuades.

External organizational communication, in the forms of advertising, public relations, and personal sales, involves persuasion. Both the rhetorical and social science traditions in the field of communication give us insight into how these processes work, how we might seek to be effective, and what the broader societal implications of these messages might be. Scholars and practitioners alike will probably never be satisfied with the current state of knowledge we have about these persuasive forms because the world is ever-changing and new understandings are always needed. As will be discussed later, new technologies, a greater recognition of diversity, and globalization are examples of trends that may alter what we consider to be conventional wisdom or common sense. In addition, the same may also be said of internal organizational communication.

LABOR NEGOTIATIONS

Historically, the term labor negotiations has referred most often to management–union contract bargaining. The negotiations for a labor contract between the management of General Motors and the United Auto Workers is an example of such a situation. While some aspects of labor negotiations are external, because they involve the work within the company itself, they may be considered internal communication. The main reason for viewing them as internal is that the rules and regulations that the respective parties agree to in the contract will have their greatest impact on the day-to-day work life of each member of the organization. Although the number of workers represented by union contracts has declined in recent years, we still have a substantial number of U.S. workers either in, or working with, labor unions, making such contracts an important aspect of organizational communication. While many people think of factory workers as the only union members, many office workers, police, firefighters, health care workers, and university professors belong to unions as well. Thus the persuasion which occurs in contract bargaining directly affects the lives of millions of people.

Bargaining may be defined as "a process whereby two or more parties attempt to settle what each shall give and take or perform and receive" (Putnam & Jones, 1982, p. 262–263). Although wages often receive the most headlines, just about every aspect of worksite procedure is potentially a bargaining issue. This may include safety factors, job descriptions, and contingency plans for financially difficult times. The intent is to give the worker, through collective action, a voice in the decisions concerning organizational rules and regulations. This does not necessarily equalize the power gap in the relationship, but often brings the sides closer together in this regard. While some believe that unions have become too powerful in certain situations, others believe that unions are a response to management exercising too much power (Holley & Jennings, 1980). In either case, the hope is that persuasion at the bargaining table will be effective in creating a fair and equitable work environment in which both the company and the workers may profit from the venture.

When the two parties enter into labor negotiations each side usually has some notion of what they consider to be an acceptable agreement. Within these boundaries lies the range of possible settlements (Holley & Jennings, 1980). Research supports the position that the greater your ability to predict at what point the other side will maximally settle, the more likely you are to achieve an agreement favorable to your side (Donohue, 1981). This suggests that while power in the management union relationship may be inherently unequal, favoring management, that union negotiators can enhance their position by greater understanding and execution of the communication skills in bargaining situations. Management on the other hand, has an incentive to protect shareholder value, thus they need to understand the persuasive process in negotiation as well.

Reiches and Harral (1974) developed a model of the negotiation process that focuses on arguments as the key to understanding the entire process. Their framework grows out of the their "concern for a communication-centered theory of negotiation derived from a recognition that negotiation models often ignore interaction of the negotiators and instead focus on a determination of outcome" (p. 36). They advance the perspective that negotiation is best understood as argumentation. Each participant presents a set of arguments that "can increase the number of choices available to his [*sic*] opponent, can increase the uncertainty about some choices, and can foster the awareness that any range of alternative outcomes presents a more desirable solution than no agreement at all" (p. 37). As Aristotle (1954) suggested, it is up to the negotiators to construct arguments that embody the available means of persuasion.

Threats, promises, and thromises (a combination of threats and promises) are all tactics that one may employ to advance your position at the bargaining table (Murdock, Bradac, & Bowers, 1984). With each, the effect is enhanced if the other side perceives that you have high levels of ethos. For example, a union threatening a strike action that the other person knows is not likely because the membership will not walk out, is an ineffective tactic. Furthermore, it is important to construct the arguments supporting the threats, promises, and thromises in a compelling manner. To illustrate, imagine the difference between someone simply claiming that they know you can afford to give raises versus a person who can demonstrate the claim with financial data. All of this implies that you will be more successful if you have done your homework. In other words, it is difficult to create a compelling argument without good evidence. It is also difficult to attack your opponent's argument without good evidence. Thus, just as we found with advertising, public relations, and sales, doing background research and listening to the other person are critical keys to effective persuasion.

ORGANIZATIONAL INFLUENCE

Perhaps the area of organizational persuasion that piques the interest of people the most is that of influence between and among organizational members. Some scholars claim that interest in organizational influence by researchers may be great because it has replaced formal authority as the means of achieving goals (Keys & Case, 1990). For example, supervisors want to know how to motivate workers, employees want to know how to ask for a raise, workers often want to persuade the boss to do something different, and co-workers want to convince others to give up what they consider to be annoying practices. Research which relates to these situations exists in several areas of organizational study including leadership, motivation, and bargaining. Some of the related theories and research are discussed in this chapter; others elsewhere in this volume.

Several studies have been conducted that focus on the influence strategies people report using in organizational settings (Fairhurst, Green, & Snavely, 1984; Keys & Case, 1990; Kipnis & Schmidt, 1982). The list includes presenting a rational explanation, telling without support, presenting a complete plan, demonstrating persistence, showing support for others, using others as a platform, using examples, using threats, offering traded favors, using manipulation, evoking formal policy, demonstrating confidence, delegation, listening, questioning, rewards, and developing trust (Keys & Case, 1990). The choice of strategy depends in part on both the situation and the skills of the persuader. Even more important, however, is the relative power of each of the participants in the influence episode.

Social scientists over the past several decades have tended to work with the notion that power is something that resides in individuals. Possibly the most widely used taxonomy of power was developed by French and Raven (1968) who posit that a person has power in one of five forms, reward (the ability to give), coercion (the ability to punish), legitimate (the ability to evoke institutional position), referent (the ability to evoke identification), and expert (the ability to assert superior knowledge). The main problem that contemporary scholars have with this vision of power is its linear construction and implicitly simplistic definition of communication (Mumby, 1988). It is not so much that we cannot view a given person as being in a more powerful position than their counterpart, but that power is more complex and pervasive than definitions focused on individuals imply.

Pearce (1989) and Carey (1989) in different approaches similarly express the notion that we do not merely transmit communication but rather live in communication. This perspective is consistent with the work of Giddens (Cohen, 1989) and Clegg (1989), which suggests that power lies in the very structure of the organization. This means that power is developed by and functions through communication practices. All of the rules, regulations, procedures, titles, and other labels help to define and construct the nature of power in the organization. Thus power in a given situation may be embodied less in the individuals involved than in the larger organizational context in which they operate. For example, a manager may have been responsible for granting raises to employees, what might be described as reward power in the French and Raven (1968) taxonomy. However, if others in the organization have determined the size of raises possible or the criteria that determine the amount, then the rules and structure of the organization convey more power than the individual manager holds. When choosing influence strategies, systemic power is an important consideration.

Organizational influence strategy choice is affected by a member's sense of power (Keys & Case, 1990). Power, however, is not the only contextual factor that should impact on the choice of strategy by either a labor union when bargaining or an individual organizational member. In the next three sections of this chapter important contemporary influences on organizational persuasion will be discussed. Organizational change, diversity, and globalization, like power, all operate both in individual episodes as well as in systemic patterns to shape and influence our choices of influence strategies. Put another way, these processes play a role in our sense of all of the available means of persuasion. Further, the impact of change, diversity, and globalization goes beyond internal to external organizational communication, magnifying its importance in persuasion efforts by organizations and individuals.

ORGANIZATIONAL CHANGE

Organizational transformation, reengineering, downsizing, rightsizing, and continuous change processes are all examples of the latest buzzwords in the world of organizations (Hammer & Champy, 1993; Kochan & Useem, 1992). Even the federal government is participating in this trend with their own term, reinventing government. These terms are reflective of a massive restructuring effort across the organizational landscape. Virtually no organization is unaffected by this movement. Not since the early industrial revolution have such a broad array of changes impacted so many people in the workplace. These changes are necessitated by developments in information and communications technology, increased worldwide industrialization, and reduced trade barriers among nations. Organizations must adapt to the environment in which they operate or cease to exist. Both managers and workers are often quite resistant to the changes that are necessary for organizations to continue operations. This creates a substantial number of situations in which organizational leaders and often consultants must engage in persuasive action if the organization is to survive, much less prosper.

For some, such change is difficult because it entails giving up work habits developed over several years. One common example is the continued practice among many employees of writing memos and messages longhand even though the organization has moved to an e-mail system. Another similar situation is the desire on the part of managers to delegate typing to a secretary when they have the capability to word process sitting on their desk. In each of these cases people will often resist change until persuaded by someone else that altering their work practices is in their best interest. Many organizations have chosen to coerce their members to change, while others have attempted to persuade by less draconian means. While coercion may yield a change in work practices, a more gentle persuasion holds the potential for rapid movement to a positive work atmosphere with less hostility and fear exhibited by the organizational members.

Perhaps the most difficult act of persuasion is to convince people to shed their individual approach and learn to work in teams, as discussed in Chapter 1. Since 1980 organizations have made ever increasing attempts to use teams in all of their work processes. Many organizations have found the development of team structures to be a frustrating process because people often actively resist team membership. Some will refuse outright while others will join the team but sabotage its effort. Still others are willing to participate but do not know how to communicate in a team environment and need to develop those skills. When management, trainers, and consultants come together in an attempt to make teams functional they often find that it is difficult to tell the difference between the resisters and those who are willing but simply need to learn. The strategies you need for each group are different, but when you cannot identify who belongs in which group it is difficult to apply persuasive strategies effectively.

Once organizations convince people to participate in teams, the next problem is to teach co-workers to learn how to persuade each other in a team environment. People who have worked for several years are often expecting role authority to be exercised by a manager. Traditionally, the power to decide is defined into the leader's position. Further, workers may expect role limits, where job responsibilities are enumerated and tasks are defined as either in or out of a worker's task list. A team environment may leave all of these issues up for negotiation among the members. Such ambiguity demands that each participant develop persuasive skills as part of effective team membership. For example, when a member does not want to perform a task that the team needs that person to do, it is important that the rest of the team be able to persuade the member without creating future relational problems. Traditionally, such skills have not been considered important and therefore tend to be absent from the required university curriculum. Only recently have business schools considered the inclusion of skills that communication departments have historically viewed as essential.

An even more profound area of organizational change than the move to teams is the development of new information and telecommunications technologies as discussed in Chapter 13. Changes in computing occur so rapidly that even the most expert among us have difficulty in tracking innovations. Many people are not happy about these technological developments, and some are afraid of the changes the machines bring about. The term "technophobia" has been developed to describe such people. Convincing technophobic people to use computers is an interesting exercise in persuasion. This is particularly so when someone has a previous experience which turned out negative. Once I met a bookkeeper who refused to use a computer because once, when she tried, the whole system crashed and she lost several hours of work. The problem is that organizations are moving towards increasing computerization, and technophobic employees need to learn to use the machines. The special concerns around new technology make this a uniquely modern persuasion situation.

DIVERSITY

With immigrants from around the globe, combined with a native population, the United States has always had to cope with the problems of diversity. As discussed in Chapter 11, recent immigration and birth patterns are creating trends that will profoundly affect our national make up. As Fernandez (1993) points out:

> *By the year 2040, one-half of the U.S. population will be African American, Hispanic/Latino American, Native American, and/or Asian American.*

Women will fill 65% of the new jobs created during the 1990s; by the year
2000 nearly one-half of civilian workers will be female. (p. 11)

Historically we have used several different strategies, including both armed and legal
suppression of minorities, to manage our diversity issues. In the last half of the twentieth century several pieces of legislation, along with court support, has made it
increasingly difficult to oppress those not in the dominant group. This, along with
demographic change, has forced organizations to develop new strategies for managing a diverse workforce requiring alternative persuasive approaches. Organizations
must confront complex problems and deeply held attitudes in an attempt to sustain
productivity as well as worker harmony. These changes have not, nor do they continue to, unfold without significant efforts in persuasion.

At the core of the diversity issues are the problems associated with racism, sexism, and ethnocentrism. These concepts reflect an ideology in a communication pattern that believes that certain groups of people and ways of being are superior to
others (Fernandez, 1993; Pearce, 1989). The attitudes resulting from racism and so
forth can range from hatred, to sabotage, to inadvertently offending a person. Thus,
in addition to moral and legal arguments against racism, sexism, and ethnocentrism,
organizations have productivity issues as well. These manifest themselves in a variety of patterns. The most obvious is that of limited opportunity created when people
are discriminated against based upon their ethnicity or gender. Fernandez (1993)
gives a statistical picture of this pattern:

> *Minorities represent almost three in ten persons in the U.S. population, but*
> *few people of color have made it to the middle and upper ranks of corporate*
> *America. Only about 8 percent of the middle-level managers and less than*
> *2 percent of upper-level managers were people of color in the 15 major cor-*
> *porations we have studied. (p. 11)*

These statistics are consistent with those of other researchers, and they suggest that
the opportunity for advancement is not evenly distributed across the population. The
opportunity to advance is one of the major motivators available to organizational
management. The absence of motivation that can result from limited opportunity
among workers can be a serious problem. With the growing number in this nation
of people of color this problem will become worse unless some change is made in
organizational attitudes.

Many are frustrated because they want to respond to diversity in a positive way,
but they find it difficult to get advice that fits their situation. This is in part a result of
years of social science research that has not taken diversity issues into account when
studies are conducted. For example, a great deal of research on media effects, persuasive processes, and organizational behavior completely ignore diversity along race,
gender, and ethnic lines. One of our major modern persuasion problems is to convince
scholarly researchers to account for these issues when they conduct investigations.

Although this is not directly an internal organizational communication problem, it affects how we understand internal organizational communication and how training workshops might be conducted if such issues were considered when the curriculum is developed.

One example of a communication framework which helps us understand how discriminatory dialogue can characterize organizational discourse was developed by W. Barnett Pearce (1989). In introducing his taxonomy Pearce suggests that:

> *Communication is not everywhere and at all times the same thing.... it takes on different forms.... Successful participation in any society requires an ability to detect (and respond appropriately to) the differences between a lecture, a sales presentation, a sermon, and a helpful hint. Sometimes "the boss" is engaging in casual chat, sometimes making a suggestion, and sometimes giving an order-it helps to know the difference. (p. 91–92)*

Diversity among organizational members adds complexity to those differences in communication patterns that must be understood if successful persuasion is to take place. As Kenneth Burke (1974) stated "You persuade a man [*sic*] only insofar as you can talk his language by speech, gesture, tonality, order, image, attitude, idea, identifying your ways with his" (p. 55).

Pearce's (1989) proposed taxonomy of patterns takes into account diversity and contains four types of communication—monocultural, ethnocentric, modernist, and cosmopolitan. Briefly defined, monocultural patterns recognize only one way of interacting, ethnocentric at least two but tends to privilege one's own pattern, modernist recognizes diversity but creates little means of connecting people, and cosmopolitan recognizes diversity and creates ways of connecting those of different groups. As you can see, from Burke's perspective persuasion of those who communicate differently from us is extremely difficult unless one engages in a cosmopolitan pattern. By interacting in a manner that acknowledges and accepts alternative ways of communicating, you enhance your ability to identify your ways with the other person and create the framework for persuasion. As organizations attempt to persuade employees to be more productive and work in teams, and in turn, as workers in teams attempt to persuade each other, this issue becomes more critical.

Jackson and Hardiman (Ayvazian, 1992) bring this thinking into the organizational context with their six stage model of moving towards being a multicultural organization. Their stages include the following:

The Exclusionary Organization	Devoted to maintaining the dominance of one group over another. This may be the purpose of the organization (such as the KKK) or related to organizational policies (prohibiting the hiring or promoting of certain groups).

The Club	This organization is not explicitly exclusionary but maintains policies and practices that have that effect.
The Compliance Organization	This organization will eliminate some of the discriminating practices of the club, but only inasmuch as it can be done without changing the fundamental nature of the organizational structure. This often results in the hiring of women and people of color at the bottom of the organization, but maintains the glass ceiling.
The Affirmative Action Organization	This organization is more actively involved in creating diversity among members than the compliance organization, but still requires communicative practices that adhere to a dominant norm.
The Redefining Organization	This is an organization in transition. It is not satisfied with communication that does not encourage the distribution of power among diverse groups. Further, it encourages members to speak up and suggests alternative ways of organizing that create inclusion and empowerment.
The Multicultural Organization	This organization encourages communicative practices which reflects the various cultures and social groups that make up its membership. Further, it supports efforts to eliminate social oppression.

The first stage corresponds to Pearce's monocultural pattern, the second with ethnocentric, the third and forth with modernist, and finally the fifth and sixth with cosmopolitan.

These authors are suggesting that diversity has everything to do with organizational persuasion. This is partly because the diversity orientation of the organization is related to the fundamental ways of interacting among members. This creates parameters around the available means of persuasion. In addition, if an organization wishes to change diversity perspectives, then members must learn to interact in ways more consistent with the change of pattern. As indicated in the previous section, organization change is not always an easy persuasion process.

Sensitivity to diversity concerns is not sufficient to achieve productive change. Members of the organization need to be persuaded that communication patterns that reflect concern for diversity are in their best interest. If everyone or even most people engaged in diversity-sensitive interaction, we would not have problems associated with racism, sexism, and ethnicity. However, many are resistant to the behavioral changes necessary to manage these problems, creating the need for persuasion. As with other organizational changes, coercion is not likely to be as functional as persuasion. People cannot develop sensitivity as a result of heavy pressure, they must come to it by gentle persuasion along with training that provides communication alternatives. In what has become a recurring theme in this chapter, first and foremost we can develop a diversity-sensitive communication style if we learn about those different than us and listen to what others have to say. Information is a valuable asset in effective communication, whether we are attempting to persuade or simply trying to understand those different than us.

GLOBALIZATION

Along with the changes resulting from diversity, is the increasing interconnection between people around the world (Parrish-Sprowl, Carveth, & Desiderio, in press). This is known as globalization, and it is a communication process that is both political and economic in nature. It is a process that creates interdependence among both businesses and countries and interconnects them through formal treaties such as the European Union and NAFTA. Communication and transportation technology have made this interconnection possible, and one result has been the development of several international companies that tend to view national boundaries as business problems to solve rather than as barriers to the conduct of commerce. International companies may produce in one country or ten; they will export all over the world; their officers may come from six countries on three different continents; and their headquarters may be in a country altogether different from the above. We know that globalization encompasses many peoples, nationalities, and countries and this process will only spread in the future.

Globalization is not only a process of growing international interdependence, it may also be considered an attending perspective from which one may understand and frame communicative activity. To envision ourselves as members of a global society we must think of ourselves as citizens of the globe more so than of nations or regions. From this perspective we must understand and respond to situations as worldly people not bound by ethnocentric or nationalistic limits in our thinking and communicative practices. In Pearce's (1989) terms this requires us to become cosmopolitan communicators. This is a difficult concept for many to accept and incorporate into their perspective; however, as the world becomes more tightly linked, we function better if we rid ourselves of the ethnocentrism that pervades the human condition. We can no longer construct identities solely as Americans, Cubans, Koreans, or Poles but as members of a larger interdependent community. Thus the society that we consider to be ours covers the world and all of the multicultural elements which make up humanity.

Organizations must play a significant role in convincing their members to take on a global perspective. First, because organizational members may work side by side or for someone who is from another country. As organizations become more involved in international manufacturing and trade, labor pools tend to become more global as well. The issues of global workers are somewhat different than domestic diversity in that national identity adds a layer of complexity. Second, organizations owned by people in other countries are increasingly operating within the United States, and a greater number of citizens never need to leave town to work for a foreign corporation. However, the path to advancement may lead the worker to make a choice to work outside of the United States for a period of time. Employees with a global perspective will be more comfortable with these opportunities and motivated to perform when presented with the chance to advance.

To compete in global markets, organizations must employ people with the skills to negotiate in international markets. Persuasion in this arena is more complex than it is in a domestic situation. The legal environment is different, national customs are different, and the costs are high. A person who is an expert at negotiating in the United States may be completely inept outside of the borders. Knowledge of intercultural communication is important as is experience working in other nations. For example, I once consulted with a person from the United States who needed to negotiate a contract with a counterpart in Korea. Every time the person flew to Korea he would let them know his time schedule including his departure date as a practice of courtesy. What he did not realize is that the person from Korea saw this as an opportunity to outwait him and force him to negotiate a deal with less favorable terms. Once the American discovered what was happening he discontinued the practice of informing his host that he had a schedule to keep and subsequently bargained to better settlements.

Americans have a strong tendency to assume that the rest of the world looks at life from the same value perspective. As a consequence they often offend people quite unintentionally. In 1993 and 1994 I spent several months working in Poland. A frequent topic of conversation among some of the Poles I met was the frustration that resulted from working with people from the United States who did not take the time to understand Polish perspectives and conditions. Frequently consultants would provide advice that simply was not practical in the Polish context. To illustrate, one consultant suggested to several Polish business executives that they obtain a bank loan to solve their immediate problem. Unfortunately, at the time it was virtually impossible to obtain a loan in Poland because of the financial conditions stemming from the transformation from a centrally planned to a market economy. Americans make a number of mistakes in foreign countries because they do not take the time to investigate local conditions and practices. Again, as Burke (1974) suggests, you may be able to persuade a person when you have a sufficient understanding of their situation that you can identify with them. As the future unfolds, a significant area of organizational study, including persuasion, will be the issues that arise from a changing global environment.

CONCLUSION

Persuasion and organizational communication are both broad areas of study representing thousands of investigations. In this chapter we have briefly covered some of the major contemporary themes that reside at the intersection of these two areas of study. While topics important to some may be missing, the subjects of the present chapter represent a broad view of the theory and research related to persuasion in and by organizations. Scholars from rhetoric, nominological social science, and critical/interpretive backgrounds have contributed to the rich literature in this important area. While definitive prescriptions for persuasive practice are difficult, if not impossible, we are not without substantial insight. From rhetoric perspectives we learn to examine all of the possible ways in which we might develop the quality of our ethos, pathos and logos. From social scientists we develop a recognition of the complex processes of attitude formation and change and are provided with several theoretical frameworks from which to analyze and influence. Critical/interpretive perspectives remind us to remember that communication constructs our collective sense of the world and that the impact of interaction pervades our environment, which both liberates and constrains our persuasive choices.

As we enter the post–Industrial Age it is particularly important to ponder the problems of new technology, organizational change, diversity, and globalization. Persuasion is not only important to consider within the framework of these topics, the areas themselves will change the way we think about persuasion. For example, requesting a raise in a team structured organization is different than in a traditional bureaucracy, and persuading people from different cultural orientations may entail rhetorical choices not considered when interacting with someone of a similar background. Thus, as time passes, the knowledge and ability that constitute rhetoric skill is constantly being reconstituted.

Even as we enter a new era, the traditional areas of organizational persuasion still deserve our attention. Advertising, public relations, and personal sales attract a growing number of people to their professions, many of whom major in communication. You or someone you know will work a large percentage of their career in one or the other of these areas and knowledge of the communicative resources and practices necessary for successful persuasion will be of particular importance. Although you may never become a professional in advertising, public relations, or sales, these occupations will exert a profound influence on your life; hence insight into the their nature will help you make decisions that serve you well.

Persuasion within the organization is important as well. Many of us are affected by labor negotiations and how they are conducted is a critical concern. Many, if not all, of the workers in the United States will soon be or already are involved in teamwork. Several have found it to be a wonderful experience, many more feel only frustration with the attending difficulties of learning new work interaction patterns. We benefit from understanding the possible processes of persuasion in team settings as we attempt to have a successful experience. To improve your professional performance and satisfaction I suggest you make it a personal goal to learn all that you are able about persuasion in organizations.

GLOSSARY

Advertising—organizational persuasion aimed at changing or reinforcing existing behavior in the consumer.

Compliance gaining strategies—methods used to get targets to engage in activities they would not have on their own.

Ethos—how a person establishes credibility.

Globalization—the increasing interconnection among people around the world, which is both political and economic in nature.

Interpretive research—a perspective of research in organizations that aims at capturing the nature of the organization, rather than specific bits and pieces of organizational life.

Logos—the logic of a persuasive strategy, a system of reasoning.

Pathos—persuasive appeals directed at stirring emotions.

Public relations—organizational efforts aimed at persuading various constituencies that the organization is a good community member.

Rhetoric—all the available means of persuading others.

Technophobia—a fear of the changes resulting from the technologies used in contemporary organizations.

Thromis—a combination of threats and promises.

CASE STUDY—CREATING THE SUCCESSFUL TEAM PROJECT

You have been assigned to a team with four other co-workers. Your task is to create a training manual that improves the diversity sensitivity of the sales force. You are excited about the project because you recognize the importance of the subject and realize that this will be a high profile project, one that may help you earn a bonus.

Your co-workers, however, are not equally excited. One thinks that diversity is an annoying topic that wastes too much company time. Another believes that this is your chance to make a political statement. Thus, rather than learn practical skills in the training seminar they want to focus on teaching ideology. The other two feel as you do and hope to create a successful program.

Discussion: 1. Identify the points of persuasion. 2. Develop a strategy to achieve your goals.

REFERENCES

Ajzen, I., & Fishbein, M. (1980). *Understanding and Predicting Social Behavior.* Englewood Cliffs, N.J.: Prentice-Hall.

Aristotle (1954) *The Rhetoric.* (W. Rhys Roberts, trans.). New York: Modern Library.

Ayvazian, A. (1992). *Stages of multicultural development in organizations: An adaptation from the work of Bailey Jackson and Rita Hardiman.* Unpublished handout, Smith School of Social Work, Northampton, Mass.

Bandura, A. (1972). *Social Learning Theory.* Englewood Cliffs, N.J.: Prentice-Hall.

Booth-Butterfield, S., Cooke, P., Andrightetti, A., Casteel, B., Lang, T., Pearson, D., & Rodriquez, B. (1994). Simultaneous versus exclusive processing of persuasive arguments and cues. *Communication Quarterly, (42)*1, 21–35.

Burke, K. (1974). *A Rhetoric of Motives.* Berkeley: University of California Press.

Carey, J. W. (1989). Communication as culture: Essays in media and society. Boston, MA: Unwin Hyman, Inc.

Clegg, S. R. (1989). *Frameworks of Power.* Newbury Park, Calif.: Sage.

Cohen, I. J. (1989). *Structuration Theory: Anthony Giddens and the Constitution of Social Life.* New York: St. Martin's Press.

Dilenschneider, R. L., & Forrestal, D. J. (1987). *Public Relations Handbook* (3rd ed.). Chicago: The Dartnell Corporation.

Donohue, W. A. (1981). Analyzing negotiation tactics: Development of a negotiation interact system. *Human Communication Research, 7*(3), 273–287.

Fairhurst, G. T., Green, S. G., & Snavely, B. K. (1984). Face support in controlling poor performance. *Human Communication Research, 11,* 272–295.

Fernandez, J. P. (1993). *The Diversity Advantage.* New York: Lexington Books.

Festinger, L. A. (1957). *A Theory of Cognitive Dissonance.* Evanston, Ill.: Row Peterson.

Fishbein, M., & Ajzen, I. (1975). *Belief, Attitude, Intention and Behavior.* Reading, Mass.: Addison-Wesley.

French, J. & Raven, B. (1968). The bases of social power. In D. Cartwright & A. Zander (Eds.), *Group Dynamics: Research and Theory* (3rd. ed.). New York: Harper & Row, 259–269.

Golden, J. L., Berquist, G. F., & Coleman, W. E. (1983). *The Rhetoric of Western Thought* (3rd ed.). Dubuque, Iowa: Kendall/Hunt.

Hammer, M., & Champy, J. (1993). *Reengineering the Corporation.* New York: Harper Business Books.

Heider, F. (1958). *The Psychology of Interpersonal Relations.* New York: John Wiley.

Holley, W. H. & Jennings, K. M. (1980). *The Labor Relations Process.* Hinsdale, Ill.: The Dryden Press.

Jhally, S. (1987). *The Codes of Advertising.* New York: St. Martin's Press.

Keys, B., & Case, T. (1990). How to become an influential manager. *Academy of Management Executive, 4,* 38–51.

Kiesler, C. A., Collins, B. E., & Miller, N. (1969). *Attitude Change: A Critical Analysis of Theoretical Approaches.* New York: John Wiley.

Kipnis, D., & Schmidt, S. M. (1982). *Profile of Organizational Influence Strategies.* San Diego Calif.: University Associates.

Kochan, T. A., & Useem, M. (eds.) (1992). *Transforming Organizations.* New York: Oxford University Press.

Kotler, P. (1986). *Principles of Marketing* (3rd ed.). Englewood Cliffs, N.J.: Prentice-Hall.

Leiss, W., Klein, S., & Jhalley, S. (1986). *Social Communication in Advertising.* Toronto, Canada: Methuen Publications.

Levine, T., & Boster, F. (1993, May). *Putting the compliance back in compliance-gaining: The effects of power and message variables on compliance.* Paper presented at the annual meeting of the International Communication Association, Washington, D.C.

McGuire, W. J. (1964). Inducing resistance to persuasion: Some contemporary approaches. In L. Berkowitz (ed.), *Advances in Experimental Social Psychology,* vol. 1 (pp. 191–229). New York: Academic Press.

McGuire, W. J. (1969). The nature of attitudes and attitude change. In G. Lindzey & E. Aronson (eds.), *The Handbook of Social Psychology* (2nd. ed.), (vol. 3, pp. 136–314). Reading, Mass.: Addison-Wesley.

Miller, K. (1995). *Organizational Communication: Approaches and Processes.* Belmont, Calif.: Wadsworth Publishing Company.

Mumby, D. K. (1988). *Communication and Power in Organizations: Discourse, Ideology and Domination.* Norwood, N.J.: Ablex.

Murdock, J. I., Bradac, J. J., & Bowers, J. W. (1984). Effects of power on the perception of explicit threats, promises, and thromises: A rule-governed perspective. *The Western Journal of Speech Communication, 48*(4), 344–361.

Norton, R. (1995, February 6). Winning the game of business. *Fortune.*

Osgood, C., & Tannebaum, P. (1955). The principle of congruity in the prediction of attitude change. *Psychological Review,* (62), 42–55.

Pacanowsky, M. E. (1983). A small-town cop: Communication in, out, and about a crisis. In L. L. Putnam & M. E. Pacanowsky (eds.), *Communication and Organizations: An Interpretive Approach.* Beverly Hills, Calif.: Sage.

Parrish-Sprowl, J., Carveth, R. A., & Desiderio, S. (in press). The post-communist transformation: The challenge of creating a discourse of advertising in Poland. In W. Sitek (ed.), *Kulture i Strukture II: Spoleczenstwo Wobec Wyzweu Ryuku.* Wroclaw, Poland: Instytut of Socjoloii, Uniwersytet Wroclawski.

Parrish-Sprowl, J., Carveth, R., & Senk, M. (1994). The effect of compliance gaining strategy choice and communicator style on sales success. *Journal of Business Communication, 31*(4), 291–310.

Parrish-Sprowl, J., & Senk, M. (1986). Sales communication: Compliance gaining strategy choice and sales success. *Communication Research Reports, 3,* 64–68.

Pearce, W. B. (1989). *Communication and the Human Condition.* Carbondale, Ill.: Southern Illinois University Press.

Petty, R. E., & Cacioppo, J. T. (1986). *Communication and Persuasion: Central and Peripheral Routes to Attitude Change.* New York: Springer-Verlag.

Putnam, L. L., & Jones, T. S. (1982). The role of communication in bargaining. *Human Communication Research, 8*(3), 262–280.

Putnam, L. L., & Pacanowsky, M. E. (1983). *Communication and Organizations: An Interpretive Approach.* Beverly Hills, Calif.: Sage Publications.

Redding, W. C. (1985). Stumbling toward identity: The emergence of organizational communication as a field of study. In R. D. McPhee & P. K. Tompkins (eds.), *Organizational Communication: Traditional Themes and New Directions.* Beverly Hills, Calif.: Sage.

Reiches, N. A., & Harral, H. B. (1974). Argument in negotiation: A theoretical approach. *Speech Monographs, 41,* 36–48.

Schudson, M. (1984), *Advertising: The Uneasy Persuasion.* New York: Basic Books.

Sherif, M., & Sherif, C. (1967). *Attitude, Ego Involvement and Change.* New York: John Wiley.

Simons, H. W. (1986). *Persuasion: Understanding Practice, and Analysis* (2nd ed.). New York: Random House.

Snyder, M., & DeBono, K. G. (1985). Appeals to image and claims about quality: Understanding the psychology of advertising. *Journal of Personality and Social Psychology, 49,* 586–597.

Snyder, M., & DeBono, K. (1989). Understanding the functions of attitude: Lessons from personality and social behavior. In A. R. Pratkanis, S. J. Breckler, & A. G. Greenwald (eds.), *Attitude Structure and Function* (pp. 339–360). Hillsdale, N.J.: Lawrence Erlbaum.

Soldow, G. F., & Penn Thomas, G. (1984). Relational communication: Form vs content in the sales interaction. *Journal of Marketing, 48,* 84–93.

Spiro, R., & Perreault, W. (1979). Influence use by industrial salesmen: Influence, strategy mixes and situational determinants. *Journal of Business, 52,* 435–455.

Sprowl, J. P. (1985). *The use of compliance gaining strategies in personal sales: An exploratory analysis.* Paper presented at the International Communication Association Conference, Honolulu, Hawaii.

Wells, W., Burnett, J., & Moriarty, S. (1992). *Advertising: Principles and Practice* (2nd ed.). Englewood Cliffs, N.J.: Prentice-Hall.

Wood, J. T. (1994). *Gendered Lives: Communication, Gender, and Culture.* Belmont, Calif.: Wadsworth Publishing Company.

RECOMMENDED READINGS

Eisenberg, E. M., & Goodall, H. L. (1993). *Organizational Communication: Balancing Creativity and Constraint.* New York: St. Martin's Press.

Frank, A., & Brownell, J. (1989). *Organizational Communication and Behavior.* New York: Holt, Rinehart and Winston.

Moemeka, A. (ed.) (1993). *Development (Social Change) Communication: Building Understanding and Creating Participation.* New York: McGraw Hill.

Putnam, L. L., & Poole, M. S. (1987). Conflict and negotiation. In F. Jablin, L. Putnam, K. Roberts, & L. Porter (eds.), *The Handbook of Organizational Communication* (pp. 549–599). Newbury Park, Calif.: Sage.

Rubin, J., & Brown, B. (1975). *The Social Psychology of Bargaining and Negotiation.* New York: Academic Press.

Shavitt, S., & Brock, T. C. (1994). *Persuasion: Psychological Insights and Perspectives.* Boston: Allyn & Bacon.

Young, O. R. (ed.) (1975). *Bargaining: Formal Theories of Negotiation.* Urbana, Ill.: University of Illinois Press.

► 8

Organizational Culture

ANGELA TRETHEWEY

Perhaps more than any other, the term culture has been used to describe organizations over the course of the past decade. To describe the term merely as a buzz word diminishes the widespread impact that culture has had on the study of and practices in organizational life. The concept of organizational culture has served several diverse purposes among academics and practitioners alike. Managerially biased scholars and practitioners have treated culture as a variable to be manipulated by individual managers to create a strong, effective, and competitive organization (Deal & Kennedy, 1982; Ouchi, 1981; Peters & Waterman, 1982). Others have treated organizational cultures as shared systems of symbols and meanings that must be described and interpreted to be understood. The value of this approach rests in its ability to "demonstrate how symbols are intertwined in meaningful relationships and how they emanate from the activities of people in a particular [organizational] setting" (Smircich & Calás, 1987, p. 241). Still other critically oriented thinkers view organizational cultures with often well-founded skepticism. For them, organizational cultures are potentially oppressive and, therefore, need to be understood, critiqued, and ultimately changed (Deetz & Kersten, 1983). This chapter will explore organizational culture from these three perspectives to provide a full and rich understanding of the concept. The chapter will conclude with two recent developments, namely postmodern and feminist analyses, in organizational culture studies. First a brief overview of organizational culture is offered.

CULTURE DEFINED

Culture "refers to all the accepted and patterned ways of behavior of a given people. It is a body of common understandings...the sum total and the organization and arrangement of all the group's ways of thinking, feeling and acting" (Brown, 1963, pp. 3–4). An organizational culture can be thought of as a mini-society that has its own distinctive patterns. Morgan (1986), an organizational theorist, argues that one of the easiest ways to appreciate the nature of an organizational culture is to "observe the day-to-day functioning" of an organization *as if one were an outsider.* Adopt the role of anthropologist. The characteristics of the culture will gradually become evident as one becomes aware of the patterns of interaction between individuals, the language that is used, the images and themes explored in conversation, and the various rituals of daily routine" (p. 121). In brief, organizational culture can be understood as the " 'unique sense of place' that each organization seems to offer" (Pacanowsky & O'Donnell-Trujillo, 1983, p. 128). An organization's unique sense of place is made up of several elements.

Elements of Organizational Culture

Organizational cultures are a combination of many inextricably related elements. The following list, while not exhaustive, describes several cultural elements:

1. Metaphors—The language that members use to describe their experiences of organizations shapes the organizational reality or culture. For example, organizational members may use metaphors of family, teams, the military, or the jungle to describe and characterize their work lives (Morgan, 1986; Smith & Eisenberg, 1987).
2. Rituals—Organizational rituals are practices that are performed regularly or occasionally in the organization (for further discussion of rituals and rites see Beyer & Trice, 1987; Deal & Kennedy, 1982; Pacanowsky & O'Donnell-Trujillo, 1983; Trice & Beyer, 1984). Rituals are "dramatizations of the company's basic cultural values...[that] provide the place and script with which employees can experience meaning" (Deal & Kennedy, 1982, p. 62). Rituals can range in scope from personal to organizationwide practices. Individualized trademark performances, day-to-day routines for accomplishing work, Friday afternoon pub runs, and the annual organizational holiday reception are a few examples of rituals that contribute to the culture by "orient[ing] members temporally, synchronizing their focus and introducing a sense of regularity" (Pacanowsky & O'Donnell-Trujillo, 1983, p. 135).
3. Stories—Storytelling is a significant feature of organizational life. Stories are "important indicators of the values the participants share, the social prescriptions concerning how things are to be done, and the consequences of compliance or deviance" (Wilkins, 1983, p. 82). Stories may serve a variety of functions in organizations, including control or system maintenance, motivation, legitimation, integration of members into the organization, and representing important or valued aspects of

the culture (Martin et al., 1983; Wilkins, 1983). Stories are thought to be a particularly effective means of transmitting culture because as stories are retold over time, the themes and values they express become real to members.

4. Heroes—Heroes are organizational members who are held up as exemplary role models. Quite often, these heroes hail from the executive or managerial ranks, and therefore, embody and personify managerial values (Schein, 1991). Mary Kay Ash of Mary Kay Cosmetics, who "trains sales women not simply to represent her but to believe that they *are* Mary Kay," is just one such hero (Deal & Kennedy, 1982, p. 40). The founders of Hewlett-Packard, "Bill and Dave," have become company legends, exemplars of the firm's values including innovation and a "people orientation" (Peters & Waterman, 1982, p. 244).

5. Cultural Artifacts—Tangible and physical features of the organization may also contribute to the organization's culture. Furnishings, corporate artwork, and even place settings at company breakfasts have been studied as cultural artifacts that contribute to the organization's unique sense of place (Barley, 1983; Rosen, 1985).

6. Performances—Performances are the dynamic, processual, and creative communicative events that members engage in when socially constructing organizational cultures. Members may enact a variety of performances including rituals, passion, sociality (or organizational etiquette), politics, and enculturation of new members (Pacanowsky & O'Donnell-Trujillo, 1983).

7. Values—Values are a shared set of beliefs about what is and is not appropriate organizational behavior. Values are derived from charismatic leadership or organizational tradition. A set of values might include a commitment to quality, customer service, and innovation (Deal & Kennedy, 1982; Schein, 1991; Shockley-Zalabak & Morley, 1994).

LOOKING AT CULTURE THROUGH MULTIPLE LENSES

Organizational cultures can be examined from a variety of perspectives. Three theoretical approaches—functionalist, interpretive, and critical—have dominated organizational culture studies in the field of speech communication. Exploring organizational cultures from functionalist, interpretive, and critical perspectives provides a full and adequately complex understanding of the phenomenon. Each perspective highlights as well as hides aspects of organizational culture, and each has implications for the way we understand and behave in organizations.

Functionalist Approach to Organizational Culture

The functionalist approach to the study of organizational communication has a long and rich tradition. Early organizational communication research, dating back to the 1940s, developed from a rather mechanistic and linear view of communication that resulted in the development of the functionalist or logical positivist research tradition. The functionalist tradition has been and continues to be the dominant perspective in most organizational communication research. Those who adhere to this perspective treat communication as a tangible, measurable, and knowable product that is transmitted within organizations. The organization is conceived as a fixed container in which messages are transmitted. Functionalists conceive of communication and other "social phenomena as concrete, materialistic entities" (Putnam, 1983, p. 34) and "reify social processes by ignoring the creation of structures" (Putnam, 1983, p. 85).

Functionalists treat communication as a variable that can be manipulated. More specifically, "functionalists study the relationship between communication variables and organizational outcomes in order to predict and control those outcomes" (Fine, 1993, p. 135). This research is often conducted to give managers practical advice and strategies for using communication to create effective organizations. While a bias toward management and the maintenance of the status quo is not an inherent feature of the functionalist paradigm, "the scientific concerns for administrative and technical efficiency have led to managerial based-definitions of organizational concepts" (Putnam, 1983, p. 37). Closely related to the implicit managerial bias that underlies the functionalist approach is a "unitary" view of the organization in which the organization is conceived of as a unified, cooperative entity whose members pursue common goals (Putnam, 1983, p. 37).

The functionalist approach that has permeated communication studies, in general, has also found widespread acceptance in the study of organizational cultures in particular. Adherents of functionalism believe that culture is a variable, like technology or management style, that can be manipulated or changed by managers to create strong, effective, and competitive organizations. The assumption is that "managers can control culture through controlling communication practices, and thus influence organizational performance" (Smircich & Calás, 1987, p. 234). More specifically, functionalists try to establish quasi-causal relationships between particular cultural events such as rituals or storytelling and organizational outcomes, including employee commitment and increased productivity. For example, management theorists Trice and Beyer (1984) contend that managers can use rites to change and improve their corporate cultures. Kunda, a management scholar who researches organizational cultures (1992), provides an account of how one high-tech firm's management attempted to "engineer culture" by using rituals and other cultural events to foster a strong culture. For this company, whose culture is described in metaphors of "family" and even "religion," "'the culture' is a gloss for an extensive definition of membership in a corporate community that includes rules for behavior, thought, and feeling, all adding up to be what appears to be a well-defined as widely shared 'member role'" (Kunda, 1992, p. 7).

The functionalist perspective suggests that a strong culture is characterized by organizationwide consensus, consistency, and clarity where "members share the same values and understandings, promoting a shared sense of loyalty, commitment, and—hopefully—productivity" (Frost et al., 1991, p. 11). In addition to providing members with the knowledge of who they are, what they do, and why they do it, a strong culture is also presumed to be an effective means of control. Organizations with strong cultures are said to have less need for policy manuals, organizational charts, or detailed rules; instead, "people way down the line know what they are supposed to do in most situations because the handful of guiding [cultural] values is crystal clear" (Peters & Waterman, 1982, p. 76). When members develop strong emotional attachments to their culture and internalize the organization's values, formal control strategies are deemed less effective and less necessary. "In the view of proponents of strong cultures, work in such companies is not merely an economic transaction; rather, it is imbued with a deeper personal significance that causes people to behave in ways that the company finds rewarding, and that require less use of traditional controls" (Kunda, 1992, p. 10).

Strategies for Building Strong Cultures

According to many authors, the rewards for creating and maintaining strong cultures include increased competitiveness and increased member satisfaction. These authors provide managers and consultants with several strategies for creating strong cultures, some of which are described below.

Deal and Kennedy's (1982) *Corporate Cultures: The Rites and Rituals of Corporate Life* is a prescriptive managerial guide for developing strong cultures. More specifically, this popular text outlines five elements of strong cultures, including the business environment, values, heroes, rites and rituals, and the cultural network. The business environment determines, in large part, what an organization must do to succeed, which in turn determines the nature of the organization's culture. For example, companies that depend on their ability to sell a particular product often develop work hard/play hard cultures that are designed to keep their sales forces selling. Organizational values are the heart of the corporate culture. "These are the basic concepts and beliefs of an organization...[that] define 'success' in concrete terms for employees" (p. 14). At Proctor & Gamble, key values such as, "the consumer is important," "things don't just happen, you have to make them happen," and "we want to make employee interests our own," are said to undergird the company's culture. The culture's values are personified by heroes who provide role models for employees. "These achievers are known to virtually every employee within a few months' tenure in the company. And they show every employee 'here's what you have to do to succeed around here'" (p. 14). Rites and rituals are programmed and planned "routines of day-to-day" life that make manifest important company values and behavioral expectations (p. 14). According to Deal and Kennedy (1982), "strong culture companies go to the trouble of spelling out in copious detail, the routine behavioral rituals they expect their employees to follow" (p. 15). Rituals can prescribe and celebrate behavior regarding communication, work procedures, managerial processes, and special achievements worthy of recognition. Rituals can range in scope from daily greeting rituals to lavish cultural extravaganzas. Deal and Kennedy (1982) describe in detail the lavish rituals at Mary Kay Cosmetics where:

> *Awards for the best sales are given—pink Buicks and Cadillacs. One year the cars simply 'floated' down onto the stage from a 'cloud'—a weighty touch of hoopla that produced an overwhelming response from the crowd. But the biggest night is a five-hour spectacular when the company crowns the Director and Consultant Queens (supersaleswomen) in each category. They're given diamonds and minks and surrounded by a court of women who have also achieved terrific sales. At the end of this extravaganza, everyone understands that the challenge of this company is in sales. (p. 74)*

Finally, strong cultures require a cultural communication network or an informal grapevine that carries organizational values and the company's cultural mythology. The characters in the network are described as storytellers who can help define and describe organizational reality, priests who are the guardians and keepers of cultural values, gossips who pass on the everyday details and happenings of organizational life, and others. The savvy manager is one who knows how to tap the informal network by recognizing its existence, cultivating it, and in fact relying on it for most of his or her communicative needs.

A central figure in Deal and Kennedy's (1982) scheme is the "symbolic manager." The symbolic manager is said to shape, support, or change the culture by thinking about, acting out, and adopting a zealous willingness to speak about the corporate culture. The symbolic manager literally manages the symbolic or "soft side" of the organization. "Symbolic managers see themselves as players—script-writers, directors, actors—in the daily drama of company affairs...Each day is a new scenario; each meeting a new setting for dramatic action. No events are too trivial for the great actor as he [or she] strides across the stage of the corporate set" (p. 142). His or her task is to articulate the organization's key values, to personify those values in dramatized events, and to change or reshape the culture when necessary.

Tom Peters and Bob Waterman provide practitioners with a similar set of guidelines for managers interested in developing strong cultures. Peters and Waterman's (1982) *In Search of Excellence: Lessons from America's Best Run Companies* is the best-selling popular management text of all time in which the authors outline eight attributes that characterize "excellent" companies. Like Deal and Kennedy, Peters and Waterman assume that managers are capable of manipulating and molding their organization's culture. It is the manager's capacity to shape a particular culture based on the eight essential characteristics, in fact, that determines whether or not an organization will be successful. Those attributes include the following (Peters & Waterman, 1982, pp. 13–16):

1. *A bias for action*—Instead of deliberating and agonizing over every decision excellent companies simply and rapidly come up with answers and implement solutions.
2. *Close to the customer*—Excellent companies regularly and intently listen to and learn from their customers in order to provide "unparalleled quality, service, and reliability."
3. *Autonomy and entrepreneurship*—Creativity and innovation are encouraged at all levels in excellent companies. These companies foster practical risk-taking and reward individuals for "good tries" even if they are not always successful.
4. *Productivity through people*—Respect for individual employees permeates excellent companies. This respect is manifest when the "rank and file" members are treated as the "root source of quality and productivity gain."
5. *Hands-on, value-driven*—Stellar organizations are often host to managers who articulate the organization's values and who immerse themselves in the day-to-day operations of the organizations to ensure those values are being upheld.
6. *Stick to the knitting*—Strong companies "stay reasonably close to the business that they know." In other words, these organizations do what they do best.
7. *Simple form, lean staff*—Excellent companies' organizational structures are "elegantly simple" and lean.
8. *Simultaneous tight-loose properties*—Simultaneous centralization and decentralization characterize strong performers. The organizations are decentralized in that they allow those on the shop floor to make decisions about work processes, but they are centered on their core values.

In addition to these key attributes, Peters and Waterman (1982) suggest that, more than anything else, excellent companies are characterized by a palpable intensity. The task of the manager is to spread, encourage, dramatize, and reward intensity—in the form of employee commitment, increased productivity, or innovation—among organizational members.

Clearly, the functionalist approach to organizational culture requires that managers pay special attention to the human side of organizational life, its mythology, heroes, values, stories, vocabularies, rites, and rituals. From a managerial perspective, the functionalist approach is attractive as it encourages managers to "see themselves as symbolic actors whose primary function is to foster and develop desirable patterns of meaning," rather than as "more or less rational men and women designing structures and job descriptions" (Morgan, 1986, p. 135). In so doing, symbolic managers are believed to increase organizational performance and affect organizational change.

Critique of the Functionalist Approach

While the functionalist approach is appealing, it has been critiqued for its mechanistic conception of communication, its failure to address the socially constructed nature of organizational culture, and its managerial bias (Martin, 1985; Morgan, 1986; Putnam, 1983). Too often, organizational culture is treated as a static set of reified, thing-like artifacts that can be simply passed from one organizational member or from one organizational generation to the next. Here culture is "viewed as a set of distinct variables, such as beliefs, stories, norms, and rituals, that somehow form a cultural whole. Such a view is unduly mechanistic" (Morgan, 1986, p. 139). This mechanistic, linear view fails to capture the complexity and holistic quality of organizational cultures. While outsiders may succinctly describe an organization's culture, these descriptions are often patterns that are imposed retrospectively. Members' experiences of cultures are often much more complex, subtle, and fragmented than many functionalist authors might have us believe.

Many have critiqued the functionalist assumption that managers are capable of engineering, changing, or controlling culture (Kunda, 1992; Smircich & Calás, 1987). Critics argue that culture is not something that can simply be imposed from the "top down"; culture is too holistic and too pervasive to be managed or controlled by any single individual or management team. Instead, culture is something that is socially constructed in day-to-day communicative behaviors among all members of the organization. Culture emerges out of the processes of sense-making and interaction among members. "Cultural purists . . . find it ridiculous to talk of managing culture. Culture cannot be managed; it emerges. Leaders don't create cultures; members of the culture do" (Martin, 1985, p. 95).

Perhaps the most damning critique of the functionalist perspective centers on the implications of its managerial bias. Oftentimes, the culture becomes equated with management's value systems to the exclusion of other members' values. This perspective limits the range of shared understandings and experiences that receive attention from researchers and practitioners. The focus on management's attempts to control culture blind us to the sense-making practices of other organization members that may or may not jibe with management's culture. Another, more startling, implication of the functionalists' managerially-biased approach is that it advocates "ideological manipulation and control" as an "essential managerial strategy" (Morgan, 1986, p. 138). Critics suggest that attempts to manipulate culture inherently include attempts to manipulate organizational members' thoughts, feelings, emotions, experiences, and indeed their very selves. In *Engineering Culture,* Kunda (1992) suggests that the functionalist approach to culture may in fact be a "sophisticated and manipulative form of tyranny in the workplace, a threat to both freedom and dignity, an unwarranted invasion of privacy" (p. 15). The debate over whether organizational cultures provide members with positive experiences of community or limiting and constraining experiences continues to be a hotly contested one. More will be said regarding this issue in later sections. First, we will turn a different lens on organizational culture.

Interpretive Approach to Organizational Culture

During the early 1980s, as a result of dissatisfaction with functionalism, research in organizational communication took an interpretive turn. Interpretive researchers became less concerned with the problems that managers faced and more concerned with understanding the complex, processual nature of organizational life (Putnam & Cheney, 1985). Interpretive researchers seek to understand the rich, dynamic, and socially constructed nature of organizational life. Following sociologists Berger and Luckman (1966), interpretivists argue that the reality of everyday life is a social construction reproduced and maintained through communication. Thus, in organizations, members of all hierarchical levels, not just management, are thought to create and shape organizational culture through everyday communicative practices.

Interpretivists explore "the subjective, intersubjective and socially constructed meanings of organizational actors" (Putnam, 1983, p. 44). In brief, the interpretive approach centers on the processes through which organizational members construct or make sense of their experiences. Rituals, myths, jokes, and other cultural performances are not viewed as static entities to be transmitted from management to the lower levels of the organization nor are they treated as mere reflections of organizational meanings (Pacanowsky & O'Donnell-Trujillo, 1983). Instead, elements of culture are understood as ongoing, dynamic, communicative processes that constitute organizational life. While the process of organizational sense-making is partial and ongoing, it also creates for the members a very tangible and objective structure. Organizational members, after all, do not respond to what they think is a creation of their consciousness, but to what is real for them (Mumby, 1988). Organizational reality, or organizational culture, is then at once subjectively real and socially objectified (Berger & Luckman, 1966); it is the shaper of human interaction and its outcome (Jelinek, Smircich, & Hirsch, 1983). The organizational chart, for example, is a symbolic, social construction that has real consequences for everyday interaction. As a case in point, "The chart is symbolic in that it represents previous and potential relationships, but it is also structural in that the use of or reference to it impacts on daily actions among members" (Putnam, 1983, p. 35).

Many interpretive researchers study organizational cultures and organizational symbolism. For interpretivists, culture is not merely another variable that the organization has; rather, culture is something that the organization is. As a culture, the organization requires description and interpretation in order to be understood. Interpretive researchers often develop "thick descriptions" of cultures (Frost et. al., 1991; Geertz, 1973). Their descriptive accounts of culture provide rich and often complex portraits of members' experiences of organizational life. While these interpretive accounts are not necessarily anti-management, they often provide multiple conceptualizations or versions of organizational reality. Interpretivists, more than functionalists, recognize that organizations are coalitions of participants with different aims and priorities, not monolithic, unified entities. As a result, interpretivists often adopt a pluralistic perspective by exploring members' sense making practices at all levels of the organization.

The pluralistic view or "differentiation perspective" of culture is highlighted in Smith and Eisenberg's (1987) interpretation of Disneyland's organizational culture (Frost et. al., 1991, p. 8). The differentiation perspective suggests that members' shared understanding and experience of the organizational culture is not the same across the organization; instead consensus only emerges in within subcultures. "At the organizational level of analysis, differentiated subcultures may co-exist in harmony, conflict, or in indifference to each other... subcultures are islands of clarity; ambiguity is channeled outside their boundaries" (Frost et. al., 1991, p. 8). In the case of Disneyland, the employees and management reached consensus regarding what it meant to be a member of that organization within their own subcultures. The ambiguity and conflict emerged between the two groups' cultural boundaries. Smith and Eisenberg (1987) describe the root-metaphors that Disneyland employees used to make sense of their organization. The authors assert that a change in emphasis of root metaphors from drama to family reflected fundamental differences in the employees' and management's world view. The managerial use of the drama and "business of show business" metaphor implied structure, conformity, and a bottom line orientation. This metaphor was in opposition to the employees' emphasis on family, which suggested uncritical support of fellow employees. The employees' use of the family metaphor grew out of Walt Disney's desire to build an organization that provided family entertainment and friendly employee–customer relations. After Walt's death, employees began to interpret the family metaphor to mean that relations among Disney employees and management were friendly, uncritical, and supportive. The employees' interpretation of family was one that Walt Disney might not have intended or embraced. The conflicting metaphors and attendant conflicting realities employed by both groups ultimately led to a strike. Smith and Eisenberg's study points to the material consequences of socially constructed reality.

Pacanowsky (1983) provides another example of how the interpretive approach can provide a fuller understanding of organizational culture. Rather than reporting his findings in traditional social scientific forms, Pacanowsky's "A Small Town Cop" used the genre of fiction to display the detail, richness, and complexities of a policeman's organizational life. His study involved 160 hours of observation in a police department in which the focus was on "symbolic processes, a central concern for the social construction of meanings in organizational life, an aim to understand how organizational life is constituted, and the use of methods consistent with inquiry from the inside" (p. 261). In this study, Pacanowsky describes, among other things, a police officer's reaction when his partner is shot. His artful interpretive analyses "heighten our sensitivities to the excitement, depression, agony, and boredom of modern organizations" and capture "the complexities and richness of organizing by allowing readers to vicariously experience the emotional dilemmas of organizational actors" in ways that traditional, functionalist accounts cannot (p. 261).

Interpreting Culture
Interpretivists view cultures as systems of shared symbols and meanings to be described and interpreted in order to be understood. Therefore, interpretivists adopt naturalistic or ethnographic methods to investigate cultures, including participant observations, interviews, and interpreting organizational documents, outputs, mem-

oirs, and training/instruction manuals (Bantz, 1983). Aspects of organizational life that may have once been considered mundane have taken on added significance as communicative practices that constitute the organization's culture. Personal rituals (Pacanowsky & O'Donnell-Trujillo, 1983), organizational furnishings (Barley, 1983), storytelling, and jokes, are all fruitful areas of inquiry in the interpretive approach. In brief, interpretivists study everyday, "naturally occurring phenomena; they become immersed in the lives of the people they study; and they approach their task in a more flexible, iterative manner than do the functionalists" (Putnam, 1983, p. 44).

Ethnographic research requires that the investigator learn about the culture by living it. The researcher is not a detached, objective scientist; rather, he or she attempts to close the gap between the observer and the observed by embracing the culture and immersing himself or herself in it. This inquiry from the inside enables the researcher to explore, understand, and interpret the lived experiences of everyday organizational actors. Kunda (1992) adopted ethnographic methods in his study of a high-tech firm's culture. During the course of his year-long fieldwork, Kunda acted as an "unstructured observer," "a free management consultant," (p. 234), an "individual contributor," and even a "quasi-therapeutic" consultant to some organizational members (p. 236). Kunda's ethnographic methods of collecting data included full-time participant observation in which he participated in a variety of "public" activities including training seminars, sporting events, workshops, design meetings, review meetings, and other group meetings. He also participated in "private" situations such as lunching with informants and acting as a driver. Kunda also spent a significant amount of time interviewing several members of the organization, many of whom became key informants.

The ethnographer's task does not end with collecting data. He or she must also find a way to re-present that data to the reader. Kunda (1992, p. 238) describes the interpretive, analytic and iterative process of "writing it up":

> *I began the analysis and writing during the last months of my field work... The first step was reading and cataloguing my fieldnotes, creating, combining, redefining, and discarding numerous categories and groupings. It was in the course of this process that the main analytic categories—ideology, ritual, and the self—emerged. Next, I wrote a short ethnographic description of Tech... This became the basis for a rather frenzied, apparently directionless, yet satisfying process of writing descriptions that I engaged in after the field work was (arbitrarily) terminated. The final version of the thesis emerged after repeated writing and rewriting...*

Kunda's statement points to the common ethnographic treatment of cultures as texts that require "reading" and interpretation (Geertz, 1973; Goodall, 1984, 1989; Van Maanen, 1988). As texts, cultures can be interpreted in different ways, and thus there are often many tales to be told about the same culture (Van Maanen, 1988).

Just as interpretivists often adopt a pluralistic or differentiated view of organizational cultures, they also adopt pluralistic methods for analyzing and interpreting culture. Organizational communication scholars Krone, Jablin, and Putnam (1987) assert that, "no perspective is right or wrong" (p. 38); instead, interpretivists embrace any method that contributes to our understanding of organizational life. In addition to the ethnographic methods described above, researchers have also employed metaphor analysis (Feldman, 1991; Smith & Eisenberg, 1987), fantasy theme analysis (Bormann, 1983), semiotic analysis (Barley, 1983; Sless, 1986), and other interpretive methods to describe and understand cultures.

Critique of the Interpretive Approach

Interpretive studies of organization culture have been lauded for providing the in-depth understanding of the complexities of organizational life that is not possible in functionalist research. While interpretive studies are often interesting and insightful descriptions of culture, many argue that interpretive approaches are politically naive because they fail to address the power dimensions of organizational cultures (Deetz & Kersten, 1983; Fine, 1993; Mumby, 1987, 1988). Nor do interpretive studies adequately address the relationship between the larger social context and the particular culture in question (Fine, 1993). Finally, while interpretive studies provide us with rich understandings and thick descriptions of organizational life, they offer little in the way of prescriptive guidelines for improving organizational performance or facilitating organizational change as functionalist approaches claim to do.

Critical Approach to Organizational Culture

The critical approach to culture is an outgrowth of the interpretive approach in that it also aims to describe and interpret organizational culture, but critical research extends the interpretive tradition into the realm of critique and evaluation. The critical approach is a relative newcomer to organizational culture studies, but it is gaining increasing prominence in the field. Where interpretive research is descriptive, critical research is evaluative. Interpretivists make sense of organizational reality through an understanding of the symbol systems that account for organizational actions. Here "the investigator accepts the organizational reality as it is without questioning its potential" (Putnam, 1983, p. 200). In contrast, the critical researcher becomes an active critic of the status quo. More specifically, critical studies examine and call into question the ideologies and power structures that undergird organizational cultures. In so doing, the seemingly natural and taken-for-granted organizational reality is revealed as systematically distorted, constraining, and power-laden (Deetz & Kersten, 1983).

Organizational Culture and Ideology

The critical approach views communication and communicatively constituted organizational cultures as ideological or systematically distorted. Moreover, critical researchers assume that ideological communication produces conditions of domination and oppression. Ideology is "the medium *through which* social reality [or culture], consciousness, and meaningfulness are constructed. Through ideology we not only come to see the world around us in a particular way, we also become a part of that world and define ourselves in terms of it" (Deetz & Kersten, 1983, p. 162). Ideology tells us what exists, what is good, and what is possible in organizations (Therborn, 1980). It limits the social construction of reality by preventing other equally possible but not yet articulated conceptions of organizational reality from coming to fruition. By constraining and limiting our understanding of and experiences in organizational culture, ideology contributes to organizational oppression and domination.

The critical approach is grounded in an emancipatory drive to free people from domination and oppression. Critical theorists and researchers hope to expose the ideologies that exist in organizational cultures by examining "the deep structure process through which certain organizational realities come to hold sway over competing world views" (Mumby, 1987, p. 113). Mumby's (1987) explanation of the ideological function of narrative in organizations is an exemplar of the critical approach. Extending a descriptive study by Martin and colleagues (1983), Mumby (1988) analyzes an IBM story that reads as follows:

> *The supervisor was a twenty-two year old bride weighing ninety pounds whose husband had been sent overseas and who, in consequence, had been given a job until his return... The young woman, Lucille Burger, was obliged to make certain that people entering security areas wore the correct identification. Surrounded by his usual entourage of white-shirted men, Watson approached the doorway to an area where she was on guard, wearing an orange badge acceptable elsewhere in the plant, but not a green badge, which alone permitted entrance at her door. "I was trembling in my uniform, which was far to big," she recalled. "It hid my shakes, but not my voice. 'I'm sorry,' I said to him. I knew who he was, all right. 'You cannot enter—you're admittance is not recognized.' That's what we were supposed to say". The men accompanying Watson were stricken; the moment held unpredictable possibilities. "Don't you know who he is?" someone hissed. Watson raised his hand for silence, while one of the party strode off and returned with the appropriate badge. (pp. 117–118)*

According to Martin and colleagues' (1983) interpretive account, the story provides members with two related messages regarding IBM's culture. To higher status members, the story says, "Even Watson obeys the rules, so you certainly should" (p. 440). The message to lower status members is, "Uphold the rules, no matter who is disobeying" (p. 440). Mumby (1987, 1988), however, critiques the story as an ideological device that reinforces the power of the elite members of the organization. He goes beyond simply interpreting the story or describing how the story functions to produce an organizational reality at IBM. His analysis suggests that "Narratives punctuate and sequence events in such a way as to privilege a certain reading of the world. They impose order on 'reality' that belies the fact that such a reading is a largely ideological construction that privileges certain [managerial] interests over others" (1988, p. 126).

More specifically, Mumby (1987, 1988) outlines the four functions of ideology as they are manifest in the IBM story. First, the story functions ideologically by representing sectional interests as universal. In other words, ideology serves to make the interests of the managerial elite appear to be the interests or needs and concerns of all organizational members. The story suggests that all IBMers need to be concerned with upholding the rules; what the story obscures, however, is that the rule system itself was created by the corporate elite to protect their own interests. Second, ideology functions to deny contradictions that are often inherent in organizational life. According to Mumby (1988), the story itself is contradictory because it suggests that at IBM "no one is above the law," but if "Watson *was* subject to corporate rules in the same way as other employees, then this story would have little significance" (p. 120). The third function of ideology evident in the story is the naturalization of the present through reification. Through the process of reification socially constructed phenomena come to be perceived as objective realities separate from people who created them. Critical organizational communication scholars Deetz and Kersten (1983) explain, "Even though organizational members participate in the construction of social reality, the results of these constructions become natural and eventually dominate them" (p. 164). In the IBM story, the organizational hierarchy, the rule system, and traditional gender roles are reified. Finally, the story performs the ideological function of control. Ideology creates a consensus regarding the way the world is. "This consensus, expressed in thought and action, shifts control away from the explicit exercise of power . . . and places it in routine practices of everyday life" (Deetz & Kersten, 1983, p. 164). Ideological control is subtle and indirect, but effective and powerful. Ideological control, also known as hegemony, "works most effectively when the world view articulated by the ruling elite is actively taken up and pursued by subordinate groups" (Mumby, 1988, p. 123). In the IBM story, the rule system that supports the dominant organizational elite is actively upheld by a subordinate; thus, the "rules are enforced from the bottom up rather than from the top down" (Mumby, 1988, p. 123). The legitimacy of IBM's (reified) structure and rule system is reinforced in the telling of the tale.

The four functions of ideology—representing sectional interests as universal, reification, denying contradictions, and control—are often articulated in narrative form. Organizational stories are, in this sense, political because they are a "powerful means of constructing and maintaining an organization's underlying mode of rationality, providing a vision of the organization which is relatively complete, stable, and removed from scrutiny" (Mumby, 1988, p. 125). Mumby's analysis provides researchers with a model for understanding how other organizational texts, including stories, jokes, memos, rituals, and mission statements, can be critiqued to reveal the underlying ideology that privileges the interests of dominant groups over those of others.

Rosen's (1985) "Breakfast at Spiro's: Dramaturgy and Dominance" is an analysis of an advertising agency's culture in which the relationship between organizational symbolism and ideology is critiqued. Rosen's unit of analysis is a "social drama," or the ritualized annual company breakfast. More specifically, Rosen demonstrates how the "social drama" legitimizes and supports the extant power structure, which privileges the interests of management. For example, management's public speeches, performed in front of the Spiro's audience over eggs Benedict, serve as "pep rallies" and, more importantly, as a means of making the power structure evident. The ideological impact of these social dramas is articulated concisely by Rosen (1985) who says: "Managerial domination in practice is maintained not by an excited audience rushing back to the agency to work energetically, but by a workforce accepting the defined terrain. Culture, creating, and being the terrain for [member] consciousness here is a mechanism for control" (p. 48).

Critical researchers and theorists hope to go beyond simply exposing ideologies. The goals of critical research include understanding, critique, and education (Deetz, 1985; Deetz, 1992; Deetz & Kersten, 1983). The first goal of understanding refers to the creation of insight. Deetz (1985) cautioned that "merely understanding the means by which consensual realities are formed and perpetuated says little about whether such a [false] consensus adequately represents competing interests" (p. 268). Instead, critical researchers are interested in reframing knowledge of the organizational culture and exploring choices that are otherwise hidden by the culture's standard, and often unexamined, practices. Without such understanding "members remain in a sense victims of meaning structures that were developed in response to past situations and perpetuated in their talk and actions" (Deetz, 1992, p. 86). The second goal of the critical researcher is criticism. Like Mumby's (1987, 1988) analysis of the IBM narrative, critique involves holding the taken for granted culture up for careful scrutiny to determine whose interests are represented and whose are blocked within that reality. "Critique itself operates as part of a participative communicative act, the act of reopening effective communication to productive conversation" where all organizational members' interests are represented (Deetz, 1992, p. 87). Education is the third goal of critical research. Here the goal is to form "new concepts for organizational members and researchers in such a way as to enhance understanding of organizational life and to allow for undistorted discourse," and to enable members to employ alternative responses to organizational life (Deetz, 1982, p. 140). The role of the intellectual in critical organizational culture studies is not simply to produce new theories of oppression and domination; instead, as an educator, the role involves forming new ways of "seeing and thinking and contexts for action in which groups can express themselves and act" (Deetz, 1992, p. 88). Education might include providing organizational members, other researchers, practitioners, and students with alternative organizational discourses, strategies for engaging in productive and constructive conflict, and participative decision-making skills (Deetz, 1992). These are the tools that can help to free organizational members from ideological domination by enabling them to critique the meaning structures in which they find themselves and to develop alternative, fully participative, and ultimately less constraining organizational cultures.

Critique of the Critical Approach

The critical approach to organizational culture brings into sharp relief the inextricable relationship between organizational culture, power, and ideology. It forces us to take seriously the dark side of otherwise excellent or strong organizational cultures and suggests that this dark side should be a mainstream concern for managers and organizational researchers and theorists (Morgan, 1986). While this approach provides us with useful ways of thinking about the influence of culture, many critical studies and essays are theoretical and based on conceptual models rather than empirical data collected in real life organizations (Fine, 1993). One explanation for the paucity of empirical critical studies is that it may be more difficult for critical researchers, who do not write from the managerial point of view and indeed critique that point of view, to gain access to organizations. Critical researchers have also been critiqued for failing to write in forms that are accessible to organizational members and to develop practical strategies for helping members restructure their organizations in ways that serve the interest of members and the organization (Fine, 1993). Finally, Morgan (1986) cautions that we should not blind ourselves to the fact that nondominating forms of organizational cultures are possible and that perhaps more enlightened cultures do exist. Fully participative cultures in which the interests of all members are represented should be held up as models; those that do not, however, should continue to be exposed and critiqued.

RECENT TRENDS IN ORGANIZATIONAL CULTURE

The functionalist, interpretive, and critical approaches continue to frame the study of organizational culture. Very recently, however, two relatively new theoretical perspectives have begun to influence they way we think about organizational cultures and their influence. In the following section two new trends, feminist and postmodern analyses of organizational life, will be addressed.

Feminist Analyses of Organizational Culture

At its core, feminism is about creating equal opportunities for self-expression for both women and men in a variety of contexts, including organizations. It is important to note here that a single, unified feminism or feminist theory does not exist; rather, several partial and provisional answers to the woman question have been forwarded by Marxist, psychoanalytic, postmodern, liberal, radical, and other varieties of feminism. Yet all these different brands of feminism intersect to "lament the ways in which women have been oppressed, repressed, and suppressed and to celebrate the ways in which so many women have 'beaten the system,' taken charge of their own destinies, and encouraged each other to live, love, laugh, and be happy" (Tong, 1989, pp. 1–2). Feminist studies of organizations are only now beginning to have an impact on the field, and very few studies in speech communication have examined organizational culture through a feminist lens.

FOUR LINES OF FEMINIST RESEARCH IN ORGANIZATIONAL COMMUNICATION STUDIES

In organizational communication, four lines of feminist research have emerged (Fine, 1993). The first line of research examines the larger organizational context rather than organizational communication per se (Acker, 1990; Ferguson, 1984; Hearn et al., 1989). These studies suggest that organizations are gendered. While traditional conceptions of organizations seem to suggest that organizations are rule-governed, rational, and gender-neutral, an increasing number of communication scholars argue that "the prevailing [organizational] context within which women and men communicate is dominated by male values and forms" (Marshall, 1993, p. 126). In a very real sense, organizations valorize traits and characteristics that are stereotypically masculine, including an emphasis on rationality, long-range and abstract concerns, assertiveness, and the drive for individual success. In contrast, the traits that are typically attributed to women, such as an emphasis on feeling or emotion, devotion to detail and to practical, immediate needs, and orientation toward affiliative relationships, are often denied legitimacy in organizational life. When organizational cultures, however unwittingly, privilege that which has been constructed as masculine and marginalize that which has been constructed as feminine, problematic gender stereotypes are reproduced and reified (Fine, 1993; Hearn et. al., 1989; Martin, 1990; Mumby & Putnam, 1992; Pringle, 1988; Smircich & Calás, 1990).

Organizational stereotypes are problematic for men and women because they limit and constrain opportunities for self-expression. Wood (1994) identifies three stereotypes of men: sturdy oaks, fighters, and breadwinners. The sturdy oak is tough, unaffected by problems, always in control, in short a pillar of strength. While this stereotype is one that is often valued in organizations, it can contribute to poor performance and poor health. The sturdy oak stereotype may encourage men to take unnecessary risks rather than admitting doubts or fears and may contribute to poor decision-making when men refuse to ask others for help or important input. The cultural values that encourage men to be sturdy oaks may also contribute to men's stress-related conditions. The fighter is the warrior who goes to battle in the competitive world of the organization. This stereotype encourages men to put the organization first and to "fight for it with everything they have" (Wood, 1994, p. 269). As a result, men are often less able to take off time from work to devote time to their families. Finally, men are still stereotyped as breadwinners, as primary wage earners for families. Because earning income is a significant part of masculinity in our society, men feel enormous pressure to succeed economically. These stereotypes make it difficult for men to find legitimate alternative self-definitions and to facilitate policies that enable men to reduce time at work and to spend more time developing relationships with children and others (Wood, 1994).

Kanter's (1977) seminal work, *Men and Women of the Corporation,* suggests that women, too, are cast in outmoded and constraining stereotyped roles, including mother, seductress, pet, and iron maiden. Unfortunately, these stereotypes are far too common in organizations of the nineties (Wood, 1994). The mother stereotype pigeonholes women as nurturers. The negative consequences the mother faces are threefold: (1) She is rewarded for service to others rather than for independent action; (2) She is expected to act as an accepting, "good mother" or lose her rewards; and (3) She becomes an emotional specialist (Kanter, 1977, p. 234). Rarely will a "mother" be rewarded for "critical, independent, task-oriented behavior" (p. 234). The seductress or sex object is often caught in a double-bind: If she is viewed as sexually desirable and available, "she risks the debasement of the whore," but if she forms an alliance with a particular man, she may arouse jealousy and resentment (p. 235). Like the mother, the seductress is valued or devalued for her sexuality, not her competence. The pet is a childlike, humorous, amusing plaything. Any displays of competence on the part of the pet are "treated as special and complimented just because they [are] unexpected" (p. 235). Finally, the iron maiden may be viewed as a competent or "good" employee because she is tough, but she is simultaneously seen as a "bad" woman, lacking in femininity or sexuality. These stereotypes have material consequences for women, some of which will be taken up in the following section.

The second line of feminist research in organizational communication concerns "women's problematics" or experiences that are significant to and relevant for women in organizational contexts (Fine, 1993). These experiences include sexual harassment, gender discrimination, lack of family care and family leave policies, inflexible work schedules, and others (Fine, 1993; Wood, 1994). Organizational cultures that privilege masculinity can exacerbate these problems for women. For example, a culture that informally supports stereotypes of women might discourage employers from perceiving women primarily as employees or from taking them seriously. As a result women's contributions may be deemed less worthy and less valuable than their male counterparts who more closely fit the masculine norms of the culture. In fact, there are several empirical studies indicating that women still are not equally valued in organizational contexts. Women are paid less, their career ladders are shorter, their upward mobility is slower than in the case of men, and promotional outcomes between men and women still exist in the workplace. More specifically, women doctors earn 63 cents for every dollar that their male counterparts earn; women managers earn approximately 65 cents for every dollar earned by male managers; and a saleswoman earns 58 cents to a salesman's dollar (Wood, 1994). Unfortunately, the disparities are even greater when racial discrimination is considered. "On average, white women and black men are paid 25% less than their white male peers, and black women make 36% less. The disparity is even greater for Hispanic men, who make 32% less, and Hispanic women, who make 43% less" (Wood, 1994, p. 265).

Sexual harassment is another problem that feminist researchers have brought to the fore. Sexual harassment has been occurring for decades, but it was not until feminists identified, named, and legitimized the problem that we began to take it seriously. Sexual harassment is a problem that is often subtly fostered by organizational cultures that normalize masculine sexuality (Clair, 1993; Cockburn, 1991). Clair (1993) interviewed women about sexual harassment and found that these women often actively participated "in the production and reproduction of the dominant [masculine] organizational ideology" by sequestering their own stories of sexual harassment (p. 113). Clair argues that we should begin to "think culturally" about sexual harassment by viewing sexual harassment, not as a reified "thing" that happens in organizations, but rather as a discursive or communicative action that reproduces oppressive organizations (p. 115). In so doing, organizational members may begin to expose and legitimate stories of harassment and the women (and men) who share them. Fortunately, corporations are beginning to respond to this problem by developing preventive measures including training programs, education, and "consciousness raising" for all employees, not just management (Aburdene & Naisbitt, 1992, p. 96). What was once considered a private matter between the harasser and harassed is now a matter that is increasingly and rightly subject to public scrutiny.

A third line of feminist research aims to document women's voices by identifying the meanings and values women bring to the workplace that may be different from but equally appropriate as masculine values and meanings (Fine, 1993). In *Megatrends for Women: From Liberation to Leadership,* Aburdene and Naisbitt (1992) suggest that women's leadership is characterized by an "inspire-and-communicate" approach rather than a traditional masculine "command-and-control" model. Moreover, it is the inspire-and-communicate model that is predicted to prevail in the 1990s. Connectedness or community-mindedness is another example of a feminine value. For most women, connection with others is a primary given, not just a secondary option to be contracted at will. Similarly, women tend to judge themselves by standards of responsibility and care toward others (Ferguson, 1984; Gilligan, 1982). A redefined conception of leadership, compassion, nurturance, and caring are feminine values that are useful for both men and women and are worthy of incorporating into organizational cultures.

The final line of feminist studies centers on alternative organizations based on feminist principles. Feminist organizations are "pro-woman, political and socially transformational" (Martin, 1990, p. 184). They are profit and nonprofit, hierarchically structured and collectivist, national and local, legal and illegal, and dependent and autonomous (Martin, 1990). An organization can be characterized as a feminist organization if it meets one of the following criteria (Martin, 1990): "(a) has feminist ideology; (b) has feminist guiding values; (c) has feminist goals; (d) produces feminist outcomes; (e) was founded during the women's movement as part of the women's movement (including one or more of its submovements, e. g., the feminist self-help health movement, the violence against women movement..." (p. 185). Feminist organizations include the National Organization for Women, rape crisis centers, Weaver's Guilds (Wyatt, 1988), bookstores (Seccombe-Eastland, 1988), and record companies (Lont, 1988). All these organizations "reveal organizational structures and enactments that challenge traditional conceptions of organizations" and provide researchers, theorists, and practitioners with alternative models of organizing and organizational cultures (Fine, 1993, p. 147).

While significant inroads have been made and organizations are beginning to be transformed, feminist analyses will continue to be needed in the future. More precisely, Fine (1993) calls for future feminist research to document the organizational experiences of women and other marginalized groups, to examine the social construction of race, gender, and class as it is enacted in organizational contexts, to contribute to the development of multicultural organizations in which diversity (of gender, ethnicity, sexual orientation, age, and class) is valued and celebrated, and to uphold the feminist "ethical imperative for the researcher to work *within* organizations to study real people in real situations and to work for changes that will improve the lives of those people" (p. 154). Feminist approaches may ultimately facilitate the move toward increasingly responsive organizational cultures that will better serve the increasingly diverse and complex workforce.

Postmodern Analyses of Organizational Culture

Postmodern thinkers have produced provocative, challenging, and sometimes jarring accounts of organizational life (Foucault, 1978, 1979). Postmodern analyses of organizational cultures question the assumptions of "unified" cultures and instead formulate culture in terms of irony, paradox, seduction, difference, and otherness (Calás & Smircich, 1991; Cooper & Burrell, 1988; Deetz, 1992; Linstead & Grafton-Small, 1992; Meek, 1988; Shultz, 1992). The "fragmentation perspective" outlined by Frost and colleagues (1991) captures a postmodern orientation to organizational culture (p. 8). This perspective views ambiguity as a significant and pervasive aspect of organizational life, and studies using this lens focus on cultural expressions of ambiguity. Here, "consensus and dissensus co-exist in a constantly fluctuating pattern... Any cultural manifestation can be, and is, interpreted in a myriad of ways. No clear organization-wide or subcultural consensus stabilizes when a culture is viewed from a fragmentation point of view" (p. 8). Postmodern thought forces us to radically reconceive the way we think about organizational culture, to question the very notion of culture itself. Although the works of postmodern writers do not represent a unified theory, they do offer a related set of approaches to a similar problem. What unifies diverse postmodern theorists is their "suspiciousness against everything previously accepted" (Simonsen, 1990, p. 53). Several postmodern concepts, including difference, deconstruction, discourse, and disciplinary power, as well as their implications for the study of organizational culture, will be addressed in the following section.

Difference and Deconstruction

The concept of *différance* or difference asks the critic to consider what is absent as equally significant to what is present in any text or discourse. In a very simplistic sense, what is not said is often as meaningful as what is said. Derrida (1976), a contemporary continental philosopher, posited that meanings are not immediately present in signs because there is no fixed distinction between a signifier (a word) and a signified (that which a word represents). Presence or meaning seems fixed and ontologically stable only because it appears to stand in opposition to another fixed term—absence. Derrida (1976) reminds us that presence or meaning is always elusive and is dependent on absence for its (relational) definition. "Positively marked terms 'signify' because of their position in relation to what is absent, unmarked, the unspoken, the unsayable. Meaning is relational within an ideological system of presence and absences" (Hall, 1985, p. 109).

Difference has many implications for the way we conceptualize and research organizational cultures. Linstead and Grafton-Small (1992) are organizational communication scholars who argue that studies of organizational culture have focused on the "concept of 'shared meaning' as definitive of cultural forms," but difference suggests that such "shared meaning' is impossible, always incomplete," a fiction (p. 345). Using difference as a lens through which to view organizational culture, we might expect to find paradox, ambiguity, instability, and fluidity of meanings in place of shared meanings. Cooper (1989), a thoughtful critic of contemporary organizations and management practices, applies difference to organizational life by demonstrating that "an organization always harbours within itself that which it transgresses, namely, disorganization" (p. 480). Similarly, the formal organization is only meaningful in relation to the often hidden and "absent" informal organization. Obviously for the traditional, functionalist organizational communication researcher an unstable, floating definition of "organization" (heretofore a fixed, certain, and knowable identity) may cause no small amount of concern.

Furthermore, the relational meaning of a term is hierarchically ordered such that one term is dominant or subordinate to its opposite. Binary pairs such as presence/absence, male/female, management/union, and superior/subordinate are examples of these apparently fixed and hierarchically arranged oppositional terms. Derrida argues, however, that these binary pairs conceal the degree to which the things that are presented as oppositional are in reality interdependent. This interdependence means that neither term is autonomous, but instead meaning is scattered in an endless play of signifiers. Meaning cannot easily be located because, "it is never fully present in any one sign alone, but it is a kind of constant flickering of presence and absence" (Sarup, 1989, p. 35).

It is through Derrida's (1976) method of deconstruction that difference, the flickering meaning of a term, can be addressed. Deconstruction actively challenges traditional boundaries between oppositions such as reason/emotion, masculine/feminine, superior/subordinate, and self/other (Tong, 1989). Deconstruction consists of two interrelated movements, the overturning and "metaphorization" of the binary opposition (Cooper, 1989, p. 481). "To deconstruct the opposition, first of all, is to overturn the hierarchy at a given moment" (Cooper, 1989, p. 483). The critic, however, must not stop at simply replacing the dominant term with the subordinate term, but must move to metaphorization. Metaphorization problematizes the very idea of oppositional logic and thereby allows for a space or a "middle-voice" to emerge in between the oppositional terms (Poovey, 1988). Derrida (1976) terms this space *différance* or difference. Thus, deconstruction enables us to move away from binary or either/or thinking to embrace both/and, multiplicitous, ambiguous thinking.

Recently, organizational theorists have begun to deconstruct organizational texts. Organizational communication researchers, Mumby and Putnam (1992), deconstructed Simon's formal concept of bounded rationality, which describes the predilection of actors to suffice rather than maximize their organizational behaviors. Bounded rationality is rooted in and provides a justification for bureaucratic structures of meaning. Mumby and Putnam's (1992) postmodern feminist critique demonstrates how bounded rationality privileges the formal terms such as male, public, mind, and rational over their informal opposites—female, private, body, and emotional. The subordinated terms are subsequently marginalized and "constituted as 'other,' or as supporting but not essential to organizational life" (p. 466). Their deconstruction attempts to overturn bounded rationality by articulating "bounded emotionality" as an alternative mode of organizational experience (p. 466). Bounded emotionality—characterized by relatedness, the integration of mind, soul, and body, communality, tolerance of ambiguity, a hierarchy of goals and values, and nongendered institutional forms—represents an oppositional way of knowing (speaking about, conceiving of, and developing) organizations. Mumby and Putnam's (1992) reading is an example of how similar organizational meaning systems might be deconstructed, thereby creating a space for the rearticulation of subordinated voices in organizations. Martin's (1990) deconstruction of gender conflicts in organizational life also employs a postmodern–feminist lens. Difference and deconstruction are fruitful constructs for organizational theorists who are interested in constructing alternative, liberating, and enabling organizational discourses and organizational cultures. More empirical studies of organizational culture using a postmodern lens are needed, however, before we will be able fully to assess the contribution of this new and novel approach.

Discourse and Disciplinary Power

Foucault (1978, 1979, 1980) provides a new vocabulary for discussing, and thus a new way of understanding, organizational communication and organizational culture. Foucault's *Discipline and Punish: The Birth of the Prison* (1979) and *The History of Sexuality* (1978) are thought-provoking organizational/institutional analyses in which "normal" practices like sexuality and punishment come to be seen in an entirely novel and often exceedingly disturbing light. Both texts force us to radicalize our thinking by vividly illustrating how organizations operate as discursive sites in which individuals' subjectivity or identity is produced. For Foucault, communication or "discourse" is more than a system of shared meanings; rather, discourse is a site of power, a struggle among competing versions of "truth" and a site in which individuals are literally created or constituted. Discourse is defined by Flax (1990b, pp. 205–206) as a

> *system of possibilities for knowledge. [Discourses] are made up in part of sets of usually tacit rules that enable us to identify some statements as true or false, to construct a map, model, or classificatory system in which these statements can be organized, and to name certain "individuals" as authors...All [discourses] simultaneously enable us to do certain things and confine us within a necessarily defined system.*

Discourses are ways of constituting knowledge or "truth." The problem for Foucault (1980) lies in "seeing historically how effects of truth are produced within discourses which in themselves are neither true nor false" (p. 118). Discourses have both ideational and material or practical effects or "truths." As organizational communication scholars, we must ask questions such as, "How is knowledge or 'truth' produced through organizational discourse?," "What types of discourses are accepted as 'true' in the organization?," and finally, "Whose 'truth' counts?" Deetz (1992) suggests that managerial discourse is typically valued, perhaps unnecessarily, over other marginalized discourses in contemporary organizations. Thus, managerial discourse becomes the "truth" for all organizational members. Similarly, the popular management press is an organizational discourse in which often only males are able to produce knowledge. In texts *In Search of Excellence* (Peters & Waterman, 1982) and *Thriving on Chaos* (Peters, 1987), organizations' protagonists are almost exclusively male, and management is described in typically masculine terms (i.e., managers must attack, confront, and take control of the organizational environment). This discourse produces a masculine model of leadership and subsequently any other possible alternatives such as a feminine model of management is denied (Trethewey, 1992).

Discourses create what Foucault (1980) would call the "subject" or the individual. For this reason, discourses are highly political. "Discourses are more than ways of thinking and producing meaning. They constitute the 'nature' of the body, unconscious and conscious mind and emotional life of subjects which they seek to govern. Neither the body nor thoughts and feelings have meaning outside of their discursive articulation" (Weedon, 1987, p. 108). The way we speak, read, write and listen is always done in ways that are discursively determined and have social effects. Even when we are most conscious of our individuality, for example, in our most intimate encounters, we communicate in ways that are socially and conventionally determined, which in turn helps to reproduce, maintain, or change social relations (Fairclough, 1989).

Foucault (1979, 1980) would argue that our sense of self or our identity is produced discursively, and modern organizations are an increasingly important site of subjectivity formation. For Foucault discourses are not powerful because they can deny or repress our desires or interests, nor are they powerful because they prevent us from discovering our true interests or true self (because, according to Foucault, there is no true or essential self to be found). Instead, discourses are powerful in that they produce identity. This form of productive power Foucault (1979) terms "disciplinary power." Deetz's (1992) explanation of disciplinary power is particularly insightful, "[It] is thus a configuration of power inserted as a way of thinking, acting, [feeling], and instituting. It is shared by both those who control and are controlled; in fact it defines what control will be in its realm and the parts [the] subject [or organizational member] may play" (p. 259).

Although Kunda (1992) does not use the term disciplinary power, his discussion of normative control provides a compelling account of disciplinary power at work. He persuasively argues that organizational cultures are forms of normative control that shape the employees' very selves in the corporate image. Kunda's (1992) insightful definition of normative control is worth citing here at length:

> *Normative control is the attempt to elicit and direct the required efforts of members by controlling the underlying experiences, thoughts, and feelings that guide their actions. Under normative control, members act in the best interest of the company not because they are physically coerced, nor purely from an instrumental concern with economic rewards and sanctions. It is not just their behaviors and activities that are specified, evaluated, and rewarded or punished. Rather, they are driven by internal commitment, strong identification with company goals, intrinsic satisfaction from work. These are elicited by a variety of managerial appeals, exhortations, and actions. Thus, under normative control, membership is founded not only on the behavioral or economic transaction traditionally associated with work organizations, but, more crucially, on an experiential transaction, one in which symbolic rewards are exchanged for a moral orientation to the organization. In this transaction a member role is fashioned and imposed that includes not only behavioral rules but articulated guidelines for experience. In short, under normative control it is the employee's self—that ineffable source of subjective experience—that is claimed in the name of corporate interest. (p. 11)*

In today's world, there appear to be a variety of reasons that individuals are willing to and, in fact, enjoy subjecting themselves to normative control. Many people are looking for meaning, community, and involvement in causes larger than themselves (Alvesson, 1990). Increasingly organizations are providing individuals with those important needs for meaningful lives and involvement. Primary meaning-giving institutions such as the family, the community, and the church have, in many ways, been eclipsed by their corporate counterparts (Deetz, 1992). "As different forces in society, including corporate practices themselves, lead to the erosion of stable production of meaning and identity in the home and community, the corporation becomes ever more central in the process of coordinating individual activity" (Deetz, 1992). As a result, modern public organizations are encroaching into arenas that were once considered the domain of the individual's private life. Family life, for example, is now structured around the needs of the corporation. Where we live, how we live, and even the timing of children are choices that are more closely tied to work than to community or kinship ties (Deetz, 1992). Even the areas of the self that were once considered private are subject to corporate scrutiny, including thoughts and feelings. This is disciplinary power at work.

The problem with normative control or disciplinary power comes into view when members "allow corporate definitions of reality to serve as unquestioned criteria for their self-definition and their world view" (Kunda, 1992, p. 225). The ability of the subject to form his or her identity through alternative discourses is constrained when organizational discourse constitutes the subject in the corporation's image. Moreover, not only does normative control undermine the individual's ability to form an alternative identity, such control might also undermine the "foundations of collective action" in the larger society when corporate subjects respond to family, community, and the body politic in the way that corporate discourse demands. Without alternative discourses through which members can choose various subject positions or identities, the fear is that the normative control mechanisms, such as strong cultures, that are so pervasive in organizational discourse, may ultimately "narrow the human character" (Deetz, 1992, p. 43). It is indeed difficult to find an organization in which bodies are not subject to normative control or, in Foucault's (1979) terms, disciplinary power. Foucault's (1979, 1980) work enables organizational communication scholars to conceive of a wide variety of organizational practices such as training and development, performance appraisals, rituals and ceremonies, and newcomer orientations as manifestations of disciplinary power through which organizational subjects are produced.

As a form of disciplinary power, organizational culture is "partially constitutive of the subjectivity of those who are involved in its production... As members [of a culture], be they managers, professionals, superiors, subordinates, or amenable to any other taxonomy, they are immersed in this unselfconscious negotiation and emergence of their own identities within and without the corporation" (Linstead & Grafton-Small, 1992, p. 344). Organizational cultures are powerful and influential because they have the capacity to shape our very individuality. Fortunately, while individuals are influenced and shaped by organizational discourse (discourses that are themselves multiple and conflicting), the self is not completely determined or fixed by organizational discourse. Instead, organizational members often employ a variety of resistance strategies. Few organizational members engage in outright acts of rebellion, revolt, or uprising; however, in the space between passive acceptance of disciplinary power and revolt, members often use strategies such as gossip, rumor, the creation of social spaces for the assertion of dignity, parody, and even the decoration of desk tops and office space as means of asserting, and in fact defining, one's self in the face of pervasive, normalizing organizational cultures. The Foucauldian lens is one that is certainly worth looking into, and we can expect more and more organizational culture theorists and researchers to do just that in the coming years.

CONCLUSION

Because we literally spend our lives in organizations, it behooves us to study and understand their cultures. Organizational cultures are clearly complex human creations that require examination from a variety of perspectives to be fully understood and appreciated. The five theoretical perspectives presented in this chapter—functionalist, interpretive, critical, feminist, and postmodern—represent different lenses through which we can examine culture. Certainly no one perspective is the right or best perspective; instead, each lens provides us with a different view of the multifaceted phenomenon that is organizational culture.

GLOSSARY

Critical approach—an approach to organizational communication that assumes that organizational reality is shaped by deep structures of power. The goal of critical research is to emancipate organization members. Communication is conceived as ideological and power-laden, not as a neutral medium for transmitting information or creating shared realities.

Deconstruction—a method for analyzing and critiquing organizational texts that actively challenges traditional boundaries between oppositions such as reason/ emotion, masculine/feminine, superior/subordinate, and self/other (Tong, 1989). The goal of deconstruction is "undermining the imposition of a veneer of reality of texts" and showing how a given text undermines the very "philosophy it asserts, or the hierarchical oppositions on which it relies" (Mumby, 1988, p. 161).

Difference—Derrida's (1976) conception of difference refers to the idea that absence is as important as presence in understanding and evaluating language. Difference embodies both meanings of the French verb "'différer': to defer, or to postpone, in time, and to differ in space" (Cooper, 1989, p. 488). As Mumby and Putnam (1992) explain, "The meaning of a text consists of both a system of differences and the constant deferral of any fixed meaning" (p. 468). The French term describes the instability of meaning in any given text.

Discourse—in the Foucauldian sense of the term, discourse is a way of conceiving of language as a social practice that has a variety of effects, including the production of "truth," knowledge, and the self.

Feminism—a political movement and a set of theories that attempt to account for women's and other marginalized groups' subjugated status and to find ways to overcome oppression and domination based on gender, race, and other differences.

Functionalist approach—an approach to organizational communication that assumes organizational reality is given and knowable. The goal of functionalist research is to predict and control organizational behavior by establishing causal relations between communicative acts and organizational outcomes. Communication is conceived in mechanistic and linear terms.

Ideology—a system of meanings that makes us see the world in a particular way. Ideological meanings are pervasive because they assume that mantle of "the natural for which there is no alternative" (Fiske, 1982, p. 153). Critical theorists remind us, however, that there are always alternative meanings that normally lie unrecognized or unacknowledged.

Interpretive approach—an approach to organizational communication that assumes organizational reality is socially constructed. The goal of interpretive research is to understand or to provide insight into humanly constructed phenomena. Communication is conceived of as a form of sense-making.

Normative control—"The attempt to elicit and direct the required efforts of [organizational] members by controlling the underlying experiences, thoughts, and feelings that guide their actions" (Kunda, 1992, p. 11). Normative control claims the member's very self in the name of the corporation.

Postmodernism—a (non)philosophy, a way of thinking that rejects traditional; assumptions about truth, reality, and the nature of the self. All postmodern discourses "seek to distance us and make us skeptical about beliefs concerning truth, knowledge, power, the self, and language that are often taken for granted within and serve as legitimation for contemporary Western culture" (Flax, 1990a, p. 41).

CASE STUDY

Wisner Shaw Press is a family-owned printing company in Northern California that prides itself on delivering outstanding customer service and quality products. The Wisner Shaw premises house the executive offices, as well as design, sales, estimating, and other administrative offices. The facility also boasts impressive, state-of-the-art presses and printing equipment. Mr. Shaw, the owner and president of the company, believes that providing potential clients with tours of the Wisner Shaw facility is an effective way to make clients feel welcomed, to showcase their equipment and products, and to enable salespersons to provide information about Wisner Shaw's services.

In the past, the four full-time sales associates (all men) provided tours on a rotating basis (historically Wisner Shaw has had trouble retaining and promoting women sales associates). Recently, however, a new sales associate, Candy Murdock, has been hired. After several clients commented on Murdock's informative and enjoyable tours, Mr. Shaw asked Murdock to assume more responsibility for the tours. Not wanting to disappoint her new boss or co-workers, Murdock agreed. Now every time a client comes to the facility, all the sales associates, including Murdock, simply assume that Murdock will provide the tour. The sales staff and Mr. Shaw refer to these tours as "Candy's famous in-house tours." Murdock takes pride in her ability to perform this task effectively, but as a salesperson whose salary is based on commission she also feels her time could be more productively spent working "in the field" on new accounts.

At the last Wisner Shaw holiday reception, Mr. Shaw introduced each member of the sales team by name and sales figures for the past year. For example, he said, "Let's hear it for Mr. Jeff Brown who sold $1, 300, 000 worth of Wisner Shaw printing last year!" When he introduced Murdock, however, he said, "And this is Candy, our favorite little hostess who is well known for her 'famous in-house tours'." Murdock left the reception feeling ambivalent about both her responsibility for the tours and her future at Wisner Shaw Press.

Discussion: 1. What elements of organizational culture seem to be at work at Wisner Shaw Press? 2. Imagine that you have been hired as a communication consultant by Wisner Shaw Press. How would you help Mr. Shaw and other senior level managers understand the impact of this particular ritual? What strategies might you suggest to improve or strengthen the sales team's subculture? 3. Examine this case study through each of the five "lenses" discussed in Chapter 8, including the functionalist, interpretive, critical, feminist, and postmodern approaches. What aspects of the case are highlighted by each lens? What is the value of looking at a cultural phenomenon through a variety of theoretical lenses?

REFERENCES

Aburdene, P., & Naisbitt, J. (1992). *Megatrends for Women: From Liberation to Leadership.* New York: Fawcette Columbine.

Acker, J. (1990). Hierarchies, jobs, bodies: A theory of gendered organizations. *Gender and Society, 4,* 139–158.

Alvesson, M. (1990). On the popularity of organizational culture. *Acta Sociologica, 33,* 31–49.

Barley, S. R. (1983). Semiotics and the study of occupational and organizational cultures. *Administrative Science Quarterly, 28,* 393–413.

Bantz, C. R. (1983). Naturalistic research traditions. In L. L. Putnam & M. E. Pacanowsky (eds.), *Communication and Organizations: An Interpretive Approach* (pp. 55–72). Newbury Park, Calif.: Sage.

Berger, P., & Luckman, T. (1966). *The Social Construction of Reality: A Treatise in the Sociology of Knowledge.* Garden City, New York: Doubleday.

Beyer, J., & Trice, H. (1987). How an organization's rites reveal its culture. *Organizational Dynamics, 15,* 4–35.

Bormann, E. G. (1983). Symbolic convergence: Organizational communication and culture. In L. L. Putnam & M. E. Pacanowsky (eds.), *Communication and Organizations: An Interpretive Approach* (pp. 99–122). Newbury Park, Calif.: Sage.

Brown, I. C. (1963). *Understanding Other Cultures.* Englewood Cliffs, N.J.: Prentice-Hall.

Calás, M., & Smircich, L. (1991). Voicing seduction to silence leadership. *Organizational Studies, 12,* 567–601.

Clair, R. P. (1993). The use of framing devices to sequester organizational narratives: Hegemony and harassment. *Communication Monographs, 60,* 113–136.

Cockburn, C. (1991). *In the Way of Women: Men's Resistance to Sex Equality in Organizations.* Ithaca, N.Y.: ILR Press.

Cooper, R. (1989). Modernism, postmodernism and organizational analysis 3: The contribution of Jaques Derrida. *Organization Studies, 10,* 479–502.

Cooper, R., & Burrell, G. (1988). Modernism, postmodernism and organizational analysis: An introduction. *Organization Studies, 9,* 91–112.

Deal, T. E., & Kennedy, A. A. (1982). *Corporate Cultures: The Rites and Rituals of Corporate Life.* Reading, Mass.: Addison-Wesley.

Deetz, S. (1982). Critical-interpretive research in organizational communication. *Western Journal of Speech Communication, 46,* 131–149.

Deetz, S. (1985). Ethical considerations in cultural research in organizations. In P. J. Frost, L. F. Moore, M. R. Louis, C. C. Lundberg, & J. Martin (eds.), *Organizational Culture* (pp. 253–269). Newbury Park, Calif.: Sage.

Deetz, S. (1992). *Democracy in an Age of Corporate Colonization: Developments in Communication and the Politics of Everyday Life.* Ithaca, N.Y.: State University of New York Press.

Deetz, S., & Kersten, A. (1983). Critical models of interpretive research. In L. L. Putnam & M. E. Pacanowsky (eds.), *Communication and Organizations: An Interpretive Approach* (pp. 147–171). Newbury Park, Calif.: Sage.

Derrida, J. (1976). *Of Grammatology* (G. Spivak, trans.). Baltimore: Johns Hopkins University Press.

Fairclough, N. (1989). *Language and Power.* New York: Longman.

Feldman, M. S. (1991). The meanings of ambiguity: Learning from stories and metaphors. In P. J. Frost, L. F. Moore, M. R. Louis, C. C. Lundberg, & J. Martin, (eds.), *Reframing Organizational Culture* (pp. 14–25). Newbury Park, Calif.: Sage.

Ferguson, K. E. (1984). *The Feminist Case Against Bureaucracy.* Philadelphia: Temple University Press.

Fine, M. G. (1993). New voices in organizational communication: A feminist commentary and critique. In S. Perlmetter Bowen & N. Wyatt (eds.), *Transforming Visions: Feminist Critiques in Communication Studies* (pp. 125–166). Cresskill, N.J.: Hampton Press.

Fiske, J. (1982). *Introduction to Communication Studies.* London: Methuen.

Flax, J. (1990a). Postmodernism and gender relations in feminist theory. In L. Nicholson (ed.), *Feminism/Postmodernism* (pp. 19–38). New York: Routledge.

Flax, J. (1990b). *Thinking Fragments: Psychoanalysis, Feminism, and Postmodernism in the Contemporary West.* Berkeley: University of California Press.

Foucault, M. (1978). *The History of Sexuality* (R. Hurley, trans.). New York: Pantheon.

Foucault, M. (1979). *Discipline and Punish: The Birth of the Prison* (Alan Sheridan, trans.). New York: Vintage.

Foucault, M. (1980). *Power/Knowledge* (Ed. Colin Gordon). New York: Pantheon.

Frost, P. J., Moore, L. F., Louis, M. R., Lundberg, C. C., & Martin, J. (eds.) (1985). *Organizational Culture.* Beverly Hills, Calif.: Sage.

Frost, P. J., Moore, L. F., Louis, M. R., Lundberg, C. C., & Martin, J. (eds.) (1991). *Reframing Organizational Culture.* Newbury Park, Calif.: Sage.

Geertz, C. (1973). *The Interpretation of Cultures.* New York: Basic Books.

Gilligan, C. (1982). *In a Different Voice: Psychological Theory and Women's Development.* Cambridge: Harvard University Press.

Goodall, H. L., Jr. (1989). *Casing a Promised Land.* Carbondale: Southern Illinois University Press.

Goodall, H. L., Jr. (1984). The status of communication studies in organizational contexts: One rhetorician's lament after a year-long odyssey. *Communication Quarterly, 32,* 133–147.

Hall, S. (1985). Signification, representation, ideology: Althusser and the post-structuralist debates. *Critical Studies in Mass Communication, 2,* 91–114.

Hearn, J., Sheppard, D., Tancred-Sheriff, P., & Burrell, G. (eds.) (1989). *The Sexuality of Organization.* Newbury Park, Calif.: Sage.

Jelinek, M., Smircich, L., & Hirsch, P. (1983). Introduction: A code of many colors. *Administrative Science Quarterly, 28,* 331–338.

Kanter, R. M. (1977). *Men and Women of the Corporation.* New York: Basic Books.

Krone, K. J., Jablin, F. M., & Putnam, L. L. (1987). Communication theory and organizational communication: Multiple perspectives. In F. M. Jablin, L. L. Putnam, K. H. Roberts, & L. W. Porter (eds.), *Handbook of Organizational Communication: An Interdisciplinary Perspective* (pp. 18–40). Newbury Park, Calif.: Sage.

Kunda, G. (1992). *Engineering Culture.* Philadelphia: Temple University Press.

Linstead, S., & Grafton-Small, R. (1992). On reading organizational culture. *Organization Studies, 13,* 331–355.

Lont, C. (1988). Redwood records: Principles and profit in women's music. In B. Bate & A. Taylor (eds.), *Women Communicating: Studies of Women's Talk* (pp. 233–250). Norwood, N.J.: Ablex.

Marshall, J. (1993). Viewing organizational communication from a feminist perspective: A critique and some offerings. In S. Deetz (ed.), *Communication Yearbook, 16* (pp. 122–143). Newbury Park, Calif.: Sage.

Martin, J. (1985). Can organizational culture be managed? In P. Frost, L. Moore, M. Louis, C. Lundberg, & J. Martin (eds.), *Organizational Culture* (pp. 95–98). Beverly Hills, Calif.: Sage.

Martin, J. (1990). Deconstructing organizational taboos: The suppression of gender conflict in organizations. *Organization Science, 1,* 339–359.

Martin, J., Feldman, M., Hatch, M. J., & Sitkin, S. B. (1983). The uniqueness paradox in organizational stories. *Administrative Science Quarterly, 28,* 438–453.

Martin, P. Y. (1990). Rethinking feminist organizations. *Gender and Society, 4,* 182–206.

Meek, V. L. (1988). Organizational culture: Origins and weaknesses. *Organization Studies, 9,* 453–473.

Morgan, G. (1986). *Images of Organization.* Newbury Park, Calif.: Sage.

Mumby, D. K. (1987). The political function of narrative in organizations. *Communication Monographs, 54,* 113–127.

Mumby, D. K. (1988). *Communication and Power in Organizations: Discourse, Ideology, and Domination.* Norwood, N.J.: Ablex.

Mumby, D. K., & Putnam, L. L. (1992). The politics of emotion: A feminist reading of bounded rationality. *Academy of Management Review, 17,* 465–486.

Ouchi, W. (1981). *Theory Z.* Reading, Mass.: Addison-Wesley.

Pacanowsky, M. (1983). A small town cop. In L. L. Putnam & M. E. Pacanowsky (eds.), *Communication and Organizations: An Interpretive Approach* (pp. 261–282). Newbury Park, Calif.: Sage.

Pacanowsky, M. W., & O'Donnell-Trujillo, N. (1983). Organizational communication as cultural performance. *Communication Monographs, 50,* 126–147.

Peters, T. (1987). *Thriving on Chaos: Handbook for a Management Revolution.* New York: Harper & Row.

Peters, T. J., & Waterman, R. H., Jr. (1982). *In Search of Excellence: Lessons from America's Best Run Companies.* New York: Harper & Row.

Pringle, R. (1988). *Secretaries Talk.* London: Verso.

Poovey, M. (1988). Feminism and deconstruction. *Feminist Studies, 14,* 51–65.

Putnam, L. L. (1983). The interpretive paradigm: An alternative to functionalism. In L. L. Putnam & M. E. Pacanowsky (eds.), *Communication and Organizations: An Interpretive Approach* (pp. 31–45). Newbury Park, Calif.: Sage.

Putnam, L. L., & Cheney, G. (1985). Organizational communication: Historical developments and future directions. In T. W. Benson (ed.), *Speech Communication in the 20th Century* (pp. 130–156). Carbondale, Ill.: Southern Illinois University Press.

Rosen, M. (1985). Breakfast at Spiro's: Dramaturgy and dominance. *Journal of Management, 11,* 31–48.

Sarup, M. (1989). *An Introductory Guide to Post-Structuralism and Postmodernism.* Athens, Ga.: University of Georgia Press.

Schein, E. H. (1991). The role of the founder in the creation of organizational culture. In P. J. Frost, L. F. Moore, M. R. Louis, C. C. Lundberg, & J. Martin (eds.), *Reframing Organizational Culture* (pp. 14–25). Newbury Park, Calif.: Sage.

Schockley-Zalabak, P., & Morley, D. D. (1994). Creating a culture: A longitudinal examination of the influence of management and employee values on communication rule stability and emergence. *Human Communication Research, 20,* 334–355.

Seccombe-Eastland, L. (1988). Ideology, contradiction, and change in a feminist bookstore. In B. Bate & A. Taylor (eds.), *Women Communicating: Studies of Women's Talk* (pp. 251–276). Norwood, N.J.: Ablex.

Shultz, M. (1992). Postmodern pictures of culture. *International Studies of Management and Organization, 22,* 15–36.

Simonsen, K. (1990). Planning on "postmodern" conditions. *Acta Sociologica, 33,* 51–62.

Sless, D. (1986). *In Search of Semiotics.* London: Croom Helm.

Smircich, L., & Calás, M. (1987). Organizational culture: A critical assessment. In F. Jablin, L. Putnam, K. Roberts, & L. Porter (eds.), *Handbook of Organizational Communication* (pp. 228–263). Newbury Park, Calif.: Sage.

Smircich, L., & Calás, M. (1990, August). *What feminist theory offers organization and management theory, or why go from culture to gender?* Paper presented at the annual conference of the Academy of Management, San Francisco.

Smith, R. C., & Eisenberg, E. M. (1987). Conflict at Disneyland: A root metaphor analysis. *Communication Monographs, 54,* 367–380.

Therborn, G. (1980). *The Ideology of Power and the Power of Ideology.* London: Verso.

Tong, R. (1989). *Feminist Thought: A Comprehensive Introduction.* Boulder, Colo.: Westview Press.

Trethewey, A. (1992, November). Re-reading/re-writing managerial discourse: A semiotic critique of *Thriving on Chaos: Handbook for a Management Revolution.* Paper presented at the annual convention of the Speech Communication Association, Chicago, Illinois.

Trice, H. M., & Beyer, J. M. (1984). Studying organizational cultures through rites and rituals. *Academy of Management Review, 9,* 653–669.

Van Maanen, L. (1988). *Tales of the Field: On Writing Ethnography.* Chicago: University of Chicago Press.

Weedon, J. (1987). *Feminist Practice and Poststructuralist Theory.* Oxford: Basil Blackwell.

Wilkins, A. (1983). Organizational stories as symbols which control the organization. In L. Pondy, G. Morgan, P. Frost, & T. Dandridge (eds.), *Organizational Symbolism* (pp. 81–92). Greenwhich, Conn.: JAI Press.

Wood, J. T. (1994). *Gendered Lives: Communication, Gender, and Culture.* Belmont, Calif.: Wadsworth.

Wyatt, N. (1988). Shared leadership in the Weavers Guild. In B. Bate & A. Taylor (eds.), *Women Communicating: Studies of Women's Talk* (pp. 147–176). Norwood, N.J.: Ablex.

RECOMMENDED READINGS

Cooper, R., & Burrell, G. (1988). Modernism, postmodernism and organizational analysis: An introduction. *Organization Studies, 9,* 91–112.

Deal, T. E., & Kennedy, A. A. (1982). *Corporate Cultures: The Rites and Rituals of Corporate Life.* Reading, Mass.: Addison-Wesley.

Fine, M. G. (1993). New voices in organizational communication: A feminist commentary and critique. In S. Perlmetter Bowen & N. Wyatt (eds.), *Transforming Visions: Feminist Critiques in Communication Studies* (pp. 125–166). Cresskill, N.J.: Hampton Press.

Frost, P. J., Moored, L. F., Louis, M. R., Lundberg, C. C., & Martin, J. (eds.). (1991). *Reframing Organizational Culture.* Newbury Park, Calif.: Sage.

Linstead, S., & Grafton-Small, R. (1992). On reading organizational culture. *Organization Studies, 13,* 331–355.

Mumby, D. K. (1987). The political function of narrative in organizations. *Communication Monographs, 54,* 113–127.

Putnam, L. L., & Pacanowsky, M. E. (eds.). (1983). *Communication and Organizations: An Interpretive Approach.* Newbury Park, Calif.: Sage.

Sathe, V. (1983). Implications of corporate culture: A manager's guide to action. *Organizational Dynamics, 12,* 5–23.

Organizational Creation and Evolution

TIMOTHY NEAL THOMPSON

Creativity is happening in organizations. It happens in many ways, from the clerk in a mom and pop shop doing the window display to corporate giants creating new products and sending new images over networks of light and sky. It happens as the organization's members describe their mission ("what we do") and construct their vision ("where shall we go?"). Organizational creativity is people producing—individuals and groups inventing, experimenting, trying new combinations of things and ideas. In our heads, in conversations, and in the doings of each new day, we're all creating in one way or another.

We are all a part of numerous organizations right now, all of them creative at many levels. Our family, peer groups, schools, clubs, where we work, and the places in which we socialize all have organizational structure, and all are organizing and creating in different ways. We flow through and change (and change with) these organizations. We are doing things, making things, putting ideas together to solve problems; possibly making it up as we go, as each organization must be recreated by new members across time. In a very real sense we are creating our organizations, doing our part or playing our role in the drama and stories of those organizations.

Organizations are evolving, attempting to achieve a better fit within the shifting situations of the social environment. Whether it be putting together products and marketing plans to better fit the targets, or refurnishing office space to better fit our needs, organizing is directed "toward a better fit." The continual push to fit, to adapt, to do it differently and better, is the birthplace of creativity. And if we take all the separate acts of creativity and put them together in one big ball of change, we have social evolution. Creation and evolution are not necessarily contradictory terms.

Creativity happens in mind and interaction. It is a *psychological process,* occurring within individuals, and a between-person or *social process.* It happens in our thoughts, in dyadic discussions, in groups, in organizations, in mass media, and in global social networks. Creativity is happening in each communication context, at all levels as it all evolves.

Creation and evolution in organizations are in focus here, but that does not exclude the individuals, groups, media, and cultures we interact with and within. We can't ignore systems thinking. The organization is a system of so many individuals and groups and a subsystem of other sociopolitical and cultural systems. Organizations are many circles of interaction moving in larger circles. This chapter is about those circles of creative and communicative action and the larger circles of change, and evolutionary form, in which they occur. What is organizational creativity and how is it enhanced? Can organizations and individuals think and act in more creative ways? How does that creativity influence and get influenced by other social systems? How are creativity and communication evolutionary processes? We'll begin with some notes on creativity and organizing, work our way through evolution theory, then conclude by applying those notes in an example of a creative, evolving organization.

CREATIVITY AND ORGANIZING

"Create" has roots in the Latin *creatus* and the Sanskrit *creare,* both meaning "to produce" or "to make." It implies doing. Ideas are wonderful and plans can be great, but creativity implies putting ideas and plans into practice. That's creativity—putting ideas into practice—doing things, thinking about them, doing some more. In composing a letter, playing with computer graphics, revising a report, giving a speech, proposing plans, or evaluating "how things are going," we are putting ideas into action. That's the general form of creative, evolutionary social systems: action-reflection-action, and so on. We do things, we think and talk about them, we do some more.

Typically the creative process is discussed in terms of *initiation* of an idea, *preparation* for working on the idea, *incubation* as the idea meshes with others in the subconscious, *illumination* if the idea gets to that "aha!" stage, and *action* whenever we *do* something with the evolved idea. All parts of the process are important, but action does hold a prominent position.

Just as the physical body gains range of motion from exercise, the mind and social systems can also gain range. Through practice, or *doing,* we gain flexibility. Thinking is important, but saying and doing complete the circuit. Some Eastern philosophers have taught us of meditative states for the mind, such as Zen, transcendental meditation, yoga, and the many variations of Tao. Most masters will emphasize the importance of moving meditation, ways of doing that promote ways of thinking. Tai Chi, for example, with its emphasis on slow moving stretches, promotes an awareness of the limits and limitlessness of our physical being and the here and now environment surrounding us. Ways of doing promote ways of thinking and feeling.

What exercises creativity? Reading, reflecting, and talking are exercise, as are making, doing, inventing, and playing. Writing your notes is exercise. Thinking about what you're thinking right now is exercise. We do, we think, we do some more. Doing and thinking are exercise, and adding flexibility to action and thought is how we expand our range of creative options.

Exercises that promote creativity include writing, sketching, drawing, walking, stretching, playing, building, gardening, painting, computing, making music, and other activities. Even watching television, an act that usually takes a beating from those promoting creativity, can be exercise that makes us aware of more options. Each activity can be grounds for growth, expansion, opening our realm of experience. Or each activity can become routine and stabilized. Thus, it is important to exercise creativity regularly but just as important to add variations to our exercises. All actions can be considered opportunities for creative exercise, all interactions are food for thought.

For groups, activities like brainstorming, improvisational "jam session" discussions, and playfulness can enhance creativity. Moreover, the environment of social relations in groups can enhance or inhibit creativity. Groups that are loosely coupled, with interdependent yet independent members socially relaxed, and tolerant of deviation, tend to demonstrate more creative action than groups that are uptight, intolerant of disorder or deviation, with members who are socially stressed in various ways. For instance, if you find yourself in an organization of members who think their answers are the right answers, and no other interpretations are acceptable; or where conflict overrides cooperation to the point of paranoia, and large chunks of each day are spent on "the battle;" or where the nasty things said to nice things said ratio for the group is typically 9:1, then you may be in an uptight group situation.

How can we distinguish organizational creativity from individual and group creativity? We can't, and even if we can, it is probably not necessary. Essentially, organizations are the product and process of individuals and groups organizing, and most of what we call creativity occurs in the individual and group communication context. The organization has impact, there can be no doubt, in the rules, norms, traditions, culture, and other organizational variables that impact on individuals and groups. But it is in individual minds and interactions between people that ideas are born and put through the creative paces; it is at these levels that creative potential may be exercised.

For the physical body, it's good to maintain stability and strength and to develop flexibility or freedom of motion. The same is true of things mental and social. Exercising flexibility while remaining relatively stable is the balance Gregory Bateson pondered, as he talked and wrote of evolving social systems. Bateson was an anthropologist who danced on the cutting edge of communication and other disciplines for a good part of this century. He wove his way through anthropological field studies (with his wife, Margaret Mead, in earlier years), evolution theory, cybernetics, art, literature, and other fields. If he didn't discover the idea, he surely made us more aware of the "content" and "relational" levels of communication and the need to understand communication as being more relational than individual. In this piece from *Steps to an Ecology of Mind* (Bateson, 1972), he's talking of human behavior as a variable, and how lack of stretching in relation to other variables can limit our freedom to vary:

> *In other words, the variable which does not change its value becomes* ipso facto *hard programmed. Indeed, this way of stating the genesis of hard-programmed variables is only another way of describing* habit formation.
>
> *As a Japanese Zen master once told me, "To become accustomed to anything is a terrible thing."*
>
> *From all of this it follows that to maintain the flexibility of a given variable, either that flexibility must be* exercised *or the encroaching variables must be directly controlled. (p. 511)*

This battle between stability and flexibility wages on in all evolving systems. It's the opposition between order and disorder, organizing and disorganizing, composition and decomposition. Stability is found in habits, rules, traditions, and norms. Flexibility is found in the changes we make and the exercising of options in doing something new that doesn't quite fit within the existing structures. Both are necessary. As with Yin and Yang, night and day, and the cycles of growth and decay in the changing seasons, creativity occurs within a dialectic of opposites that need each other. "Dialectic" here refers to opposing forces working together, or unified opposition, or the ways in which opposites in a process need each other. We need stability and we need flexibility.

Dialectical Influences in the Creative Process

Certain attitudes and actions can help maintain our flexibility. An openness to variety and learning from others helps, as opposed to absolute acceptance of one perspective or one group's interpretations, and other habits that get in the way of learning. Remaining open and continually learning is difficult in many ways. We each have habits of thought, and partake in developing group habits of thought. Dynamics such as groupthink and other social-limiting patterns—like pressures toward conformity, normalcy, and continuity—can cage creativity. But again, we can see that conforming, being normal, and having a sense of connection between past and present are functional. We can be creative and still conform to certain ideals.

All that enhances creativity may hinder it if taken too far. For instance, learning our profession, the rules, games, technologies, trends, and big ideas, can stimulate creative thought. Training is good. But too much training in a single domain can be debilitating. Kenneth Burke (1984), one of our century's most creative communication scholars, wrote of the "occupational psychosis" that develops from prolonged focus in a narrow specialization, as we begin to talk about and think about the world according to our job and training, and *not see* the many other possibilities for thinking and doing. The more we become accustomed to one way of thinking, the more difficult it becomes to think in other ways. Hence Burke treats us to Thorstein Veblen's oxymoron, "trained incapacities," to remind us of the dangers in overspecialization. Training is good, but too much training in one area can be a detriment to creative growth.

The same is true of so many other influences in the creative process. Time plays a role. Deadline pressures, for instance, can constrict creativity insofar as they cut our time to create. But deadlines also are given credit for many creations, by those who "work best under pressure," and in the frenzy of social activity that sometimes occurs as we near a deadline. The way we think about and "use" or "spend" time can enhance or inhibit creativity as well. A constant sense of time anxiety, too much to do in too few hours of the day, can make us feel harried, stressed, trying to "just catch up" let alone be creative. A more relaxed view of time might let us see the opportunities in each new moment. I'm not saying "take time to smell the flowers" all the time, or some other timely cliche; just that time, the impact of clocks on our life, can be experienced differently, and can be friend or foe to the creative process.

Action is another area of dialectical concern in the creative process. To this point "doing" has been emphasized; the idea that we must act, make, do something!, if creative growth is a goal. Activity is good, and laziness or complacency can be habits that hinder creative action. But a little laziness may be a good thing; a bit of time spent procrastinating, "not producing," not working, may be just the ticket for some fresh meanderings in our mind. Many creative souls, from Henry David Thoreau to the Beatles' John Lenon, promoted the benefits of aimless sauntering, purposeless sitting, and other forms of inaction. It is noble to act, and choose not to act, as we balance the needs to work, rest, think, and dream. Sometimes the best way to work on a problem or project is to quit working and to let the subconscious streams take over for a period of incubation.

The dialectic is also present in the simultaneous convergence-divergence of the creative process. Creativity converges on the new form being created, and yet the process includes divergent patterns. In other words, the creative process is stochastic, much like the form of a branching decision tree. Stochactic refers to converging on a decision by exploring divergent paths. We make decisions (converge) about what to do, what to think, what to say, and so forth, and each of those decisions open up new possibilities and probabilities (diverging opportunities). Each decision made makes certain courses of action more likely, and other paths less likely. The decision to go to school opened up possibilities, set up new branches of decisions to be made (such as major/minor, career, specialization, groups to join, and other decisions), and made it less likely that you will travel the same path that you would have had you not gone to school. Like any other course of action that we put together, career decision-making is a creative process, and those unfolding pathways of fresh possibilities are part of the stochactic creative process.

The list of dialectical influences can go on, such as the impact of rules, argumentation, and goal-directedness on creativity. Rules are necessary for social stability, and the awareness of the "rules of play" in our profession is important, but a rigid reliance on rules can stunt creativity and bind our ability to adapt. Argumentation can be productive, but too much argument may blind us of the agreements necessary to coproduce creative projects with others. Having goals is a very good thing, but being stuck on a goal so much as to miss the whole adventure is not good. Creativity happens within this dialectic, between opposing yet necessary "forces." Creativity is a balancing act, an ongoing blending of organizing with disorganizing, believing and disbelieving, following and leading, pulling reality apart and putting it back together again. Probably most of all, it is a balance between the current order and the emerging new order, where we are and where we are going, the "what?" and the "toward what?" of our evolving systems.

To summarize, creativity is making something new in thought and action; blending old ideas in new ways and new ideas in old ways; the process of transforming ideas and things into new forms. The creative process entails doing something, thinking about it, and doing some more; cycles of action/reflection. The process is dialectical, where opposites are attracted, working together, in the build up, breakdown, converging, diverging patterns of creation. We can also note the dialectical tensions between what enhances creativity and what inhibits creativity:

Enhances Creativity	*Inhibits Creativity*
Action	Stagnation
Relaxed environment	Uptight environment
Mental freedom	Mental imprisonment
Awareness of variety	Narrow realm of knowledge
Constructive argumentation	Groupthink
Training	Trained incapacities
Tolerance for disorder	Strict adherence to order
Knowing the rules	Completely rule-driven
Exercise	Habitual laziness

Many influences impact on creativity for us and our organizations, some physical, some psychological, and some social. Many models have been and can be made of the creative process as well, but one that is especially helpful for understanding creativity is the model of evolution.

Evolutionary Process in Organizing

The evolutionary process of organizing has been described eloquently by Karl Weick. In his landmark book, *The Social Psychology of Organizing* (1979), we are given history and application of evolution theory for organizations. Weick, like Burke and Bateson, is a key player in this century's emergence of communication as critical discipline. And like Burke and Bateson, his influence has spilled across disciplines, supplying scholars and practitioners with useful information in the Information Age. In essence, Weick says that organizations evolve and survive by continually making new sense of their environment. People in organizations are asking "What's going on here?" and attempting to adapt by finding (or creating) answers. Marketers are asking what consumers are doing, thinking, buying; accountants are pondering better ways to line up the numbers; legal counsel is determining how the latest rulings should be interpreted; research and development is talking about developments in other companies. All are making sense of their domain, and attempting to achieve a "better fit" within that domain, just as you, me, and others are looking for answers, interpretations, for the present scene. Organizations, groups, and you and I evolve by making sense of our environments.

Weick (1979) likens organizational sense-making to an evolutionary process by explaining the cycles of enactment, selection, and retention. Normally, evolutionists talk of *variation,* selection, and retention, so Weick's model is a variation on evolution theory (meta-evolution?). That is, Weick's ideas are a creative blend of old with new, part of the evolution of organization theory, and to the extent that we find his ideas useful, they may become part of our own creative evolutionary growth.

Enactment, Selection, and Retention

Enactment, selection, and retention are three identifiable activities tied together in the process of sense-making. Enactment means "attending to" a part of the Big Picture, and the domain being attended to is the "enacted environment." Selection is choosing rules and interpretations for the enacted environment, determining which ways of thinking and doing are best for situations. Retention is like the memory process, as retained images developed in the past are applied to the present sense-making situation. We are involved in the process right now. The enacted environment is organizational communication; we are reading, talking about, and choosing different interpretations; and we have a retained vocabulary and rules for thinking about organizing that we've brought from the past to this present situation. Those retained maps may be the product of a long history or may have been freshly developed earlier in this book. So now leadership, conflict, persuasion, and culture are familiar terms as we come across them again, as we make sense of this and other domains.

Weick (1979) expands our vocabulary for each term, connecting enactment, selection, and retention to other areas of knowledge. The terms relate to creativity, for in the creative process retained ideas are combined as we act and interact and interpret those interactions. Creativity is doing, and talking, and thinking, and doing some more, as past interactions and thoughts are used in making sense of, and making something new in, the present.

Enactment is "acting that sets the stage for sense-making. [We have seen] exhibits of enactment in the activities of saying, doing, spinning webs of significance, adapting, and producing variations. In each case enactment served to bracket and construct portions of the flow of experience" (Weick, 1979, p. 147). Enactment is the way we frame an event by naming and thinking about only certain aspects out of all possible aspects. Korzybski (1958), as discussed in Chapter 1, would say we're "abstracting" by talking about only a few characteristics from the infinite characteristics of any given event. Enactment is abstraction, as we frame reality within the words and visuals used to name it. That is not to say that the "stuff" of our enactments is not real. Perceptions are very real, and enacting is perceiving.

For example, let's say a news story has just been released about dirty deeds going on in local government. The mayors administration is accused of financial, sexual, and drug- related crimes. As the mayor reads the story, she thinks: "What is this?! I'm innocent! Who's responsible for this slander?!" As the mayor's most ardent enemy reads the story, he thinks, "Ah, now we've got you! I've always said you were crooked." Two people, attending to the same news story, but attending to it in very different ways. They are enacting different realities around the same event.

Selection is the process of choosing interpretations, the choices we make while answering the question "What's going on here?" Selection is the process of interpreting the enacted environment, as we select how things will be named, and give meaning to the flow of events by drawing from the pool of all possible meanings. We select how things will be interpreted, whether something is right or wrong, functional or dsyfunctional, comic or tragic, or otherwise. For instance, right now quality is the rage in many circles, from business to ways of life. But quality is enacted differently by different people and organizations, some selecting statistical applications and others choosing to focus on the humanistic aspects of the quality movement. Some associate it with "zero defects" and focus on quality product, while others associate quality with people and ways of life, talking of empowerment, continuous education, and other "god terms" clustering around quality. Robert Pirsig, in *Zen & the Art of Motorcycle Maintenance: An Inquiry into Values* (1974), selects different meanings all together for quality, treating it as an elusive term that can only be measured when we impose our systems of measurement—only given meaning when we apply our systems of meaning. We select meanings, from quality to other questions about "What's going on?" and "How can we do better?"; we choose how everything will be interpreted. How do people in our organizations talk? Are they positive, negative, hopeful, doubtful, or what? In all organizations we find variety in the ways different members talk, differences in the realities people choose by the words they use.

We pay attention to some things and do not pay attention to others. We select some meanings and not others. What we attend to (enact), and what meaning we give it (select), are largely directed by our retention system. Retention is memory and recall, maps developed in the past that are used in making sense of the present. But those maps are not exact, memory is in no way perfect. Weick argues retention is itself a constructive process, as we put images together to form memories. Individual and organizational memory are reconstructive processes, and the maps we construct become inputs into the sense-making process. Our retained maps, images in mind, are like lenses through which we perceive and name our world, and they influence how we enact and select interpretations for our world. For example, I've read and taught some things about advertising, about aesthetics (What makes an artistically good ad?), and about social criticism (Are advertising and consumerism good, bad, or "both and _____"?). The things I've read and said are retained images that influence how I look at advertising and how I interpret it. I can talk of ads from a financially functional point of view—did they help sales/revenues? or take a more critical viewpoint to discuss the proliferation of pollution and junk that accompany models that emphasize consumerism. Or choose any number of other interpretations and ways of attending to or thinking about advertising. My ways of thinking about the topic of advertising are only limited to the extent that my retained maps are limited or that my sources for new maps get cut off.

Retention can limit or provide freedom/range to our enactments and selections. A variety of available images in retention gives variety to enactment and selection processes. The more we know about an area or topic, the more ways we can name it and think about it. Variety in our retained images gives us variety in the ways we interpret and adjust to the events of the world. This is what "requisite variety" refers to, having variety inside of the system so the system can recognize and adapt to variety outside of the system. The more knowledge and experience members have about their field, the better they can adapt. Ideally. But people can have all kinds of knowledge and experience and still not be able to adapt. Having a variety of images or meanings available does not mean people will use them, and it's in the using, the doing, where adaptation occurs. Thus, knowing more can help us achieve a better fit in our organizational domain, but it's in doing that we achieve the fit. Requisite variety is being aware of variations for knowing and doing, having and using a variety of maps as we think and act in various sense-making scenes.

Weick's (1979) maps of evolutionary process in organizing help us make sense of what's going on in organizations. Enactment, selection, and retention give us a way of naming the process, and other terms he reviews help us to understand that process. When he writes "complicate yourself with respect to organizing" (p. 261), Professor Weick suggests we should develop our own requisite variety, learn many ways for talking and thinking and doing, as we adapt in many organizing environments.

Organizing, Balancing, and Changing

The connections between evolution and organizing are plentiful. For instance, Weick (1979), the philosopher anthropologist Gregory Bateson (1972), and others talk of the cybernetic cycles of evolving organisms. Cybernetics deals with self-correcting systems. In the process of adaptation, both physical and social, we see cybernetic self-correcting circuits toward "homeostasis," as systems attempt to maintain the "moving balance" discussed in Chapter 1. As we organize, in business, pleasure, or whatever, we attempt to achieve some level of expectations, and our expectations set the level at which we will feel "things are going as they should," the steady state or homeostatic point of "balance" for the system. What is the point of balance for us, or our groups and organizations? Is balance when things are slow-paced, laid-back, and mellow, or does it happen when the action's moving fast? Does balance occur when we're not inundated with information, or does our system need a generous amount of symbolic goods and a lot of information to keep sailing at an even keel? Different people, and groups, and organizations live and act in different environments, and their points of homeostasis, or balance, or sense that "things are all right" are different. One couple needs more argumentation while another couple needs lack of conflict to feel things are going all right. One group may feel "staying cool" is the point of balance while another group needs the heat of preparing for battle to experience "normalcy." I've been in organizations in which the pace was slow and that was normal, and where the pace was fast, such as the newsroom of a newspaper, and that was normal. Social and biological systems have different points of balance, and adaptation is the system "correcting" toward the point of balance. Of course, that point of balance may be different for individuals and groups within the organization, and so the "balance" is always being negotiated, defined, and redefined across time.

Change is what sets organizing into action. We attempt to determine "what's going on here" within shifting social conditions, changes within the ecology of the organization, and the systems it interacts with and within. The ecology of an organization is the everything of the organization—the culture, other organizations in the suprasystem, the profession, the place and time, people, stories, past history, present action, and future visions. Organizations, as examples of organizing systems, are part of a larger social-ecological system, or as Bateson (1972) called it, the eco-mental system. We are connected with other people, our mind is a part of the larger social mind that is developing now and has been developed in the past. Through language and other symbols we are connected with many others; we are being influenced by and influencing the systems of thought we act within. These systems of thought comprise much of the ecology we are discussing. Our ecology is physical, consisting of trees, rain, birds, other people, and all of the elements in the cycles of composing and decomposing life. But the ecology of concern here is the social, as our mind and actions are both product and part of the process of social interaction. What music do you listen to? Which media do you gravitate toward? Who do you socialize with? What do you talk about? What do you hear? What are the typical patterns of stories that flow through the news you watch? What do you like to read? What are the typical patterns of symbols, ideas, thoughts that dance in your head? Who has influenced you and who do you influence? All are part of the social ecology, the eco-mental systems in which you play your part.

Creative Cybernetic Cycles

Cybernetics is the study of self-correcting systems. That's what evolving organizations do, they correct themselves toward ideas of what should be happening, or toward expectations of what is normal, in balance, or OK. Consultants, communication specialists, and professionals of all sorts visit organizations to show them how to be OK, how to achieve a better business balance as they adapt to changes. Various therapists help individuals and groups achieve some sort of better fit with their scene. All are trying to reach "good fits" of various kinds. One group's trying to fit by making more money while another group tries to get their minds off money to adapt. One scholar seeks to perfect statistical applications for a problem, another tries to adapt by perfecting language. We're all "correcting" toward something, some point of balance or bliss. This process of monitoring our environment, and trying to correct toward our bliss, is creative.

We're monitoring what's going on in our ecology, trying to put things together in satisfying ways. I monitor what the rain and sun and running feet do to my lawn and flowers and make adjustments according to what I think lawns and gardens should look like. I do something, spread some grass seed, rake on topsoil, transplant flowers. I'm creating something, putting seed and earth and roots together in new combinations. Likewise, I monitor what's going on with my family and at work, tending to the seeds I've sewn in those scenes. These are parts of my ecology, and they're changing, and I try to change with them. I calibrate my thoughts and actions with changes in the physical and social ecology, *creating* all the while.

Organizations are changing. New people, ideas, technologies, and information flow in and out of organizations. We're adapting within the changing ecology by choosing and using some of the ideas and things. Like awareness of the interaction between sun, rain, and earth, we try to figure out what interacts to make our organizations grow and thrive, then we create, plant the seeds of ideas and tend to the garden through our actions. Things are changing, and we're creating changes to fit the changes.

So, what are we saying and what's in it for us? Our organizations are organizing and reorganizing toward moving ideals, forever adjusting, calibrating the system to fit the changing scenes. The process of putting ideas together is creative within our evolving ecology, as is the way organizations co-create our existence by naming and acting in the larger scene in certain ways. For instance, members of military and political systems are enacting "safety" and "threats" in different ways, and the ways they interpret various conflicts and borders does much to create our global military–political environment. Business executives, market analysts, and financial institutions are helping create local and global markets. Government agencies are enforcing rules (and selectively not enforcing the rules sometimes), helping to create the order; meanwhile, radical groups, terrorist groups, and other oppositional groups are trying to create a new order. All kinds of people are together creating the order of things through their actions and interactions, and to a certain extent we make choices about what order we will create. We can choose to creatively blend the "stuff" of our existence toward a better way.

We create our ecology and it creates us. Humans have created all kinds of technologies and ideas, and these technologies and ideas structure our lives to a certain extent. It is quite a different thing to live with phones, faxes, fiberoptic networks, a vast repertoire of media, and the ideas that accompany the Information Age, than it is to live in the forest, dessert, or water in a more Agricultural Age frame of mind. Cars, credit cards, guns, and other products of our creation now partly create us or at least structure our choices. Some people are creating and created by the global marketplace, while some are creating and created by their local weather and crop yields. We've created our ecology in the choices we made to put us where we are now, and where we are going in the future. The ecology of people and ideas from our past, in our present, and toward our future all partly create us. We create the evolving eco-mental system and it creates us.

Order/Chaos and Stability/Flexibility

We're making choices about certain paths to follow in thought and deed. Along what paths shall we seek knowledge? How shall we proceed with relationships? What shall I say next? We're choosing among new unfolding pathways, the stochastic process or branching decision trees of life, organizing, evolution. As with the self-similar fractal patterns of chaos theory, we see the choices people make branch out before them as they do something (enact), choose interpretations for it (select), and reflect (the back and forth retention process between now and then), and continue to see new choices. We've made choices that have brought us this far and have a fresh menu of choices in adapting to our here and now. Each branch we climb on the decision tree sets up the probability that we'll climb within a certain range of future branches and not others. That's stochastic process, the unfolding of new probabilities that develop in the interacting elements of our ecology. Our choices, each of our decisions, are an element in the evolving ecology of ideas; part of the order within the grand chaotic mishmash of ideas (or are we the chaos within the grand order?).

Chaos used to be a bad thing. For quite some time, from the boom years of the industrial revolution, to the rapid growth following the Second World War, organizations strove toward order—putting things and people in their place, using time and motion in the most efficient ways, defining and enforcing rules—keeping chaos out. Organizations are still into creating order (after all, that is what organizations do), but attitudes about chaos have changed. In some circles, chaos is the welcome state of affairs. In hard sciences like physics, geology, and biology, chaos theory has had an impact on the way scientists "see" and think about their universe. Rather than seeking the underlying order of things, those in the chaos camp look at the neverending birth of randomness and newness in the interactions of things. Rather than seeing direct or linear causal chains of events in the world, chaos theory redirects attention to nonlinear causal circuits, where small beginnings can cycle forward into huge endings, where the flapping of a butterfly's wing in Cleveland can amplify forward, and interact with other "causes" to create the weather in Boston (see Briggs, 1992; Briggs & Peat, 1989; Gleick, 1987; Stewart, 1990).

Weather is often used to illustrate chaos theory. Weather systems are not completely predictable because so many different conditions are interacting all at once. Cold and warm fronts, high and low pressure areas, moisture and dryness, and other aspects are all moving and mixing. Many dynamic subsystems are interacting in the total system of weather, and because they are dynamic and interactive, moving and mixing, we cannot predict past a very few days with high probability. The probability of predicting the weather accurately is difficult due to the infinite possibilities that are born each moment in the interaction of all factors producing the weather. Next week's weather is not very predictable because of changes that will occur when things interact.

We could go on to discuss how chaos theory has influenced computer technology, art, fashion, and other fields. Most to the point here is the way the ideas behind chaos theory have been iterating through the academic and business communities. From Karl Weick's (1979, p. 245) advice that "chaotic action is preferable to orderly inaction," to Tom Peters' (1987) lessons for *Thriving On Chaos: Handbook for a Management Revolution,* those influencing organizations are recommending that organizations grow accustomed to chaos. Changes are happening rapidly and regularly, so set up organizations that are ready to change—creative organizations.

The readiness to change with new demands from the environment implies flexibility. Organizations gain flexibility by maintaining enough chaos in their system to meet the demands of the chaos in outside systems. What is that point of "enough chaos" is as good a question as what is the proper balance between flexibility and stability. We never quite know, and the best we can do is to be always "finding out," as we take our readings of the changes out there and create our changes in the organization.

To a degree, we are structured and limited by the environments we create, and to a degree we have freedom to create those environments differently. On the one hand, certain dictates from the higher system, our suprasystem, are limiting choices and stabilizing social structures; but on the other hand, we see individuals and organizations exercising flexible options within the constraints of social structures. Stability and flexibility are forever moving in the balancing act of organizing, sensemaking, adapting, and evolving: forever making the new, the same old way, in the Grand Old Dialectic.

Creativity is blending old and new, chaos and change within the order of things; an evolving, stochastic decision tree of choosing and using variations. Creativity is born in the choices we make when doing, thinking, and saying. The following is an example of a creative, evolving organization, born in the actions, thoughts, and words interacting between several organizing systems. The example, a festival created by students, was born in interaction, the dialectical dance between minds, symbols, and action.

CREATION AND EVOLUTION
IN ORGANIZING A FESTIVAL

As I write this my wife is due with our fourth child, we're completing some construction on our house and barn, and I just completed the final report on the results and future of a festival I helped create. It sounds kind of busy, but they're not all happening at once so much as developing through time. Just as the baby has been through a nine moon gestation, the house and the festival have evolved over time.

At home we're reorganizing, making changes in getting ready for the change. Likewise, the festival committee is reorganizing, reading the signs from this year's festival while getting ready for next year's event. We're creating the festival, making choices about who, what, where, when, how, and why. Those choices are influenced by what has happened, retained images of past festivals, what worked and what needs work, as we put ideas into action. What events were successful? Did the advertising work? Was our organization efficient and cost-effective? We look at what we've done (retention) as we choose what we will do (enactment).

The festival has a past and we're planning a future in the here and now of our present. Creativity happens now, influenced by what was and what is to be. We do, make, think new thoughts, and build new things based on the knowledge, experience, and wisdom from our past while working on some vision of the future. Retention and variation play together as we select our paths of adaptation.

The festival is the Spring Highlands Festival, named during a brainstorming session in a graduate public relations class at Edinboro University. We were working on developing a celebration of spring for the university, and since the school and community have roots in Scotland, a Scottish theme was chosen. This story of the festival's origin and genesis is the story of a creative, evolving organization.

Theme and Variation in an Evolving Idea

The first Spring Highlands Festival at Edinboro University was held in April, of 1993. Formal planning began September 1992. What started as an idea, conception, was brought to fruition after nine cycles of the moon, so the connections between making festivals and birthing babies are even stronger than I first imagined.

Formal planning for the birth took place in two public relations courses, then the carrying through on the advertising and implementation of the event was done by an advertising class and other groups who clustered around the idea as it progressed. What started as a few people talking about things ended up being many people doing things. The idea evolved as it interacted with others' ideas.

The idea did not begin in the classes. Ideas for festivals and Scottish games have been around for centuries. My initial thinking and interest in a Scottish celebration for Edinboro began when attending the Ohio Scottish Games in Oberlin, Ohio, the summer before beginning work at Edinboro. After a year of living and teaching here, and having not seen such a festival in this Scottish borough, I wrote the university president a letter asking if we should try to start a Scottish Festival. In consequent conversations with him and other administrators, I was told the idea had been thought about but not tried, mainly due to the costs involved and the difficulty justifying expenditures on such a frivolous thing as a festival in tight economic times. The variation, or idea, had been explored but not selected. The idea had a history in the retained images of the University.

I came into that year's public relations courses with the idea that we would create a student Scottish festival; nothing big or expensive, just a celebration of spring with Celtic themes. As we talked about the festival and started doing things to make it happen, the ideas expanded and mutated. It got messy. We were trying to create order amid the chaos of so many possibilities. Many ideas for "what you do" at festivals were suggested: have a parade through town and build floats; sell t-shirts and cups and hats, and give the money to charity; sports, games, and prizes; plenty of food and beer—a festival's gotta have beer! All kinds of things were suggested, and variations were spun, as we brainstormed what the festival would be.

We soon realized we were not acting in a vacuum, that our decisions were influenced by the larger university system and the system of Scottish games and festivals. One member of our graduate public relations class had been to a Scottish festival, and through her fairly efficient network for finding information (she's an investigator with the state district attorney's office) found out who was in charge of that festival and put me in contact with him. That phone call was to David Peet of the Ligonier Highland Games, provided me with an hour full of new information about activities and costs and changed my thinking about what our festival needed. He talked about pipe and drum bands and contests; highland dance competitions; heavy athletes throwing the caber, stone, weight, and sheaf; travel money and cash prizes; judges; lodging; and other aspects of putting on a festival. That phone conversation was enactment. It spun out new variations that challenged the retention system of "what our festival will be". Talking was *doing* that presented fresh choices to the system as we calibrated our way toward a destination, and with one phone call the destination changed, the target moved.

Calibration refers to monitoring and adjusting. Organizations are calibrating toward some vision, monitoring the way things are and adjusting toward the way things should be. Calibrating toward "normal" or "good," correcting for deviations and what the system defines as bad, this is what organizations do. In profit-making systems, losing money is bad; in educational systems, failing grades and grade inflation are deviations away from what some have codefined as standards. Look at whatever system you choose, from the biology and social influences in a community of ants, to your organizational communities, or the community of planets in our solar system, all have points of homeostasis. As communities create something new they are maintaining a balance with old ideals. All systems experience loops of deviation and correction, cycles of deviation-amplification and counteraction. Evolution and information theorists would name these positive (deviation away from homeostasis) and negative (correction back towards homeostasis) feedback loops. Our festival planners were trying to calibrate toward some ideal of a Scottish festival, going through positive cycles of change toward "a good festival".

Chaos theorists would remind us of interaction effects, that the feedback loops of one system are interacting with and within many other systems, and these interactions keep us guessing. As with the weather that becomes unpredictable, unfolds in new ways in the interaction of all variables, social systems unfold along branching and somewhat unpredictable paths in the interaction of people, symbols, and ideas. Our festival was a new variation on an old theme, just another celebration or event in the history of festive events. The idea of our festival interacts with the ideas and ideals established by other festivals. The Spring Highlands Festival committee calibrates toward "a good festival" while monitoring other festivals, selecting some of "what they do" to be be part of the retained actions which comprise "what we do." This creation of "what we do," who we are, our mission and vision and all that, progresses along chaotic branches yet is structured by evolutionary form. Each human, like each snowflake, like each organization, is a new variation within an established form. The festival is a variation of an established pattern, a new weave in an old tartan cloth.

So we're trying to adapt by choosing and using characteristics that move toward a "successful festival". Some choices we make can enhance creativity and the exercising of options, and some choices are limiting, encroaching on our freedom to vary.

Playing, talking, drawing, building, and other exercises were mentioned as ways to enhance creativity. Making the festival has been a playful conversation, with plenty of sketching and building and revising. The festival logo, "Nessy," went through four iterations of change before we locked into a design.

The chosen Nessy design was then part of our newly forming organization's retention system (Figure 9-1). The design structured how Nessy would look, to a certain extent, but variations have developed.

The variations shown in Figure 9-2, new enactments of the Nessy domain, are the result of playing around with images and ideas, as are the video and radio ads, news features, posters, and signs that festival volunteers create.

Continuous involvement in the learning process helps creativity, as systems seek variety to match the variety of their environment. We started out knowing little of the Scottish festival domain, and have learned from attending other events like ceilidh (a Scottish party with music, dance, traditional foods, plenty of scotch, and a ceremonious dish called haggis), Scottish country dance workshops, Robert Bums birthday celebrations, and other festivals. Going to these events feeds our system with fresh possibilities, awareness of other things that are going on. Looking at the brochures and ad executions from other festivals enhances the image pool for our festival advertising. Creative systems are learning systems, people who are looking around and blending ideas from the many surrounding environments.

Learning occurs as the festival is recreated each year. Learning occurs in the advertising and public relations areas as well as the structuring of the new organization. What started as a loose conglomeration of people handling many tasks has

FIGURE 9-1 **Evolution of the festival logo.**

evolved into more people performing specialized roles to handle the various events within the event. We've created an organizing structure, an adapting new order within the orders of the university, the community, and the system of Scottish festivals. Our festival group interacts with and within many other groups, as mapped on the group relations chart (Figure 9-3).

FIGURE 9-2   **Creativity as variations on a theme.**

Each group (organizing unit) on that chart is changing, and the festival is changing with them, being influenced by and influencing other networks of people. All
organizations are being created anew, as people and ideas and places and things
interact in the evolving order, with its sidekick chaos. Newness is happening as we
select what the festival will be from the menu of choices, what our organizations will
be from the menu of futures, and what each of us individually will be in the decisions
we make from our menu of paths. We create, it all evolves, we create some more.

Edinboro University

Institute for Research
and Community Service

Students Clubs
Faculty/Staff
Alumni Association
Facilities/Housekeeping
Volunteers

Borough of Edinboro

Mayor, Manager, Council

Business
Schools
Churches
Police/Fire
Volunteers

Spring Highlands Festival

Director

Coordinators of:
Public Relations/Advertising/Sales
Volunteers
Pipe Bands
Highland Dancers
Scottish Athletes
Kids' Games and Crafts
Musicians
Historical Re-enactments

Musicians and Dancers

Scottish Clans and Societies

Other Scottish Festivals

Scottish Publications

Local and Regional Media

Food Vendors
Celtic Gift/Clothing Vendors

Association of Scottish
Games and Festivals

Pennsylvania Travel
and Tourism

U.S. and Canadian Tourism
Agencies

FIGURE 9-3   **Chart of individual and group relations for the festival.**

The festival is evolving, changing, and we're revising as we go. To a certain extent, the scripts are written and we're trying to learn them, but to a greater extent, we are writing the scripts. We're reading the music of Old as we improvise our variations of the New. Festivals have happened and are happening, and we learn from their scripts and scores as we write ours.

CONCLUSION

Is there a formula for creativity? Can we say "do this: _____ and "don't do that: _____" and you'll be more creative? I think so. I really think that playing, stretching, walking, running, doodling, sketching, writing, and talking can enhance creative action. All are forms of exercise that help us maintain flexibility.

Think about it, talk about it, and do it. Read a little, write a little; look, listen, reflect on what is and what needs to be; then read more, write more, and talk more as you figure out what's going on. I guess I'm saying communication is the key to creativity. Talking, reading, writing, drawing, thinking—blending and reblending symbols—as we make our way through and make sense of our world. We communicate, we create, it all evolves.

We're creating by communicating, being affected by and affecting the circles of evolving systems we're organizing. Organiz*ing!* Weick (1979) says to keep the emphasis on the "ing." All are moving, changing, flowing, dynamic systems; working toward some semblance of balance, but never quite balanced, forever balanc*ing*. Creating, evolving, changing is what organizations do.

Organizing is creation, communication, and evolution. We create our organizations and they create us amid the eternal dancing of symbols, in the choices we make from the variety of interpretations. "What's going on here?" and "what shall we do?" are our Creation, fashioned in communication, within the grand evolution.

GLOSSARY

Chaos theory—a relatively new paradigm in the arts and sciences that focuses on nonlinear, iterative processes of change rather than stable order.

Creativity—the process of transforming ideas and things; the act of making original products, be they symbolic, material, or both.

Dialectic—narrowly defined as the art of examining questions logically through question and answer, or where conflict between opposing ideas or entities (thesis and antithesis) is resolved in the formation of new ideas or entities (synthesis). More widely defined as opposing yet interdependent forces, such as Yin and Yang, or the dynamic composing and decomposing of seasonal changes and life cycles.

Enactment—as used by Weick (1979), in the socio-evolutionary process, enactment is bracketing a piece of the flow of events for closer inspection and attending to or perceiving part of a domain. The aspects attended to are the enacted environment.

Retention—in Weick's (1979) evolutionary scheme, retention refers to the memory process, or the storage and usage of retained images, when enacting and selecting interpretations of a domain.

Selection—for Weick (1979), selection is the process of interpreting the enacted environment, choosing some interpretations from the pool of all possible meanings.

Stochastic—the process of choosing the probable best course, given many possible courses of action, in which each choice opens up a range of new choices. Metaphorically, new branches on the decision tree grow with each decision we make.

CASE STUDY

You've been hired by the Spring Highlands Festival committee to do the advertising for this year's event. Committee members believe that past advertising has effectively reached the Scottish communities and groups in the state and region, but tell you that thus far they have not been successful at reaching students at the university. Put together a rough advertising plan to present to the committee. Include the following: (1) definition of the problem; (2) goals and objectives for your advertising; (3) analysis of the target audience and other potential publics; (4) media you will use to reach your audiences; (5) the message plan, including theme, slogan, key words/copy, and visuals to be used in various media, such as the script for a video ad, or a rough draft of a poster or brochure; (6) a budget, including how much things will cost, and how much extra revenue you intend to generate through increased attendance; and (7) evaluation plans for how you'll measure whether your advertising was successful. Discussion can include questions about what motivates students, what visual appeals could be created to get student attention and interest, and what media should be used around campus to reach students.

REFERENCES

Bateson, G. (1972) *Steps to an Ecology of Mind.* San Francisco: Chandler Publishing.

Briggs, J. (1992) *Fractals: The Patterns of Chaos.* New York: Touchstone.

Briggs, J., & Peat, D. F. (1989) *Turbulent Mirror: An Illustrated Guide to Chaos Theory and the Science of Wholeness.* New York: Harper Collins.

Burke, K. (1984) *Permanence and Change: An Anatomy of Purpose* (2nd ed.). Berkeley: University of California Press.

Gleick, J. (1987) *Chaos: Making a New Science.* New York: Viking.

Korzybski, A. (1958) *Science and Sanity: An Introduction to Non-Aristotelian Systems of General Semantics* (4th ed.). Lakeville, Conn.: International Non-Aristotelian Library Publishing Company.

Peters, T. (1987) *Thriving on Chaos: Handbook for a Management Revolution.* New York: Harper Perrenial.

Pirsig, R. (1974) *Zen and the Art of Motorcycle Maintenance: An Inquiry into Values.* New York: Bantam Books.

Stewart, I. (1990) *Does God Play Dice: The Mathematics of Chaos.* Cambridge, Mass.: Basil Blackwell.

Weick, K. E. (1979) *The Social Psychology of Organizing* (2nd ed.). Reading, Mass.: Addison-Wesley.

RECOMMENDED READINGS

Dewine, S. (1994). *The Consultant's Craft: Improving Organizational Communication* New York: St. Martin's Press.

Eisenberg, E., & Goodall, Jr., H. L. (1993) *Organizational Communication: Balancing Creativity and Constrain.* New York: St. Martin's Press.

Peppers, D., & Rogers, M. (1993) *The One to One Future: Building Relationships One Customer at a Time.* New York: Currency Doubleday.

▶ Part III

Contemporary Issues

▶ 10

Gender Issues: Management Style, Mobility, and Harassment

CYNTHIA BERRYMAN-FINK

There are a variety of gender and communication issues affecting contemporary organizations. These stem from increasing numbers of women entering the workforce but encountering barriers of equal opportunity compared to men. This chapter examines the status of women in organizations, factors affecting their mobility, men's and women's roles in organizational cultures, the treatment of women managers, behavioral styles of male and female managers, the sexes' participation in informal communication systems, work–family conflicts, sexual harassment, and organizational romance. In some cases, these issues have implications for macro-level communication in the entire organization. In other cases, micro-level gender issues relate to intrapersonal or interpersonal communication in the organization. The chapter concludes with a forecast of how gender issues will be handled in organizations of the future.

THE ENTRANCE OF WOMEN INTO THE WORKPLACE

In the last few decades, women have entered workplace organizations in large numbers. This burgeoning entrance of women into the workforce constitutes a major change in organizational life. Let us look at the extent to which women participate in workplace organizations. By the late 1980s, women comprised about 45 percent of the United States workforce (U.S. Department of Labor, 1989). By 1992, 50 percent of mothers with preschool children worked outside of the home (Shelton, 1992). Demographic projections indicate that by the year 2000, over 60 percent of all women in the United States will be working outside of the home.

THE ENTRANCE OF WOMEN INTO MANAGEMENT

While women's participation in the workforce has increased dramatically in the second half of the twentieth century, their movement into management and executive levels has been slower. By the late 1980s, women held about 38 percent of all administrative, managerial, and executive jobs (U.S. Bureau of Labor Statistics, 1987). The majority of these positions were at low and middle levels of management, however. A 1991 investigation revealed that women comprised only 2.6 percent of the corporate officers of the top Fortune 500 companies and only 4.3 percent of the corporate officers of Fortune 500 service companies (*Women and the Workplace: The Glass Ceiling,* 1991). By 1992, only one in thirteen female law associates was a partner in her firm, and of partners at major accounting firms, only 3.7 percent were women (White, 1992). Even in organizations in which the number of female employees far exceeds the number of male employees, men tend to assume the leadership of those organizations (Powell, 1993). So we see large numbers of women entering organizations, but only some of them serving as managers and relatively few of them reaching executive levels.

SEX SEGREGATION OF OCCUPATIONS

In addition to the concentration of women at lower levels of management, we see some degree of sex segregation of occupations in today's workplace organizations. According to Powell (1993), more than one quarter of the female labor force works in clerical occupations while only 6 percent of the male labor force holds clerical positions. Women dominate half of service occupations, while only 10 percent of all engineers are women. Over half of the male or female labor force would have to change jobs for sex segregation of occupations to be eliminated. Women are overrepresented in such professions as elementary teaching and underrepresented in the construction fields, for example (Haslett, Geis, & Carter, 1992). There exists an expectation that men are best suited for certain kinds of jobs and women are best suited for other kinds of jobs. Many people automatically expect engineers, mechanics, and surgeons to be male and day-care workers, nurses, and receptionists to be female (Pearson, West, & Turner, 1995). To a large extent, these expectations hold true with the sexes occupying these professions in vastly different numbers. Men's jobs typically have more power, status, and prestige, while women's jobs often have more pleasant working conditions and emphasize the woman's appearance (Haslett, Geis, & Carter, 1992).

SALARY DIFFERENCES IN ORGANIZATIONS

In addition to the concentration of women at lower organizational levels and the sex-segregation of occupations, we see a third factor describing contemporary organizations. This is the salary inequity between male and female employees. In 1991, women earned 72 cents for every dollar earned by a man (Women and the Workplace: The Glass Ceiling, 1991). Now, if women and men work in different kinds of occupations, we would expect some differences in pay levels. But even when the sexes have comparable educational status, job categories, and job credentials, there is still a disparity between salaries (Doyle & Paludi, 1991). Men typically earn more than women for the same job (Powell, 1993). A study by Marini (1989) showed that full-time female employees in various occupations earn a percentage of what their male counterparts earn. For example, female physicians earn 54 percent as much as male physicians; female computer operators earn only 76 percent of the salaries of their male counterparts; female lawyers earn 75 percent of what male lawyers earn. Female managers earn only 66 percent as much as male managers earn.

THE FEMINIZATION OF OCCUPATIONS

As occupations become more female-oriented, the prestige and salaries in those fields decline. An interesting example of this phenomenon can be found in the public relations field. The public relations profession, once a male-dominated occupation, is rapidly becoming a female-dominated career. Evidence shows that women in public relations have lower salaries than men in the same field. As this feminization of public relations is occurring, concerns about the status and credibility of the profession have begun to emerge (Nadler & Nadler, 1993). This example lends support to the view that women's jobs are less prestigious and lower paying than men's jobs.

THE GLASS CEILING

Thus far, our portrait of organizational life shows women working at lower organizational levels than men, holding lower prestige jobs, and earning less money than men. The phenomenon for women in the workplace has been called the "glass ceiling" (Women and the Workplace: The Glass Ceiling, 1991). The glass ceiling is a metaphor for the invisible but impermeable barrier that prevents women from advancing beyond middle levels in organizational hierarchies. The ceiling is glass because women can see the higher level, more prestigious, and greater paying jobs above them, but they cannot attain them in any large numbers.

Causes of the Glass Ceiling

Let us examine various reasons for the existence of this glass ceiling. By discussing possible causes of the glass ceiling, we can understand the complex dynamics of gender issues in organizations. One explanation for the shortage of women in upper levels of management is called the "pipeline theory" (Karsten, 1994). Since it takes twenty to twenty-five years for the average man to climb the corporate ladder to reach senior executive levels, women have not been in the executive pipeline long enough to attain such levels. There is a natural time lag between entry into a profession and attainment of senior level status in that profession. This theory predicts that in time, as men and women enter occupations in equal numbers, then equal numbers of the sexes will attain executive levels in their organizations. A second explanation for the glass ceiling is the homogeneity principle (Karsten, 1994; Sitterly & Duke, 1988). This theory explains that since white males traditionally have held the upper level positions in organizations, they naturally seek out other individuals who are similar to them to join the executive ranks. Group dynamics principles tell us that it is human nature to feel more comfortable with and to more favorably perceive people who are similar to us. According to this theory, males perceive other males as executive material more easily than they would perceive females as capable executives. Because a woman executive is different from the norm, other executives, who tend to be male, would be less likely to promote women into the ranks of senior management. A third possible explanation for the glass ceiling relates to the expansion of part-time work for women (Asplund, 1988). More women than men work in part-time jobs, because of childbearing and childrearing responsibilities. During childrearing years, part-time work can be a viable option for balancing work and family for many women. But part-time work does not carry the credibility in most organizations that full-time work does. Family demands, which may force some women into part-time positions, presents risks for career growth (Warme, Lundy, & Lundy, 1992). Working part-time in any profession for any length of time probably reduces one's chances for promotion into the ranks of management. The demands of positions at the levels of vice-president and above most likely preclude part-time work. This explanation claims that women's choices of part-time work reduce their likelihood of attaining upper level positions. A fourth explanation for the glass ceiling relates to the choice of self-employment which many women have made (Asplund, 1988). Increasing numbers of women are starting their own businesses in which they are the sole employee. Thus, by opting out of the corporate hierarchy, these women reduce the potential numbers of women in senior level positions in organizations.

The fact that many occupations are still sex-segregated may be another explanatory factor. We have seen that sizable numbers of women occupy clerical positions, an occupation for which there is little opportunity for advancement into management, especially senior level management. A sixth explanation for the glass ceiling concerns the climate of interaction for women and men in their jobs. Compared to men, women have fewer role models and mentors to assist them in their career advancement and are less involved in informal communication networks (Carr-Ruffino, 1993; Sitterly & Duke, 1988). Later in this chapter, we will elaborate on the differences in mentoring for male and female employees. An informal network of contacts and communication is essential for anyone who seeks to advance in the ranks of management. Evidence shows that women are less integrated into informal communication networks in organizations than are men. Consequently, they may not be getting the information they need to advance in their careers.

A seventh possible cause for the connections of women at lower organizational levels relates to the demands of balancing work and family for women (Doyle & Paludi, 1991; Karsten, 1994). Since men do not bear children and they traditionally assume less responsibility than women for raising children, they do not have the same extent of conflict between work and family roles that women do. Many women opt for less demanding careers, interrupt their careers for childbearing, or, as we have seen, seek to work part-time as strategies for balancing the demands of work and family. Family responsibilities for women, coupled with work-related choices for accommodating those family responsibilities, may be partially responsible for their lesser representation at executive levels. In a controversial article in 1989, Felice Schwartz argued that organizations ought to offer women a career path that is less demanding so that women can balance career and family needs. Dubbed the "mommy track," this alternative was criticized by many women as leading to a second-class status in the workplace. There is a particular work-family conflict unique to women (Bailyn, 1982). Typically, a women's childbearing years (twenties and thirties) coincide with the early and most demanding stage of her professional life. One's performance in the first ten to fifteen years of a career set the stage for later career success such as advancement into senior ranks. Yet this is often the period in which a woman's biological clock is ticking away before childbearing becomes dangerous or impossible. Because men can become fathers at any age, there is not as strong a fatherhood pressure during the early career years.

Finally, a category of explanations for the glass ceiling involve issues of overt or subtle discrimination. Perhaps, women reach a barrier in their career advancement because organizations discriminate against women. That is, attitudes and behavior of decision-makers in organizations and the ways that organizations are structured may contribute to the glass ceiling (Gutek, 1985; Kanter, 1977; Karsten, 1994). Karsten (1994) argues that men and women are not presumed to be equally capable in organizations. Men will be evaluated for promotions on their perceived potential while women will be judged on past accomplishments. There is an expectation that men are more capable managers, especially at higher levels of management, than are women. Kanter, in a classic 1977 book titled *Men and Women of the Corporation,* discussed a form of organizational discrimination based on the ratio of males to females in an organization. If there are relatively few women in a job category, for example, senior management, then any women who hold that position will be stereotyped, will face greater performance pressures, and will be tested more than the males who occupy that position in large numbers. Gutek (1985) offers a sex-role spillover theory for why women receive discrimination in the form of fewer promotions in the workplace. She claims that many men have impressions of women related to women's roles as mother and wife. The expectations associated with these traditional roles for women spill-over to influence the impressions that individuals have of women managers and executives. Traditional expectations may limit women's roles and opportunities in the workplace. Because of the association of women with traditional roles of wife and mother, organizations may inadvertently place women in supportive or nurturing roles such as clerical or human resources jobs rather than in more challenging or fast-track jobs. Seeing a woman in sexual terms, a traditional way for men to perceive women, might result in her competence being overlooked.

Thus we have seen a wide array of possible explanations for the fact that women are less likely than men to occupy top level jobs in organizations. Realistically, no one explanation can fully account for the glass ceiling phenomenon. Many of these factors may interact to explain why women face a ceiling in their career promotions. Individuals and organizations seeking to determine reasons for promotion barriers experienced by women should consider how societal roles, individual choices, sex-role stereotyping, and organizational structures combine to create and perpetuate the glass ceiling.

GENDER AND ORGANIZATIONAL CULTURE

As explained in Chapter 8, a popular and useful approach to studying organizational communication is to examine the culture of an organization. Regarding organizational culture, an important question becomes, "What is the role of gender in creating and sustaining organizational culture?" Traditionally, the cultures of most workplace organizations have been based on male models of organizing and of managing (Haslett, Geis, & Carter, 1992). This makes sense, since at one time, the workforce and especially management, was comprised almost exclusively of men. Despite the fact that women have entered the workplace in large numbers, the culture of most organizations is still based on male norms and assumptions. Because workplaces have historically been designed by and for men, they may include behavior and communication patterns familiar and comfortable to men but not to women (Wood, 1994).

Masculine Organizational Cultures

The predominant organizational structure of hierarchy with inherent competition is considered a masculine model (Astin & Leland, 1991; Asplund, 1988). Deborah

Tannen, in her best-selling book *You Just Don't Understand: Men and Women in Conversation* (1990), explains how females tend to see the world as a series of individual connections while males more often see the world as a hierarchical social order. Even in organizations that have adopted flatter, more decentralized structures, hierarchy is still a fact of life. Positions, responsibility, and authority are structured such that some people are higher or lower than others in the hierarchy. Male-oriented metaphors borrowed from military or sports domains also prevail in many organizational cultures (Rizzo & Mendez, 1990). Examples of military language used in the workplace include "sales force," "in the field," "chain of command," "under fire," and "front line." Many organizations use sports terminology such as "ballpark figure," "game plan," "teams," and "score." Organizational structures and symbolic language are just two examples of how workplace cultures follow masculine assumptions and styles.

The Assimilation of Women in Organizations

To be successful in most organizations, women are expected to assimilate into masculine organizational cultures (Rizzo & Mendez, 1990). They must enter hierarchically structured organizations, be competitive to climb the hierarchy, and speak the language of the organization, even if such a culture is foreign or uncomfortable for them. Such masculine assumptions of organizational culture are so ingrained that people do not realize the degree to which organizations adopt male norms and styles. We erroneously believe that organizations are neither masculine nor feminine in their structure and philosophies. Because of tradition, we come to see hierarchy and competition as just the way organizations are.

Feminine Organizational Cultures

Karsten (1994) offers a feminist view of organizational culture. Such a culture would include the absence of hierarchy, participative decision-making, few rules, lateral communication, interaction as the mode of conflict resolution, power based on expertise not position, cooperation, teamwork, corrective rather than punitive discipline, and flexible schedules and benefits.

Some organizational culture theorists claim that the increasing numbers of women going into management serve as a catalyst for changing organizational cultures. They explain that women challenge the dominant (male) culture of organizations by bringing unique styles to the workplace and by questioning unconscious views of how things are done in organizations. They predict that in time, organizational cultures will evolve into less masculine, more feminine, and more androgynous environments (Asplund, 1988; Astin & Leland, 1991; Carr-Ruffino, 1993; Grant, 1988; Johnson, 1989; Rizzo & Mendez, 1990; Sargent, 1981). Indeed, a few progressive organizations seem to be evolving toward the structure and styles described by Karsten in the feminist view of organizations, though they do so not for gender-related reasons but because such styles promote organizational excellence (Wood, 1994). As organizations adopt collaborative and participative styles, they move toward feminine organizational styles, though gender issues inherent in organizational cultures are rarely perceived.

So we have seen that, for the most part, workplace organizations operate on masculine assumptions and approaches to life and that women are expected to adjust to this male model if they are to be successful in the workplace. Feminine approaches to organizing are different from traditional male styles, though, to a slight degree, companies may be beginning to incorporate some feminine assumptions into organizational cultures.

PERCEPTIONS OF WOMEN MANAGERS

Since women managers are becoming more commonplace, with 38 percent of all management jobs held by women, we can ask how women managers are perceived and treated? Are they viewed or treated any differently from their male counterparts? Let's examine some of the research evidence on this question. Research shows that most people prefer working for male managers and have more positive perceptions of male managers, though this will vary between male and female employees and according to how much experience one has had with women managers (Ely, 1988; Haslett, Geis, & Carter, 1992; Powell, 1990; Sutton & Moore, 1985; Wheeless & Berryman-Fink, 1985). In a 1985 survey of attitudes toward women managers, only 47 percent of the men but 82 percent of the women surveyed reported that they would feel comfortable working for a woman (Sutton & Moore, 1985). In 1989, business students described a good manager in mostly masculine terms (Powell & Butterfield, 1989). Most studies of hiring for managerial jobs have found a preference for male applicants (Powell, 1988). Some studies show that even female subordinates prefer male managers (Haslett, Geis, & Carter, 1992). One study showed that even liberal women reported that they felt less comfortable working in female-led groups than in male-led groups (Ely, 1988). Wheeless and Berryman-Fink (1985) found that while women had more favorable attitudes toward women managers than men had, anyone who had experience with a woman manager held a more favorable attitude than individuals who had no experience with women managers. Powell (1990) corroborates this by showing that stereotypes about women managers diminish after employees work for them. Fear of the unknown and the reliance on stereotypes probably account for the negative attitudes among those who have no experience with women as managers. Perhaps as women managers become more prevalent at all levels of management, negative perceptions of and discomfort toward women as managers will diminish. On the other hand, stereotypes may not diminish no matter how many women become managers. Powell (1993) echoes this concern when he says: "Our research shows that managerial stereotypes have stayed essentially the same despite the considerable increase in women managers in recent years.

We have little reason to believe that the stereotypes change if even more women become managers." (p. 156)

BEHAVIORAL EXPECTATIONS
FOR WOMEN MANAGERS

It has been speculated that women managers have a more difficult job than male managers do because of the expectations and restrictions that are placed on women. According to Karsten (1994), there is a narrow range of acceptable behavior allowed for women managers. They must be tough and independent (traditionally masculine qualities), yet also feminine. They must be masculine enough to perform managerial duties, yet be feminine enough not to be aggressive or offensive in the performance of those duties. Women managers must balance masculinity and femininity and carefully monitor how they are coming across to others. Male managers, on the other hand, have the freedom to be masculine, since organizational cultures and management principles are based on male norms. There is not as much pressure on male managers to project a gender-appropriate image and to monitor their behavior. Research shows that subordinates prefer gender-appropriate behavior from their managers (Stratham, 1987). This means that they expect female managers to be feminine and male managers to be masculine. This expectation poses no problem for male managers, where masculine behavior is ingrained and the organization operates by and rewards male-oriented behavior. For women, however, there is a dilemma. Women managers are expected to conform to sex-appropriate behavior and thus to act feminine. Yet, workplace organizations operate on masculine assumptions and good managers are seen as displaying masculine-oriented behaviors such as competitiveness, aggression, and independence. One study showed that women leaders who did not conform to sex-role stereotypes suffered dislike, hostility, and reprisal (Buder & Geis, 1990). Thus societal stereotypes present a no-win situation for women managers and a more comfortable situation for male managers.

EVALUATIONS OF MALE
AND FEMALE MANAGERS

We have seen that people have different perceptions and expectations for male and female managers. Now let us examine how male and female managers are treated. Do people behave differently toward managers based on the sex of the manager? The important question here concerns the evaluation of the performance of female and male managers. Research results are mixed on the question of whether male and female managers are evaluated differently. Some studies show that men are judged more favorably for the same performance as women (Lott, 1985; Nieva & Gutek, 1980; Paludi & Strayer, 1985). This means that work, when attributed to a male, receives a higher rating than identical work attributed to a female. Yet, other studies show little evidence of evaluation bias in favor of either sex (Powell, 1993). According to Lott (1985), there is a tendency to under-rate and under-reward women compared to men when credentials are equal. In a review of the extensive literature on gender and leadership, Dobbins and Platz (1986) conclude that male leaders are rated as more effective than female leaders when studies are done in laboratory settings. This pro-male bias disappears when studies of actual managers in the field are conducted. This may be because in laboratory research, respondents rely more on stereotypes to form their evaluations. In organizations, there are more opportunities to observe actual performance, so evaluations need not be based on stereotypical assumptions. Eagly and Johnson (1990) found that subordinates evaluate male and female leaders as equally effective. Haslett, Geis, and Carter (1992) claim that women are less likely to be hired for leadership and managerial positions than equally qualified men. So we can conclude that there may be some differential evaluation of male and female managers, though judgments of women and men in the actual workplace seem more equitable than judgments made in laboratory studies.

MALE AND FEMALE MANAGERIAL BEHAVIOR

So far, we have discussed how women and men in management are perceived and evaluated. Let us now examine whether female and male managers actually behave in similar or in different ways. This is a complex question, since there are countless types of behavior that can be examined. The issues of sex differences in managerial and leadership behavior have been investigated extensively. Next we will try to summarize areas in which differences have been obtained and areas in which no differences have been found.

Behavioral Differences

Research has revealed differences in male and female managers' career development, bases for promoting subordinates, leadership styles, and communication styles. Concerning career development issues, male managers may have higher aspiration levels than female managers (Harland & Weis, 1982). Powell (1993) indicates that several studies reveal that females aspire to managerial careers to a lesser degree than males do. A recent study showed that male and female middle managers differ on managerial momentum (Cannings & Montmarquette, 1991). This refers to sustained career progress and is affected by the manager's performance, ambition, and organizational rewards. One study has found that male and female managers use different bases for deciding to promote subordinates. Men may rely on informal means and women on formal means in promotion decisions (Cannings & Montmarquette, 1991).

The question of sex differences in leadership style has been studied extensively. Basically, results show that differences in leadership behaviors between men and women are small and tend to appear more in laboratory studies than in actual organizational settings (Powell, 1993). There seem to be some differences in leadership style with men exhibiting more autocratic and women more democratic leadership styles (Powell, 1993). This style difference has been found in studies of actual managers as well as in laboratory studies. This style difference corresponds to the male and female approaches to organizational cultures described earlier, with women favoring more participative decision-making than men do. Rosener (1990) describes sex differences in leadership styles. According to her, a woman's leadership style is transformational and interpersonal while a man's style is based on command and control. Women managers promote positive interactions with subordinates, encourage participation, and share power and information more than men do. Other studies corroborate this by reporting that women leaders use collaborative, participative communication that enables and empowers others while men use more unilateral, directive communication in their leadership (Helgesen, 1990; Lunneborg, 1990). Such leadership style differences may be based on some basic communication style differences which seem to exist between women and men. Case (1988) found women managers' communication patterns to be personal, facilitative, relational, and integrative while men managers were assertive, authoritative, directive, depersonalized, and commanding. In other words, the women were more interpersonally cooperative and the men more communicatively direct. These communication differences parallel the differences in autocratic and democratic leadership styles for males and females. Women managers bring unique communication skills to organizations, including human resource skills of communication, cooperation, affiliation, attachment, emotionality, and intimacy (Grant, 1988).

So we see that female and male managers do behave differently in a number of ways. They differ somewhat in career aspirations and momentum, the information they use to make promotion decisions, their autocratic versus democratic leadership styles, and their interpersonal versus authoritative communication styles.

Behavioral Similarities

A number of studies of managerial behavior have found no differences between the sexes. Male and female managers do not seem to differ significantly on the need for achievement, power, or affiliation (Harland & Weis, 1982). That is, they are similar in the degrees to which they want to achieve, the power they want to attain, and the extent to which they want to associate with people. No sex differences have been found in attributions for success (Harland & Weis, 1982). In other words, men and women cite similar reasons for their career success. Male and female managers do not seem to differ in their influence behavior (Vilkinas, 1988), their personal goal setting (Harland & Weis, 1982), or their personality traits (Astin & Leland, 1991).

GENDER AND MENTORING

Now we will discuss issues of gender and informal communication, particularly how women and men participate in mentoring and informal communication networks in the workplace. Women are less likely to have mentors than are males (Wood, 1994). Because there are fewer women than men at higher organizational levels, there are fewer female mentors available in most companies (Noe, 1988). Certainly women employees can have male mentors, but there are unique problems associated with cross-gender mentoring relationships (Clawson & Kram, 1984). Part of a mentor's job is to be a role model for the junior employees. Men cannot be as effective role models for women as women can. It may be difficult for a male mentor to help women with issues of femininity, male-based organizational cultures, work–family role conflicts, and sexual harassment and discrimination. The lack of mentorships for women hinders their job effectiveness and career advancement (Noe, 1988). Another sex difference in mentoring concerns the ways that women and men see mentoring relationships. According to Burke and McKeen (1990), women see mentoring related to friendship and connection while men see mentoring as a task-oriented alliance.

GENDER AND NETWORKING

Another area of informal communication involves networking. Much important information in a workplace is exchanged in casual and social interaction. Sometimes, decisions are made and alliances formed behind the scenes rather than in formal meetings. The informal relationships among colleagues provides access to important information that cannot be gained through formal channels. Women may be excluded from informal networks, which because of their traditional masculine nature, have been called "old-boy networks" (Benokraitis & Feagin, 1986; Harriman, 1985; Wood, 1994). It may be more difficult for women than for men to get into organizational networks. Women need to make a conscious effort and to work at getting into informal networks while men get network membership without effort (Harland & Weiss, 1982). This may be due to the principle of homogeneity whereby people are more comfortable associating with others who are similar to them. There may be a natural tendency for men to interact informally with other men, a tendency which inadvertently excludes women. Noe (1988) found that women have fewer interactions with powerful individuals in organizations. Once women are involved in informal networks, their behavior in those networks may differ from men's. Some researchers claim that women are actually better at networking, especially with other women, than are men (Brass, 1985). If women are more interpersonally oriented, more cooperative, and more concerned with connection, as we have discussed previously, than it makes sense that they may be skilled at building a network of informal contacts. Networks may serve different purposes for women and men. Women's networks are more likely to provide a social function, while men may look to networks for more task-oriented purposes (Campbell, 1988).

In summary, women are less involved in mentoring and in networking than are men. When they do participate in mentoring and in networking relationships, they perceive different functions and motives for mentors and network contacts than men do.

BALANCING CAREER AND FAMILY ROLES

Another major issue related to gender and organizations is the need to balance career and family roles. While men and women typically have both work and family responsibilities, the conflicts between these two roles are greater for women. Most men who are highly successful in their careers feel little conflict between their work role and their family roles (Doyle & Paludi, 1991). This is because working wives are responsible for about 70 to 80 percent of household and childcare responsibilities (Carr-Ruffino, 1993). Women are much more likely than men to take time off from work when children are sick or day-care is unavailable (Wood, 1993). As we discussed earlier, household responsibilities account, in part, for the fact that few women are in executive roles in organizations. As long as women are expected to take primary responsibility for the family, they will not be able to meet the requirements of jobs in higher levels of organizations (Bailyn, 1982). Women who choose to combine a career and a family often are treated as second-class employees. They receive less salary, status, benefits, and job opportunities (Shelton, 1992).

A profile of the typical woman executive shows that, in order to become executives, many women must choose between a career and a family. The typical woman executive is less likely than a man to be married and to have children, thereby having an uninterrupted work history (Karsten, 1994). Women with husbands and children are less likely to make it to the top levels of organizations. On the other hand, marriage has a positive influence on men's careers (Harlan & Weis, 1982). The fact that for women the extremely demanding work periods of the early career coincide with childbearing and childrearing years creates additional stress of balancing careers and families (Bailyn, 1982).

SEXUAL HARASSMENT IN ORGANIZATIONS

Definition of Sexual Harassment

Any discussion of gender issues in organizations would be incomplete without a discussion of sexual harassment in the workplace. The Equal Employment Opportunity Commission published guidelines in November of 1980 defining sexual harassment. Sexual harassment is defined as any unwelcome sexual advances, requests for sexual favors, and other verbal or physical conduct of a sexual nature. Such behavior is illegal when (Equal Employment Opportunity Commission, 1980):

> *Submission to such conduct is made either explicitly or implicitly a term or condition of employment; submission to or rejection of such conduct by an individual is used as the basis for employment decisions affecting such individuals; such conduct has the purpose or effect of unreasonably interfering with an individual's work performance or creating an intimidating, hostile, or offensive working environment.*

Let us examine the components of this definition to understand the range of behaviors considered to be sexual harassment. First, sexual harassment must be *unwelcome* behavior. If physical or verbal behavior of a sexual nature is welcomed by the recipient, then the behavior is not sexual harassment. One could question the professionalism of such behavior in the workplace, though it would not legally constitute sexual harassment. Next, sexual harassment can take the form of physical or verbal behavior. This means that sexual language constitutes harassment as much as physical assault does. The definition refers to two types of sexual harassment called quid pro quo and hostile work environment. Quid pro quo means that the sexual behavior is tied to job consequences such as hiring, firing, promotions, raises, or work schedules, for example. In this type of sexual harassment, the harasser may directly state what job consequences will be given or withheld in exchange for sexual favors. Or the harasser, if that person is a superior, need not directly state job consequences because the power to affect job outcomes is an implied part of a supervisor–subordinate relationship. In quid pro quo harassment, the harasser has some type of authority over the recipient of harassment. The second type of harassment refers to the uncomfortable work environment that can result from persistent sexual behavior by co-workers. In this type, there are no explicit or implicit job consequences related to the harassment. This is because the harassers are not in a position of authority to affect job outcomes. An example of a hostile work environment related to harassment would be a situation in which one or more co-workers told sexual jokes frequently enough to interfere with the job productivity of others or to make others feel uncomfortable in the work environment.

Prevalence of Sexual Harassment

Many studies have been conducted to try to assess the prevalence of sexual harassment. A classic study that is often cited was conducted by the Merit Systems Protection Board (1981). This survey of 20,000 federal government workers found 42 percent of the women and 15 percent of the men reporting that they had experienced some form of sexual harassment in the previous two years. In a review of the literature on the prevalence of sexual harassment, York (1989) concludes that about 50 percent of women respondents to sexual harassment surveys report having experienced harassment.

Targets of Sexual Harassment

Is there a profile of the typical recipient of sexual harassment? It is important to note that anyone can become a target of harassment. Targets cross gender, race, age, education, occupation, and income levels. However, research shows that the most common target of sexual harassment is a women, younger than thirty-five, with a college or graduate degree. The higher a woman is in the corporate hierarchy, the more likely she is to be harassed. Harassment is more likely to occur in sex-segregated occupations and organizations (Karsten, 1994).

A Profile of Harassers

Research has revealed a profile of the typical harasser. Again, we must caution that this is only a generalization. The vast majority of men, whether they fit this description or not, do not engage in sexual harassment. Estimates reveal that fewer than 5 percent of men have sexually harassed someone (Webb, 1991). Most commonly, however, harassers are male, older than their targets, and married. It is more common for a co-worker than a supervisor to be a harasser. This is due, in part, to the fact that employees have many more co-workers than they do bosses. So the probability of harassment by a co-worker is greater than the probability of harassment by a supervisor. Harassers frequently bother more than one person (Webb, 1991).

Causes of Sexual Harassment

Virtually all studies that examine the reasons or motives for sexual harassment conclude that harassment stems from power more than sexual motives (Stringer et al., 1990). This means that harassers use sexual behavior as a way to intimidate, threaten, humiliate, or retaliate against others in the workplace. Supervisors may abuse their role power and legitimate authority by linking job consequences to sexual behavior. Or males, by virtue of the perceived power they have compared to women in our society, may intimidate or embarrass women in the workplace through sexual remarks or behavior. Power differences between women and men inherent in society's sex-role socialization provide males with the natural gender power to harass and deprives females or the power to resist or report harassment.

Another explanation for why sexual harassment occurs comes from Gutek's (1985) sex-role spillover theory. Remember that this concept says that perceptions of women in traditional roles in society may spill over into the workplace and lead men to see women in unprofessional ways. Men who have been conditioned by expectations of masculinity may see women in sexual ways. So even a woman manager at work will be perceived somewhat in sexual terms.

A third possible explanation for sexual harassment encompasses the other two causes and relates to the general culture of communication between women and men in society and, consequently, in the workplace. This means that typical communication styles of women and men position men in assertive, direct, and superior roles and position women in polite, submissive, and cooperative roles. These communication styles create and reinforce power imbalances that can contribute to sexual harassment in the workplace. Until organizational cultures of more powerful men and less powerful women are altered to create equitable relationships between the sexes, sexual harassment will persist (Berryman-Fink, 1993). Lewis and Johnson (1991) argue that sexual harassment based on hostile work environment will not be eliminated without a change in organizational cultures.

Male and Female Perceptions of Sexual Harassment

Because sexual harassment can encompass a variety of behaviors that range from mild to severe, and because sexual harassment is dependent on the target's perception that such behavior is unwelcome, there can be disagreement about what constitutes sexual harassment. Research shows that men and women differ significantly in their perceptions of whether a particular behavior constitutes sexual harassment. Women consistently perceive and label more behaviors as sexual harassment than men do (Booth-Butterfield, 1989). Studies have shown that 75 percent of women say they would be offended by sexual advances at work while 75 percent of men say they would be flattered (Karsten, 1994).

The Reasonable Woman Standard

In trying to determine whether certain behaviors generally would be considered offensive or hostile, court cases of sexual harassment typically have asked whether a "reasonable person" in the workplace would consider such behaviors as hostile. But the research indicating that women and men see sexual harassment differently has led to a "reasonable woman" standard to determine whether behaviors constitute sexual harassment. The question now becomes, would a reasonable woman working under the same conditions and experiencing the same sexually oriented behaviors as the plaintiff consider such behavior to be hostile and intimidating to her job performance (Karsten, 1994)?

Communication Relationships between Harassers and Harassed

Gutek (1985) did an interesting analysis of the kinds of interaction between individuals at work that precede sexual harassment. She hypothesized that, after months or years of working together, sexually oriented behavior does not just suddenly appear.

Rather, there is probably a pattern of communication that makes sexual harassment possible. Indeed, her research showed that men who harass women rarely talked about the woman's work performance or career with her. Instead, the men talked about themselves, their personal lives, and the woman's personal appearance and clothing. She concludes that men who engage in sexual harassment emphasize a woman's femaleness over her role as a worker.

Preventing Sexual Harassment

What can organizations do to prevent sexual harassment? For companies to eliminate the incidence of sexual harassment and to reduce their legal liability concerning harassment, they should create and distribute a policy statement regarding sexual harassment. Such a statement should provide the legal definition of harassment, prohibit such behavior in the workplace, and explain the options that employees have should they believe that they have been harassed. Secondly, organizations should have systems in place for handling sexual harassment complaints, investigating charges, and disciplining harassers. Such systems should be objective, fair, confidential, and timely. Finally, organizations desiring to prevent sexual harassment should educate employees about appropriate and inappropriate workplace behavior. Training sessions can help employees understand the complexities and legalities of sexual harassment and can help supervisors understand their role in monitoring, dealing with, and preventing sexual harassment (Berryman-Fink, 1993).

ORGANIZATIONAL ROMANCE

Another complicated issue facing contemporary organizations is romantic relationships between employees. Organizational romance refers to the sharing of welcome sexual behavior between employees in an organization. It is not uncommon for individuals to meet dates or mates in the workplace. Indeed, some organizational specialists conclude that organizational settings are a natural setting for the emergence of intimate relationships (Quinn & Lees, 1984). The workplace is a setting in which people have much in common and they are in frequent proximity with each other. People are well dressed and on their best behavior. Employees who spend long hours at work may have little free time in which to meet partners elsewhere.

Individuals and organizations are unsure about how to handle intimate relationships that develop in the workplace. Neville, author of the book *Corporate Attractions* (1990), claims that people are unclear about what is or is not proper behavior between men and women at work. Some people believe in separating workplace from personal relationships. Others look to the workplace as a good source of social relationships. Because of this, human resource specialists agree that corporations must develop guidelines about organizational romances.

Attitudes Toward Organizational Romance

The issue of organizational romance is a controversial one. Men and women differ in their opinions on the issue. One study (Powell, 1986) surveyed business students' beliefs about dating in the workplace. Results revealed that women perceived workplace intimacy less positively than men did. Women were less inclined than men to become involved in organizational romances, and they expressed a greater desire for organizational policies prohibiting intimate workplace relationships.

Effects of Organizational Romance

The evidence is mixed on the question of how organizational romances affect organizations. Much evidence shows negative effects such as favoritism, less productivity, and a loss of others' respect (Quinn & Lees, 1984) as well as co-worker jealousy and damage to one's professional image (Lowndes, 1993). However, there can be some positive outcomes such as people becoming easier to get along with and increased productivity (Quinn & Lees, 1984). The greatest risk seems to be for the woman involved in workplace relationships. Most organizational relationships are between higher-level men and lower-level women on the job (Anderson & Hunsaker, 1985). This is to be expected, because there are more men than women at higher organizational levels. Since women are often typically the lower-status individuals in organizational romances, women are twice as likely as men to loose their jobs because of organizational romances (Quinn & Lees, 1984). The male, who is higher on the organizational hierarchy, is seen as the more valuable individual and is less likely to be terminated.

Homosexual romances in organizations present even greater complexities and risks. Because of homophobia in society and in the workplace, participants in gay organizational romances suffer more negative consequences than do heterosexual couples (Mainiero, 1989).

Organizational Strategies for Dealing with Organizational Romance

Perhaps it is time that organizations begin to examine the assumptions and responses regarding workplace romances. Managers can no longer ignore organizational romances, but must be attentive and responsive to such issues. Managers must, without value judgments, intervene when romances are negatively affecting participants' or co-workers' productivity or when one partner in the relationship is supervising the other (Jamison, 1983; Westhoff, 1986). Horn and Horn (1982), authors of one of the earliest books on the topic, advise that organizations can take neither a hand-off approach nor an obsolete forbidding of workplace intimate relationships.

They believe that men and women employees should be allowed to date as long as they do their jobs and don't interfere with how others do their jobs. American business needs to develop mature and professional attitudes toward office romance and communicate clearly what distinguishes appropriate from inappropriate workplace behavior.

GENDER, ORGANIZATIONS, AND THE FUTURE

Some writers predict that in the future organizations will be more hospitable to women and women's needs than they are now. Advances in information technology allow for more flexible work locations and work hours. Employees can work at distant locations or at home and communicate via computers or fax machines. Some say that such flexible work arrangements are more compatible to family demands (Asplund, 1988). Perhaps companies will *have to* accommodate the needs of working women more in the future, since new entrants into the workforce increasingly will be women (Rizzo & Mendez, 1990). Companies will need women employees more in the future as a source of labor. As we move from a manufacturing to a service-based economy in the United States, the typically feminine skills of relationship building and interpersonal sensitivity become more essential (Rizzo & Mendez, 1990). Many organizations are moving from autocratic to democratic styles of management. We can expect that women's people-oriented and collaborative skills will become more valuable in participative organizations (Carr-Ruffino, 1993). As organizations decentralize, hierarchy becomes less prevalent and feminine skills related to teamwork become more necessary (Asplund, 1988). Thus, where women once were criticized or rejected for exhibiting feminine behavior in the workplace, such styles are now and increasingly will be considered the preferred management behavior (Astin & Leland, 1991). Without acknowledging the feminine nature of these styles, organizations continue to adopt feminine ways of behavior (Wood, 1994). It seems inevitable, therefore, that organizations of the future will value the contributions that both women and men bring to the workplace.

CONCLUSION

More women than ever before in history work outside of the home. While many women work as managers in organizations, few hold upper level management or executive jobs. Many occupations are segregated by sex, with women occupying more clerical and service positions than men, for example. For every dollar earned by a man in the workplace, a woman earns just 72 cents. Salary inequities occur for employees with the same levels of education in the same professions. As occupations become more female-dominated, the prestige and salaries in those fields decline. Women tend to hit an invisible, but impermeable barrier, called the glass ceiling, in their promotion attempts in organizations. A variety of factors such as past history, women's work patterns, occupational segregation, the climate for women at work, family demands, and attitudinal and structural discrimination have created the glass ceiling. The cultures of most organizations, which are based on male assumptions and behavior, expect women to assimilate into masculine-oriented workplaces. Feminine organizational cultures reject hierarchy and favor participative decision-making. Women may be slowly altering traditional organizational cultures.

People prefer to work for male managers, see managers in masculine terms, and indicate discomfort with female managers. However, women more than men and individuals familiar with women managers have more favorable attitudes toward women in management. Women managers must display enough feminine behaviors in order to conform to sex-role expectations, yet they must adopt masculine-oriented behaviors by which organizations operate. Male and female managers behave differently in a number of ways, yet they have areas of behavioral similarity also. The sexes seem to differ in leadership and communication styles. Women are less involved than men in mentoring and networking relationships. When women do form such relationships, they attribute different meanings and motives than men do to these relationships. For men, conflicts between work and family roles are minimal, while for women, balancing work and family roles is a source of stress. Marriage has a more positive effect on men's careers.

Sexual harassment is a fact of organizational life, though definitions of harassment are complex and perceptions of harassing behavior vary between women and men. There are two types of sexual harassment, quid pro quo and hostile work environment. Profiles of typical harassers and targets have been developed. Power is the major contributing factor to the prevalence of sexual harassment. The culture of communication for women and men creates power imbalances fueling sexual harassment. Harassment may also occur because traditional role expectations for women spill over into the workplace, causing women employees to be viewed in sexual rather than in professional ways. Men who sexually harass women emphasize the women's femaleness over her role as a worker. To prevent sexual harassment, organizations should develop policy statements; establish complaint, investigation, and disciplinary procedures; and educate employees about sexual harassment. Organizations face an additional gender issue of intimate relationships in the workplace.

Men and women differ in their views of organizational romance, and the effects of occupational romance can vary form negative to positive outcomes. Women face greater risks in organizational romances than men do, though homosexual relationships in organizations receive the most negative sanctions. Organizations are unclear about how to handle organizational romances, but they will need to develop positions and policies for handling the issue in the future. Organizations of the future, because of technological innovations, service emphases, and changing organizational structures, philosophies, and needs probably will become more hospitable and accommodating to women employees.

GLOSSARY

Feminization of occupations—the tendency for the salary and prestige of an occupation to decline as more women enter the occupation.

Glass ceiling—the tendency for women to work at lower organizational levels, to hold lower prestige jobs, and to earn lower salaries than men. To see the upper levels, but to be unable to reach them.

Hostile work environment—a type of sexual harassment in which co-workers make the organizational environment uncomfortable through pervasive and persistent sexual behavior.

Homogeneity principle—the tendency to feel more comfortable with, and to more favorably evaluate, those who are similar to us. An explanation for the glass ceiling and for old-boy networks.

Mommy track—the suggestion that organizations should make less demanding career paths available to women so that they can balance career and family responsibilities.

Old-boy network—the tendency for informal communication networks in organizations be be comprised predominantly of men.

Organizational romance—the sharing of welcome sexual behavior between employees in an organization.

Pipeline theory—an explanation for the glass ceiling that says women have not been in organizations long enough to receive promotions to top levels of responsibility.

Quid pro quo harassment—a type of sexual harassment in which a supervisor associates job consequences with sexual behavior of a subordinate.

Reasonable woman standard—the determination of hostility in a work environment by courts asking whether another woman experiencing the same sexual behaviors under the same work circumstances would reasonably perceive hostility.

Sex-role spillover—the tendency to let expectations associated with traditional roles for women affect perceptions of women in organizational roles.

Sex segregation of occupations—the tendency for large numbers of women to be employed in certain occupations and for large numbers of men to be employed in different occupations.

CASE STUDY

The Ajax Corporation is a multinational manufacturing organization in the top Fortune 100 companies. It dominates the world market in the manufacture and marketing of household cleaning products, gardening and farming chemicals, and food additives and preservatives. In 1979, it started an aggressive campaign of recruiting women and minority employees, which continues today. It has been regarded as one of the most innovative and progressive corporations concerning organizational diversity. A 1994 analysis revealed that women employees at all levels are leaving the

Ajax Corporation at a rate that is nearly double the rate of male attrition. While the company's personnel selection records show that, on average, equal numbers of males and females are hired into the corporation, the lower retention rate for women leads to a prediction that, in five years, seventy-five percent of the company's employees will be male. Currently, about 35 percent of all managers in the organization are female and 3 percent of all positions at the level of vice-president or higher are held by women. The household cleaning products division markets almost exclusively to women consumers.

You are a consultant brought into the Ajax Corporation to diagnose its gender-related personnel problems. How will you collect information to assess the causes of the the female attrition? What specific questions need to be asked? What recommendations would you make for retaining women employees and for promoting them in numbers equal to male promotions?

(*Note:* Either the instructor or a small group of students can represent the Ajax Corporation in answering questions. The information reported can thus provide the basis for consultant recommendations for change.)

REFERENCES

Anderson, C. I., & Hunsaker, P. L. (1985). Why there's romancing at the office and why it's everybody's problem. *Personnel, 62,* 57–63.

Asplund, G. (1988). *Women Managers: Changing Organizational Cultures.* New York: John Wiley.

Astin, H. S., & Leland, C. (1991). *Women of Influence: Women of Vision.* San Francisco: Jossey-Bass.

Bailyn, L. (1982). The apprenticeship model of organizational careers: A response to changes in the relationship between work and family. In P. A. Wallace, (ed.), *Women in the Workplace.* (pp. 45–58). Boston: Auburn House Publishing Company.

Benokraitis, N., & Feagin, J. (1986). *Modern Sexism.* New York: Harper & Row.

Berryman-Fink, C. (1993). Preventing sexual harassment through male-female communication training. In G. L. Kreps, (ed.). *Sexual Harassment: Communication Implications,* (pp. 267–280). Cresskill, N.J.: Hampton Press.

Booth-Butterfield, M. (1989). Perceptions of harassing communication as a function of locus of control, work force participation, and gender. *Communication Quarterly, 37,* 262–275.

Brass, D. J. (1985). Men's and women's networks: A study of interaction patterns and influence in an organization. *Academy of Management Journal, 28:2,* 327–343.

Burke, R., & McKeen, C. (1990). Mentoring in organizations: Implications for women. *Journal of Business Ethics, 9,* 317–332.

Butler, D., & Geis, F. L. (1990). Nonverbal affect responses to male and female leaders: Implications for leadership evaluation. *Journal of Personality and Social Psychology, 58,* 48–59.

Campbell, K. E. (1988). Gender differences in job-related networks. *Work and Occupations, 15:2,* 179–200.

Cannings, K., & Montmarquette, C. (1991). Managerial momentum: A simultaneous model of the career progress of male and female managers. *Industrial and Labor Relations Review, 44:2,* 213–228.

Carr-Ruffino, N. (1993). *The Promotable Woman.* Belmont, Calif.: Wadsworth Publishing Company.

Case, S. S. (1988). Cultural differences, not deficiencies: An analysis of managerial women's language. In S. Rose & L. Larwood (eds.), *Women's Careers: Pathways and Pitfalls,* (pp. 41–63). New York: Praeger.

Clawson, J. G., & Kram, K. E. (1984, May-June). Managing cross-gender mentoring. *Business Horizons, 27,* 22–32.

Dobbins, G. H., & Platz, S. J. (1986). Sex differences in leadership: How real are they? *Academy of Management Review, 11,* 118–127.

Doyle, J. A., & Paludi, M. A. (1991). *Sex and Gender.* Dubuque, Iowa: William C. Brown Communications.

Eagly, A. H., & Johnson, B. T. (1990). Gender and leadership style: A meta-analysis. *Psychological Bulletin, 108,* 233–256.

Ely, R. J. (1988). Attitudes toward women and the experience of leadership. In S. Rose & L. Larwood (eds.), *Women's Careers: Pathways and Pitfalls.* (pp. 65–81). New York: Praeger.

Equal Employment Opportunity Commission (1980). *Sexual harassment guidelines.* 29CFR, CHAPTER XIV, Part 1604.11. Washington, D.C.: U.S. Government Printing Office.

Grant, J. (1988). Women as managers: What they can offer to organizations, *Organizational Dynamics,* 56–63.

Gutek, B. (1985). *Sex and the Workplace: The Impact of Sexual Behavior and Harassment on Women, Men, and Organizations.* San Francisco: Jossey-Bass.

Harland, A., & Weiss, C. L. (1982). Sex differences in factors affecting managerial career advancement. In P. A. Wallace (ed.), *Women in the Workplace.* (pp. 59–100). Boston: Auburn House Publishing Company.

Harriman. A. (1985). *Women/Men Management.* New York: Praeger.

Haslett, B. J., Geis, F. L, & Carter, M. R. (1992). *The Organizational Woman: Power and Paradox.* Norwood, N.J.: Ablex.

Helgesen, S. (1990). *The Female Advantage: Women's Ways of Leadership.* New York: Doubleday Currency.

Horn, P. D., & Horn, J. C. (1982). *Sex in the Office.* Reading, Mass.: Addison-Wesley.

Jamison, K. (1983, August). Managing sexual attraction in the workplace. *Personnel Administrator, 28,* 45–51.

Johnson, F. L. (1989). Women's culture and communication: An analytical perspective. In C. M. Lont, & S. Friedley (eds.), *Beyond Boundaries: Sex and Gender Diversity in Communication* (pp. 301–316). Fairfax, Va.: George Mason University Press.

Kanter, R. M. (1977). *Men and Women of the Corporation.* New York: Basic Books.

Karsten, M. F. (1994). *Management and Gender.* Westport, Conn.: Quorum Books.

Lewis, K. E., & Johnson, P. R. (1991). Preventing sexual harassment complaints based on hostile work environments. *SAM Advanced Management Journal, 56,* 21–36.

Lott, B. (1985) The devaluation of women's competence. *Journal of Social Issues, 41:4,* 43–60.

Lowndes, L (1993). Dangerous office liaisons. *Legal Assistant Today,* 64–70.

Lunneborg, P. W. (1990). *Women Changing Work.* Westport, Conn.: Greenwood Press.

Mainiero, L. A. (1989). *Office Romance: Love, Power, and Sex in the Workplace.* New York: Rawson Associates.

Marini, M. M. (1989). Sex differences in earnings in the United States. *American Review of Sociology, 11,* 343–380.

Merit Systems Protection Board (1981). *Sexual harassment in the federal workplace: Is it a problem?* Washington, DC: U.S. Government Printing Office.

Nadler, M. K., & Nadler, L. B. (1993). Feminization of public relations: The relationship of sex, job titles, and status perceptions of the field. In C. Berryman-Fink, D. Ballard-Reich, & L. H. Newman (eds.), *Communication and Sex-Role Socialization* (pp. 185–200). New York: Garland Publishing Company.

Neville, K. (1990). *Corporate Attractions.* Washington, D.C.: Acropolis Books.

Nieva, V. F., & Gutek, B. A. (1980). Sex effects on evaluation. *Academy of Management Review, 5,* 267–276.

Noe, R. A. (1988). Women and mentoring: A review and research agenda. *Academy of Management Review, 13,* 65–75.

Paludi, M. A., & Strayer, L. (1985). What's in an author's name? Differential evaluations of performance as a function of author's name. *Sex Roles, 12,* 353–361.

Pearson, J. C., West, R. L., & Turner, L H. (1995). *Gender and Communication.* Dubuque, Iowa: Brown and Benchmark.

Powell, G. N. (1988). *Women and Men in Management.* Newbury Park, Calif.: Sage.

Powell, G. N. (1990). One more time: Do female and male managers differ? *Academy of Management Executive, 4:3,* 68–75.

Powell, G. N. (1993). *Women and Men in Management.* Newbury Park, Calif.: Sage.

Powell, G. N., & Butterfield, D. A. (1989). The good manager: Did androgyny fare better in the 1980s? *Group and Organization Studies, 14,* 216–233.

Quinn, R. E., & Lees, P. L. (1984). Attraction and harassment: Dynamics of sexual politics in the workplace. *Organizational Dynamics, 13,* 35–46.

Rizzo, A., & Mendez, C. (1990). *The Integration of Women in Management.* New York: Quorum Books.

Rosener, J. B. (1990, Nov.-Dec.). Ways women lead. *Harvard Business Review,* 119–125.

Sargent, A. G. (1981). *The Androgynous Manager.* New York: AMACOM.

Schwartz, F. N. (1989, Jan.-Feb.). Management women and the new facts of life, *Harvard Business Review,* 65–76.

Shelton, B. (1992). *Women, Men, and Time: Gender Differences in Paid Work, Housework, and Leisure.* Westport, Conn.: Greenwood Press.

Sitterly, C., & Duke, B. W. (1988). *A Woman's Place: Management.* Englewood Cliffs, N.J.: Prentice-Hall.

Stratham, A. (1987). The gender model revisited: Differences in the management style of men and women. *Sex Roles, 16,* 409–426.

Stringer, D. M., Remick, H., Salisbury, J., & Ginorio, A. B. (1990). The power and reasons behind sexual harassment: An employer's guide to solutions. *Public Personnel Management, 19,* 43–52.

Sutton, C., & Moore, K. (1985, Sept.-Oct.). Executive women 20 years later. *Harvard Business Review,* 43–66.

Tannen, D. (1990). *You Just Don't Understand: Women and Men in Conversation.* New York: William Morrow and Company.

U.S. Bureau of Labor Statistics. (1987).

U.S. Department of Labor (1989, August). *Handbook of Labor Statistics.* Washington, D.C.: U.S. Government Printing Office.

Vilkinas, T. (1988). Do women use different influences? *Women in Management Review, 3:3,* 155–160.

Warme, B. D., Lundy, K. L. P., & Lundy, L A. (eds.) (1992). *Working Part-Time: Risks and Opportunities.* Westport, Conn.: Praeger.

Webb, S. L. (1991). *Step Forward: Sexual Harassment in the Workplace.* New York: Master-media.

Westhoff, L. (1986, Feb.). What to do about corporate romance. *Management Review, 75,* 50–55.

Wheeless, V. E., & Berryman-Fink, C. (1985). Perceptions of women managers and their communicator competencies. *Communication Quarterly, 33:2,* 137–148.

White, J. (1992). *A Few Good Women: Breaking the Barriers to Top Management,* Englewood Cliffs, N.J.: Prentice-Hall.

Women and the Workplace: The Glass Ceiling. Hearing before the Subcommittee on Employment and Productivity of the Committee on Labor and Human Resources of the United States Senate, October 23, 1991.

Wood, J. T. (1993). *Who Cares: Women, Care, and Culture.* Carbondale, Ill.: Southern Illinois University Press.

Wood, J. T. (1994). *Gendered Lives: Communication, Gender, and Culture.* Belmont, Calif.: Wadsworth Publishing Company.

York, K. M. (1989). Defining sexual harassment in workplaces: A policy capturing approach. *Academy of Management Journal, 32,* 830–850.

RECOMMENDED READINGS

Carr-Ruffino, N. (1993). *The Promotable Woman.* Belmont, Calif.: Wadsworth Publishing Company.

Haslett, B. J., Geis, F. L., & Carter, M. R. (1992). *The Organizational Woman: Power and Paradox.* Norwood, N.J.: Ablex.

Karsten, M. F. (1994). *Management and Gender.* Westport, Conn.: Quorum Books.

Powell, G. N. (1993). *Women and Men in Management.* Newbury Park, Calif.: Sage.

White, J. (1992). *A Few Good Men: Breaking the Barriers to Top Management.* Englewood Cliffs, N.J.: Prentice-Hall.

▶ 11

Cultural Diversity and Organizations

ALBERTO GONZÁLEZ, JENNIFER WILLIS,
AND CORY YOUNG

The Cleveland, Ohio, office of a large corporation was assigned the task of providing technical and organizational support to an electric company in China. A team of four managers was sent to China. The U.S. managers assumed that the Chinese desired to expand their service in the U.S. fashion that emphasized quickness, efficiency, and the attainment of short-term goals. After all, the managers reasoned, the Chinese had hired U.S. experts. But soon the U.S. managers perceived resistance from the Chinese managers. After one month, the U.S. managers saw that their efforts were leading nowhere and decided to return home. Shortly after their return, the corporation purchased for the managers a day-long cultural sensitivity seminar that focused on China. The seminar addressed topics such as "The Chinese Management Style," "Appropriate Emotions in Interactions," and "Chinese History and Worldview." Armed with this training, the managers now were deemed fit to resume their project.

This actual case illustrates three general issues relating to communication and organizations that we wish to explore in this chapter. First, the organization that relies on and thrives solely within a locality is rare, if not totally extinct. The interrelated and ever-expanding interests of organizations often entail transfers to positions overseas, the placement into the organization of nonlocal consultants, technologies, and methods of working, and the entry into and investigation of new markets. A mobile workforce and shifting demographics in the U.S. shift attention to new relevancies among employees. So it is not surprising that a manager from Cleveland is sent to China to provide advice about service development. Our first issue, then, is, "What is the relationship between the organization and its diverse cultural environment?"

Organizations increasingly understand that respecting domestic co-cultures and international cultures requires attention not simply to the language one speaks, but to *how one communicates* (Is the individual accepting of differences or opposed?) and to the *nature of the communication contexts* fostered within the organization (Is discussion open to all or restricted?). This latter emphasis implies consideration of everything involved in the creation of meaning. Our second issue is, "What is the role of communication in diversity training programs for organizations?"

A third issue pertains to the shifting locus of expertise in organizations. In the example above, the organization deferred to a local consultant whose specialty is providing information about cultures outside of the United States. Organizations differ in their statement of mission, management styles, and climate. Human resources officers, trainers, and the programs they deliver also differ in their assumptions about the nature of organizations, the responsibilities of managers, and choices on how and what about cultures is to be presented. Yet there is little effort to achieve compatability between the organization and the program. Our final issue is, "What do diversity programs offer organizations and how are they to be selected and assessed?"

We address these issues in the following way: First, we offer our initial assumptions about the relationship between communication, organizations, power, and diversity; second, we summarize the domestic demographic changes and the increasing internationalization of U.S. business; third, we describe the various assumptions, objectives, and delivery styles of training programs along with criteria for selection and assessment; finally, we advance an ethical perspective for communication in a culturally diverse organization.

INITIAL ASSUMPTIONS

George Cheney, in his book *Rhetoric in an Organizational Society: Managing Multiple Identities* (1991), observes that:

> *when we remove the physical environment of an organization and take away the parts of its members' lives that are not included within the organizational context, what we have left is a communicative system as the essence of the organization.*

With Cheney, we believe that the business of most organizations is the creation and exportation of meanings. Yet, this creating and exporting of meanings is no random activity; meanings are associated with interest and power. Cheney states (p. 8), "The organization seeks to establish or reinforce certain value premises in the minds of its audiences so that the members of the audience will make decisions in accord with the preferences of the controlling members of the organization." An organization's "audience" may be its own employees, its own investors, a consumer market, business subsidiaries, or a government regulatory agency.

Mumby's analysis of organizations, in *Communication and Power in Organizations: Discourse, Ideology, and Domination* (1988), reveals how the "value premises" of the controlling members also are communicated by the organization's very structure. Office meetings

> *are examples par excellence of the symbolic structuring of power, and of the reification of organizational hierarchy. As such, meetings can be viewed as important not so much by virtue of what they accomplish, but because they provide a context in which various organizational issues can be played out between those members and interest groups that structure organizational agendas. Meetings are symbolic insofar as those people who occupy positions of power in the organizational hierarchy use this context to signify their power, and thus to reaffirm their status. (p. 68)*

The routine, taken-for-granted practices of the organization facilitate certain interests and obstruct the emergence of others. Further, these routine practices seem to make concrete or "natural" what actually is an interpretation and prescription of values. As Stanley Deetz reminds us in *Democracy in an Age of Corporate Colonization: Developments in Communication and the Politics of Everyday Life* (1992), "the corporation is about more than efficiency and profit" (p. 335). From this perspective, we may view with skepticism the assessment by R. Roosevelt Thomas, Jr., in "Managing Diversity: A Conceptual Framework" (1992, p. 307) that one "can conclude that corporate America has not failed in managing or understanding diversity, but rather that it simply has not had these tasks on its agenda."

Because the corporate organization is a concentration of social and cultural meanings and interests, its practices often mirror the political issues of the society that sustains it. There are few social issues today that are as fraught with controversy and potential gain as the efforts by organizations to realize democratic ideals in hiring, promotion and retention, and respecting the relevancies of employees. These efforts are controversial because implied in the appearance of diversity training programs is an indictment of corporate America: Power has been used to dominate and exclude on the basis of race, gender, and cultural affiliation. The recent lawsuits against the Denny's restaurant chain and the court ruling that found that the FBI discriminated against Latino agents in promotions and job assignments (Flynn, 1988) are only two prominent instances of corporate and governmental failure to create organizational climates that are free of domination.

We view cultural diversity as part of an ongoing discourse that is critical of domination and allied with the goal of supporting the free and open participation of all members in the symbolic life of the organization. Carnevale and Stone in "Diversity: Beyond the Golden Rule" (1994) adopt a view of diversity that stresses the pervasiveness of change entailed by this goal. They state that diversity:

implies differences in people based on their identifications with various groups. But it is more. Diversity is a process of acknowledging differences through action. In organizations, this involves welcoming heterogeneity by developing a variety of initiatives at the management and organizational levels as well as the interpersonal (individual and intergroups) levels. (p. 22, emphasis added)

Below we summarize the data that have generated intense rethinking of organizational management.

DEMOGRAPHICS AND THE NEED FOR DIVERSITY TRAINING

The United States has always been a multicultural society. In recent reports, demographers note the increasing populations of traditionally marginalized groups. According to the U.S. Department of Labor in *The American Workforce* (1994), in 1992, over 21 percent of the people in the United States were Black, Hispanic, Asian, or of another ethnic group. By the year 2000, projections are that nearly one in four Americans will be a member of a co-culture. In 1992, co-cultural members (C-CMs)[*] made up nearly 20 percent of the civilian labor force, and that figure is projected to rise (U.S. Department of Labor, 1994). According to the U.S. Department of Labor (1989) in *Workforce 2000,* C-CMs may soon make up more than half of new entrants into the workforce.

While the number of C-CMs in the workforce is rising, there are still relatively few people of color in key positions within organizations (Cantor, 1989; Dodd, 1993). In 1990, 13.2 percent of whites employed in private industry held positions classified as officials and managers, while only slightly more than 5 percent of C-CMs employed in private industry held similar positions. In contrast, according to the U.S. Equal Employment Opportunity Commission (1990) in *Job Patterns for Minorities and Women in Private Industry,* only 13.5 percent of whites in this category held jobs classified as labor or service, compared to 29.3 percent of C-CMs. Clearly, while overall numbers of C-CMs in the workforce have increased, there is still great disparity regarding the types of positions C-CMs hold. This disparity can cause isolation of C-CMs, which can make survival in the business world more difficult.

---

[*]·We choose the term co-cultural member (C-CM) in place of the commonly used "minority." We do this for two reasons. First, C-CM emphasizes the cultural-historical component of shared identity that escapes "minority." Second, "minority" stresses a quantity, in this case less representation, less population, less money, etc. From the standpoint of culture, each person's shared identity is equally central, vital, and orienting. There isn't one worldview that is somehow more comprehensive, more explanatory, or qualitatively better than another. C-CM acknowledges this reality.

Another area of difficulty lies with the unwritten rules and rituals that are part of all organizations. In *Corporate Cultures: The Rites and Rituals of Corporate Life* (1982), Deal and Kennedy note that these rituals are at the core of an organization. They state, "Mostly social in context, one purpose (these rituals) serve among others is to introduce newcomers to the culture. When the newcomer is different... no rituals exist to socialize the individual" (p. 78). Deal and Kennedy believe that these rituals are a major barrier, not only for C-CMs and others of diverse backgrounds, but for organizations as a whole. "Failure to accept women and C-CMs into the mainstream culture hurts not only those victimized but the long-term viability of the business itself" (p. 82). According to Fernandez, in his book *Managing a Diverse Workforce: Regaining the Competitive Edge* (1991), accommodating diversity can improve the bottom line: "Companies that are willing to accommodate diversity will reap rewards in dollars-and-cents terms because they will fully utilize their most valuable resource—people" (p. 2).

Organizations that rely heavily on international assignments can also improve their bottom line through diversity training. Rosita Albert, in her book chapter "Cultural Diversity and Intercultural Training in Multinational Organizations" (1994), estimates the cost to organizations that do not have intercultural training. She states (p. 154):

> It has been estimated that between 20% and 50% of personnel sent overseas by U.S.-based multinational corporations return early; more than half of U.S. multinational corporations had failure rates of 10% and 20%, and about 5% had failure rates of 30%.... The cost of these failed sojourns are considerable... almost a quarter of a million dollars per expatriate failure when the cost of unrealized business is included.

Attitudes on race and ethnicity may be one reason why disparities between whites and C-CMs still exist. While many Americans support issues that increase opportunities for C-CMs, many Americans still hold negative attitudes about race and ethnicity. These attitudes often carry over into the working world, making it difficult for many C-CMs to get jobs (Edwards, Rosenfeld, & Thomas, 1991; Fullwood, 1991; Holmes, 1994; Kravitz & Platania, 1993; Ticked Off, 1994). Many Americans believe that there is no longer discrimination in the workplace (Brown, Minor, & Jepsen 1991; Scherer, 1994). However, attitudes are not the only problems C-CMs face when trying to advance in the workforce. Because there are few C-CMs in high positions, the opportunities for mentoring and word-of-mouth hiring, both very influential areas in the job market, are diminished (Maynard, 1994; Thornburg, 1994). Even C-CMs who do get hired often do not actively seek out members of their own race or ethnicity to mentor because of possible negative labeling by others in the company (Thornburg, 1994). These problems can also lead to higher stress (Brown, Minor, & Jepsen, 1991) and more health problems (James & Khoo, 1991).

Ethnic and racial C-CMs are not the only groups who make up a diverse workforce. As discussed in Chapter 10, women have also been stifled in the working environment. Fernandez (1991) studied responses to the following statement: "The increasing employment of women has led to the breakdown of the American family." Nearly 40 percent of the respondents agreed with the statement (p. 78). These negative attitudes in organizations continually have led to discriminatory practices towards women in the workforce. While this discrimination exists, it is often not blatant in practice. Subtle differences in behavior can also carry discriminatory overtones. Fernandez identifies one such discriminatory practice in which a position's authority is decreased if held by a woman (Fernandez, 1991, p. 109):

> *There are two main sources of power and authority at work—institutional (vested in the position) and personal. But, because of sexist attitudes, the authority inherent in a position if held by a man does not necessarily apply for a woman. The effect of this lessened authority (as the jobholder and others perceive it) is to stifle a woman's confidence and effectiveness. Then if her performance worsens, some co-workers feel justified in their original sexist evaluation of the jobholder—a vicious circle.*

Increasing the numbers of C-CMs is not sufficient for ensuring that negative attitudes are changed. A company cannot successfully adapt to a demographically changing society by merely hiring a more diverse workforce. Contact with people of diverse cultural backgrounds often does little, if anything, to dispel prejudices or stereotypes that may be held by others in the working environment (Fernandez, 1991). Also, simply having rules on how to "deal with" people of different backgrounds is not the answer. Rules, according to Fernandez (1991, p. 23) "can be transformed into absolutes and become ends in themselves. When this occurs, bureaucracies have great difficulty in adapting to special conditions and new situations not envisioned by the rule makers" (p. 23). Instead of rules, Fernandez argues that companies must be willing to work with employees on all levels, educating them about the values of having a diverse workforce.

Many companies have recognized the need for hiring a more diverse workforce. However, while many training programs may focus on hiring for diversity, few focus on how to keep these employees once they are hired. This may be due in part to the fact that many people have negative views on special training and hiring programs for C-CMs (Albert, 1994; Kravitz & Platania, 1993). Diversity training programs are becoming more prevalent in the workforce. However, many agree that training programs need to focus on training their employees to value cultural differences rather than simply to focus on hiring a larger number of minority workers (Brislin et al., 1986; Thornburg, 1994).

Training can help organizations focus on retaining new employees. Companies can often experience greater success in promoting C-CMs when they develop programs specifically designed to enhance retention. One study showed that companies that implemented career outreach programs that prepared C-CMs for advancement to management positions promoted 33 percent more minority managers compared to companies without a program which achieved only 15 percent more minority managers (Maynard, 1994).

Training is a necessity in today's society. According to the Hudson Institute in *Opportunity 2000: Creative Affirmative Action Strategies for a Changing Workforce* (1988), "Companies that fail to acculturate individuals who come from backgrounds different than those they encounter in the workplace—or to acculturate supervisors and other employees who are not used to a Multicultural workforce—will invariably face problems." (p. 90). Training could be the key to unlocking the potential of diversity within the organization. The next section describes the content and delivery of prevalent training programs.

THE HISTORY OF DIVERSITY TRAINING AND COMMUNICATION

Wendy Leeds-Hurwitz, in her article "Notes in the history of intercultural communication: The Foreign Service Institute and the mandate for intercultural training" (1990) traces the origins and development of cultural training programs. Training in intercultural communication began with the Foreign Service Institute FSI, established in 1947. During the 1940s, government analysts began to realize that American diplomats were not fully effective abroad because they did not speak the language and knew little about the host culture. Reevaluations of training procedures led to passage of the Foreign Service Act in 1946. With the implementation of this bill, training and in-service training were established to increase the diplomat's understanding of the language and the host culture.

When the Foreign Service Institute was formally established, it employed a language training program that had been developed, tested, and proven effective by the Army. The Army method employed native speakers and trained linguists, providing an innovative approach to learning that focused on idiomatic expressions and pronunciation of the language. Complementing the linguistic approach was Edward T. Hall's practical application of anthropological principles of culture. Working closely with the Foreign Service Institute under the division of the Technical Cooperation Authority, Hall facilitated a four-week modified program that included instruction in the language, orientation to the mission and its philosophy, limited study of the country and area, as well as anthropological and linguistic generalizations. These generalizations included culture as a concept, change as a process, and common American assumptions (Leeds-Hurwitz, 1990).

Leeds-Hurwitz argues that Edward T. Hall's anthropological contributions in the Foreign Service Institute were instrumental in shaping the field of intercultural communication, "because intercultural communication grew out of the need to apply abstract anthropological concepts to the practical world of foreign service diplomats" (p. 262). The early focus on training American diplomats has led to the later, now standard use of intercultural communication training.

There are several important connections between Hall's work at the Foreign Service Institute and current intercultural communication research and diversity training programs. While traditional anthropological researchers viewed cultures separately, Hall viewed cultures as interacting with one another in distinct temporal and contextual frameworks. This is also the viewpoint taken by much current intercultural research and training. Hall also expanded the concept of culture to include communication which is "patterned, learned, and analyzable" (Leeds-Hurwitz, 1990, p. 263). Finally, Hall believed that only behavioral portions of the interaction were necessary to gain competence in intercultural interactions. While this is contrary to some current intercultural research, most training programs are competency-based (Leeds-Hurwitz, 1990, p. 263–264). Thus, Hall's operationalization of culture has provided the basis for intercultural communication and training as it has been popularly conceived.

Communication Issues

Trainers often have been conditioned to isolate communication, viewing it as an entity separate from culture rather than as simultaneously influenced by and shaping cultural practices. What is not addressed in rules-based programs is the reciprocal nature these culturally-based behaviors have on communication encounters. For example, from the premise that Germans are very formal in their address while Americans are informal, the trainer may conclude that this information should enable one to interact successfully with Germans in the workplace. However, using only prescriptive rules such as this may lead to a puzzling question for the trainee: Who is supposed to adapt, the German or the American? This type of training may also lead to reinforcement of stereotypes, since a generalization is made about a nation with no consideration for regional or ethnic variations or changing social contexts.

It is this traditional conceptualization of culture and communication that has been the guiding impetus for diversity training. This type of training assumes that cultural knowledge and ways of speaking are stable across time and across social contexts. Little attention is paid to the significance or value of these particular cultural practices within a context or to variations across contexts. It is not enough to know that a different behavior exists. To be successful in intercultural interaction, we must understand how this practice operates within the given cultural context.

CORPORATE RESPONSES TO DIVERSITY TRAINING

Cultural diversity seems to be the buzz word for companies today. With the workforce demographics changing rapidly, training programs designed to "manage" diverse cultures are becoming increasingly important for an organization's economic survival. To date, much of the literature on cultural diversity training has focused on what constitutes diversity, how to manage it, how to assess the effectiveness of programs, and the "do's and don'ts" of training.

Assumptions of Traditional Training Programs

In the corporate United States, diversity is often managed through the human resources department. Ferris, Frink, and Galang in their article "Diversity in the workplace: The human resources management challenges," (1993) define human resource systems as the "policies, practices, and decisions employed to process human resources into, through, and out of the organization" (p. 43). They note that "because the human resource systems are the principal vehicles of access into and mobility through the organizations, we must examine them more closely with regard to the notion of diversity. If diversity in the workplace is to be achieved, it is these human resource systems that will facilitate the achievement of this objective" (p. 43). According to Ferris, Frink, and Galang (1993), there are two conflicting objectives operating in human resources today: organizations that claim they seek to maximize diversity in the workplace (heterogeneity), and the traditional approach to diversity that will not allow true diversity, only similarity (homogeneity).

Though diversity issues may be formulated through the human resource department, top management ultimately shapes the final decisions on the desired characteristics of the future employees. Practices for hiring and promoting are often based on those who qualify as "similar" and are willing to support objectives. Blanchette (1994) believes that "in organizations that value assimilation over diversity, emphasis is often placed on changing the people to conform to an organization's norms and performance expectations" (p. 31). Organizations often manage diversity through the reduction of cultural differences through conformity (assimilation) rather than changing the structure of the organization to manage and benefit from diversity (acculturation). There is a tendency for companies to "systematize thought, to restrict imagination, to stifle ideas, to adopt customs and rituals which become inbred and self-serving, to reinforce an ethic that is antagonistic to outsiders, newcomers and strangers" (Sussman, 1994). The organization tends to force all employees into similar molds rather than using the unique individual means found within a diverse organization to maintain the bottom line as well as other organizational objectives.

When examining corporate responses to diversity, there are many factors to take into account. Companies are motivated to acknowledge diversity issues mainly due to the changing demographics in the workforce, affirmative action laws, and the international interdependence of businesses. In order for organizations to be competitive in the global market, sensitivity to cultural issues is fast becoming an economic imperative.

Monocultural values are often at the core of many organizations and their training programs. While these values may serve as a tie for those who share the dominant culture, they often serve as obstacles for those with different backgrounds. Organizations tend to approach this division in one of two ways: assimilation or acculturation.

According to Simons, Vázquez, and Harris (1993), assimilation is "one culture swallowed up by another. The values, customs, language, and ideas of one group are exchanged for those of the mainstream" (p. 10). Ferris, Frink, and Galang (1993) note that some people may consider diversity a problem or a challenge that lessens organizational effectiveness. Others perceive the attention to diversity as an external imposition due to Equal Employment Opportunity Commission and Affirmative Action requirements. The goals for companies that operate from this definition are likely to be surface level and maintenance of status quo. Sussman (1994) claims that "if there is no change, there has been no learning. Most training does not involve learning. Much effort is spent developing routines and standardized procedures that reduce the incidence of any quirks or idiosyncrasies, thereby treating diversity as a threat or attack" (p. 48).

Training can also be conceptualized in surface level terms because those are the terms in which the company defines diversity. "Most organizations are woefully lacking in diversity besides gender or skin color. They are lacking in diversity of other qualities of people" says Sussman (1994, p. 47). For example, a company may employ several African Americans. While the color of their skin may be diverse from the rest of the employees, cultural and ethnic variables within this group of people are taken for granted. These African Americans may have Jamaican, Haitian, Cuban, or even South African influences. Attention is paid only to the numbers summarizing gender or race representation rather than understanding what this diversity means.

Assumptions of Nontraditional Training Programs

A company whose goal is acculturation, heterogeneity, and acceptance of differences, will likely have a definition similar to that of Carnevale and Stone, which we cite above. Implicit within this definition is an understanding of diversity as a supportive environment in which all people are valued and accepted. Differences are described as resources that both employees and employers may draw upon. According to Foeman (1991), organizational objectives operating from this perspective will offer: "(a) discussions of race-related issues (demystification); (b) articulation of other groups' perspectives; (c) examination of other groups' perspectives; (d) finding validity in other groups' perspectives; (e) utilizing others' perspectives in order to work together more effectively...." (p. 256).

An inherent assumption that exists in most nontraditional training programs is the conceptualization that diversity is not entirely a characteristic of non-native individuals. Diversity can exist in individual characteristics like sexual orientation, religious affiliation, age, gender, education, and social class. Programs that address diversity may include a variety of aspects. Karp and Sutton (1993), in the article

"Where diversity training goes wrong," explain that most programs are "dealing with polices and focus almost entirely on legal issues concerning diversity. They are designed to inform managers about equal employment opportunity laws and their applications, as well as affirmative-action rules" (p. 30). These programs primarily focus on rules and regulations that affect organizations, not the different ways to incorporate those with diverse backgrounds into the workforce.

There is also a temporal assumption prevalent in organizations that posits a quick easy fix to diversity issues. A cross-cultural specialist notes that a one-shot program will not completely address cross-cultural issues in an organization. Instead, a long-term approach will most likely be more productive (New Survey Results, 1993). Nontraditional approaches conceive diversity training as an ongoing investigation of cultural values that are constantly being revised and applied to new conditions.

What are the roles of trainers? How do they view diversity? According to Foeman (1991), the role of a trainer is to "establish, articulate, and reiterate group goals throughout training. Trainers also facilitate discussion, comment on group process, encourage the participation of all members, move discussion toward mutual understanding and respect, and provide contextual information" (p. 261). Although trainers supposedly assume an objective position, they do approach diversity with beliefs about the nature and goal of race relations training. Foeman cites Banks' continuum in which trainers attitudes' reflect: "(a) the assimilationist positions [which assumes] that the minority member must learn to blend into the larger society; (b) the multiculturalist position [assumes] that many cultures must coexist; and (c) the cultural pluralist position [assumes] that cultures should be separate" (p. 261).

TRAINING PROGRAMS—THREE APPROACHES

What kinds of training programs exist? There are a multitude of trainers and programs that are currently being used. Foeman (1991) categorizes them into three groups according to the manner of delivery: (a) the didactic model; (b) the experiential model; and (c) the groupwork model.

The Didactic Model

The didactic model is structured around the trainer who presents factual information in a linear, narrowly defined, lecture style manner. This is a less effective approach because interpersonal goals, such as discussing race relations, are not modeled by the trainer. Although the factual information may be important, it is insufficient to bring about change. This kind of approach is privileged to majority members because there is a comfortability factor.

A few examples of didactic models include the following: (1) awareness-based training; (2) cultural-general approaches; and (3) the "how to" and "do's and don'ts" types of programs. Carnevale and Stone (1994) define awareness-based training as a program that is "designed to increase employees' knowledge, awareness, and sensitivity to diversity issues" (p. 30). It aims to reveal worker's unexamined assumptions and commonly held stereotypes. Individuals are seen as individuals rather than members of a group. The cultural general approach (Brislin & Pedersen, 1976) encompasses self-awareness and sensitivity in preparation for interaction with any culture. It also promotes the growth of a perspective that recognizes differences. An example of this approach would be the book entitled *The Art of Crossing Cultures* (Storti, 1990). This book gives a basic introduction to traveling and living abroad and of general cultural differences. An example of the "how to" type of training can be seen in the cultural sensitivity program that Marriott International has developed. In 1994, a program was designed to teach employees how to become more sensitive to international guests. Each department was given a training booklet complete with guidelines and protocol on handling international guests. Information on such things as greetings, tone of voice, proxemics, and gestures was provided.

The Experiential Model

The second approach to training is the experiential model. In this model, interaction among participants is encouraged in order to help modify the outlooks and behaviors of others within the group. Often personal experiences are used to foster discussion about race issues. While this is a central link to changing racial attitudes, Foeman (1991) cites research from Peppard, which indicates that people of color may be placed in the position of teacher or counselor to whites while their basic concerns remain unaddressed. Simply talking about race issues is not sufficient to attend to deep interpersonal needs of those in the minority. Examples of the experiential training model include: (1) skills-based training and (2) the adversarial approach (Brislin & Pedersen, 1976; Hepworth, 1993). Focusing on behaviors, skills-based models provide tools to promote effective interaction to mediate differences and misunderstandings (Brislin & Pedersen, 1976). Because skills-based training is relatively new, experts differ as to which skills are more effective. According to Brislin and Pedersen (1976), some critical skills may include a collaborative environment, cross-cultural understanding, intercultural communication, flexibility, self-awareness, adaptability, and openness. The adversarial approach provided by Hepworth (1993), is designed to foster open communication. Here, trainers and trainees talk about stereotypes and prejudices and their feelings and emotions on these topics.

The didactic and experiential models exhibit several shortcomings that need to be addressed. Foeman contends that there is:

> *A paradox between a focus on creating a sense of sociopolitical context and the need for interpersonally satisfying communication. If we attempt an information-giving model to impart knowledge and provide context, we may ignore and subjugate people of color while miseducating white participants*

and limiting their potential for change. If we move toward a more relational model, we may achieve limited or irrelevant change in white participants and further damage people of color by exploiting their pain. (p. 259)

The didactic and experiential models both focus on disseminating information about particular cultural groups either through the trainer or through the experiences of particular group members. This information is provided to the participants in order to broaden their understanding of other cultures. However, these approaches do not inform the participants how understandings of different cultures are constructed in both society and in the organization. Nor do these approaches allow the participants to create their own understanding of cultural groups. In both the didactic model and the experiential model, the participants are *told* new ways of thinking about culture, rather than constructing this new way of thinking themselves.

The Groupwork Model

An alternative program that holds considerable potential is the groupwork model. Foeman (1991) describes the groupwork model as a "multifaceted, interactive approach" which uses a variety of techniques for training including films, role play, and discussions. This method attempts

to infuse additional information into group experience in order to help participants identify the social contexts within which interracial contacts occur, expand participants' frames of reference, and increase their options for understanding and responding to cross-race issues.... The multifaceted, interactive approach also encourages individuals to "own their attitudes and behaviors both in the group and in the larger society." (p. 260)

Another benefit of the groupwork model is its ability to be used for the examination of culture from the participants' perspective. In other words, through groupwork, participants are able to understand their *own* cultural assumptions while understanding the assumptions underlying other cultures. Edwards (1991) emphasizes the importance of examining our own cultural behaviors. "... it is crucial that we first understand how we have been shaped by our own culture and begin to recognize some of the biases and stereotypes we often bring to our interactions with others who are unlike us" (p. 47). By examining our own cultural assumptions, Edwards believes that people will develop understandings of other cultures, which, is "crucial for managing cultural diversity" (p. 47).

The central goals of the groupwork model are directed toward: "(a) establishing an information base and social context for training participants, (b) increasing cross-racial dialogue, and (c) encouraging participants to experience themselves as active both in the larger social system and interpersonal cross-racial relations" (Foeman, 1991, p. 260). In addition, this model may create an environment in which participants will be able to effectively evaluate the skills and abilities of individuals with varying cultural styles and avoid making mainstream/non-mainstream assessments of others. These goals are grounded in the ideology that diversity is something positive and that people should be valued for their differences. Carnevale and Stone (1994) write: "Valuing diversity involves treating others as they wish to be treated... It means recognizing that other people's standards and values as valid as one's own" (p. 24). To value diversity, initiatives must be implemented at all levels in an organization. This allows the company to develop an environment that works for all employees. Carnevale and Stone say that

> *in most organizations, valuing and managing diversity requires nothing less than cultural transformation. This is a prodigious task, for it requires people—especially those of the dominant culture—to let go of their assumptions about the universal rightness of their own values and customary ways of doing things in order to become receptive to other cultures. (p. 24)*

By examining diversity through different formats, participants acquire the tools needed to gain greater insight into the context that constructs particular understandings of culture and diversity. Foeman admits that there may also be limits regarding the implementation of this type of program. She notes that the goals of the program may be "constrained by the organizational goals of the institution sponsoring the training," but goes on to state that "reasonable tasks and goals should be established based on existing constraints" (p. 261). We extend the groupwork model by inviting both the trainer and the participants to examine how these constraints are constructed within the organization.

Foeman identifies three aspects regarding the implementation of a groupwork program: the trainer, the participants, and the training situation. The trainer in the groupwork model takes on a more facilitative, guiding role rather than one of instructor. Foeman notes that the trainer should be open about his or her agenda or beliefs on cultural diversity thus enabling the participants to examine that point of view and through the training, make an informed choice to either subscribe to or reject that perspective. Another step that this model invites is the examination of the organization's perspective. Examining the underlying assumptions constructed through communicative acts in the organization allows the participants to explore the different ways in which these assumptions are created and supported within the organization.

In the groupwork model, the participants also examine their own underlying assumptions about culture and diversity. These issues are examined not only on an individual level, but with regard to the makeup of the group as well. The training situation, as mentioned before, includes a wide variety of techniques enabling the participants to examine a variety of perspectives on diversity and culture. Some of these techniques are prearranged, tailored towards concerns which may be generated within the group. Some suggestions that Foeman puts forth include icebreakers, question and answer sessions, mixing up activities, same race caucuses, and wrap-up activities.

The groupwork model, in effect, revises the concept of training. It allows the participants to become the trainers, not necessarily of each other, but of themselves. By inviting the participants to examine the underlying assumptions of their own beliefs, those of others and those of the organization, participants are able to make an informed decision about the particular perspectives they choose to accept.

ASSESSMENT

Selection of Training Programs

When selecting a program, there are several important characteristics that need to be considered. Criteria for selection is used to ensure that the trainers are qualified and that the training program is legitimate. Brislin and Pedersen (1976) provide one model that suggests certain aspects that are desirable for a trainer and a program:

Trainers must also ensure that the organization is committed to diversity. From the article in *New survey results* (1993) one diversity specialist explains: "You have to ask yourself, 'Is this organization really serious? Does it feel like they're saying 'Let's just get this over with and check if off the list,' or are they doing it because they know they need to do the work'" (p. 11). It is also important that the trainer analyze the needs of the organization to clarify the purpose of the training towards the organization and towards the participants as well. Organizations should ask the trainer to provide credentials and experience, as some people are defining themselves as "diversity trainers" with minimal qualifications (p. 13). The trainer chosen should also support the operating organizational objectives. These criteria represent the most important characteristics that the trainers should employ in their research and that organizations should be aware of in their selection of programs.

TABLE 11-1   **Selection of training programs.**

Before Training	**During Training**	**After Training**
Gather data on assumptions	Provide transfer from training to real world	Evaluate effectiveness
Set up reasonable goals	Provide social support	Replicate findings
		Provide follow-up training

From R. W. Brislin and P. Pedersen (1976). *Cross-Cultural Orientation Programs,* New York: Gardiner Press, p. 6.

Evaluation of Training Programs

The evaluation of these programs is an important next step in the development of diversity training. Brislin and Yoshida (1994) offer some criteria for evaluating training programs. They state that evaluation is necessary, due to decreased economic allotments, for training programs to survive in organizations. Intercultural communication specialists, when evaluating programs, should try to answer these questions (Brislin & Yoshida, 1994, p. 147):

1. Can the training program be improved?
2. Have the goals of the training program been achieved?
3. Is the cross-cultural training program being evaluated of higher quality than other programs that could have been chosen for implementation?
4. Are there evaluation designs that allow for information to be gathered on program effectiveness and that allow busy trainers to schedule their time efficiently?
5. Can the training program being evaluated provide guidance for setting up programs for other types of people? Can a program for business people provide guidance for programs aimed at international students?
6. What are the beneficial effects of intercultural training as documented in good evaluation studies?

Brislin and Yoshida (1994) describe two ways to evaluate training programs, "in formative and summative evaluation refers to two different types of information that program planners can use" (p. 148). Formative evaluation provides insight into what can be improved. Questions that might be posed in this type of evaluation are: "Do [the trainees] find the material presented useful and interesting or do they view the program as a waste of time?; Are goals being met?; What is perceived as important?; and What material can be deleted or added?" (p.149). Summative information is gathered to address whether the program is effective. This information can include how effective people are in "communicating with culturally diverse individuals, how long it takes them to perform effectively on their job in the other culture, how effective people are in solving problems, how they deal with stress of intercultural living and so forth" (Brislin & Yoshida, 1994, p. 150). Examining how values are addressed is an important consideration in the evaluation of training programs. Elashmawi and Harris (1993) see values as crucial to diversity training. "Throughout the training process, from design to implementation, the consideration given to cultural values determines the success or failure of the program" (p. 138). Without consideration of cultural values, a diversity training program is destined to have problems.

Brewster and Pickard (1994) provide additional information on assessment through their evaluations of expatriate training programs overseas. The method of analysis used centered around training courses offered at the Centre for International Briefing at Farnham Castle in England. Various hypotheses were tested on the provision of training, the importance of the role of the partner, age, previous experience, perceptions of the training course, location, type of organization, and degree of social interaction with host nationals. The results indicated that there were significant positive attitudes exhibited by the expatriates and their partners.

In summary, organizations must learn to assess training programs beginning with a candid understanding of the particular conditions of employment experienced by C-CMs. Organizations must be prepared to finance long-term studies of the impact of training initiatives since diversity implies ongoing attention and pervasive change.

CONCLUSION: TOWARD ORGANIZATIONAL ETHICS AND DIVERSITY

The critiques of domination are based on conflictual social theories. As John Fiske argues in his essay "Writing ethnographies: Contribution to a dialogue" (1991), these theories "claim that white, patriarchal, capitalist societies are structured around conflicting social interests and that their stability and coherence is achieved by the ability of the power-bloc to promote and hold its interests against those of subordinated social groups" (p. 331). Within this conflictual interpretation of societies, Mumby (1993) asserts that organizations "reflect the struggle to fix and institutionalize the dominance of certain groups and meaning structures over others" (p. 21). In considering diversity, we are faced with an immediate question. If corporate and governmental organizations are structured to establish and maintain privilege for the few and are further structured to gain the consent of the many in the establishment and maintenance of privilege, how possible is the democratic participation of diverse cultural groups? Deetz (1990) notes how "the lack of any possible non-arbitrary, non-privileging foundation in nature can easily lead to giving up on moral questions altogether" (p. 50).

Yet Deetz, in his article "Keeping the conversation going: The principle of dialectic ethics" (1983) advances an ethic for communication in contemporary organizations. His principle states that: "Every act should have as its ethical dimension an attempt to keep the conversation going—that is, communicative action and communication research should have as a normative aim an attempt to establish the conditions for further less restrained communication" (p. 279). In *Democracy in an Age of Corporate Colonization: Developments in Communication and the Politics of Everyday Life,* Deetz (1992) calls for a concept of "balanced responsiveness" that is the opposite of domination and privileges, "care and moral direction" over "instrumentality and decisional rules" (p. 338). In this perspective the context in which communication occurs is as salient as the content of specific utterances.

As we have seen, didactic and experimental diversity programs do not seriously challenge traditional authority structures of organizations. These programs provide a mechanism whereby organizations can address diversity issues without significant change. We look to the groupwork model of diversity training to lead the way for significant change. The capacity of the groupwork model to form, dissipate, and reform, to call upon a variety of informational sources from an assortment of media, to call upon experience as a resource, and to develop individual processes for dialogue, conflict resolution, and appeal, offers the best chance to accomplish acceptance and open participation.

GLOSSARY

Assimilation—one culture being swallowed up by another.
Acculturation—heterogeneity and acceptance of differences.
Co-cultural member—member of an underrepresented or marginalized culture.
Didactic model—a model structured around the trainer who presents factual information in a linear, narrowly defined, lecture style manner.
Diversity—knowledge of and respect for cultural differences and a process of acknowledging differences through action (from Carnevale and Stone, 1994).
Experiential model—a model in which self-disclosure among participants is encouraged in order to help modify the outlooks and behaviors of others within the group.
Groupwork model—a model that uses a multifaceted approach through which participants are encouraged to "own" their attitudes and behaviors.

CASE STUDY

AJC Inc. has become increasingly diverse over the last five years. Company executives had been concerned because the demographic makeup of the company did not reflect that of the community that the company served. Executives encouraged personnel managers to implement hiring practices that would rectify this situation. For the past five years the company has been actively recruiting C-CMs and older workers for various positions, including those on the fast track to management. However, since implementing these hiring guidelines, problems have surfaced. Many of the C-CMs and older workers have been leaving the company within a year. Those who have stayed often have had less than favorable reviews. Only a few of those actively recruited have been promoted to management, though many were hired for this fast track. There have also been complaints by the union about "favored" hiring status for C-CMs and older workers. At this point, there is no training program in diversity. The only mention of diversity is in discussions of EEO guidelines in the personnel training program.

Discussion: How should AJC Inc. approach this problem? Give examples using both a traditional and a critical approach.

REFERENCES

Albert, R. D. (1994). Cultural diversity and intercultural training in multinational organizations. In R. L. Wiseman, & R. Shuter (eds.), *Communicating in Multinational Organizations* (pp. 153–165). Thousand Oaks, Calif.: Sage.

Blanchette, D. P. (1994, July/Aug.). Technology transfer in a culturally diverse workforce (Part I). *Industrial Management*, pp. 31–32.

Brewster, C., & Pickard, J. (1994, Oct.). Evaluating expatriate training. *International Studies of Management & Organization, 24*(3), 18–35.

Brislin, R. W., & Pedersen, P. (1976). *Cross-Cultural Orientation Programs.* New York: Gardner Press.

Brislin, R., & Yoshida, T. (1994). *Intercultural Communication Training: An Introduction.* Thousand Oaks, Calif.: Sage.

Brislin, R. W., Cushner, K., Cherrie, C., & Yong, M. (1986). *Intercultural Interactions.* Beverly Hills, Calif.: Sage.

Brown, D., Minor, C. W., & Jepsen, D. A. (1991). The opinions of minorities about preparing for work: Report of the second NCDA national survey. *The Career Development Quarterly, 40,* 5–19.

Cantor, B. (1989, July/Aug.). Minority hiring shows problems in corporate America. *IABC Communication World,* pp. 22–25.

Carnevale, A. P., & Stone, S. C. (1994, Oct.). Diversity: Beyond the golden rule. *Training & Development,* pp. 22–39.

Cheney, G. (1991). *Rhetoric in an Organizational Society: Managing Multiple Identities.* Columbia, S.C.: University of South Carolina Press.

Deal, T. E., & Kennedy, A. A. (1982). *Corporate Cultures: The Rites and Rituals of Corporate Life.* Reading, Mass.: Addison-Wesley.

Deetz, S. (1983). Keeping the conversation going: The principle of dialectic ethics. *Communication, 7,* 263–288.

Deetz, S. (1992). *Democracy in an Age of Corporate Colonization: Developments in Communication and the Politics of Everyday Life.* Albany, N.Y.: State University of New York Press.

Deetz, S. (1990). Representation of interest and the new communication technologies: Issues in democracy and policy. In M. Medhurst, A. Gonzalez, & T. R. Peterson (eds.) *Communication and the Culture of Technology* (pp. 43–62). Pullman, Wash.: Washington State University Press.

Dodd, M. (1993, Jan.). Survey finds minorities rare in "power" positions. *USA Today,* p. 6.

Edwards, A. (1991, Jan.). The enlightened manager: How to treat all your employees fairly. *Working Woman,* pp. 45–51.

Edwards, J. E., Rosenfeld, P., & Thomas, P. J. (1991) Hispanic and non-Hispanic white new hires in the Navy's blue-collar civilian work force: A pilot study. *Hispanic Journal of Behavioral Sciences, 13,* 412–421.

Elashmawi, F., & Harris, P. R. (1993). *Multicultural Management: New Skills for Global Success.* Houston, Tex.: Gulf Publishing.

Fernandez, J. P. (1991). *Managing a Diverse Workforce: Regaining the Competitive Edge.* Lexington, Mass.: Lexington Books.

Ferris, G. R., Frink, D. D., & Galang, M. C. (1993). Diversity in the workplace: The Human resources management challenges. *Human Resource Planning, 16*, 41–51.

Fiske, J. (1991). Writing ethnographies: Contribution to a dialogue. *Quarterly Journal of Speech, 77,* 330–335.

Flynn, K. (1988, Oct. 1). Hispanics win bias suit against FBI. *Houston Post,* p. A1.

Foeman, A. K. (1991). Managing multiracial institutions: Goals and approaches to race-relations training. *Communication Education, 40,* 255–265.

Fullwood III, S. (1991, Jan. 9). Attitudes on minorities in conflict. *Los Angeles Times,* p. A13.

Hepworth, J. (1993, May). The cultural context of change: Do trainers get it? *Cultural Diversity at Work, 5:5,* 5.

Holmes, S. A. (1994, March 3). Survey finds minorities resent one another almost as much as they do whites. *New York Times,* p. B-8.

Hudson Institute (1988). *Opportunity 2000: Creative Affirmative Action Strategies for a Changing Workforce.* (USDL Publication No. 746-C-1). Washington D.C.: Government Printing Office.

James, K., & Khoo, G. (1991). Identity-related influences on the success of minority workers in primarily nonminority organizations. *Hispanic Journal of Behavioral Sciences, 13*(2), 169–192.

Karp, H. B., & Sutton, N. (1993). Where diversity training goes wrong. *Training,* pp. 30–34.

Kravitz, D. A., & Platania, J. (1993). Attitudes and beliefs about affirmative action: Effects of target and of respondent sex and ethnicity. *Journal of Applied Psychology, 78*(6), 928–938.

Leeds-Hurwitz, W. (1990). Notes in the history of intercultural communication: The Foreign Service Institute and the mandate for intercultural training. *Quarterly Journal of Speech, 76,* 263–281.

Maynard, M. (1994, September). Diversity programs work, where they exist. *USA Today,* p. 5.

Mumby, D. K. (1988). *Communication and Power in Organizations: Discourse, Ideology and Domination.* Norwood, N.J.: Ablex.

Mumby, D. K. (1993). Critical organizational communication studies: The next 10 years. *Communication Monographs, 60,* 18–25.

New Survey Results. (1993, May). *Cultural diversity at work, 5:5,* 1, 10–14.

Scherer, R. (1994, March). First national survey of minority views shows deep racial polarization in US. *Christian Science Monitor,* p. 4:3.

Simons, G. F., Vázquez, C., & Harris, P. R. (1993). *Transcultural Leadership: Empowering the Diverse Workforce.* Houston, Tex.: Gulf Publishing Company.

Storti, C. (1990). *The Art of Crossing Cultures.* Yarmouth: Intercultural Press.

Sussman, H. (1994). Is diversity training worth maintaining? *Business & Society Review, 89,* 48–49.

Thomas, Jr. R. R. (1992). Managing diversity; A conceptual framework. In S. E. Jackson and Associates (eds.) *Diversity in the Workplace: Human Resources Initiatives.* New York: The Guilford Press (pp. 306–318).

Thornburg, L. (1994, February). Journey toward a more inclusive culture. *HR Magazine,* pp. 79–86.

Ticked Off. (1994, Sept.). *Wall Street Journal,* p. 14.

U.S. Department of Labor. (1989). *Workforce 2000: Work and workers for the 21st century.* (USDL Publication No. 0-186-705 QL 3). Washington D.C.: U.S. Government Printing Office.

U.S. Department of Labor. (1994). *The American workforce: 1992–2005* (USDL Bulletin No. 2452). Washington, D.C.: Government Printing Office.

U.S. Equal Employment Opportunity Commission. (1990). *Job pattern for minorities and women in private industry.* (USEEOC Publication No. 1059 A-10. Washington, D.C.: Government Printing Office.

RECOMMENDED READINGS

Borucki, C., & Barnett, C. K. (1990, February). Restructuring for survival—The Navistar case. *Academy of Management Executive,* 36–49.

Clarke, C. (1994, Sept.). Making diversity more manageable. *Training and Development,* 53–58.

Foeman, A. K., & Pressley, G. (1987). Ethnic culture and corporate culture: Using black styles in organizations. *Communication Quarterly, 35,* 293–307.

Jackson, S. E., & Associates. (1992). *Diversity in the Workplace: Human Resource Initiatives.* New York: The Guilford Press.

Lincoln, J. R., & Kalleberg, A. L. (1990) *Culture, Control, and Commitment.* Cambridge: Cambridge University Press.

Martin, J. (1992). *Cultures in Organizations: Three Perspectives.* Oxford: Oxford University Press.

Moran, R. T., & Harris, P. R. (1982). *Managing Cultural Synergy.* Houston, Tex.: Gulf Publishing Company.

Mumby, D. K. (1993). *Narrative and Social Control: Critical Perspectives.* Thousand Oaks, Calif.: Sage.

Pfeffer, J. (1981). *Power in Organizations.* Cambridge: Ballinger.

Schreiber, C. T., Price, K. F., & Morrison, A. (1994). Workforce diversity and the glass ceiling: Practices, barriers, possibilities. *Human Resource Planning, 16,* 51–69.

The Organizational Consultant

JAMES WILCOX AND ETHEL WILCOX

During the course of your professional career you will inevitably be functioning within one and probably more organizational environments. Chances are extremely high that you will employ or interface with many organizational consultants, some claiming expertise in human communication processes and problems. These consultants may be internal or external to your organization(s). They may rely upon you as a source of information; you may not only provide information but attempt to provide influence as well. Perhaps you will be a consultant at some point or for a portion of your career. In any case, organizational consulting, often communication consulting, has become a staple of organizational life and it is well to understand what it involves and how you might either use one or be one.

Your authors for this chapter are two professors of communication, both of whom actively consult with a wide variety of organizations, small and large, private and public, product-oriented and service-oriented. Between us we have forty-seven years of academic experience specializing in interpersonal and organizational communication and forty years of organizational communication consulting experience. We have engaged in a wide range of consulting activity, specializing in seminars and training programs as well as conducting marketing research from a consumer standpoint. Somewhat less often we have been conflict intervention specialists. We have not done readership surveys, speech writing, preparation or analysis of company newsletters, or personal counseling, to name a few recognized communication consulting activities. In recent years we have specialized in the health care industry.

Our experiences have led us to a conception of consulting as teaching, facilitating, and making problem-solving organizational communication recommendations.

We agree with Redding's (1979) position that consulting is a "helping" activity that "draws upon a body of conceptual and practical insights that go far beyond those of the casual, friendly neighbor" (p. 348). Redding, who passed away earlier this year, is viewed as the "Father of organizational communication" by several. He was an active consultant throughout his career. We have evolved in our thinking about consulting to the point that we believe that we can "help" best when we enjoy a long-term, in-depth relationship with an organization, which allows for sufficient time to grasp the systemic factors interacting within both the internal organizational and the external environments, to employ multiple methods of information gathering, to work in concert with clients in defining and framing problem situations, and to conduct follow-ups to determine the effectiveness of implemented solutions. Obviously, this ideal relationship is unlikely to occur overnight and may require several years of experience (as well as a track record on the part of the consultant) to develop. But in our judgment it represents a worthy goal to which to aspire. Often the consultant, at least in the short run, must accept less.

Our purpose in this chapter is to acquaint you with the following:

- Why organizations use (or misuse) communication consultants
- What are the various types of consulting relationships with what advantages and disadvantages for both consultants and clients
- What are the kinds of communication consulting activities for which communication consultants are likely to be hired
- What should the ideal organizational consultant aspire to by way of educational background
- How does the organizational communication consultant develop and maintain relationships with clients?

For illustrative purposes, as we begin this chapter we would like to present a situation in which we are (and have been for four years) involved with as organizational consultants. Once the case study is described, we will provide tentative answers to the above five inquiries.

GENERAL HOSPITAL: A CASE STUDY

General Hospital is a private hospital situated on 100 acres in a beautiful suburban area of a mid-size Midwestern city. One of eight hospitals in the metropolitan area, General moved from its inner city location in the mid-1970s and relocated to a rapidly growing and very affluent suburb. General's grounds are lovely: There are huge expanses of rolling grass lawns, ponds and lakes with high spraying fountains, with a backdrop of heavily wooded forest. Dozens of brightly colored ducks and geese make the hospital grounds their home.

At a time when there was a citywide "boom" in emergency department (ED) usage, with ED visits up 20 percent, General's ED census was falling. There was clearly a negative downward trend in General's ED market share:

Year	Market Share (percent)
1986	8.0
1987	7.8
1988	7.7
1989	7.6

In 1989, an independent market survey showed General to be at the bottom in terms of patient satisfaction experienced throughout the city with ED care. A significant number of patients who had visited General's ED indicated they would not be inclined to return; individuals who lived close to the hospital drove right past the ED entrance to go elsewhere for emergency care.

With a falling ED census (and a corresponding decrease in hospital admissions), the hospital board "sat up and took notice." A medical consultant was hired to review emergency services and to identify the specific problems causing the falling census. This consultant identified the following five major problems:

- *Physical plant deterioration*—General's ED waiting area was small, the surroundings "dingy," the lay-out not conducive to effective emergency care, and the facility "out of date."
- *Personnel issues*—There were a number of interpersonal communication problems in the ED. Individuals suffered from what they perceived to be an exceptionally heavy workload, insufficient support from administration, excessive patient complaints, patients not having true emergencies, and lack of positive feedback from management.
- *Staff attrition*—In just over a two-year period of time, General's ED lost nearly twenty of its experienced emergency care nurses (leaving a core of only six ED-dedicated nurses) and one exceptionally well-liked physician. The resultant staff shortages and attendant problems of nurse recruitment, retraining, and staff adjustment to the unit resulted in increasingly severe internal interpersonal problems.
- *Negative public perceptions of the hospital:* The community perception of General's ED as a place that "didn't have its act together," was an external manifestation of the internal problems facing the department. Patient evaluation forms from that time are full of anecdotal evidence of staff strife and dissatisfaction. In any community bad news travels fast.
- *Physician issues:* Physicians were concerned with such things as what they perceived to be poor management in the ED, scheduling issues, disciplinary issues, and poor nurse-physician relations.

Although the hospital board members, the hospital executive team members, the ED director, and the physicians were in agreement that the consultant had done a good job of identifying problems, they were disappointed with a lack of direction as to how to resolve the problems. The hospital board and hospital executive team members made a quick decision to build a new state of the art ED facility, but realized that unless the other four issues were addressed, the census was likely to continue falling. A local psychologist was hired to conduct support sessions for the nurses, but after the first mandatory session, nurses failed to attend other sessions, expressing displeasure with what they thought was "touchy-feely, feel-good nonsense."

It was finally decided (how the decision was reached is a fuzzy one with virtually everyone involved taking credit for reaching it) that with the exception of the physical plant problem, all of the major problems facing the ED were communication problems, perhaps best addressed by specialists in the area of health communication. At that point, the authors of this chapter were hired by the hospital to "turn the ED around." The authors knew *we* couldn't turn things around . . . that if change were to occur, it had to come from the ED staff itself. The question then faced was: How to achieve buy-in from a burned-out, angry, bickering staff that was plagued by a community image of being affiliated with a third-rate ED?

Background Information

With approximately 40 percent of all admissions to hospitals coming from emergency visits, emergency departments are literally the hospital's "front door." As a "primary feeder," the ED plays a critical role in determining the financial success of the hospital as a whole. It probably is not overstating the case to say that "As the ED goes, so goes the hospital."

For other than severe traumas and true emergency cases, patients often have a choice of which emergency department they will use. In this midwestern city area, for instance, there are eight hospital emergency departments, all of which can be reached from virtually all of the surrounding communities and outlying population centers within no more than a 30-minute drive. If an individual is not happy with the service received at one hospital, it is easy to go elsewhere to receive emergency care.

Because most patients are unable to judge the actual quality of medical care delivered in an ED, they base their opinions of the facility largely on communication factors they are familiar with and can judge. For instance, patients will often assess their medical care by judging such factors as friendliness of the staff, whether questions are anticipated and answered in a satisfactory manner, the amount of concern they find being expressed, how long they have to wait, how understandable they find their bill to be, and so forth.

Unfortunately, the ED is not an environment conducive to good communication. ED personnel are often faced with a number of difficult and sometimes conflicting demands such as the following:

- The ED staff is expected to provide timely care without being able to predict patient demand; sometimes the ED may be "packed" with patients, at other times the ED may be "dead."
- Patients often have to wait. ED care is *not* "first come, first served." Unfortunately, what patients may believe to be an "emergency" may be considered "minor" by ED personnel.
- Patients using the ED come from every walk of life with every conceivable problem. Some use the ED as their "doctor's office," some have true emergencies.
- Often EDs are not set up to facilitate customer focus. Many hospital emergency facilities are too small for the current patient demand. ED departments are often far removed from supporting departments such as the pharmacy, lab, and x-ray, and ED departments often have small and cramped waiting areas.
- The ED is staffed by individuals who have different educational levels, different goals, and differing degrees of loyalty to the department. Who reports to whom is not always clear and a number of individuals (physicians and nurses alike) may "float" through the department as demand dictates. Interpersonal communication problems are commonplace in emergency departments.

Intervention: Multiphase, Multimethod Interviews

We conducted interviews of approximately sixty minutes each with:

- The vice president of patient relations (nursing)
- The vice president of marketing
- The nursing manager of the emergency department
- The emergency department physician chief of staff

The purpose of these interviews was to obtain much of the background information (earlier described), to develop a collaborative relationship, to define appropriate goals, and to secure the willingness of each to serve as contact points. These interviews were of great assistance in helping us develop a proposal that would specify objectives, identify time frames and phases, stipulate what would be delivered by way of our consultation services, show cost of complete intervention (broken out in phases), demonstrate value or benefit to the hospital, and show how "success" would be measured.

Analysis of Documents and Other Written Materials

Several years earlier we had spent the better part of a sabbatical year as participant observers in another area hospital's ED. We had begun this endeavor for the purpose of analyzing conflict patterns and ended by describing the ED subculture in terms of all the communication activity participants employed to create and maintain their organizational reality. This prior experience had given us some familiarity with the operation of an ED, had shown us the kinds of communication "challenges" that are inherent within the situation, and alerted us to the existence of both library literature and hospital-generated patient satisfaction information.

A trip to the library refamiliarized us with the books and publications that a professional interested in emergency medicine might read. Our analysis of quarterly patient satisfaction data for the prior year familiarized us with the recurring patterns of patient response to the quality of medical attention and care they believed they had received.

The purpose of reviewing these two bodies of information was to allow us to develop an ideal model—how *should* (in the best of all worlds) communication processes occur in an ED? Then the patient satisfaction data, as well as other data we would gather, would reveal a picture of what was *actually* happening in General Hospital's ED from the perspective of those to whom it was happening. Then we could observe discrepancies between "ideal" and "real" and develop estimates of what it might take and how long to achieve reduction of that discrepancy.

Observation

We became regular observers in the ED, appearing at various times of day and night, stationing ourselves in various strategic locations and watching people interact with and within the ED environment. To reduce the obtrusive nature of our observations, we donned "scrubs" and ran errands for the ED staff. A total of eighteen hours of observation covered the approach to the facility, the reception and check-in area, the waiting area, the triage area, ED personnel interaction, ED personnel, patient, and family interaction, interaction with other departments (especially those interactions that might be witnessed by a patient or family member), and discharge processes. An example of a waiting area observation follows:

> *Other than the small rack beside the security desk, which appears to be used by security, there is no place to conveniently hang coats and hats. When one is seated there are no signs immediately apparent indicating directions to either public phones or restrooms. Signage needs to clarify the two available restrooms in the hallway—Are they both unisex or is one for each gender? As it is, many visitors seem confused. There should be a second pay phone, perhaps to the far left of the television in the waiting room. Pay phone service should also provide access to long distance lines. That these conditions are not currently present creates the potential for time-wasting questions of registration clerks or security personnel and creates the impression of a less than customer-focused facility. There are many magazines and newspapers, most relatively current, but the rack of brochure materials seems little used and perhaps needs attention directed toward it, that is, "Feel free to take a brochure." The hospital publication*

is currently folded for mailing and needs to be folded in the opposite direction for public display. It should not be covered by other materials, as both information and marketing opportunities may be missed. While coffee is obviously available, soft drinks are not. The tissue boxes need regular replacement, one for each table. Videos on ED orientation or common ailments and the ED Visitor Information Brochure are not yet available.

Focus Groups

The use of internal focus groups was a major component of the intervention. Four focus groups of ED personnel, approximately ten per group, for approximately ninety minutes discussed such questions as:

- How long have you been working in General's ED?
- What are the most and least satisfying aspects of work in the ED?
- What negative (and probably unintentional) messages do you believe patients and their families receive when they visit General's ED?
- What may be current barriers to achieving a high degree of customer focus?

Information gained from these groups was vital both in terms of our ability to create training approaches that "rang true" to staff members and to begin laying the foundation for staff buy-in to the change recommendations we would ultimately develop. We knew that employees would be more committed to decisions they had played a part in making.

Training

Sifting through the observations made by participants in the initial internal focus groups, the authors made decisions as to how to approach the training sessions. Training concepts were carefully illustrated by examples from the focus groups and were exceptionally well-received by nurses and physicians alike. Concepts that seemed particularly relevant included the following:

- We have no choice but to communicate something; our only choice is what and how we will communicate.
- There is probably no such thing as perfect communication.
- Unintentional messages can be especially counterproductive in terms of patient and employee satisfaction.
- Defensiveness may be the single greatest barrier to effective communication.
- Communication problems are generally not resolved by trying to determine "who started it."
- Improvement in communication proficiency "pays big dividends" in terms of patient satisfaction and more importantly in employee satisfaction.

Problem Solution Implementation Sessions

Both in the initial focus groups and during training sessions, ideas for ED improvement were garnered from ED physicians, nurses, technicians, clerks, and patients. Recommendations were compiled into a short report. An illustration of a recommendation follows:

> Patients should be given reasonable overestimates regarding the amount of time before treatment will begin and how long it will take to get lab reports, etc.

Patients need to be communicated with on a regular enough basis to answer for them the question inevitably in their minds: What, if anything is happening relevant to my situation. What might happen next and about how long must I wait for information? What patients are most concerned about is not just the amount of time—it is not knowing how much time and not knowing if anything is happening. Helping the patient to "structure" time in this fashion will help reduce their very natural uncertainties and will help give them the impression that they are being cared for in an organized way by an organized group of health care practitioners. The same principle applies to waiting family members or friends.

As a way of underscoring the importance of this recommendation—*Modern Health Care* of October 7, 1991, reports a survey of 21,000 former emergency patients at fifty-two hospitals nationwide. The survey showed that the following factors had the most influence on whether a patient would recommend the emergency department:

- The staff cared about the patient as a person.
- The staff kept the patient informed about delays.
- The patient felt the care was worth the amount charged.
- The nurses were knowledgeable about treatments.
- There was adequate information provided to family/friends.

To better structure waiting periods for patients, family and friends, the following recommendations were endorsed:

1. Overlap of physicians on weekends is necessary to keep waiting times reasonable. Physicians should be scheduled in such a way as to ensure that no one physician is overworked and that patients do not have to wait excessive amounts of time before seeing a physician.
2. Volunteers could be used to talk with people and to relay information. These volunteers would need to be well-trained, and perhaps could be retired nurses or students with medical interests. This function could be coordinated with the volunteer supervisor as well as with the head nurse of the unit.

3. A greater variety of magazines and newspapers could be placed in the reception area and consultation rooms—particularly reading material that may be of interest to males. Given that theft and mutilation of reading materials are facts of hospital life, increased magazine and newspaper subscriptions may require administrative funding.

4. Pamphlets on common illnesses and injuries as well as information on General Hospital and its services could be made available—this would serve both patient education and marketing functions. Pamphlets should be coordinated through the public relations department.

In a second set of internal group discussion sessions, employees reacted to the recommendations. Sessions were characterized by agreement, argument, humor, and lively debate. As a result of these focus group discussions, some recommendations were scrapped, some new recommendations evolved, and almost all recommendations were enhanced from their original form. Focus group questions centering around the recommendations included the following:

- How do you react to the goal or change desired as a result of the specific recommendation?
- Provided appropriate support, is it possible to accomplish the desired goal?
- What obstacles exist to the accomplishment of the goal?
- What specific steps should be taken to implement the change?
- What should be done to maintain the change?
- How should the change be evaluated over time?

When consensus had been achieved as to which recommendations to accept, an action plan was developed. This comprehensive plan called for some significant and fundamental changes in approaches used by all ED personnel.

The most difficult problem we faced throughout the entire intervention was a logistical one: How to ensure that *all* employees were a part of the process. Working with the nursing director of the unit, sessions were scheduled at various hours during the day *and* night. We realized that change in the ED was a process that could not be accomplished in a few days. We knew sessions had to be scheduled in such a way that agreements reached in one group could be taken to other groups and then back to the original group. We made sure the hospital administrators, the unit director, and others realized that no "quick fix" would be forthcoming *before* embarking on this intervention. The process took six months.

Report to Management

Both a written document of approximately fifty pages and an hour-long oral presentation comprised the report to management. The written report was fairly detailed and comprehensive; orally we covered the highlights and responded to questions. The oral component was important because it focused the attention of key decision-makers and allowed us to elaborate what was not clearly understood and to convince where convincing was needed. Our presentation also helped to encourage everyone to read the document in order to be prepared for the session. We have learned that recommendations often don't get implemented, even with staff buy-in, unless key decision-makers are sold and willing to authorize, encourage, direct, etc.

Follow-up

By virtually any measure, the results of this approach were successful. While there were some positive outside influences that no doubt impacted outcomes (i.e., the publicity associated with the opening of the new ED facility), most of the following results would not have been possible without the buy-in and work of the ED staff itself. By 1993:

- *The ED census improved*—The negative trend reversed itself with a census that is now higher than ever before.
- *Staff attrition declined*—Within nine months of this communication intervention, several of the experienced ED nurses had returned along with an especially popular ED physician who had left because she just couldn't take the "bickering and turmoil any longer."
- *The General Hospital ED market share improved*—Almost $2 million in *new* revenues to the hospital were generated in the first year following the intervention as a result of increased hospital admissions from ED visits.
- *Patient satisfaction with the ED is up significantly*—In the most recently conducted independent survey, satisfaction with General's ED was the *highest* in the city, completely reversing earlier findings in which General received the lowest ratings. Far fewer patient complaints are now received and positive patient comments are commonplace.

In fact, the very success General Hospital is experiencing may be leading to new problems: The stress of increased patient loads may be leading to new demands on the staff in terms of interpersonal relationships and their ability to provide customer-focused communication. The authors have been asked to return to the ED to assess the situation and to make recommendations for improvement. Much of the same process, multi-phase and multi-method, will probably be repeated.

WHY ORGANIZATIONS USE (OR MISUSE) COMMUNICATION CONSULTANTS

Organizations employ consultants for a variety of reasons, some more laudable than others. The chief reasons, however, include support for the corporate education system (i.e., the training function); expert (and presumably objective and impartial) advice to reduce the risks and uncertainties of organizational decision-making (whether structural, personnel, product, or service oriented); and to provide guidance, rationale, or reinforcement for decisions almost or already made. While the relationships between communication and organizational effectiveness may be uncertain, equivocal, or tenuous (from a communication theorist's perspective), there is nonetheless a widespread belief in the organizational world that better or improved communication may lead to better or improved organizational effectiveness. Please note that there are multiple definitions of "better" communication as well as organizational effectiveness. Yet the organizational expectation almost always exists (as a matter of faith) that one leads to the other—hence the demand for the communication consultant.

Training programs and seminars constitute the bulk of what many organizational communication consultants are hired to do on either a one-time only or a continuous basis. The October 1992 issue of *Training* magazine featured a special section on "What Employers Teach" (Filipczak, 1992). The survey of nearly 1600 U.S. organizations with one hundred plus employees breaks out data in terms of what kinds of workers receive training (by job category), general types of training, what percent of training is delivered by external suppliers and what percent by in-house staff only for both job category and training type, and what instructional methods are used.

According to the survey, some $45 billion was spent in 1992 on some 41 million workers. The types of training most often provided were management skills/development (86% of all organizations surveyed), basic computer skills (86%), communication skills (84%), supervisory skills (83%), customer relations/services (73%), and sales skills (55%), to identify a few. It should not be difficult to envision a place for the organizational communication consultant in this range of training activity. More organizations than ever before are providing customer service training. Most of the organizations surveyed used some combination of in-house and external suppliers for the training function. Most often used methods of training included videotapes (92% of all surveyed organizations), lectures (90%), one-on-one instruction (79%), role-plays (62%), games/simulations (54%), and audiotapes (51%). Again, we see a place for the particular skills and expertise of the communication consultant.

Whereas training emphasizes the consultant's teacher/educator role, provision of expert advice aimed at uncertainty and risk reduction of organizational decision-making emphasizes the data gathering and interpretation role—in short, the researcher role. In the organizational environment we are talking about applied research, that which gathers information and offers a tentative prediction; a prediction which says that, for example, if we market Product X it should sell, or if we mount Image Campaign Y more people will choose this hospital, or if we make this personnel change, job satisfaction will increase. Here the consultant's role is akin to that of a physician who diagnoses and prescribes antibiotics to eliminate a bacterial infection or to an exercise program to reduce stress and lower blood pressure or to a particular diet to improve one's health.

Basically, the organizational communication consultant is called upon to predict that some messages or constellations of messages, delivered in some particular way, through some channel or combination of channels, might have a desired effect on some particular target group, or that some patterns of interacting or some set of communication behaviors are associated with desired outcomes. Moreover, and more tentatively, these desired effects or outcomes are likely to be linked to some indices of organizational effectiveness. We feel constrained to point out that the art of communication is not as advanced as the art of medicine. We are in less a position to diagnose, prescribe, and predict outcomes than medical doctors. Nonetheless, organizations do rely upon our practice.

The reliance is a mutual one, of course, and at times organizations rely upon consultants for questionable reasons. There are three possible situations that we have witnessed or encountered that pose problematic concerns.

The first, and perhaps least problematic, occurs when the client is already, for whatever reasons, committed to a particular decision (sometimes even beyond the point of no return) and seeks confirmation for this decision from the consultant. This situation is loaded with potential biasing effects. It is somewhat easier to agree with the client and offer rationalization or confirmation for the decision than to do the opposite. This is not to suggest that the client is wrong, only that the consultation or intervention commences without the open-minded investigativeness that ideally characterizes decision-making. Of course the consultant can, and should, make a contrary recommendation if appropriate, but he or she needs to be cognizant that it takes both strength of character, evidence, and/or argument not to be a "yes-person."

The second situation is a little more problematic. This involves the use of a consultant to assist in an organizational client's internal political maneuvers. Such maneuvers may include convincing relevant constituencies or third parties that problem situations are being addressed or resolved, or that personnel or programs should to be eliminated. The consultant may initially be an unwitting collaborator—it is unlikely the client will say, "Please help me with my Machiavellian strategies to gain political influence within my organization." The external consultant especially may fall prey to this problem, lacking comprehensive knowledge of the organization's political system. Again, it takes strength of character and a strong moral sense to resist, if one is aware.

The third, and most problematic, especially from the consultant's perspective, is the situation in which the consultant's recommendation creates scapegoating opportunities and self-absolution for the client. This situation really represents a possible extension of the previous two. It is likely when the consultant has limited access to relevant information and is excessively influenced by the individual client's position.

There is no foolproof detection system for these kinds of situations. Fortunately, the inter-organizational network is active enough that clients who put consultants in these situations often become known. And consultants who acquiesce, unwittingly or not, develop a reputation for so doing. So there is within the macroenvironment an informational system of checks. The wise and successful consultant is aware of these possibilities, does not accept uncritically the client's definition of the situation, and learns to build in to the agreement negotiated with the client the kinds of safeguards that minimize misuse of consultants.

WHAT ARE THE VARIOUS TYPES OF CONSULTING RELATIONS AND WITH WHAT ADVANTAGES AND DISADVANTAGES FOR CLIENTS AND CONSULTANTS?

The most important distinguishing features of consulting relationships, with advantages and disadvantages for both parties, include duration, depth of organizational penetration, internal or external relationship to the organization, and individual versus collective consultation. To begin with, duration of the consulting relationship is an obvious way of distinguishing relationships. Some consultations are brief, single-project consultations that can be executed in a matter of hours or a few days. If brief, contact with the organization is likely to be surface (even superficial) that requires little knowledge of the organization (function, structure, people) and involves a generic program or product. It will probably be training as opposed to an applied research/advice giving contact and will probably involve little risk. The client investment is usually low; consultant involvement also low. The consultant thus functions primarily as the seller of a previously developed product or service and not an active problem solver. If the consultant is successful at selling, this category of relationship may be of greater consultant than client benefit. The consultant can move from organization to organization, collecting fees and never living with the consequences of the consultation. The client may benefit as well if what was sold was of tangible and of enduring value to the organization. However, if a training program in guest relations in which front line people are taught how to smile and employees receive no reinforcement from the organization they will probably stop smiling and experience negative morale.

Likewise, if nurses are given assertiveness training that results in conflict with unsuspecting physicians, then the effort may have been counterproductive. Some consultants prefer this kind of relationship, developing a line of products (such as assertiveness training, effective listening, guest relations) and maintain high autonomy with their client organizations.

By contrast, a relation of longer duration will probably involve a greater likelihood of some problem-solving activity, some advice giving, in-depth penetration requiring detailed information about many people at many hierarchial levels, and a more tailored approach. At an extreme, this kind of relationship can be akin to a marriage with many of the joys and perils of connubial bliss. There is an advantage to both parties in that long duration (perhaps years) results in mutual understanding that may enhance collaborative problem identification and solution efforts with the recognition that organizational problems tend to be connected. Higher long-term commitment may produce greater specialized expertise and higher security for the consultant because of greater dependence on the organization. On the downside, the long-term relationship can deprive the organization of a fresh perspective, and the consultant may begin losing "objective" distance and disinterested impartiality. At worst, the consultant can inadvertently "become part of the problem."

A second significant relational issue is the external/internal perspective. Most organizations use both. The external consultant (an individual or agency hired from outside the organization) may be able to provide expertise otherwise unavailable to the organization, with either new and creative approaches to "old" problems or with expertise the organization is unlikely to have readily available within its membership. Further, the external consultant, as a "prophet from another land" may be seen as a highly credible source of information.

At the same time there may be very real pitfalls in hiring external consultants. Unlike internal programs, designed with the organization's needs, norms, and corporate culture in mind, external programs are often generic with only minor modifications made by the outside consultant hired by the organization. The external consultant may unwittingly offer advice that may be incompatible with the prevailing management philosophy and may directly violate organizational norms and procedures. Often the internal consultant is a far better source of organizational information and has a far better notion of what, realistically, is possible.

Further, to the extent that the contract of the external consultant is of short duration, the external consultant does not have to live with the consequences of the intervention. If an intervention adversely impacts an organization, the worst thing that can happen (to the consultant) is that the consultant will not be rehired by that organization. While that may be a substantial loss to the consultant, it probably is not the loss of a livelihood for him or her.

The Questions To Be Considered in Using External Consultants section that follows should be of interest to organizational consultants, though these questions are aimed at organizations which, after all, make the decision as to who will be retained, internal or external.

QUESTIONS TO BE CONSIDERED IN USING EXTERNAL CONSULTANTS

Questions to be asked before seeking an outside consultant:

1. What are specific intervention objectives? What behavioral changes are anticipated as a result of the projected intervention?
2. How can these objectives be specified? How will success be measured?
3. What can an outside consultant provide above and beyond what can be provided by internal consultants (i.e., high credibility, expertise)?
4. Are advantages of outside intervention great enough to warrant potential longer-term problems?

Questions to be asked in selecting and using an outside consultant:

1. What experience does this person have that is industry-specific? If he or she does not have experience in your industry, is he or she willing to spend the time needed to understand the unique needs of the participants that he or she will be training or advising?
2. Has the consultant been carefully briefed as to existing conditions (Does he or she know of "budget battles," of on-going "turf struggles," and of other sensitive issues)?
3. Has the consultant developed an approach that will satisfy original objectives? Has a conscious effort been made to determine if approaches are compatible with existing managerial philosophy and practice in the organization?

Questions to be asked in selecting program participants, if the intervention involves the training function:

1. Is the proposed training of specific and current value to the participant? Can it be clearly shown that proposed training will enhance job performance of the participant?
2. Has a conscious effort been made to show the relevance of training to selected participants before the actual training session?
3. Has a commitment to attend been made by managers of program participants?

Questions to be asked after the program:

1. Have program participants been carefully debriefed? Do they have a clear understanding of changes that are expected of them as a result of this training and intervention?
2. Do participants know people to contact should they have a follow-up question about the training or intervention?
3. Are incentives in place that will reward program participants who put desired behavioral changes into practice?
4. Has a follow-up session been scheduled to reinforce ideas presented in the program/intervention?

The third relational issue is that of collective versus individual consultation, that is, does the consultant work alone, as part of a partnership, or with a small or large firm? While a consulting firm usually has greater depth and resources than the individual consultant and offers a greater appearance of institutional status and credibility (high-rise office suites, sophisticated equipment, etc.), it also has greater overhead costs and the less obvious problem of coordinating relationships between consulting agency and client. This potential problem is one that two or more consultants, working together on a project, must make a conscious and systematic effort to work to eliminate. Twenty years of joint experience has resulted in our being quite well-coordinated, but occasionally it happens that one of us will neglect to tell the other of something a client said or requested or agreed to. Clients, we have found, seem to assume that if one of us is told, then both of us know.

As earlier indicated, our own preference as consultants has been to work with an organization as external consultants who maintain durable ties over a long period of time, achieving high organizational penetration, seeing the organization as a system with an interdependent set of subsystems and operating within a larger environmental system, and tailoring our interventions, programs, etc. to what we believe are the demand characteristics of the organization. This is not to suggest that short-duration, surface-penetration, generic product kinds of consultants are undesirable or to be avoided. We have done them and probably will continue to do so. We simply find the former more professionally satisfying.

To the extent that the client relationship is consistent with our preferences, we have found it particularly essential to uncover and understand client assumptions about both organizations and communication within organizations. Our own understanding of organizational communication theory is almost inevitably more complex, abstract, and academically sophisticated than theirs. That could be disadvantageous (and perhaps has been) as we may have been insensitive to naive client images and assumptions about communication and organization. That should, however, be advantageous in helping to understand the kind of "theories" clients may have about organizations and the nature of organizational communication.

As professional students of communication theory we, far more than our clients, recognize the extent to which we are dependent upon images or perspectives in visualizing, analyzing, diagnosing, and making recommendations. A perspective refers to a "place to stand" when viewing a phenomenon, or a set of assumptions that influence the way in which we "see" that phenomenon. Alternative perspectives allow us to view the phenomenon from different angles, each emphasizing and focusing on aspects of the phenomenon that others de-emphasize. We, as communication scholars, are well aware of alternative and multiple perspectives; we are aware that we can apprehend neither the processes of communicating or organizing without benefit of some perspective. We, as consultants, are also aware that our clients generally do not recognize "perspectivisim" and are usually unaware of the underlying perspective from which they are operating. Many clients see the organization in a mechanistic way, others in an organic way, others in general systems terms, still others in a political way. For a thorough and intriguing discussion of alternative perspectives or metaphors, see Morgan's (1986) *Images of Organization* in which a chapter is devoted to each of eight "images" and the implications of each image for organizational practice are elaborated.

Not only are there alternative perspectives on organization, there are on communication itself as well. Fisher's (1978) *Perspectives on Human Communication* identifies and elaborates four such perspectives. The mechanistic perspective sees the communication process as resembling the operations of a machine; a sender encodes a message, the message is transmitted or conveyed via one or more channels, and reaches a receiver who presumably responds with feedback. According to the mechanistic perspective, when communication fails it is usually because of barriers or breakdowns in the channel that prevent the message from getting through, or from some sort of interfering "noise." From a psychological perspective, by contrast, the greater the similarity of values, attitudes, past experiences, the greater the likelihood that the intended and received messages will correspond. Messages directed at changing another's internal states should result in the creation of desired behavior. An interactional perspective will focus on the symbolic creation of shared reality and role-taking as appropriate organizational behavior. A pragmatic perspective, derived from general systems theory, concentrates on interdependence of individuals, departments, divisions, and so forth, and on the organization's interfacing activities with its external environment.

A client wedded to Fisher's mechanistic perspective will probably see communication problems as originating within the "channel." One subscribing to the psychological perspective will probably identify communication problems as deriving from the internal, psychological "conceptual filter" and look to employee attitudes and morale as areas for improvement. An interactional client might look to problems of role conflict or organizational consensus and identification. A pragmatist may look to dysfunctional patterns or sequences of behavior by way of diagnosis and prescription.

The point is that not all of us see either communication or organization the same way. We are not always even aware of our different perspectives. When a client identifies a "communication problem" or a consultant diagnoses one, they should be aware of the perspective(s) from which they are operating. The burden of responsibility rests upon the consultant—to understand the client's perspective and adapt to it or "educate" the client that another perspective may be more useful.

Our experience has been that many of our clients tend to be mechanistic in their orientation both to organization and to communication. They emphasize hierarchy, superior–subordinate status, chain of command, and structure. They see communication as an overlaid function traveling downward and upward and are often more interested in downward directed messages. The task of educating clients to both the possibility and the utility of viable alternatives can be challenging and formidable. Sometimes it is not possible. It is gratifying to be working with a client such as General Hospital (refer to case study at the beginning of the chapter) where the chief executive officer subscribes to the principles articulated in Senge's (1990) *The Fifth Discipline: The Art and Practice of the Learning Organization*—a clear, contemporary alternative to the traditional mechanistic perspective as discussed in Chapter 1.

WHAT ARE THE KINDS OF COMMUNICATING CONSULTING ACTIVITIES FOR WHICH COMMUNICATION CONSULTANTS ARE LIKELY TO BE HIRED?

There are six areas of consulting opportunity that we will highlight as common for us and others we know. They are not the only available opportunities but they are ones we believe are viable. They include seminars and training programs in communication skills, interventions in group processes, consumer research, community and public relations, diagnosis of communication processes and problems, and facilitating mergers. This clearly is neither an exhaustive nor a mutually exclusive listing of possibilities. Some consulting relationships are likely to involve several of the above activities.

Communication Skills Training

1. Public speaking training—The ancient art of rhetoric continues to be in demand. Physicians associated with hospitals, corporation executives, community action groups, politicians, and sales personnel are among those who regularly employ consultants for public speaking training, especially if they do not have local university continuing education, Toast Masters, or Dale Carnegie as suppliers. Training in the use of visual materials (slides, graphs, overheads) is especially in demand. Videotaped presentations accompanied by consultant critiques are common enough to justify purchase of video equipment by the consultant wishing to be involved in the teaching of public speaking.

2. Interviewing skills training—Whether for employment, appraisal, orientation, reprimand/correction, or termination, many organizations have consultants to assist in development of one-on-one skills for their supervisory employees.

3. Conflict management skills—There appears to be a very high demand for learning skills of managing intra- and interdepartmental conflict within organizations. Understanding win/win outcome possibilities and a working knowledge gained from such works as Fisher and Urey's *Getting to Yes* (1981) and Fisher and Brown's *Getting Together* (1988) help organizational members to negotiate differences and work for mutual gain.

4. Customer service skills—Interacting with customers is a communication process. Eliminating unintended messages, establishing a good customer–supplier relationship, are among those skills many organizations have come to value highly in recent years. Communication specialists should be well-equipped to help individuals improve customer communication.

5. Group deliberation and decision-making—Working together is a demand in almost every organization. Frustration with wasted time and low output is high on the list of organizational complaints.

6. Other possible skill areas include listening, assertiveness, coping with difficult people, and developing sensitivity to racial, cultural, and gender issues within the organization.

Interventions

Three types of interventions in group processes that we have conducted are dispute mediation or arbitration (fact finding, assisting disputants in resolving conflict issues, recommendations), team building (assisting groups to coordinate efforts and function as teams), and facilitation of group brainstorming or problem-solving activities. These interventions can be lengthy and time-consuming, sometimes resulting only in temporary states of harmony, teamwork, and creative group productivity. Clients should be given reasonable and realistic estimates of probable outcomes and the need for maintenance of desired collaborative behaviors.

Consumer Research on Products and Services

This area has been one of our mainstays and, in fact, was our initiation into the consulting world when we began moderating focus groups for local market research firms. Before long it became apparent to our clients that we also possessed research design and data gathering/interpreting skills. In addition to focus group work, we have designed phone and mail surveys, simulated stores, consumer clinics, and taste tests. All of these endeavors have been aimed at testing consumer responses to products or services (current or projected) and offering recommendations designed to reduce producer decision-making risk. Our contention has long been that communication specialists can naturally adapt to the consumer research process with the special skills they possess of information acquisition, data gathering, and in general understanding how messages function to elicit responses.

Community/Public Relations

Organizations project images, both to their publics and to their employees. Ideally, these images are not discrepant—the first should be an approximate reflection of the second. Communication consultants are often called upon to assess the internal or the external or both of these images, providing the client with data or information that might be useful in developing an image campaign or effective in adapting the organization's periodic publications to its membership and its external publics. Additionally, communication consultants might help in planning events, openings, press conferences and in responding to crisis situations within the community. The communication consultant has much to offer by way of augmenting the role of the traditional public relations professional.

Diagnosis of Communication Problems and Processes

The most familiar and used set of diagnostic instruments to communication consultants is the International Communication Association (ICA) Audit. This is a package of five instruments, developed by the ICA in the early 1970s that may be used singly or in combination. The instruments include a 122-item questionnaire that elicits respondent perception of the current status of the organizational communication system, as well as desired or ideal status. Interviews (structured and unstructured) provide follow-up to survey items. Network analysis examines communication linkages (who talks with whom) and identifies communication roles of isolate, liaison, or group member. Critical incident study asks organizational members to recall and reconstruct typically effective or ineffective communication incidents and to explore these incidents evaluatively. Communication diaries ask respondents to record specified communication activities for a period of time to discover what kinds (with what frequencies) of communication exchanges are occurring. Goldhaber's *Organizational Communication* (6th ed., 1993, Chapter 10) is an excellent source of ICA audit information.

Auditing procedures can be very useful in highlighting possibly problematic areas of communication, in providing reasonably accurate descriptive information about communication systems, in suggesting solutions and identifying relationships between communication processes and perceptions, and with such factors as decision-making, resistance to innovation, stress, technological advances, leadership or managerial style, etc. It is also probable (DeWine, James, & Walence, 1985) that the managers who read the results of an audit will incorporate findings into their own perceptions of organizational reality and interpret and select those recommendations they believe are appropriate. In short, the consultant has more control over the report of audit procedures than over the way in which the client may choose to interpret and act upon the data.

Of course, this hardly differs from the doctor–patient relationship in which, following a physical examination, the patient chooses how and when (if at all) compliance with the doctor's recommendations will occur. Moderately troubling to us is the absence of a significant data base of auditing results that might serve to provide normative standards. We know that a human temperature of 103 degrees means a serious fever. We do not know how to interpret as clearly communication audit data—it is not clear when a problem is serious enough to be organizationally life-threatening.

Facilitating Mergers

On several occasions we have had the opportunity to assist in facilitating mergers—increasingly commonplace events in today's economic climate. Our specific role has been to determine and recommend what messages are needed. When are they needed? How often are they needed? The sheer possibility of merger creates a rapidly spreading series of rumors on the informal network, and an immense amount of uncertainty is created. The challenge of the communication consultant is in helping to manage constructively that uncertainty by finding out what employees need to know and providing that as honestly and accurately as is possible. If the merger is accomplished, then helping the newly created organization to develop new and common symbols, policies, goals, and so forth becomes another area in which the communication consultant can help facilitate organizational assimilation.

WHAT SHOULD THE ORGANIZATIONAL CONSULTANT ASPIRE TO BY WAY OF EDUCATIONAL BACKGROUND?

If organizational communication consultants are to be both teachers and problem solvers regarding communication problems involving both content (creation, transmission, reception, interpretation of messages) and relationship (functional, satisfactory, reciprocal), then they should possess an academic background (at the very least baccalaureate level) in human communication study. This background should have emphasized interpersonal, group, organizational, and public communication skills. Underlying these skills is a theoretical rationale for prescriptive advice about communication. Consultants should always be capable of understanding and explaining the reasons for training or recommendations—they should know why they do what they do, why others should practice what they preach.

Beyond a comprehensive knowledge of human communication literature (both theory and skills), the consultant's education should have included two other areas. One is a knowledge of the organizational literature as contributed to by the disciplines of industrial organizational psychology, sociology, marketing, management, human resources, organizational development, and economics. Some degree of literacy with computers, accounting, and skill at technical writing is, in the 1990s, a virtual must.

The other is a knowledge, at least basic, of research methodology. Course work in qualitative or descriptive research techniques (observation, interviews, surveys, content analysis, focus group methodology) as well as quantitative research understandings (descriptive and inferential statistics, sampling, correlational studies, and significance testing) are necessary to the problem-solving component of consultancy work. Without this background the consultant will be poorly equipped to frame intelligent investigative inquiries, unable to determine what the best methods are to gather the appropriate kinds of data, and will be limited in ability to competently analyze and interpret information gathering results. Recommendations made to a client by a consultant who is methodologically ignorant are probably suspect.

One methodology with which we have had considerable experience in a variety of settings with fairly wide application potential is focus group methodology. Several years ago one of us described the following scenario as a daily occurrence (Byers & Wilcox, 1990, p. 63):

> *Eight to twelve people, usually a homogeneous grouping, are seated around a conference table engaging in discussion facilitated by a moderator they have never met. The focus of discussion may be a new product concept or prototype, an advertisement (message or campaign) or perhaps a service. Discussion will proceed for one to two hours. Group members are probed and their responses seem to stimulate discussion as to their perceptions, attitudes, and purchase intentions. The proceedings are audio (sometimes*

video) recorded and usually observed from the other side of a one-way mir-
ror by representatives of the organization which has produced the product,
ad, or service. Later, the content of the discussion (often four to eight, or
ten groups on a single stimulus) will be analyzed and interpreted in the
form of recommendations designed ultimately to reduce the client organi-
zation's risk in decision-making.

Frequently employed in marketing research efforts to gather information from consumers, the focus group has potential for the communication consultant. It is a methodology that the communication specialist should be especially adept at, and it is comprehensible to clients. The Byers and Wilcox article suggested six inquiries that could appropriately be approached by focus group methodology (pp. 71–73):

1. How do people interpret and respond to message campaigns?
2. How (and why) do people resist organizational change?
3. How can service be improved?
4. How will people respond to new technologies?
5. How effective are current corporate training/evaluation methods?
6. What issues should serve as a basis for survey questionnaire development?

Any one of these kinds of inquiries may well be a communication consultant's mission.

While one does not generalize from sample to population using focus group research, one does learn what a concept (or product, or service, or proposed change, etc.) might *mean* to groups of individuals and what issues are more or less likely to be prominent. For example, as the chapter is being written we are winding down a project for General Hospital whose objective it is to develop an overall image campaign. We have moderated nine focus groups, including physicians who are primary users of General Hospital, physicians who are not, patients treated within the last year at General, patients treated elsewhere, supervisory personnel, nonsupervisory personnel, nurses, directors, and employees with less than three years of seniority. The purpose of these groups is to provide foundational information for an image campaign. Areas of discussion and probing included the following:

- Factors that influence admission decisions, both first time and returns
- Deterrents to admission decisions
- Identification of the "customer"
- General vis-a-vis the competition
- General's strengths, weaknesses, particular products
- General's community position
- Identification of what the public should know about General

- Specific areas for probing if they do not emerge in the above areas of discussion—admissions, billing, nursing, staff, visitor accommodations, administration, location, accessibility.

From the dominant issues or themes that emerged from analysis of the audiotapes of these groups, an advertising agency will develop a proposal for a campaign. The campaign will have the advantage of being developed from information obtained from individuals both internal to the hospital and those at varying external distances. The focus group method was a relatively efficient way of obtaining in-depth responses to questions relevant to the previously mentioned topical areas.

Additionally, successful and experienced consultants need to be familiar with what their clients regard as important information sources. Such publications as the *Wall Street Journal, Training Magazine, Fortune,* and others are important sources of information. Consultants who specialize in a particular industry will read the trade journals specific to their domain of interest. (We regularly read the *Journal of Emergency Medicine,* for example). Finally, the consultant needs to be conversant with TQM (Total Quality Management) or some derivative thereof, quality circles, customer focus, empowerment, and learning organization literature, to name a few prominent areas. Clients will recognize and appreciate the consultant's attempts to orient themselves to the organizational perspective. Consultant credibility enhancement is the likely consequence.

HOW DOES THE ORGANIZATIONAL COMMUNICATION CONSULTANT DEVELOP AND MAINTAIN RELATIONSHIPS WITH CLIENTS?

In the absence of professional accrediting associations or licensing requirements, the would-be communication consultant does not complete a highly prescribed course of study, then take a state administered board exam, become licensed, then "hang out one's shingle," waiting for potential clients to call. There are many people who claim to be communication consultants who lack the credentials or knowledge bases we just described as important components of the consultant's education. The competition for clients in some markets may be great, and clients may be at a disadvantage in selecting the best consultants. The communication consultant must assume extra initiative in demonstrating a credible image as a problem solver—knowledgeable about the client's industry and problems, and as a person with a track record.

The first step to obtaining clients is twofold: work to identify market needs (both now and in the future) and work to develop products that meet those needs. Our interest in the health care industry stems in part from our ten-year association with a consultant who did a detailed study of the effects of deregulation on several industries and predicted in 1984 and 1985 that health care was where the action was going to be in the 1990s. He was aware that we might have some products relevant to hospital needs. Our association over the last several years (we have worked as consultants to a consultant) represents the result of that first step of defining needs and products.

As a second step we learned that products need to be explained, even proven, as capable of providing value or benefit to the client. Our ED work in several hospitals has put us in a position in which we can demonstrate a strong likelihood of improved morale, increased census, and higher patient satisfaction. Value or benefit is often not as immediately obvious to the client as it is to the enthusiastic novice consultant. Potential or probable bottom line impact needs to be demonstrated to the client, if for no other reason than as a tangible rationale for spending the money.

A third step is identifying potential clients. We recommend several ways of getting started. First, contact the continuing education divisions of area colleges and universities and demonstrate that you can offer an organized and credible one-day training program on, let's say, conflict management. They may be interested in supporting you. If thirty to forty participants from as many organizations attend, you have a beginning client base.

Second, contact area consulting firms that purport to do market research, marketing communications, public or community relations, or personnel training. Offer your services on a project basis to "show what you can do." Successful participation in a project may lead to employment or at least to other clients.

Third, contact potential client organizations. Be clear as to what you do, what your name or identity is, and what you can do for them. Incorporate these into a brochure that is sent with a cover letter. Follow with a telephone call. Show up in person. Be prepared for a majority of rejections! But keep in mind that all it takes is one "yes" to get you started.

Fourth, develop your own active networking skills. Offer to help others who help you. Many consultants have gotten off the ground in just this fashion as their networks expand, and they become recipients of the referrals to which these contacts can lead.

Finally, assume that your first employment positions are with corporate organizations. Several years of experience in corporate public relations, for example, may provide for you a launching pad to agency work or to beginning to establish your own agency.

Assume a contact is made and an opportunity avails itself. You are given a chance to bid for a project. Ideally, you are given the chance to confer with the client. Attempt to develop, working collaboratively with the client, a mutually satisfactory definition of the client's problem in such a way that the response can enhance functioning of the client's organizational system. Then prepare a proposal that details the following:

1. Objectives to be realized
2. Time frames and phases
3. What will be delivered and when
4. Cost of consultancy

5. Demonstration of value or benefit to client
6. Means by which success will be measured

It will probably take a lot of groundwork and a few false starts, but the preceding is basically the way the consultant proceeds.

When the project is done, it is wise to request both a letter of reference from the satisfied client and to inquire about future projects. Maintain regular contact with that client with ever-ready reminders that you are there, ready to continue helping.

Observing professional and ethical considerations is an integral part of maintaining high quality and lasting relationships with organizational clients. These considerations should regularly guide the consultant's behavior and conduct. If observed conscientiously we believe they will enhance the consultant's image of credibility and integrity and help maintain good professional relationships.

First, the consultant should adapt to the client organization by being (and staying) familiar with both industry-specific and organizational-specific information. The consultant should be familiar with the organization's history, its function, and its hierarchical structure. Additionally, the consultant should make a reasonable effort to conform to organizational norms of dress, language, and social amenities. An external consultant especially is, after all, a visitor.

Second, problem situations should be analyzed only after researching the available data and talking with the persons closest to the problem. When a report is prepared, sources of information should be identified so the data base from which the consultant is recommending is known to the client. If some information or persons are, for some reason unavailable, that should also be indicated.

Third, the client's business is the client's business and privacy and confidentiality should be maintained unless the consultant has permission to do otherwise. Exceptions, in the rare event there are any, must be considered with the best interests of the organization in mind. Gossiping about other clients is taboo. Even if the client seems to enjoy the gossip, they will long remember where they heard it.

Fourth, recommendations need to be put in clear and concrete language. This is a time during which the communication consultant should be a superior exemplar of his or her craft. All client interactions, in fact, should exemplify the best the communication discipline has to offer.

Fifth, the consultant should advise the client if there are possible difficulties of a legal, ethical, economic, or cultural consideration. To the degree that the consultant perceives possible risk to the client of following (or not following) a particular course of action, the consultant should alert the client.

Finally, the consultant should deliver a high quality product on time, fulfilling the terms of the proposal agreement. It is critical to the consultant's professional image that he or she deliver what is promised, when it is promised. Ideally, the consultant delivers a little more than promised. There is no better way, short of sheer incompetence, to lose consulting projects than being lax in quality and delivery.

CONCLUSION

This chapter has described the kinds of activities in which a communication consultant might engage, discussed major issues in consulting relationships, and recommended ways of getting started. Our approach has been, we hope, a down-to-earth and practical one—from the consultant's perspective. Following the glossary at the end of this chapter is a set of more academically oriented readings that will provide valuable detailed and in-depth information about organizational communication consulting.

GLOSSARY

Empowerment—a process whereby individuals in an organization are encouraged to assume initiative in problem-solving and decision-making.

External consultant—a consultant who is not an employee of the company in question, but is hired to perform a specified task.

Focus group research—a qualitative research methodology employing discussion groups guided by an expert moderator.

Generic program or service—a program or service that is used in a variety of organizational settings with no or very few changes.

I.C.A.—the International Communication Association, which is one of the major professional organizations to which communication consultants and scholars belong.

International Communication Association Audit—a research instrument employing procedures to audit communication from both a perceptional and observations view.

Internal consultant—an individual who is an employee of a company who serves as a problem solver for a specified task.

Organization-specific program or service—a program or service that is custom designed to meet the needs of an organization.

Perspective—an organized set of assumptions and presuppositions that will result in our viewing a phenomenon in a particular defined way.

CASE STUDY

You are an organizational communication consultant. Recently you were contacted by Mr. Robert Harris, the vice president of marketing for JRW Rentals, a large car rental company that has outlets nationwide. In the course of his conversation with you, Mr. Harris showed you two letters: one from an irate customer (Ms. Spirek) and the response written by a JRW branch manager (Sally Archer). (These letters are on the following pages). Mr. Harris said he received the letters because Ms. Spirek contacted him directly by mail after she received the response written by the JRW branch manager.

Mr. Harris indicated to you that he is, obviously, concerned. Aside from the obvious typographical and grammatical errors in Ms. Archer's letter, Mr. Harris believes her response may be indicative of customer focus problems within the company. In response to your initial inquiries, you learned that the JRW company does not have a formal program to assess customer concerns, although "Satisfaction Survey Cards" are given to customers when they pay their bills. About 5 percent of JRW's customers return the cards. Mr. Harris told you that although he has not formally analyzed the cards returned, responses appear to be mixed: Some customers are very pleased, others report perceptions of incompetent help, slow processing, and lack of "warmth" on the part of some employees.

Specific concerns of Mr. Harris include the following: How widespread are problems such as the one Ms. Spirek reports? How concerned should he be (in other words, is poor customer service hurting the bottom line)? If there is a problem, what remedies seem most appropriate?

Discussion: As an organizational communication consultant, what additional information would you like from Mr. Harris before proceeding? How might you assess customer service practices throughout JRW Rentals? How would you determine if current customer service practices are impacting the profitability of the company? What, if anything, would you suggest be done at this point about Ms. Archer's reply to Ms. Spirek? (Consider the messages being sent by the letter itself.) Based only upon the information provided to you, what key ideas might you stress if asked to provide communication training to JRW Rentals personnel?

Letter from Ms. Spirek (Irate Customer)

29072 Belmont Lake Road
Perrysburg, Ohio 43606

Mr. Robert Harris
Executive Vice President
National Marketing
JRW Rental Company
1 Plaza Central Blvd.
Chicago, Illinois 60601

Dear Mr. Harris:

I am not happy with the service I just received from JRW and think you should know why. Yesterday afternoon, while still in Toledo, I called the Indianapolis Airport JRW office, explaining that I had just learned I had less than an hour after arriving in Indianapolis to get to an exceedingly important meeting some 45 plus minutes away from the airport. My question to your representative was, "How could JRW help me get my car as quickly as possible?" Your employee said that there was "nothing she could do," and to my ear she didn't seem sorry she could not help me.

Given the urgency of my request, I persisted in suggesting that surely something could be done. Finally, I was told to "Hang on." This I did for over three minutes. Finally, another woman answered the phone. She obviously had no understanding of why I had called. After I once again explained the nature of my problem, I was told that I'd simply have to go through normal check-in procedures.

When I then asked what I could expect in terms of a wait at the Indianapolis outlet, I was told "It depends." The representative explained (as if I didn't already know) that "Sometimes lines are long, sometimes short." I asked if the line happened to be long if anything could be done to facilitate a speedy check-in. At this point I was given a condescending lecture to the effect that "I'm sure you understand that people in front of you also think their meetings are important. Surely you wouldn't expect us to let you cut in line in front of them. Surely, you wouldn't think that would be fair, would you?"

I agreed that normally one should certainly wait one's turn and that I've spent countless hours waiting in lines in airports (that's why I was calling). I also suggested that customer-focused, pro-active companies (the only companies likely to survive and thrive in today's economy) understand that clients may have extenuating circumstances that justify "rule-bending" or at least an attempt to be flexible. Think about it: How often does a person call your company from their home city hoping to resolve a problem in advance?

Perhaps to get me off her back (at least that's the way it seemed to me), the employee did say that if the line at the terminal counter was long, I could take the bus directly to the JRW car area and check in there. She indicated that she didn't think this would speed things up (and indeed she indicated that it might even slow me down), but I was welcome to try.

After answering my remaining questions in a perfunctory manner, without showing the slightest concern for my situation, the call was terminated. The only bright spot in all of my interactions with JRW personnel was an employee named Doug at the JRW check-in counter. He noticed I was in a hurry and told me he'd get to me as soon as possible (which meant completing transactions for four or five persons in front of me). Even though the line was long and my worst fears in terms of a check-in wait were realized, at least I appreciated Doug's concern.

Thinking that the individuals I had talked with on the phone could not be representative of JRW employees in general or of the way your company does business, I returned the car (around 6 A.M. this morning) determined to take a fresh look at your company. As I drove into the return area I saw a large sign that told me to drive the car up to the gas pumps. This was impossible to do as there was a line of parked cars in front of the pumps. I parked in an empty space and walked into the office. When I began to explain that I had parked in an empty space and had not pulled up to the pumps, the employee snapped, "It's not my fault! No-one has been here to move cars this morning." Tell me, what am I to think of JRW?

As a university professor and an in-demand consultant, last year I talked with 1,000 plus individuals about the importance of customer focus and satisfying the customer. My examples, both positive and negative, were chosen from personal experience. As I address the next 1,000 plus people, is there any reason why I should not use JRW as one of my colorful, memorable, and negative examples?

Sincerely,

Marie Spirek, Ph.D.

Reply to Ms. Spirek's letter

Dear Maire Spirek,

On behalf of JRW Rents please accept my apologies for the wait you had at our Airport Location. We do understand that customers do run late and need to get quick service. We do strive on Customers Satisfaction but in this case we were not the ones to make the decision to take you next in line when there were other customer in front of you. If you needed for us to take you next then you should of asked the customers in front of you, if they wouldn't mind if you were wait on next, this would not be something JRW could do. If there are any questions please write to me at JRW Rentals, Indianapolis Air Port, Indianapolis, In 46241.

Sincerely,

Sally Archer

REFERENCES

Byers, P., & Wilcox, J. (1990). Focus groups: A qualitative opportunity for researchers. *Journal of Business Communication, 28,* 63–77.

DeWine, S., James, A., & Walence, W., (1985). *Validation of organizational communication audit instruments.* Unpublished paper presented at the International Communication Association Convention, Honolulu.

Emergency Patient Survey. (1991, Oct.). *Modern Healthcare, 7,* 48.

Filipczak, B. (1992, Oct.). What employers teach. *Training, 29,* 43–55.

Fisher, B. A. (1978). *Perspectives on Human Communication.* New York: Macmillan.

Morgan, G. (1986). *Images of Organization.* Newbury Park, Calif.: Sage.

Redding, W. C. (1979). Graduate education and the communication consultant: Playing God for a fee. *Communication Education, 28,* 346–352.

Senge, P. (1991). *The Fifth Discipline: The Art and Practice of the Learning Organization.* New York: Doubleday/Currency.

RECOMMENDED READINGS

Argyris, C. (1993). *Knowledge for Action: A Guide to Overcoming Barriers to Organizational Change*. San Francisco: Jossey-Bass.

Blake, R. R., & Mouton, J. S. (1983). *Consultation* (2nd ed.). Reading, Mass.: Addison-Wesley.

Buchholz, W. J. (ed.). (1983). *Communication Training and Consulting in Business, Industry, and Government*. Urbana-Champaign University of Illinois: American Business Communication Association.

Daniels, T. D., & Spiker, B. K. (1994). *Perspectives on Organizational Communication* (3rd ed.). Dubuque, Iowa: Brown and Benchmark Publishers.

DeWine, S. (1994). *The Consultant's Craft: Improving Organizational Communication*. New York: St. Martin's Press.

Eisenberg, E. M., & Goodall, H. L., Jr. (1993). *Organizational Communication: Balancing Creativity and Constraint*. New York: St. Martin's Press.

Fisher R., & Brown, S. (1988). *Getting Together*. Boston: Houghton Mifflin.

Fisher, R., & Urey, W. L. (1981). *Getting to Yes*. Boston: Houghton Mifflin.

Goldhaber, G. M. (1993). *Organizational Communication* (6th ed.). Dubuque, Iowa: Brown and Benchmark.

Krueger, R. A. (1988). *Focus Groups: A Practical Guide for Applied Research*. Beverly Hills, Calif.: Sage.

Morgan, D. L. (1988). *Focus Groups in Qualitative Research*. Beverly Hills, Calif.: Sage.

Pace, R. W., & Faules, D. F. (1994). *Organizational Communication* (3rd ed.). Englewood Cliffs, N.J.: Prentice Hall.

Steele, F. (1975). *Consulting for Organizational Change*. Amherst: University of Massachusetts Press.

► 13

Communication Technologies in Contemporary Organizations

DAVID R. NEUMANN

There is no doubt that communication technologies will continue to be an increasingly important influence in our lives. For some of us, these technologies are very powerful channels that impact not only our work, but also our leisure time and influence our very conceptions of ourselves. It was a few short years ago that the computer was still a novelty, voice mail was in its infancy, and the fax machine seemed like a very real threat to the overnight courier businesses. Today all of these technologies and many more are part of our everyday lives and are becoming as commonplace as telephones, radios, and televisions. The Internet has become a common business tool for both huge multinational corporations and mom and pop businesses. The World Wide Web connects individuals, groups, and organizations that have some common thread of interest and allows for nearly instantaneous connections for people all over the globe.

This chapter provides us with a broad perspective of communication technologies in contemporary organizations. Within this chapter, various theories, hypotheses, research findings, predictions, and pieces of practical advice are provided. First to be discussed is the Internet, also known as the information superhighway. This global computer network is being used increasingly as a communication device.

Telecommuting, or working at a location distant from a central office, is also becoming more common as a result of the Internet. This chapter discusses various pros and cons of telecommuting, including concerns about the security of computer networks. Next, the various communication technologies that allow for teleconferencing are discussed as well as how these technologies affect human organizational communication. Selected theories, models, postulates, and hypotheses are presented to provide a foundation for understanding and predicting the effects of technology on communication dynamics. Last, implications for management training and development provide some practical advise and action steps for best managing the effects of communication technologies on organizational communication.

As our reliance on communication technologies increases, and as new technologies are developed, we must put forth significant effort into understanding the influences of these technologies on our lives as members of organizations. Examining the consequences of developing communication technologies in organizations is a difficult task. Finding an objective observation point is challenging; distancing ourselves from communication technologies is becoming more and more difficult as these technologies continue to become more ingrained in our daily activities. It is difficult to imagine going through a day without using technologies such as the telephone or television. In a few years we will probably have the same feeling about computers. Many people already have shed their computer phobia and do use the computer as a daily communication medium.

As a student of communication you probably have a prediction of how technology impacts and alters the human communication process within organizations. You may say that these technologies will dehumanize the workplace and act like a Big Brother; that technology left unchecked may run rampant and eventually take over the higher order functions of executive decision-making. Or perhaps you take a more pragmatic, cost-benefit perspective that views the many assets of emerging technology. Technology will increase productivity, reduce waste, create higher quality products, make jobs easier, free up workers, and add to leisure time. Your prediction probably falls between these diametrically opposed points of the continuum. Communication technologies, while creating distance between people, help to speed up tasks.

As communication technologies change and develop, so do the dynamics of organizational communication. There is no doubt that the invention of the computer has had a dramatic effect on most every aspect of today's organizations. Beyond being a tool to provide calculations and manage inventory, today's computers are being used more and more as a substitute for face-to-face and other traditional forms of communication. Through experience with interpersonal and telephone communication, we have come to understand the norms, rules, and other communication cultural nuances that help us to create shared meanings and to engage in effective interactions. As new communication technologies are developed and used, we must learn to understand new and evolving communication dynamics. One question surrounding the increasing use of communication technologies asks if we can keep up with the dynamics of evolving communication channels. Gerald M. Goldhaber, author of several organizational communication textbooks and may other publications, suggests that technologies that once took ten years to develop now take only one year (1993). As the development of these technologies increases, our understanding of the dynamics of human communication through electronic channels becomes of paramount importance.

One of these technological developments involves a complex system of computer networks known as the Internet, also referred to as the information superhighway. The importance of this developing communication channel cannot be understated. The Internet, also referred to as the "'national information infrastructure' and the 'mother of all networks'" (Santoro, 1994, p. 73), is receiving increased attention from the classroom, to the newsroom, to the board room, and to the White House. "Having an Internet address is rapidly becoming a requirement for doing business, especially in high-tech circles" (Wiseman, 1994a, p. B1). Since this 1994 statement it can be asserted that having an Internet address is a requirement for most every business person, teacher, student, and legislator, well beyond the parameters of high-tech circles.

INTERNET—THE INFORMATION SUPERHIGHWAY

Presently, if you have access to a personal computer, some inexpensive software, a modem, and enough money for a monthly charge less than most peoples' telephone or cable television bills, you can hook up to the Internet and take a ride on the information superhighway. For students and faculty at most colleges and universities these fees are absorbed in tuition and other charges. This computer network has quickly found its way into many businesses, universities, hospitals, news media, and other information-hungry organizations. It has also caught the eye of social critics and commentators who speculate on the ramifications of the availability of massive amounts of information to the computer privileged and computer literate.

The Internet has been in existence for over two decades and is "a web of 30,000 computer networks that dates back to when Neil Armstrong walked on the moon" (Wiseman, 1994a, p. B1). But only recently, with the proliferation of personal computers in the office, at home, in schools, and on the lap top, has this network begun to realize its potential. "During the 1980s and 1990s the Internet has expanded exponentially as other computer networks [using compatible computer languages] were connected to it" (Santoro, 1994, p. 73). As we look upon the new millennium, this proliferation is expected to continue.

One leading advance of the Internet is the introduction of the World Wide Web. While the Internet allows for transfer of text and numerical data, the World Wide Web, also simply referred to as "the Web" allows for sharing images and sound in addition to text and numbers. With the proper software, moving images, video clips, and animation can be shared over the Web. It is in part the visually-based menus and screens that make communicating over the Web more accessible to new computer users. Remembering specific text commands that resemble hieroglyphics is quickly becoming extinct and a more universal system of images and icons is evolving. This transformation is helping to propel the Internet in a new direction. Nothing demonstrates the popularity of the World Wide Web more than the amazing success of Netscape. Netscape is software that allows a computer to link to the Web. While there are other programs that do the same job, Netscape has secured 70 percent of the market. During a few week span in August 1995, Netscape Communication Corporation's stock skyrocketed from $14 to $71 a share. Advertiser and marketers are flocking to the Web which "is regarded as the next stage in the information revolution" (Quittner, 1995, p. 26).

As more and more people connect via computer, new social and professional networks develop. Small clusters of people who are geographically dispersed currently interact via computer. From a sociological perspective, it is odd to view a group, clique, or small community of people as being physically and geographically isolated from each other. But the Internet fosters this type of community growth. In essence, new communities will be developed void of traditional community factors such as neighborhoods, public transportation, and other physical manifestations that have such a strong influence on our communication. This electronic community will develop its own rules and codes of conduct dictating levels of communication appropriateness and effectiveness. The Internet is used now by a minority of the population who are pioneers in this new territory. As with all pioneers, the vast unknown is the context of their activities. We can speculate and attempt to predict what might be ahead, but uncertainty and ambiguity will provide a great deal of problems. "Right now, the super highway is used by 'we happy few.' There are very few real experts and most of us who engage ourselves with the Internet, either through academic backbones or commercial services are novices. We sometimes drive recklessly, sometimes we stay, and most of the time we are bewildered by the number and variety of ideas and information now at our fingertips" (Phillips, 1994, p. 71). But Phillips' "we happy few" are quickly being transformed into a more significant portion of the population.

It is not only the uncertainty of this new communication channel that is a challenge, but it is also the sheer volume of information choices that can be perplexing (Phillips, 1994). A quick browse of the Web will find over two hundred locations for communicating about the Grateful Dead, over one hundred locations for college rowing teams, and over fifty locations for information about the sport Ultimate Frisbee. Businesses are recognizing the tremendous marketing and commercial potential of this virtual community, not to mention its use as an in-house and intra-organizational communication conduit. As Internet success stories circulate, and as more innovative ideas are tested, Internet user numbers will rise. In January 1993 under 350,000 commercial uses were on the information superhighway. "As of January [1994], nearly 568,000 computers registered to commercial users were connected to the Internet, up 63% from a year earlier... And that figure undoubtedly undercounts businesses on the Internet because not all of them are registered as commercial users" (Wiseman, 1994a, p. B2). Using this conservative number, by the year 2000 over 10 million commercial users may be connected to the Internet. The range of services offered will only be limited by the imagination of business people and entrepreneurs.

Establishing a business using the Internet requires a fraction of the capital that it would take to start a traditional business. For this reason specialty services and ideas dictated by timeliness will proliferate. An interesting example of a specialty service dictated by timeliness is the Woodstock 1994 concert electronic bulletin board. This Internet address allowed concert ticket holders to plan their trip to the festival on-line. Ride sharing, lodging, and a host of other information services were created to help disseminate information to the over 200,000 concert goers (American Broadcasting Company, 1994).

Companies use the Internet to meet a variety of in-house communication needs. The following breakdown shows that more than half the use is for communication with colleagues and customers: 35 percent colleagues, 26 percent customers, 10 percent education, 9 percent forums and news groups, 5 percent government agencies, 15 percent other (Lottor, 1994). The information superhighway allows for easy information exchange and frees employees from the physical constraints of an office building. This will possibly lead to a rise in the number of employees who telecommute.

Telecommuting

Communication technologies, while merely a conduit for exchanging information, will force us to challenge our conceptualizations of our daily behaviors and habits. No longer will we have to leave our homes to go to work, rather we will simply telecommute. "Businesses are jumping aboard the global web of computer networks called the Internet. It gives businesses access to affluent consumers and brings together employees in far-flung offices" (Wiseman, 1994a, p. B1). Most agree that communication technologies will continue to increase the number of employees who telecommute. Instead of driving to work, employees work from home or while traveling by employing various communication technologies. Some employees may have traditional office space within an organization and telecommute part-time. Others, however, may work solely out of their homes, cars, recreational vehicles, motor homes, hotels, or small satellite offices. Telecommuting offers employment and business opportunities to many people and organizations that would otherwise be denied these opportunities. It is becoming more common for new parents to stay home with young children while maintaining their careers. Individuals who are home-bound for medical and other reasons also benefit from the technologies that allow for telecommuting. Telecommuting is also beneficial in cases of family emergencies, when there are various geographical and even meteorological constraints, and for employees who need to work flexible hours. Also, organizations that want to explore new geographical areas without committing the overhead necessary for setting up a new office can benefit by hiring on telecommuters.

The most common and simple form of telecommuting is the use of a personal computer and modem to connect the employee with the organization's mainframe computer. Most often this is accomplished via the Internet. Through this link, the telecommuter can communicate with other members of the organization. More sophisticated forms of telecommuting include conference calls, fax machines, video-conferencing, and fiber optic connections. Seen as a blessing by many, telecommuting allows employees many freedoms that would be lost if one was required to work in an office or some other particular location.

As the industrial revolution not only gave rise to mass production, mass consumption, and higher quality products affordable to the masses, it also created the economy and commodity of leisure time. Leisure time away from the workplace has grown to be an expected reward of work and is a commodity for which we bargain. Leaving a place of work at the end of the day, riding in a car, bus, or train, and arriving home provides one with temporal and physical distance from a place of work. Leisure time begins. Telecommuting has, in effect, muddled the distinction between work and leisure time. "The new office technology [of telecommuting] is having a decidedly double-edged impact.... Untethered, or mobile employees may have more freedom from supervision, but they work longer hours under more severe deadline pressure than do their tethered counterparts at the office" (Nebel, 1994, p. D4). A survey by the Daniel Yankelovich Group found that work weeks of fifty to seventy hours were not unusual for telecommuting employees (Nebel, 1994). The Yankelovich survey also suggests that telecommuters may be a self-selected group insofar as "these people tend to describe themselves as having 'higher-than-average energy levels, and the stamina to work even longer hours'" (Nebel, 1994, p. D4). Telecommuting also requires employees to work in somewhat of a social vacuum away from the central culture of the organization. Working in an office environment with other employees affords them an immediate connection to the communication practices and nuances that create symbolic and personal connections to the organization. Important connections between employees and an organization can occur in the break room, around the water cooler, at happy hour, or in a car pool commute to work. Beyond opportunities for informal interaction, the telecommuter misses more subtle communication cues that are only available by being in the continuous live presence of others. For example, the nonverbal reaction employees may have to a supervisor, seeing the company newsletter on the bathroom floor, and the pecking order displayed in the cafeteria are all subtle yet important aspects of an organization's culture. There is full bandwidth in face-to-face communication; in other words, all verbal and nonverbal communication channels are open. This increased bandwidth allows for personal relationships to develop and sophisticated interpersonal communication rules, roles, and norms to be created. The telecommuter has access to a limited bandwidth and misses the benefits of these central components of an organization's culture. Therefore, while the employee needs to work with other employees, the foundation of a shared frame of reference may be lacking.

Using the information superhighway as a telecommuting channel has many distinct economical advantages, but there are also causes for concern. There needs to be very thoughtful examination of the effects and consequences of using the Internet as a significant communication channel. Several causes for concern center around the security of communication on the superhighway.

Computer Network Security

Confidentiality and security of communication are of primary importance to many organizations. With competitors attempting to outperform one another, product and service advances can result in millions of dollars added to or subtracted from the bottom line. Dana Corporation, a multinational manufacturing operation, is planning to use the Internet as its channel for e-mail. A main concern for Dana Corporation is privacy; more specifically they question whether other organizations will be able to acquire their sensitive information (Govang, 1994).

There also needs to be a significant level of trust between organizations and their customers. "A lot of companies are wary about exposing their communications with clients and their own computer systems to the Internet" (Wiseman, 1994b, p. B2). The consequence of a breech of confidentiality between an organization and its client can be devastating. "Security from air tight eavesdroppers and thieves isn't airtight, though it's improving. . . . now sophisticated encryption technology can be used to protect e-mail and verify the identity of people on the other end of an electronic conversation" (Wiseman, 1994b, p. B2). Besides the importance of secure corporate secrets, employees need to know that their personal and informal communications are secure as well. Employees often engage in conversation concerning personal and sometimes sensitive, nonprofessional issues. Paranoia, as to the confidentiality of personal information, will undoubtedly result in lower morale, stifled creativity, and most likely decrease productivity. Nonetheless, it is reported that 40 percent of employers admit to eavesdropping on employees e-mail and 20 percent eavesdrop on employees' voice mail (Turner Broadcasting Service, 1994).

The information superhighway will continue to give us many topics to discuss and debate. With the many compelling opinions and predictions we may hold, one thing seems certain—the Internet is here to stay. As a communication tool alone it has already had a major impact on international, national, regional, and local organizations. While the Internet has developed prominence only since the late 1980s (Santoro, 1994), another method of electronically linking employees together has een in use for years—teleconferencing.

TELECONFERENCING

Teleconferencing is a generic term for any combination of electronically mediated audio, video, or computer interaction that connects two or more people at two or more locations. Teleconferencing can be either "synchronic" live interaction or "asynchronic" interaction in which each party involved can receive and send messages at their convenience; there is no real-time interaction. Messages are sent, received, and replied to in the same chronological fashion as writing and mailing letters. Complete interaction that may take several minutes face-to-face, may take several hours, days, or weeks when asynchronically communicating.

The most convenient way to discuss teleconferencing is to break it down into three main modes: two-way video-conferencing, two-way audio-conferencing, and two-way asynchronic computer conferencing, also called e-mail. "Electronic mail (e-mail) is a computer function that allows one computer user to send an online 'memo' to another computer user. It was originally developed for use by people with accounts on the same computer, however it soon spread to computer networks" (Santoro, 1994, p. 78). There are also forms of synchronic computer conferencing; "Interactive messaging is a synchronous form of computer mediated communication the sometimes is called 'chat'. With interactive messaging all parties to the communication must be online at the same time" (Santoro, 1994, p. 80).

Various combinations of audio, video, and computer channels have been used as well. For instance, one party can send video and audio messages while the other party can only reply with audio messages. This is referred to as one-way video, two-way audio-conferencing. Along with these channels come various impacts on the users' perceptions of the communication.

Teleconferencing technologies are being used by many organizations. Businesses find financial saving by reducing travel expenses via the use of teleconferencing. If an organization has managers located at one hundred branches across the country and needs to simultaneously expose them all to a new product, it could cost hundreds of thousands of dollars to fly them all to one location, house them, and feed them. This equation does not include lost work hours for travel time or consider special needs of employees who may be averse to flying or who have some other conditions that limit their travel abilities. Educational organizations tap into new populations of students who are unable to attend traditional classes. Health care and medical facilities use teleconferencing to share procedures and practices with one another.

As organizations grow, many are becoming increasingly decentralized. Methods of maintaining communication amidst decentralization needs to be implemented. Teleconferencing can serve as a viable communication link in these organizations (Johansen, 1985; Short, 1974). Personal computer networks and conference telephone calling capabilities can connect virtually everyone within an organization. Other uses of these new communication channels are still being realized. Like the television and telephone, teleconferencing may become an accepted channel in our future communication experiences. "In fact, [computer conferencing] may be losing its forbidding, impersonal image as more individuals gain experience in computer-mediated communications" (Williams, 1987, p. 231). But, as with all forms of electronically mediated communication, there are limitations on the communication bandwidth. Bandwidth is a measurement of the amount of cues that can be transmitted via a communication channel. Face-to-face communication allows for the greatest bandwidth because all verbal and nonverbal cues can be transmitted between people. All communication technologies, no matter how sophisticated, limit the transmission of some communication cues. These limitations affect communication, understanding, and relationship development.

Human Factors Research

Teleconferencing affects various aspects of the communication process including leadership emergence (Strickland et al., 1978), availability of nonverbal cues (Johansen, Vallee, & Spangler, 1978; 1979), frequency of interaction (Johansen & DeGrasse, 1978), conversation flow (Rutter & Stephenson, 1977), planning for future interaction (Greif, 1982), problem solving (Krueger & Chapanis, 1980), and the teaching process (Becker, 1978). Channels with greater nonverbal capacities allow people to create more positive perceptions of others—more favorable, friendly, pleasant, and cooperative. However, these channels also allow for more spontaneous (interruption) communication.

As discussed in Chapter 2, nonverbal communication affects all of our interactions. We use it to determine social status and power, to express confidence and trust, to communicate interest and satisfaction, and as a guide to turn-taking and synchronization of conversation (Hickson & Stacks, 1985). Teleconferencing limits nonverbal communication, and therefore, affects these and many other processes of communication.

Nonverbal communication also supplies us with structure and rules that dictate appropriate behavior and form a framework in which we create meanings. It is a strange and unique sensation engaging in one's first video conference. Many of us have a great deal of experience yelling at the television, but we are not used to talking to a television monitor and having the person on the screen look at us and respond back to us. Professionals with teleconferencing experience agree that a fairly strict set of rules needs to be created in order to have an effective meeting. The taken-for-granted process of turn-taking in a face-to-face interaction needs to be guided by agreed upon rules in teleconferencing. There is an inverse relationship between channel bandwidth and the formality of communication rules that are needed to govern interaction; decreased channel bandwidth necessitates increased rule formality. During a face-to-face encounter, turn-taking and turn-maintaining cues are communicated through vocal intonations, eye contact, and various proxemic and kinesthetic adjustments (Jaffee & Feldstein, 1970; Wiemann & Knapp, 1975). You can see that these rules of turn-taking are excluded from some teleconferencing channels with narrower bandwidths. Video-conferencing allows for many of the rules to be visually perceived, audio-conferencing only allows for vocal intonations, and computer conferencing relies solely on message content. From this example alone it is evident that teleconferencing channels can seriously affect communication processes by impacting on the cues available to the participants.

Teleconferencing and Conflict Management

As discussed in the chapter on conflict, a main function of communication within organizations is conflict management. In an environment of limited resources, differing ideas and ideals, and where the quest for meeting the bottom line is paramount, conflict is inevitable. Conflicts in organizations have been processed through mediation, arbitration, bargaining, pressure, power, and other formal and informal methods. Grievance committees, letter writing campaigns, ventilation interviews, focus groups, and other channels have been used to deal with differences. Many of these channels and techniques have been successful, but still "new methods must be considered for facilitating negotiation" (Mills, 1983a, p. 4). Mills' statement comes as organizations are committing themselves to increase dependence on technology to manage information and communication. As these technologies are implemented, they should be examined for their conflict managing capabilities. This examination should consist of research and testing—jumping to a conclusion about the effectiveness of one technology or another in the conflict management arena can lead to devastating results.

We are cautioned to question: "What is the effect on the conduct of a negotiation if communication is by [teleconferencing] instead of face-to-face?" (Short, 1974, p. 225). Studies into conflict management via teleconferencing reveal various results; employing teleconferencing in this capacity may appear appealing for various reasons. For instance, teleconferencing can allow for anonymous testing of ideas towards conflict resolution (Mills, 1983b, p. 16). One may be hesitant to suggest solutions to a conflict in a face-to-face setting. For individuals who are communication apprehensive, or fear rejection or punishment, computer conferencing may supply them with a nonthreatening channel for communication.

Negotiations and bargaining often pit two or more perspectives against each other in the division of power, money, or some other resource. Teleconferencing may be seen as an ideal channel for this form of communication as it allows people to have their required information at their disposal. Employees need not travel with their information when a computer conference can take place between or among offices. Computer conferencing allows for greater preparation and planning "away from the fury pressure of the bargaining table" (Mills, 1983a, p. 4). The psychological impact of negotiating on your own or someone else's "turf" can be reduced by teleconferencing. All parties can be located at their own private and comfortable location.

Another benefit of this technology in a formal conflict management forum is that it allows for plentiful prenegotiation interaction within the various camps engaged in the negotiation. This includes discussion between the camps and mediators concerning rules of the negotiation as well as interaction with other parties who could supply information or who would feel the consequences of the negotiation. "There are applications for teleconferencing far beyond prenegotiation discussion. Shop stewards in a multi-plant union could jointly deal with layoff or recall of workers" (Mills, 1983a, p. 60). Access to teleconferencing would allow for more frequent interaction.

Conflict management can become entangled in personal battles and vindications. Emotions rise and rational thinking may fall by the wayside. Employing teleconferencing limits the availability of nonverbal cues, and therefore, the participants become more reliant on other available information to successfully communicate. "As the visual channel appears to be particularly concerned with socio-emotional information, its removal would be expected to lead to an increased dependence on the more task-oriented verbal channel" (Short, 1974, p. 226). Audio and computer conferencing may aid in the conflict management process if a lack of task focus is expected.

"Electronic meetings ease the task of making contact; they do not, however, erase the complexity of...communication" (Johansen, Vallee, & Spangler, 1978, p. 317). Besides impacting on turn-taking, these channels may distort participants' perceptions of each other's message, thus affecting the negotiation process (Short, 1974). Conflict is often caused by inaccurate communication, misperceptions, and faulty information transmission. If, during a conflict management situation, messages continue to be distorted, the conflict could easily escalate. With strict rules guiding our interaction in teleconferences, further distortion and greater anxiety and impatience are probable.

Short, Williams, and Christie (1976), a team of researchers among the first to examine how teleconferencing affects the human communication process, state that conflict management is sensitive to the communication medium. Their work with teleconferencing and conflict has yielded some interesting results. For instance, they have found that when two groups are communicating via teleconferencing with one group at each site, coalitions are easily formed between people at the same location (Williams, 1975a). Extrapolated, this finding supports the notion that conflict management is a function of interpersonal/relationship dimensions as well as content/task dimensions. Other researchers found that audio-mediated communication leads to more task-oriented communication and less relationship-maintaining communication than face-to-face interaction (Morley & Stephenson, 1969, 1970). In one of their experimental designs they set up a weak argument about an issue of conflict and hypothesized that this weak case would be more successful in face-to-face than electronically mediated negotiations. This is based on research that found less task-focused communication and greater focus on relationship-maintenance communication in face-to-face interaction. The emphasis on the interpersonal dimension would interfere with the participants' analysis of the objective data. "It was accordingly predicted that the 'weak case' would be more successful in face-to-face than telephone negotiations—this was confirmed by the experimental results" (Short, 1974, p. 226).

Short, a researcher whose doctoral dissertation examined the effects of communication mediums on two-person conflicts, experimented with subjects who had varying levels of ego-involvement and conviction towards the case they were arguing (1974). Based on the idea that an audio channel focuses more on task and less on personal dimensions, the person with higher ego-involvement in the case would be less successful when the visual channel was lacking. This proved true: "The individual whose personal views were more consonant with the case he was required to argue [was] relatively more successful in the face-to-face condition while the reverse [held] true for the other person" (p. 233). These findings emphasize again how the communication channel affects people's perceptions. There are both positive and negative consequences associated with using teleconferencing to deal with disputes and conflict management.

Teleconferencing is a relatively new communication medium. In its many forms, teleconferencing has varied effects on communication factors such as inter-actants' perceptions, communication styles, and message clarity. Conflict management is a specific communication situation that is sensitive to message distortion and task and relationship dimensions of communications. Teleconferencing affects these sensitive areas. Future research in this area should attempt to isolate further factors and variables in order to create a clearer picture of when teleconferencing should be used in conflict management situations.

OTHER COMMUNICATION TECHNOLOGIES

There are other communication technologies in use today and some that will become common in the years to come. Telephones are becoming smaller and increasingly cordless. Cellular telephones quickly evolved from needing a bulky transmitter and receiver usually carried over our shoulder, to a telephone that can fold up and fit into our pocket. Hands-free cellular telephones are common in automobiles and are even required by law in some states.

There are also personnel monitoring systems in use. With these systems, employees wear identification tags that house a small transmitter. Located throughout an office building are receivers that monitor where personnel are and automatically direct calls to the nearest telephone. A unique ringing pattern and even a recording of persons' names signal them that they have an incoming call. Other communication technologies are being developed as well. As we continue to use and rely on these technologies, our need to understand and predict their impact on communication becomes increasingly important. Theories need to continue to be developed and tested in this search for understanding and managing communication technologies.

THEORIES, MODELS, POSTULATES, AND HYPOTHESES

Theory of Electronic Propinquity

Propinquity is a basic concept that examines how proxemics, or nearness in physical space, affects our communication patterns. In other words, your proxemic relationship to other people has a strong influence on who you will meet, how often you will engage in communication with specific people, who you will form friendships and coalitions with, even which of your neighbors you will become friends with. Thinking back to your childhood you may have become friends with your next door neighbors or with people who lived close to you. You may have even been a little suspicious of the motives of people who lived in a different part of your town or city. If this is true, then your experiences support the premise of propinquity. Physical space strongly influences with whom we interact. Once given the opportunity to interact, we may find things in common with others; past interactions alone facilitate this commonality. It is having things in common that leads to relationship development and friendships. "In its baldest form, the proposition of propinquity reads as follows: other things equal, people are most likely to be attracted to those in closest contact with them" (Newcomb, 1956, p. 575).

Filipe Korzenny, a communication theorist who was one of the first to apply face-to-face communication theories to mediated communication channels, reasserts that space, the physical proxemics and location of people, is a significant factor in our communication patterns, interaction, and outcomes of communication in general (Korzenny, 1978; Korzenny & Bauer, 1981). "Space, due to sheer accessibility, determines who and what we know" (1978, p. 5). With new communication technologies it is oftentimes easier to communicate with someone across the office, across town, across the country, or even across an ocean, than it may be to communication with a neighbor face-to-face. In Korzenny's theory of electronic propinquity, the concept of space is substituted with the idea of channel bandwidth.

With increased electronic communication our closest communication partners are no longer our neighbors or office mates, rather, they are those people on the other end of the telephone, video conference, or Internet. The factor of physical closeness is replaced with technological closeness. But it would be shortsighted to assert that relationships and friendships develop in the same manner via e-mail and face-to-face communication. Electronic propinquity examines the bandwidth of communication technologies as important factors in relationship development. The larger the bandwidth, the more communication cues available. All other factors being equal, channels that supply more cues are more likely to foster interpersonal attraction and relationship growth. Korzenney's assertions are echoed by A. Rodney Wellens (1986) discussion of psychological distance.

Generic Psychological Distancing Model

A. Rodney Wellens, as director of the Interactive Television Laboratory, University of Miami, focused on the "psychological distance" created by teleconferencing modes as compared to face-to-face interaction. In his "generic distancing model," Wellens (1986) notes the nonverbal cues that are lost as fewer senses are accommodated by the narrowing bandwidth of teleconferencing channel. He states that in face-to-face communication there are kinesic, visual, paralinguistic, and linguistic cues available. When video-conferencing only, visual, paralinguistic, and linguistic cues are available.

With audio-conferencing, only paralinguistic and linguistic cues are available. Lastly, computer conferencing allows for only linguistic cues to be communicated. This model depicts the loss in fidelity of the nonverbal channel as interaction moves further from face-to-face personal contact to solely computer interaction. The bandwidth of the channel diminishes from including a full range of available cues in face-to-face communication situations to the exchange of pure linguistic data over e-mail.

Although Wellens' list of communication cues available through each channel may be incomplete (he does not discuss tactics, oculesics, chromenics, etc.), his premise is valid; the further one moves from a face-to-face channel, the fewer nonverbal cues are available. These differences have psychological effects and impact on the communication and relationship between participants. For instance, channels that have greater nonverbal capacity lead participants to have generally more favorable perceptions of each other (Kiesler, Siegel, & McGuire, 1984; Kiesler et al., 1985; Williams, 1975b); people who communicate via face-to-face and video channels are seen as more friendly and pleasant than those who communicate via computer channels (Champness, 1973; Ryan, 1976), face-to-face channels are preferred over other channels for conflict resolution (Campbell, Kruskal, & Wallace, 1966; Hartnett, 1983; Newman, 1983), interpersonal cooperation decreases as more nonverbal cues are eliminated from the channel (Wichman, 1970), and verbal interruptions are higher in channels with greater nonverbal capacity (Lickiss & Wellens, 1978; Rutter & Stephenson, 1977; Rutter, Stephenson, & Dewey, 1981; Williams, 1978; Wilson & Williams, 1977).

Cleveland's Postulates About Information

Harlan Cleveland's article, "The Twilight of Hierarchy: Speculations on the Global Information Society," discusses the implications of information as we shift from Industrial Age organizations to Information Age organizations. He suggests several postulates that will help us to examine data, information, and communication using a new paradigm (1990, p. 329).

1. Information is expandable—As information is used and passed along, it grows. People examine the information, add to it, sometimes edit it, and send it on to the next person or group of people. As this process continues the original pool of information grows. With computer networks it is easy to send volumes of information to as many people as desired. This allows us to reduce cost and waste associated with paper and duplication expenses, but it may also reduce our motivation to send on only pertinent information. We no longer need to be as selective when transmitting information because it takes the same effort and cost to send one page of material as it does to send one hundred pages.

2. Information is not resource hungry—While many industries rely on raw materials and physical resources to create products, information may be acquired and manipulated for a relatively low cost. This factor may continue to propel the growth of the service sections of many global economies. It is also possible that this availability of information will help developing nations to prosper.

3. Information is substitutable—Information can be used to streamline productions and reduce work forces. As Taylor's Scientific Management techniques increased productivity by decreasing physical movements of laborers, as discussed in Chapter 1, communication technologies may alleviate middle managers or other levels of hierarchy in today's businesses.

4. Information is transportable—"at close to the speed of light" (p. 329). With the Internet we have access to our workplace from all over the world. Despite minor time delays and satellite availability we can teleconference around the globe at will. "In the world of information richness, you will be able to be remote if you want to, but you'll have to work at it" (p. 329).

5. Information is diffusive—Information, unlike a material substance, is not bound by the laws of physics. Rather, it becomes easily distorted and easily leaked. Due to the influence of human perception, information is interpreted differently by different people. It is also changed, slightly or dramatically, as it is transmitted from person to person. Even in the most tightly guarded systems, information often turns up outside of the system.

6. Information is sharable—Unlike a material possession that can only be owned by one person, information can be known to many people. It is difficult to govern information by the laws of supply and demand, because, disregarding copyright laws, information can be duplicated. The supply is limitless.

Cleveland's postulates imply that the dynamics of information, especially in the electronic age, need to be viewed using a new paradigm. The paradigm we use to view physical resources, supply and demand, and other manifestations of commodity is not suitable to understanding and managing information. To more fully understand communication in contemporary organizations, most information must be viewed as an important component of success that cannot be physically contained, but rather as something that permeates an organization and evolves over time.

O'Connell's Six Hypotheses About the Impact of Technology on Organizational Communication

The advent, uses, and effects of technological innovations have desirable and undesirable consequences on organizational communication (Rogers, 1983). Desirable consequences are the positive effects that a technological innovation has on the function of an organization. For instance, a voice mail system may allow employees to route various telephone inquiries to the proper office within a large organization. The positive result would be saving time and routing the incoming call to the most expert and reliable source. While these systems are time and money savers, we all have gotten lost in what seems like and endless maze of voice mail options. Frustration and a feeling of a cold and impersonal organization can be an undesirable consequence of this same technological innovation (Rogers, 1983).

Communication technologies continue to develop at a rapid rate. By the year 2000 we may look back on today's technologies as antiquated. In her chapter "Human Communication in the High Tech Office," Sandra E. O'Connell (1988) states that with the speed of technological advances, we have a lot to learn in a limited time. It is important to understand the impact of communication technologies on our communication so we can best prepare ourselves and others for the consequences of these impacts. O'Connell presents six hypotheses concerning these impacts.

Hypothesis 1: O'Connell's first hypothesis states that as the use of communication technologies increase, face-to-face communication will decrease. "Consequently opportunities for random, spontaneous information sharing will be reduced.... Meaning will be derived increasingly from text and symbols" (p. 480).

The norms that control our typical face-to-face communication, those norms that we have grown up with, will not be as prominent in our future professional lives. We will need to become more flexible and creative in our communication as the available bandwidth narrows. Written communication, the narrowest bandwidth, will become increasingly common for less formal interactions. Written communication has been the staple for formal agreements, legal matters, and the like, but it will be used more frequently as a substitute for short telephone conversations and discussions in the hallways.

The advent of communication technologies also has had a dramatic effect on the architecture and design of buildings and workplaces. The rising costs for work spaces combined with the miniaturizing of computers has reduced the amount of space designated for employees' offices and working areas. Many organizations have recognized this problem and created informal meeting places that are both comfortable and spacious, allowing employees some "breathing room" (Harney, 1982).

Hypothesis 2: O'Connell's (1988) second hypothesis states that as the use of communication technologies increase, more informal messages causing "short-circuiting" of the hierarchy will occur. "Organization structure and formal information flow will be redefined" (p. 480). Due to increased competition and operating expenses, organizational structures are being redefined, reexamined, and reengineered. Problem-solving based on informal communication may yield poor decisions created out of incomplete or distorted data.

Hypothesis 3: O'Connell's (1988) third hypothesis states that as the use of communication technologies increase, decision-making will be impaired rather than enhanced. Because more communication will be taking place through more impersonal communication channels, messages that convey an organization's values, culture, and history will decrease. "Ambiguity in interpreting information will increase, and the quality of decisions could decrease with the lack of organizational values and context.... New and improved decision-making skills will be needed" (pp. 480–481).

It will become increasingly important for information to be communicated with clarity and brevity. The presentation of formal information in this manner may serve as a check and balance system for employees to gauge the accuracy of information on which they are basing their decisions.

Hypothesis 4: O'Connell's (1988) fourth hypothesis states that as the use of communication technologies increase, "trust will play a changed role in communication" (p. 481). As electronic communication replaces traditional face-to-face communication, the informal daily interaction that helps to build trust between people will also diminish. The loss of trust or the inability to build trust between employees is a serious issue that left unchecked, can have long-term negative consequences on an organization's ability to function.

Hypothesis 5: O'Connell's (1988) fifth hypothesis states that as the use of computer technologies increase, organizations will become less tolerant of people who do not use the linear thinking paradigm. There will be "less patience and tolerance for individual styles of communicating" (p. 481). E-mail systems are linear in their design. Attempts to brainstorm via computer mail can be difficult. The spontaneity of face-to-face interaction that helps to nurture creativity is lost. Cognitive and learning styles that are more visual and less structured are stifled by linear communication channels.

Hypothesis 6: Lastly, O'Connell's (1988) sixth hypothesis states that as the use of communication technologies increase, expectations of work requirements will change. "As we become accustomed to the speed and accuracy of the computer, we may expect employees to have the same qualities and produce in a similar manner" (p. 481). Also, as stated earlier, employees may be expected to work from home, online, with increased regularity.

All of O'Connell's hypotheses lead to the conclusion that organizations will need to train their employees to understand how communication technologies affect their professional lives. New perspectives for understanding communication and information need to be developed and integrated within the culture of organizations.

IMPLICATIONS FOR MANAGEMENT AND TRAINING

If many of the predictions about the future of communication in organizations are accurate, offices of the future will require far less face-to-face interaction than the offices of today. More and more information will be disseminated and exchanged at increasing speeds. Organizational hierarchies will continue to flatten, and co-workers will be distributed across a large geographical area. Corporate cultures will change, management styles will evolve, and employees' feelings of dedication will wane.

The need to foster and nurture interpersonal relationships between employees will be more important in the Information Age than it ever has been. Electronic communication technologies will allow us to isolate ourselves from one another at home and on the job. Technology allows people to work together on tasks while keeping people physically apart. This lack of immediacy inhibits personal relationships from developing. There is a need to increase focus on personal relationships to break the barriers often produced by electronic communication. "Managers will need to structure work and relationships to provide more opportunities for face-to-face contact to occur" (O'Connell, 1988, p. 480).

Communication and management training is one step to bridging the relationship gap fostered by technology. This type of long-term training may be able to create a self-perpetuating culture based on the premise that face-to-face and informal communication are as important as getting a task completed via electronic communication.

Training should be focused on three main areas: (1) learning, accepting, and using new technologies; (2) managing large quantities of electronic information; and (3) fostering informal communication and relationship development.

Before communication technologies can realize their full potential, employees must be able and willing to use them. "The introduction of technological innovations is high risk at best, with most estimates placing the rate of success during the first introduction at less than 25 percent" (Shockley-Zalabak, 1994, p. 199). Training programs must be designed to assist employees with feeling comfortable with these new technologies. "Technology influences our behavior by creating uncertainty in our organizational lives" (Goldhaber, 1993, p. 290). Demystifying the complexity of technology, adding certainty, and reassuring employees that technologies are not meant to replace people should be central components in these training sessions. Demonstrating how the technologies can be used for informal communication should also be considered.

The second area of training should help employees to manage large volumes of information. As stated earlier, using e-mail it is as easy to send one hundred pages of documentation as it is to send one page. Training employees to deal with this vast amount of information should begin by examining how to send information. Information senders should forward the most relevant and pertinent information. It is far easier to send a lot of information than to edit out unimportant information. More training should examine issues of information overload and help employees to understand how their communication technologies can help them to organize information.

Lastly, and perhaps most importantly, training programs should be designed to increase trust-based personal relationships between employees at all level. Current training techniques of team building and role modeling can help attain this goal. Special attention should be paid to ensuring that informal gatherings become part of an organization's culture. While the benefits of technology are fairly easy to quantitatively measure, corporate trainers and managers need to focus their energy on ensuring the growth and health of the more qualitative dimension of human relationships.

CONCLUSION

Communication technologies have become an indispensable component of contemporary organizations. The Internet with the World Wide Web is quickly becoming a common communication medium for large and small corporations, colleges and universities, politicians, marketers, and community-based organizations, as well individuals without organizational affiliation. Teleconferencing technologies are being used in many corporations to save travel expenses and to connect many people from remote sites. Various new communication technologies are being introduced as the market allows. Given the proper circumstances, these technologies allow for more efficient and effective communication. As stated in this chapter, there are many benefits to the uses of communication technologies, but there are also some cautions. As we progress into the new millennium, communication students and scholars must continue to understand both the positive and negative effects on communication technologies in contemporary organizations.

GLOSSARY

Asynchronic conferencing—interaction in which each party involved can receive and send messages at their convenience; there is no real-time interaction. Messages are sent, received, and replied to in the same chronological fashion as writing and mailing letters.

Audio-conferencing—interactive audio communication channels between two or more people at two or more locations; also referred to as conference calling.

Bandwidth—a term used to describe the sheer amount of cues available in a given communication channel; the smaller the bandwidth, the fewer the cues available.

Generic psychological distancing model—a model that isolates specific verbal and nonverbal cues that are, and are not, available in various communication channels.

Internet—a network of computers designed to facilitate e-mail transactions on a global scale.

Propinquity—the theory that posits that proxemics, or the physical distance between people, is a significant factor in determining how relationships develop.

Synchronic conferencing—real-time, live conferencing in which all members of the interaction are simultaneously involved in the interaction.

Telecommuting–the use of communication technologies to allow employees to perform job-related tasks and to communicate with their organization from their homes or other remote locations.

Teleconferencing—a generic term for any combination of electronically mediated audio, video, or computer interaction that connects two or more people at two or more locations.

Video-conferencing—interactive video communication channels between two or more people at two or more locations.

CASE STUDY

FutureTech, a mid-size computer manufacturing and software development firm, employs about 150 people in its Rochester, New York, headquarters. The company was founded eight years ago and has enjoyed steady growth in the emerging high-tech field. The guiding management philosophy has been to run the company like a large family. There are frequent celebrations, informal gatherings, birthday gifts and gags, and everyday except Wednesday is dress-down day. The company dress code is very informal, except for Wednesday. FutureTech takes pride in breaking the mold of contemporary organizations. Employees respond favorably to this management style and are further reinforced by increased sales, profits, and bonuses.

Last year, FutureTech decided it was time to expand. There were many other markets across the Northeast that needed to be tapped into by FutureTech, otherwise their competitors would grow too strong. The organization's strategy was to set up five satellite offices throughout the Northeast: Pittsburgh, Boston, Portland, Hartford, and Paramus, N.J. The management of FutureTech realized that much of the organization's success was based on the corporate culture created by the informal Rochester headquarters. Part of the strategy was to transplant two or three current employees to each new office to help establish the proper culture.

For the first time in the organization's eight years, profits began to drop. While the Rochester office boasted high moral and productivity, the five satellite offices were not being profitable. A communication audit was done and the results were fairly clear; the employees away from Rochester lost their sense of connection to the corporate culture that provided a fertile climate for motivation and productivity. The management decided to implement radical changes in the communication channels among all of the offices. At great expense, each of the new offices was equipped with full-motion, state-of-the-art video-conferencing as well as access to the Internet. The FutureTech management knows that proper training is necessary in order to fully use these technological channels to their fullest potential.

Discussion: You are part of a consulting team hired to train FutureTech employees to use these new technologies. What should this training consist of? How can FutureTech's culture be nurtured given the current setup of one headquarter and five satellite offices? Should all employees be trained? Should there be regularly scheduled video conferences between all of the offices? Are there specific situations that should not be handled via electronic communication? Should employees be rotated throughout the various office locations?

REFERENCES

American Broadcasting Company (1994, Aug. 10). Turning Point: Return to Woodstock [Telecast]. New York: ABC.

Becker, A. D. (1978). A survey and evaluation. *Journal of Communication, 15,* 120–124.

Campbell, D. T., Kruskal, W. H., & Wallace, W. P. (1966). Seating aggregation as an index of attitude. *Sociometry, 29,* 1–15.

Champness, B. (1973). Attitudes toward person to person communications media. *Human Factors, 15,* 437–447.

Cleveland, H. (1990). Epilogue: The twilight of hierarchy: Speculations on the global information society. In S. R. Corman, S. P. Banks, C. R. Bantz, & M. E. Mayer (eds.), *Foundations of Organizational Communication: A Reader* (pp. 327–341). New York: Longman.

Goldhaber, G. M. (1993). *Organizational Communication* (6th ed.). Madison, Wis.: Brown & Benchmark.

Govang, P. (1994, Aug. 3). Personal communication.

Greif, I. (1982). Teleconferencing and the computer-based office workstation. In L. A. Parker & C. H. Olgren (eds.), *Teleconferencing and Electronic Communications: Applications Technologies and Human Factors* (pp. 388–397). Madison, Wis.: University of Wisconsin Press.

Harney, A. L. (1982). Why offices will never be the same. *The Washingtonian, 17,* 247–251.

Hartnett, T. F. (1983). Containing conflict: Teleconferencing and labor relations. The need for human interaction. *Arbitration Journal, 38,* 13–14.

Hickson, M. L., & Stacks, D. W. (1985). *Nonverbal Communication: Studies and Applications.* Dubuque, Iowa: William C. Brown Communications.

Jaffee, S., & Feldstein, J. (1970). *Rhythms of Dialogue.* New York: Academic Press.

Johansen, R. (1985). *Teleconferencing Success Stories.* IFTF Paper P-137. Menlo Park, Calif.: Institute for the Future.

Johansen, R., & DeGrasse, R. (1978). Computer-based teleconferencing: Effects on working patterns. *Journal of Communication, 28,* 137–148.

Johansen, R., Vallee, J., & Spangler, K. (1978). Electronic meetings: Utopian dreams and complex realities. *The Futurist, 12,* 313–319.

Johansen, R., Vallee, J., & Spangler, K. (1979). *Electronic Meetings.* Reading, Mass.: Addison-Wesley.

Kiesler, S., Siegel, J., & McGuire, T. W. (1984). Social psychological aspects of computer-mediated communication. *American Psychologist, 39,* 1123–1134.

Kiesler, S., Zubrow, D., Moses, A. M., & Geller, V. (1985). Affect in computer-mediated communication: An experiment in synchronous terminal-to-terminal discussion. *Human-Computer Interaction, 1,* 77–104.

Korzenny, F. (1978). A theory of electronic propinquity: Mediated communication in organizations. *Communication Research, 5,* 3–24.

Korzenny, F., & Bauer, C. (1981). Testing the theory of electronic propinquity: Organizational teleconferencing. *Communication Research, 8,* 479–498.

Krueger, G. P., & Chapanis, A. (1980). Conferencing and teleconferencing in three communication modes as a function of the number of conferees. *Ergonomics, 23,* 103–122.

Lickiss, K., & Wellens, A. R. (1978). Effects of visual accessibility and hand restraint on fluency of gesticular and effectiveness of message. *Perceptual and Motor Skills, 46,* 925–926.

Lottor, M. (1994, July 7). IBM Internet user survey; USA Today research. *USA Today,* p. 1B.

Mills, M. K. (1983a). Containing conflict: Teleconferencing and labor relations. *The Arbitration Journal, 38,* 4–7.

Mills, M. K. (1983b). Author's response. *The Arbitration Journal, 38,* 15–16.

Morley, I. E., & Stepheson, G. M. (1969). Interpersonal and interplay exchange, a laboratory simulation of an industrial negotiation at the plant level. *British Journal of Psychology, 60,* 543–545.

Morley, I. E., & Stepheson, G. M. (1970). Formality in experimental negotiations, a validation study. *British Journal of Psychology, 61,* 383.

Nebel, B. P. (1994). Electronic liberation or entrapment? *The New York Times,* p. B14.

Newcomb, T. M. (1956). The prediction of social attraction. *The American Psychologist, 11,* 575–586.

Newman, H. R. (1983). Containing conflict: Teleconferencing and labor relations. A dissenting view. *Arbitration Journal, 38,* 10–12.

O'Connell, S. E. (1988). Human communication in the high tech office. In G. M. Goldhaber & G. A. Barnett (eds.), *Handbook of Organizational Communication* (pp. 473–482). NJ: Ablex.

Phillips, G. M. (1994). Introduction to "the Internet." *Communication Education, 43,* 71–72.

Quittner, J. (1995, Aug. 21). Browser madness. *Time,* 26–27.

Rogers, E. M. (1983). *Diffusion of Innovations* (3rd ed.). New York: The Free Press.

Rutter, D. R., & Stephenson, G. M. (1977). The role of visual communication in synchronizing conversation. *European Journal of Social Psychology, 7,* 29–37.

Rutter, D. R., Stephenson, G. M., & Dewey, M. E. (1981). Visual communication and the content and style of conversation. *British Journal of Social Psychology, 20,* 41–52.

Ryan, M. G. (1976). The influence of teleconferencing medium and status on participants' perceptions of the aestheticism, evaluation, privacy, potency, and activity of the medium. *Human Communication Research, 2,* 225–261.

Santoro, G. M. (1994). The Internet: An overview. *Communication Education, 43,* 73–86.

Shockley-Zalabak, P. (1994). *Understanding Organizational Communication: Cases, Commentaries, and Conversations.* New York: Longman.

Short, J. A. (1974). Effects of medium of communication on experimental negotiation. *Human Relations, 27,* 225–234.

Short, J. A., Williams, E., & Christie, B. (1976). *The Social Psychology of Telecommunications.* New York: John Wiley.

Strickland, L. H., Guild, P. D., Barefoot, J. C., & Paterson, S. A. (1978). Teleconferencing and leadership emergence. *Human Relations, 31,* 583–596.

Turner Broadcasting Service (1994, July 1) Headline News [Telecast]. Atlanta, Ga.: TBS

Wiemann, J. M., & Knapp, M. L. (1975). Turn-taking in conversations. *Journal of Communication, 25,* 75–92.

Wellens, A. R. (1986). Use of a psychological distancing model to assess differences in telecommunication media. In L. A. Parker & C. H. Olgren (eds.) *Teleconferencing and Electronic Communications V: Applications Technologies and Human Factors* (pp. 347–361). Madison, Wis.: University of Wisconsin Press.

Wichman, H. (1970). The effects of isolation and communication on cooperation in a two-person game. *Journal of Social Psychology, 16,* 114–120.

Williams, E. (1975a). Coalition formation over telecommunications media. *European Journal of Social Psychology, 5,* 503–507.

Williams, E. (1975b). Medium or message: Communications medium as a determinant of interpersonal evaluation. *Sociometry, 38,* 119–130.

Williams, E. (1978). Visual interaction and speech patterns: An extension of previous results. *British Journal of Social and Clinical Psychology, 17,* 101–102.

Williams, F. (1987). *Technology and Communication Behavior.* Belmont, Calif.: Wadsworth Publishing Company.

Wilson, C., & Williams, E. (1977). Watergate words: A naturalistic study of media and communication. *Communication Research, 4,* 169–178.

Wiseman, P. (1994a, July 7). The Internet snares more business. *USA Today,* pp. 1B–2B.

Wiseman, P. (1994b, July 7). Security, culture may cause tangles. *USA Today,* pp 2B.

RECOMMENDED READINGS

Johansen, R., Vallee, J., & Spangler, K. (1979). *Electronic Meetings.* Reading, Mass.: Addison-Wesley.

Peterson, G. L. (1994). *Communicating in Organizations: A Casebook.* Scottsdale, Ariz.: Gorsuch Scarisbrick.

Postman, N. (1992). *Technopoly: The Surrender of Culture to Technology.* New York: Knopf.

Williams, F. (1987). *Technology and Communication Behavior.* Belmont, Calif.: Wadsworth Publishing Company.

► Part IV

Postscript

How to Think and Talk About Organizational Communication

PHILLIP K. TOMPKINS

Because of my status as a senior citizen of the academic field called organizational communication (by virtue of the fact that my Ph.D. was completed in 1962 at Purdue University under the "father" or "founder" of the field, W. Charles Redding), the editor of this book has given me a license to comment on the previous chapters. My purpose is to provide a historical perspective on the field and the chapters. Here and there I will take a different stance on the topics than those taken by the other authors. The reader will be the ultimate judge of which positions are more useful.

Peggy Byers' introductory chapter is so rich and stimulating that it gave me the courage to present a pattern of management theory and organizational communication that may help in understanding organizations and how people talk about them. Byers discusses such management theorists as Taylor, Fayol, Mayo, and Roethlisberger.

THE ORIGIN OF ORGANIZATIONAL COMMUNICATION

An article by Barley and Kunda (1992) treated *all* of management theory in U.S. history as so much "discourse" or "rhetoric" about management. And rather than present these as linear progressions over time, the authors argued that theories come into prominence as waves that reach a full height only to crash, recede, and return again in a different form.

Table 14-1 is taken from the Barley and Kunda (1992) article. I shall not spend much time explaining each wave of discourse because most are discussed by Byers and other authors in this chapter, but some clarification is necessary. The first wave, called industrial betterment (IB) was the first discourse about management in U.S. history. There is no single theorist we can identify for this theory. It was a rather simple and well-intentioned theory that held that if workers were treated decently they would produce more. There was also a reformist streak in this discourse, a belief expressed that if you could get workers to quit drinking, join a religion, and settle down, they would be more reliable and trustworthy. It had a normative "tenor," or theme, because of the assumption that good treatment would cause the worker to identify with company goals and values, to accept them as their norms.

The second wave of management theory was scientific management (SM), or Taylorism, discussed by Byers. The proponents of SM attacked IB for being soft and ineffective, establishing a tension between waves that is repeated in each of the following successions. Even though SM became more prominent than the first wave, IB did not completely disappear. Elements of IB were present in the human relations (HR) movement also discussed by Byers. Note that the HR movement or theory was, like IB, normative in tenor.

The fourth wave, systems rationalism (SR), is discussed by another name in this book. Angela Trethewey's chapter on culture calls this the functionalist approach to organizational communication, "a rather mechanistic and linear view of communication." What Trethewey is referring to is also called logical positivism, or empiricism, a philosophy of science that requires one to supply quantitative data and statistical tests to support one's claims. Functionalism is an unfortunate term for this approach because it is not unique in claiming that communication performs certain functions. For example, Trethewey herself, in explaining how stories are important for organizational cultures, says that "stories may serve a variety of functions in

TABLE 14-1   **Waves of managerial discourse in U.S. history.**

Theory	Era of Prominence	Tenor
Industrial betterment	1870–1900	Normative
Scientific management	1900–1923	Rational
Human relations	1923–1955	Normative
System rationalism	1955–1980	Rational
Culture	1980–present	Normative

From Barley and Kunda, 1992.

organizations." In other words, the cultural approach makes functionalist assumptions. Trethewey cannot be faulted for coining the word functionalism—it is part of the field's vocabulary—but because we have seen its problems, it is wiser to use the term systems rationalism (SR), or some other more descriptive term. And we shall return to this problem later in this chapter. SR fits this wave of management theory well. This period was dominated by systems theory (see Chapter 1) and systems thinking as well as logical positivism. The tenor for this period is, of course, rationalism. It had much in common with SM and revived the memory of Taylor. Indeed, because of the development of computers, SR was able to outdo SM in rationality.

Finally, we see the cultural approach. It was proposed as an alternative to SR in part because the United States was falling behind the Japanese in terms of productivity. Didn't the Japanese have strong cultures that conscripted commitment from their workers? Wouldn't strong cultures in U.S. companies produce the normative control the Japanese enjoyed? So began the culture movement (see Chapter 8).

Note again that these theories arrived in alternating waves. Barley and Kunda suggest that this normative–rational alternation is due to the fact that certain cultural values, for example, individualism versus communalism, can't both be satisfied at the same time. My view is that normative–rational is not a true opposition, and for that reason the alternation is probably due to a cluster of cultural antinomies, or contradictory values. I would state the cluster as individual/communal, rational/emotional, and mechanistic/organic.

What have we accomplished at this point? We have helped explain the origin and motivation for certain management theories that have been assimilated into organizational communication and discussed as such in this book by Byers, Trethewey, and others. We have also offered a cluster of antinomies to explain the back-and-forth nature of managerial discourse. Now I propose to outline some corresponding stages in the development of our own field, organizational communication, which are illustrated by topics discussed in this book.

THE DEVELOPMENT OF THE FIELD OF ORGANIZATIONAL COMMUNICATION

Table 14-2 is my adaptation of the Barley–Kunda scheme to the unique development of the field of organizational communication. There are some differences as well as similarities. I find nothing comparable to the industrial betterment period or wave of managerial discourse in organizational communication. I mark the beginning of organizational communication with the publication of an article by W. Hayes Yeager in 1929. Let me explain why.

In 1929 the field of communication was known as speech. It was largely devoted to the teaching of public speaking, argumentation, and debate. Its scholarly interests were in studying the history and criticism of historically important public speeches or public address (see Chapter 1).

TABLE 14-2   **Waves of discourse in organizational communication.**

Approach	Era of Prominence	Tenor
Business and professional Speaker (BPS)	1929–1955	Rational Rhetoric
General semantics/ human relations (GS/HR)	1955–1968	Idiographic, Understanding, Communal
Systems rationalism (SR)	1968–1980	Rational, Understanding, Nomothetic
Cultural/critical	1980–present	Emotional, Rhetoric, Communal

Yeager, along with William Sandford, proposed to change all of that with a course at the University of Illinois called Business and Professional Speaking and a textbook by the same name. Then in 1929 Professor Yeager wrote an article for the *Quarterly Journal of Speech* advocating that others create such courses. He argued that public speaking courses and textbooks dealt with political and pulpit speeches, among others, and formal addresses that few of their students would ever be expected to give.

Business speeches, he argued on the other hand, were practical. He outlined the proposed course. It was devoted to conference speaking—a dyadic or interpersonal situation—as well as group communication. It was intended to help students acquire skills needed by students and by the organizations that would hire them. Yeager described the reporting relationships of the hierarchy in a business organization so well that it could be quoted in an introductory textbook on organizational communication today (Yeager, 1929).

Speaking for the Cornell School of rhetoricians, James A. Winans offered resistance to the idea of business and professional speaking (BPS) in the same journal, the *Quarterly Journal of Speech*. He claimed to be ignorant of business practices and thus incompetent to teach such a course. His article suggested that the practical or "applied" nature of BPS was beneath the lofty aims of a liberal education. The co-author of Yeager's textbook, William Sandford, entered the exchange with an article refuting Winans in the same journal (Sandford, 1931). Sandford used humor and powerful arguments in his surrebuttal. He explained that they were applying the same rhetoric theory and principles to business speaking that Winans applied to the teaching of political speaking.

Sandford also explained their pedagogical approach. In both dyadic and group assignments, an individual student was given a business case well known to the instructor. The student analyzed the case and prepared a solution or recommendation for a superior executive or board of directors (other students played the roles of listeners). The speaker was expected to anticipate the questions and objections of the superior or board. This Case Method was, in summary, a rhetorical theory of communication and decision-making in organizations before that approach was created by Chester Barnard (1938) and continued by Herbert Simon (1976). It emphasized the rational, problem-solving approach to communication. Redding (1985) called BPS a "precursor" of the field, but I submit that this was the first stage in the development of organizational communication.

The second stage is similar yet different from the HR wave described by Barley and Kunda. I call it the general semantics/human relations (GS/HR) era. Byers discusses the teachings and relevance of general semantics to organizational communication in her introductory chapter. She correctly identifies Alfred Korzybski as the founder of this approach to language and human communication. It is my job to put this work in the historical context of the development of the field.

Two of Korzybski's prominent associates in the GS movement were professors of speech: Elwood Murray at Denver University and Irving Lee of Northwestern University. Both saw GS as a way to study speech or communication in the everyday settings of business organizations. They thought GS could help us better achieve understanding in our mundane affairs; they even thought it could improve our mental hygiene, or health. Both became interested in the human relations movement centered at the Harvard Business School. Lee was invited to Harvard to teach general semantics to business students and professors. He even provided the interpretation of data gathered in one of the most famous case studies in the HR literature, George F. F. Lombard's (1955) *"Behavior in a selling group: A case study of interpersonal relations in a department store."* The most important sentence in Lombard's book is this: "The breakdowns in communication which we diagnosed as the department's central problem followed from the lack of skillful evaluations and behavior of this sort" (1955, p. 316).

In one of my earliest articles, I showed that there was a deep interpenetration between the general semantics movement in speech and the human relations movement (Tompkins, 1965). At that point there was no hard and firm distinction between interpersonal and organizational communication. Note for example that while we today think of Lombard's case study as a classic in organizational communication, he used the term interpersonal in the subtitle of the book. Interestingly, Rawlins' history of interpersonal communication offers as a thesis that "much of the impetus for the speech field's interest in interpersonal communication arose during the 1930s from the human relations movement out to the Harvard Graduate School of Business Administration and the general semantics movement started by Alfred Korzybski" (Rawlins, 1985, p. 109). Rawlins cites my article (Tompkins, 1965) in support of his claims of an "increasing" scholarly exchange between human relations theorists and general semanticists in the speech field" (Rawlins, 1985, p. 116). (So, interpersonal and organizational communication have more in common, at least in roots, than contemporary workers in both fields believe.)

The GS/HR stage of organizational communication can be documented in many different ways. In his history of organizational communication, W. Charles Redding wrote that the first two master's theses in the field were completed in 1943 at Denver University where Elwood Murray, prominent general semanticist, was highly influential. The first doctoral dissertation was completed by Thomas Nilsen (1953) at Northwestern University under the direction of Irving Lee, whose role as a liaison between speech and human relations was discussed above (Redding, 1985). Redding himself, the "father" of organizational communication, took his B.A. and M.A. in speech under Elwood Murray at Denver and received a fellowship to study with Korzybski in Chicago. As one of Redding's early Ph.D. students at Purdue, I can assure today's students that I studied general semantics, and human relations, as preparation for helping build a field called organizational communication.

The Purdue program under Redding—he directed forty-one doctoral dissertations (and I was one of the fortunate forty-one)—also imitated the case study approach pioneered at Harvard. My own dissertation was a case study of an international labor union that pursued the problem of "semantic/information distance" or gaps between levels of an organization. I used quantitative and qualitative evidence in this case, but the "idiographic" method of the case study was the dominant characteristic of dissertation research at Purdue. Thus, the GS/HR idiographic approach, the attempt to understand organizations as wholes, was almost the only one until 1968.

Redding's history summarizes the main accomplishments of that eventful year:

> o 1968: Thayer (1968), Communication and Communication Systems, broad-ranging treatise, theory building; new major graduate program at Michigan State Department of Communication) under way, directed by R. V. Farace—first dissertation, Schwartz (1968). (Redding, 1985, p. 53)

Looking at this paragraph through the lens created by Barley and Kunda's scheme, we can see a parallel development in organizational communication of the systems rationalism stage in managerial discourse. Thayer's book applied general systems theory to organizations, as communication systems, as can be seen in the title of his book. The developments at Michigan State are perfectly captured by the terms. Textbooks in organizational communication by faculty at Michigan State—Farace, Monge, and Russell (1977) and Rogers and Agarwala-Rogers (1976)—are best characterized as a combination of systems theory and network analysis. Network analysis gathers data about who-talks-to-whom in organizations (see Chapter 2). It generates such large quantities of data that only a computer can handle the job. William Richards had the "talent and vigor that propelled the tradition of network analytic studies in organizational communication at Michigan State University.

Richards elaborated a system of vigorous definitions of network groups and roles as he devised the software now called NEGOPY" (Tompkins & McPhee, 1985, p. 9). The excellent chapter on networks written for this book by Susan Hellweg stands in that SR tradition.

By the early eighties, however, the cultural wave seemed to swamp SR. Angela Trethewey's chapter on this subject does an admirable job of explaining the rise of the cultural approach. I amend this movement to include the critical approach in communication, one aspect of which is the feminist critique of communication. Recall the cluster of dichotomies presented above to explain the alternating waves identified by Barley and Kunda: individual/communal, rational/emotional, mechanistic/organic. Rawlins' history of interpersonal communication, mentioned above, identified several "dimensions" on which theorists have taken widely different positions. One of those dimensions is the familiar individual/communal opposition we have discussed. Another is influence versus understanding. Some interpersonal theorists have stressed that understanding, a meeting of minds, should be the main purpose of interpersonal communication. Others stressed persuasion and influence as the end of dyadic communication. We can add Rawlins' dimension of understanding/influence to our cluster of dichotomies or oppositions. It helps explain the differing emphases of the stages of organizational communication and chapters in this book.

In the beginning was business and professional speaking. This era can be characterized as rational, mechanistic and aimed to influence the decision-making process in organizations. It stressed the rhetoric initiative of the individual but tried to align that with the interests of the organization.

The GS/HR era is quite different from the BPS (even though the latter coexists even today with all of the approaches even if not in an ascendant position). The goal in this period was understanding. Influence was denounced by Irving Lee as a fascist kind of goal (Rawlins, 1985). It stressed the *communal,* the work group, the organization over the individual. It was *organistic* and *emotional* to the extent that the need for social communication, for identification with the group, was thought to be basic to the human condition.

Systems rationalism in communication did not swing to an individualistic orientation because the system, the network, is all important. It was, however, decidedly rational and mechanistic, so mechanical that persons were sometimes called "nodes." SR seemed also to come down on the understanding side of the split. The cultural approach swung back to organic, the communal, the emotional. Strong cultures were thought to influence the individual. Identification with the organization is one of the most important outcomes of a strong culture. People who identify, who commit themselves, will walk the extra mile for the organization.

Let me emphasize what I see as an important point. The two existing histories of organizational communication—Redding (1985) and Redding and Tompkins (1987)—treat the different eras of organizational communication as natural stages in the life cycle of the field. The interpretation I am presenting in this chapter makes a different point. The different eras are in *antagonistic* relationships with each other.

Each thinks the other approach is in error. Was there tension between the two different approaches advocated by Purdue and Michigan State? Yes. The attack on functionalism articulated by Putnam (1983), which was really directed at systems rationalism, was rather harsh. My point today is that despite antagonisms in the past a reasonable case can be made for either alternative on the four dimensions we have expressed. Different times and circumstances call for different emphases. It is natural therefore, to swing from one side to another, from the organistic to the mechanical, for example, or vice versa. We can be sure, however, that time is running out for the cultural approach. A new approach will replace it as a dominant wave, even though the traces of the other approaches will continue to have advocates.

Turning inwardly, different chapters in this book stress different positions on our cluster of oppositions. John Parrish-Sprowl's chapter on Organizational Persuasion is an obvious instance. Should those who treasure understanding as an organizational goal deride such a chapter? Certainly not. Raymond O'Connor Jr.'s chapter on the role of communication in the leadership process is clearly on the side of influence rather than understanding. David R. Neumann's chapter on communication technology stresses understanding, even though it could have emphasized how technology influences humans.

Dale Shannon's comprehensive chapter on conflict has a difficult task to perform. Conflict is thought to be natural, perhaps desirable, in the rational, problem-solving approach of BPS. It is regarded as a cancer to be surgically removed by the GS/HR understanding-is-everything approach.

Cynthia Berryman-Fink's chapter on gender issues is a good reminder that such a chapter would not have been conceivable until the development of feminism and the cultural–critical approach. I wish I could talk about all of the chapters. I enjoyed reading each and learned from each, but my license has a page limit. I must hasten to suggest a way of thinking and talking about organizational communication today and tomorrow.

INTERPRETIVISTS VERSUS FUNCTIONALISTS

I have to admit to a bias, a previous commitment to which I am ego-involved. I shall reveal that commitment in time, but must turn to another opposition in our field. In a book chapter published in the early 1980s, Putnam (1983) divided the field of organizational communication into the interpretive and the functionalist. It was clear what side she was on. The functionalists were the bad guys and gals in black hats. The interpretivists wore the white. The basic difference was that the functionalists believed that there was a real world out there to be studied. Putnam and the interpretivists said the focus of inquiring, research, and teaching should be on the *meanings* of the members of organizations. In addition, Putnam (1983) argued "that reality is socially constructed through the words, symbols and behaviors of its members" (p. 35). Notice she did not say that "social" reality is so constructed.

There is a contradiction between these two positions. By saying that we should limit ourselves to studying the subjective meanings of organizational members, we close off an objective reality. But what if the organizational members we study believe that there is a hard, recalcitrant reality out there that is *not* socially constructed? That is exactly the condition I faced in my studies of NASA (Tompkins, 1977, 1978, 1993). The engineers, scientists, managers, bureaucrats, and other kinds of members did *not* believe in a socially constructed world. They believed the rockets they made did in fact go to the moon. Moreover, they believed that NASA and the contractor firms who worked for them were real. They believed that these organizations could succeed or fail by objective criteria and that their bosses could hire or fire, reward or penalize individuals—actions with *real* consequences.

I hope the reader can see the contradiction. For me or Putnam or anyone else to impose on the members of NASA a view of their world as socially constructed would not have been true to their subjective or "objective" meanings, what Max Weber called *Verstehen.* And, on the other hand, to say that they were wrong in believing in an objective reality would be setting oneself up as a privileged observer, a move contrary to the ambience and rationale of the interpretivist approach.

Another problem in Putnam's discussion is her assertion that the interpretivist view is "relativistic" (1983, p. 40). This is not the case. Rabinow and Sullivan (1987) dedicate an entire volume of essays to the debates between and among interpretivists since Max Weber invented the concept. The critics of the interpretivists *have often accused them of being relativists,* but to my knowledge Putnam is the only one to admit such a change. All others smeared with such a label have denied it. Why? What does it mean to admit a relativistic view of the social world? It means that such a field has no basis or grounds for discriminating between good and bad claims. All claims are thus relative. An academic field cannot continue to survive in colleges and universities if it has no convincing warrants for its claims.

In that influential book chapter published in 1983, Putnam attempted to articulate some concerns shared by many people in organizational communication about what kind of research was being conducted. The research was "scientific" in that it was conducted with the belief that there was a world of organizations out there to be observed. The observations were frequently turned into numbers or statistics and analyzed in computers. These researchers, particularly those at Michigan State University, did this from the perspective of systems theory, the assumption that in the case of organizations there are inputs, outputs, and internal operations such as communication. Each part of the system, or organization, was assumed to affect other parts. Putnam chose to call this functionalism. As we saw earlier, this was an unfortunate word choice because all approaches take a functional perspective.

Putnam posed an alternative way of thinking about, and doing research into organizational communication. She called it the interpretive approach. She said correctly that the interpretive approach began with Max Weber (Putnam, 1983, p.46). Weber developed the concept of *Verstehen,* the subjective understanding of the world developed by human beings. Another term for this would be *meaning.* In short,

Weber believed that social scientists, when studying social phenomena such as organizations, should try to discover the subjective understandings of the organization developed by the members or participants in it. Thus, we should try to interpret the interpretations of the members and other participants.

Although I agreed with Putnam's attempt to give legitimacy to the interpretive approach, I believe her approach was a bit one sided. Interpretivism became in her chapter what Kenneth Burke (1950) calls a God-term. Functionalism became a Devil-term. Let me illustrate. Functionalists, said Putnam, believe in determinism, interpretivists in voluntarism. Functionalists assume a unitary view of organizations that has a bias in favor of management. Interpretivists have a pluralistic perspective that incorporates views other than those of the managers. Functionalists are guilty of reification, making abstract notions concrete. Interpretivists do not. Putnam also says that functionalists act as consultants to organizations proving their bias in favor of managers and presumably against workers.

I could go on and on, but the reader gets the point that the interpretivists, like the good guys in early Western movies, wear the white hats while the functionalists wear the black ones. The world is a bit more complex than that. For example, I know people in the interpretivist camp who are involved in consulting. One is Michael Pacanowsky at the University of Colorado at Boulder. Another is Larry Browning at the University of Texas at Austin. So, consulting, and the danger of managerial bias, is practiced in both camps.

In fact, who is in the functionalist camp? Putnam did not name names, nor did she cite any functionalist research in the field of organizational communication. She identified only some "schools of thought" in sociology and other social sciences. In a sense one could say there weren't any functionalists in the field of organizational communication. I have never heard anyone in organizational communication admit to being a functionalist. The word is used only in a pejorative sense, a category with negative meanings.

Yes, there were and are people in organizational communication who advocate empiricism or systems theory, or even a social scientific approach. Putnam borrowed the term functionalist from writers outside the field.

Moreover, as we saw above, interpretivists themselves talk about the "functions" of culture and cultural variables or performances. So do the criticalists. Dennis Mumby's edited book, *Narrative and Social Control: Critical Perspectives* (1993), cannot avoid neither the term function nor the concept (see pp. 81, 105, 127, 145, 162, 190, 206, 222). In fact, Mumby published an article with the title, "The political function of narrative in organizations" (1987). No one involved in understanding complex phenomena can avoid the concept of functions. Try to explain the relationship between communication and organization. It may be possible to avoid using the term function—it will not be possible to avoid the concept.

In short, the interpretivist/functional dichotomy has become a privileged hierarchy crying out for deconstruction, a terministic prison that oversimplifies the world. It is also misleading and unfair to those branded with an unwanted label. And, as I am sure Putnam would agree more than ten years later, contributions to our understanding have been made by all rigorous approaches to organizational communication.

CONCLUSION

Directions in Organizational Communication Research

Charles Redding and I tried to come up with something better than the functionalist interpretive dichotomy (Redding & Tompkins, 1988). As other writers put it (Wert-Grey et al., 1991, p. 143):

> *In an attempt to expand and clarify Putnam's two-category model, Redding and Tompkins (1988) propose that organizational communication research can be divided into three categories: modernistic, naturalistic, and critical.... [T]hey argue, "in defense of our categories, we believe they have the virtue... of having emerged from within the study of organizational communication rather than from a externally defined philosophical system."*

These authors used our three-way classification system to add up how much research has been conducted in each column. I was pleased to see that they found our system more useful than the old in categorizing research in the field in 1991. Today I would modify that tripartite system by making it a four-way categorization. First is the modernist, or systems rationalism. This would include the quantitative work on such subjects as organizational assimilation, superior–subordinate communication, and network analysis. Second is the naturalistic. This includes ethnographic research, the interpretive approach, and, of course, organizational communication as culture. Third would be the critical approach. This includes the work of Deetz (1992), Mumby (1993), and Wendt (1994). Notice that as Redding and Tompkins (1988) observed in their history and analysis of the field, the critical theorists "still assume that there is a 'truth' out there to be discovered. The critical theorists act as if their version of the truth will set workers free, while the positivists [a synonym for modernists or system rationalists] use another version of the truth to effect control" (p. 23). Fourth, and here is a new category, would be the feminist approach to organizational communication. It has become clear that the feminist approach is here to stay, that it has separated itself from the critical theorists. As the father of two daughters and the grandfather of two boys and a girl, it would be satisfying in ten years or so to write that this fourth approach did its job so well it can retire.

REFERENCES

Barley, S., & Kunda, G. (1992). Design and devotion: Surges of rational and normative ideologies of control in managerial discourse. *Administrative Science Quarterly, 37,* 363–399.

Barnard, C. (1938). *The functions of the executive.* Cambridge: Harvard University Press.

Burke, K. (1950). *A Rhetoric of Motives.* New York: Prentice Hall.

Deetz, S. (1992). *Democracy in an Age of Corporate Colonization.* Albany, N.Y.: State University of New York Press.

Farace, R., Monge, P., & Russell, H. (1977). *Communicating and Organizing.* Reading, Mass.: Addison-Wesley.

Lombard, G. (1955). Behavior in a selling group: A case study of interpersonal relations in a department store. Cambridge: Harvard University Graduate School of Business Administration.

Mumby, D. (1987). The political function of narrative in organizations. *Communication Monographs, 54,* 113–127.

Mumby, D. (1993). Critical organizational communication studies: The next ten years. *Communication Monographs, 60,* 18–25.

Mumby, D. (1993). *Narrative and Social Control: Critical Perspectives.* Newbury Park, Calif.: Sage.

Nilsen, T. (1953). *The communication survey: A study of communication problems in three office and factory units.* Unpublished dissertation, Northwestern University.

Putnam, L. (1983). The interpretive perspective: An alternative to functionalism. In L. Putnam & M. Pacanowsky (eds.), *Communication and Organizations: An Interpretive Approach.* Beverly Hills, Calif.: Sage.

Rabinow, P., & Sullivan, W. (1987). *Interpretive Social Science: A Second Look.* Berkeley: University of California Press.

Rawlins, W. (1985). Stalking interpersonal communication effectiveness: Social, individual, or situational integration? In T. Benson (ed.), *Speech Communication in the 20th Century.* Carbondale, Ill.: Southern Illinois University Press.

Redding, W. C. (1985). Stumbling toward identity: The emergence of organizational communication as a field of study. In R. McPhee & P. Tompkins (eds.), *Organizational Communication: Traditional Themes and New Directions.* Beverly Hills, Calif.: Sage.

Redding, W. C., & Tompkins, P. (1988). Organizational communication—past and present tenses. In G. Goldhaber & G. Barnett (eds.), *Handbook of Organizational Communication.* Norwood, N.J.: Ablex.

Rogers, E., & Agarawala-Rogers, R. (1976). *Communication in Organizations.* New York: The Free Press.

Sandford, W. (1931). Some notes on the teaching of business speech. *Quarterly Journal of Speech, 17,* 451–458.

Schwartz, D. (1968). *Liaison communication roles in a formal organization.* Unpublished dissertation, Michigan State University.

Simon, H. (1976). *Administrative Behavior.* New York: The Free Press.

Tompkins, P. (1965). General semantics and human relations. *Central States Speech Journal, 16,* 35–37.

Tompkins, P. (1977). Management qua communication in rocket research and development. *Communication Monographs, 44,* 1–26.

Tompkins, P. (1978). Organizational metamorphosis in space research and development. *Communication Monographs, 45,* 110–118.

Tompkins, P. (1993). *Organizational Communication Imperatives: Lessons of the Space Program.* Los Angeles: Roxbury Publishing Co.

Tompkins, P., & McPhee, R. (1985). "Introduction and afterword." In R. McPhee & P. Tompkins (eds.), *Organizational Communication: Traditional Themes and New Directions.* Beverly Hills, Calif.: Sage.

Wendt, R. (1994). Learning to "walk the talk": A critical tale of the micropolitics at a total quality university. *Management Communication Quarterly, 8,* 4–45.

Wert-Gray, S., Center, C., Brashers, D., & Meyers, R. (1991). Research topics and methodological orientations in organizational communication: A decade in review. *Communication Studies, 42,* 141–154.

Winans, J. (1931). Is public speaking out? *The Quarterly Journal of Speech, 17,* 163–177.

Yeager. W. (1929). Teaching business speaking—a modern trend. *The Quarterly Journal of Speech, 17,* 485–494.

Index

Abella, R., 62, 81
abstracting, implications of, 16, 17
abstracting, process of, 13–15
Aburdene, P., 221
Acker, J., 219
act utilitarianism, 94, 95
Adler, R.B., 5, 6, 11
administrative management, 21–23
advertising, 180–183
affective states, 148
Affirmative Action Organization, The, 195
Agarwala-Rogers, R., 366
Aiken, M., 3
Ajzen, I., 176, 177
Albert, R.D., 288, 289
Altman, I., 65
Alvesson, M., 226
ambiguity, of nonverbal behavior, 66, 67
American Broadcasting Company, 339
American Workforce, The, 287
analysis of documents/materials, by organizational consultant, 309–319
Anderson, C.I., 276
Anderson, P.A., 80, 81
antecedent conditions, 147, 148
appearance, 63–64
Apple, C., 104, 105
arbitration, 163
Argyle, M., 81
Aristotle, 173, 189
Art of Crossing Cultures, The, 295
Asplund, G., 262, 264, 265, 277
assessment of diversity training programs, 298–300
Astin, H.S., 264, 265, 269, 277
attribute theory, 131–133
attribution theory, 131–133
autocratic *vs.* participative styles of leadership, 121, 122
Ayvazian, A., 194

Bach, G.R., 161
Bachrach, S.B., 3
Bailyn, L., 263, 271
Baird, J.E., 79
Bandura, A., 176
Bannister, B.D., 127

Bantz, C.R., 213
Bardack, N.R., 64
bargaining, 188
Barge, J.K., 63, 79
Barley, S., 205, 213, 361, 362
Barnard, C., 365
Barnlund, D., 11
barriers, implications of, 16, 17
Bateson, G., 238, 243, 244
Bauer, C., 347
Beavin, J.H., 4, 5
Becker, F.D., 61, 343
behavioral approach, 121–126
behavioral codes, 60–63
behavioral expectations, of women, 267
benevolent-authoritative management style, 27
Benokraitis, N., 270
Bentham, Y., 93
Berg, P.O., 126
Berger, P., 211
Berquist, G.F., 174
Berry, L.L., 79
Berryman-Fink, C., 266, 274, 275
Beyer, J.M., 204, 206
biases, positivity and negativity, 71
Bill of Rights, specific liberties, 99
Bingham, S., 80
Birdwhistell, R., 60
Blackwell, K., 106, 107
Blake, R.R., 124
Blanchette, D.P., 292
Boag, D., 60, 78, 80
body movements (Kinesics), 60
Bok, S., 101, 102
Booth-Butterfield, M., 177, 274
Boss, B.M., 50
Boster, F., 178
Bostrom, R.P., 164
Bosworth, L.K., 164
boundary spanner (cosmopolite), 44
Bowers, J.W., 189
Bowie, N., 109
Bradac, J.J., 189
Bradley, P.H., 79
Brass, D.J., 270
Brett, J.M., 0
Brewster, C., 299
bridge, 43
Briggs, J., 247

Brislin, R.W., 289, 295, 298, 299
brown bag meetings, 138
Brown, D., 288
Brown, I.C., 204
Buber, M., 93
Buller, D.B., 59, 67, 76, 79
bureaucracy, 23–25
bureaucratic organization, qualities of a, 23, 24
Burgoon, J.K., 59, 67, 73, 74, 76, 79, 81
Burke, K., 194, 197, 238, 239, 270, 370
Burnett, J., 180
Burrell, G., 222
Butler, D., 267
Butterfield, D.A., 266
Byers, P., 325

Cacioppo, J.T., 177
Calás, M., 203, 206, 210, 219, 222
Callahan, E., 106
Callister, R.R., 160
Camden, G.T., 68
Campbell, D.T., 348
Campbell, K.E., 271
Cannings, K., 268
Cantor, B., 287
Cappella, J.N., 81
career, balancing, and family roles, 271
Carey, J.W., 190
Carlson, R.E., 64
Carnevale, A.P., 286, 293, 295, 297, 301
Carr-Ruffino, N., 263, 265, 271, 277
Carter, M.R., 260, 261, 264, 266, 268
Carveth, R., 186, 196
case method, 365
case studies, 35, 55, 56, 84, 85, 111, 141, 142, 166, 167, 199, 229, 230, 255, 279, 280, 301, 306–309, 330–333, 354
Case, S.S., 269
Case, T., 189
causes of sexual harassment, 273, 274
cellular telephones, 346
Center for Business Ethics, 91
Center for Business Ethics (Bentley College), 90, 91

interaction, coordination of, 81–82
Interactive Television Laboratory, University of Miami, 347
interdependence, 29
intergroup conflict, 155, 156
intergroup conflict management, 161, 162
internal-operational communication, 7, 8
Internet-the information superhighway, 337–339
interorganizational conflict, 156
interorganizational conflict management, 162, 163
interpersonal communication, 6
Interpersonal Conflict, 150
interpersonal conflict, 153, 154
interpersonal conflict management, 159–161
interpretive approach to organizational culture, 210–214
interpretivists *vs.* functionalists, 368–371
interventions to manage conflict, 159–163
interventions, in group processes, 322, 323
interviewing skills training, 322
interviews, 77, 78
intragroup conflict, 154, 155
intrapersonal communication, 5
isolate, 43

Jablin, F.M., 214
Jaccoby, J., 40
Jackall, R., 100
Jackson, D.D., 4, 5
Jackson, P., 62, 77, 81
Jaffee, S., 343
James, A., 324
James, G., 107
James, K., 288
Jamison, K., 276
Jarke, M., 164
Jaska, J., 100
Jelassi, M.T., 164
Jelenek, M., 211
Jennings, K.M., 188
Jensen, J., 106, 107
Jepsen, D.A., 288
Jhally, S., 179, 181
Job Patterns for Minorities and Women in Private Industry, 287
Johansen, R., 342, 343, 345
Johnson, B.T., 268
Johnson, F.L., 265
Johnson, P.R., 274
Jones, E.E., 70
Jones, E.H., 164
Jones, S.E., 62
Jones, T.S., 188
Jurma, W.E., 160

Kahn, R., 122
Kant's categorical imperative, 91–93
Kant, I., 91, 92, 93, 103
Kanter, R.M., 220, 263
Kantian theory, 95
Karp, H.B., 293
Karsten, M.F., 262, 263, 265, 267, 271, 273, 274
Katz, D., 122
Katz, N.H., 160
Kaufman, M.M., 48, 49
Kellerman, K., 71
Kelley, J.R., 64
Kendon, A., 59, 60
Kennedy, A.A., 203, 204, 205, 207, 208, 288
Kenny, D.A., 120
Kerr, S., 124
Kersten, A., 203, 215, 216, 217
Ketrow, S.M., 62, 78, 81
Keys, B., 189, 190
Khoo, G., 288
Kiesler, C.A., 175
Kiesler, S., 348
Kline, S., 181
Knapp, M.L., 61, 63, 72, 81, 82, 343
Kochan, T.A., 191
Kofman, F., 29, 30, 31, 32
Korzenny, F., 347
Korzybski, A., 13, 15, 242
Kotler, P., 180
Kotter, J.P., 118
Kram, K.E., 270
Kravitz, D.A., 288, 289
Kreps, G.L., 21, 23, 26, 28
Krone, K.J., 214
Krueger, G.P., 343
Kruse, A., 162
Kruskal, W.H., 348
Kunda, G., 206, 207, 210, 213, 226, 227, 229, 361, 362

labor organizations, 18, 189
labor relations, 25, 26
Larson, L.L., 124, 125
Lawyer, J.W., 160
Leader-Match Training, 128
leadership
and seating position, 81–82
autocratic *vs.* participative styles of, 121, 122
communication strategies for better, 134–139
definition of, 117, 118
importance of, 118, 119
Ohio State studies on leadership, 122–124
recent approaches to, 129–133
University of Michigan studies on, 122
leadership approaches, contemporary, role of communication in, 134

leadership process, role of communication in, 117–145
leadership style, sex differences in, 269
leadership theories, historical review of, 119–134
behavioral approach, 121–126
contingency approach, 126–129
recent approaches, 129–134
trait approach, 119, 120
learning organizations, Key principles of, 31, 32
Leary, M.R., 61, 79
Leathers, D.G., 61
Leeds-Hurwitz, W., 290, 291
Lees, P.L., 275, 276
Leiss, W., 181, 182
Leister, A.F., 120
Leland, C., 264, 265, 269, 277
Lengel, R.H, 118
Lesikar, R.V., 7, 8, 15, 16, 17, 18
Leung, K., 64, 77
levels of conflict, 153–156
Levine, T., 178
Lewin, K., 121
Lewis, K.E., 274
liaison, 43
Lickiss, K., 348
Likert, R., 27
Linder, B., 62
Lindsay, L.L., 21
Linstead, S., 222, 223, 227
Lippert, R., 121
listening, active and attentive, 136, 137
logos, 19, 173, 174
Lombard, G., 365
Lont, C., 222
Lord, R.G., 119
Loren, E., 30
Lott, B., 267, 268
Lottor, M., 339
Luckman, T., 211
Lundy, K.L.P., 262
Lundy, L.A., 262
Lunneborg, P.W., 269

Macoby, M., 24
macro perspectives on conflict management, 159
Mahar, L., 128
Mainiero, L.A., 276
male managerial behavior, 268, 269
male managers, evaluations of, 268
male perceptions of sexual harassment, 274
Management and the Worker, 25
management development, 25
management styles, four types of, 27
management, entry of women into, 260